DIMENSIONS
IN CHUMASH

BEREISHIS · SHEMOS

MOSAICA PRESS

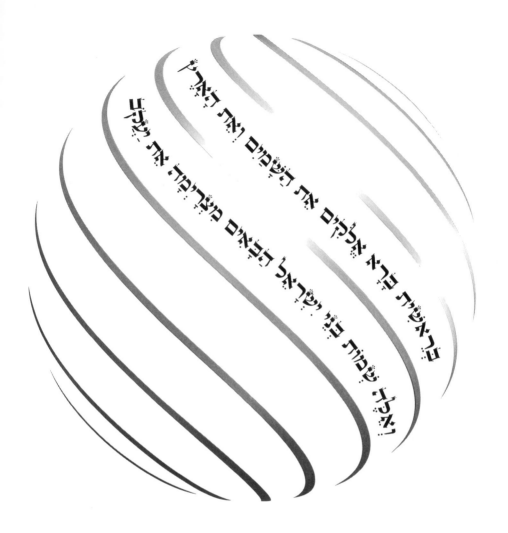

DIMENSIONS
IN CHUMASH

BEREISHIS · SHEMOS

RABBI IMMANUEL BERNSTEIN

Published by Mosaica Press, Inc.
www.mosaicapress.com
info@mosaicapress.com

ספר זה מוקדש
לזכרון עולם ולעילוי נשמת
בן איש חי רב פעלים
איש ישר ונאמן וטוב לב

ר' ישראל בן ר' אברהם ז"ל

בגיל צעיר גלה למקום תורה
היה דבוק בתורה ולומדיה כל חייו
מדריך משפחתו בדרך הישר
באהבה ובחכמה
מיצר בצרת חברתו ושמח בהצלחתו
כאב רחמן דאג לחינוך בני עירו
עושה ומעשה את האחרים
ליסד ולחזק מוסדות התורה והחסד

נלב"ע בשם טוב
ליל ש"ק ח' מרחשון תשע"ב

ת.נ.צ.ב.ה.

הונצח ע"י משפחתו

In cherished memory of our parents

MAIDIE AND MICHAEL FIDLER

and

ROSALIND AND JOSEPH ZATMAN

And in gratitude to the Almighty
for the love of our children

ELLIOT, JULIAN, AND ABIGAIL

OUR DAUGHTERS-IN-LAW

HADASSAH AND KAREN

and our grandchildren

ASAF, JOEL, MAYA, ARIELLA, ZAN, NOAM,
SKYE, GILI, EHUD, LIBBY, AND AYALA

LYNN AND JAN FIDLER
Jerusalem

In memory of Renée's parents

ANN AND CHARLES K. ADLER

And in memory of her brother

GERALD S. ADLER

RENÉE AND SHAUL MANSHEIM

Dedicated in memory of

HARAV YEHUDA COPPERMAN, zt"l

HARABBANIT TZIPORAH COPPERMAN, a"h

In appreciation of the unique flavor of Torah
they taught us, for introducing us to each other,
and by extension, the beautiful *nachas*
we've been able to share together

DANIEL AND ELISHEVA LISS
SHMUEL, YEHUDA, SUSSY, NAVA, AND AHUVA

שלום בן צדוק (סאלח) צוברי

עלה לארץ ישראל בשנת 1949 מיד שנפתחו שערי העליה. על כנפי נשרים.
בהתראה של ימים אחדים עזבו אבא ואמא שרה סעדה את כל ההיסטוריה בתימן
עם פנים לחיים חדשים בארץ הקודש. כל שהביאו איתם היה ספרי קודש טלית תפילין
ושורשים עמוקים של יהודים למודי סבל.
המשפט האהוב של אבא ואמא היה: "לא יעזוב ולא יטוש" "והבוטח בה׳ חסד יסובבנו".
מנוחתם עדן

For Saba Shalom,
Orphaned in Yemen at 13, you were raised by your
older sister, then raised your younger sister in turn,
started a family, and literally carried your children on your
back into the desert to make it to the plane to Israel.
Your dedication to your *mesorah*, your investment
in *sefarim*, and your effort in learning from them and
teaching them to your children—while feeding and
supporting them, with a heartfelt desire to connect
the new to the old—are a continued and everlasting
inspiration.

With love,
RAFAEL, NAOMI (Z"L), LIAT, CARMIT, OFIR,
EDEN, AND MA'AYAN TZOUBARI

Dedicated in loving memory of our
parents and grandparents

ISADORE AND BELLE GLASTEIN
ISAAC AND FRIEDA SUTTON

ר׳ יחזקאל ב״ר יעקב דוב ז״ל | מרת בילא בת ר׳ בנימין ע״ה
ר׳ יצחק ב״ר יוסף ז״ל | מרת פרידא בת ר׳ יוסף ע״ה

With love,
DR. CARY AND DEBORAH GLASTEIN
IAN AND SOPHIE GLASTEIN
ZACK AND RITA CARLA GLASTEIN

Dedicated to our

ODELIA SARA נ״י

May you continue to grow and bring
much light and laughter to the world.
And may you merit to emulate the qualities of your
great-grandmothers after whom you are named—
both women of dignity, determination,
and above all, kindness

IMMA AND ABBA

לז"נ

ר' ישראל בן נתן אדלער זצ"ל

R' FELIX ADLER, z"L

BY HIS CHILDREN

Dedicated to our daughters

PENINA LEAH

SHIRA ITA

ESTHER PESHA

May they grow in their love of Torah,
yiras Shamayim, and compassion for others,
ad meah v'esrim shanah.

ADAM AND CHANI SAUNDERS

אַשֶׁר זעליג וייס

כגן 8
פעיה"ק ירושלם ת"ו

ז' ניסן תשפ"ב

I have seen the wonderful *sefer* of my dear friend,
HaRav Immanuel Bernstein *shlit"a*, containing profound
discussions and insights on the Chumash drawn from the
gedolei hadoros. This sefer is simply overflowing with illuminating ideas and concepts. Indeed, it may be said that
Rabbi Bernstein has authored many works—each of them
beloved and enlightening—but this one surpasses them all.

It is my blessing to the author that this *sefer* will be
well-received and that many will benefit from its light,
and that he may merit always to spread the greatness and
grandeur of Torah in all its glory.

With love,

אסרו חג בדכ"ס

To whom it may concern

I have seen some of the writings of Rabbi Emmanuel Bernstein, shlita, and was impressed with the depth of the contents as well as the lucid presentation.

Certainly a אסרו חג בדכ"ס is in place here.

May it be the will of Hashem Yisborach that our community drink from the wellsprings that the author has dug, for the waters are mayim chayim

D Cohen
Rav of Cong Gvul Yaabetz
26th of the Omer
תשנ"ב

YISROEL REISMAN
1460 EAST 19TH STREET
BROOKLYN, NY, 11230

ישראל רייזמאן
ישיבה תורה ודעת
אגודת ישראל בפלאטבוש

To My Dear Friends,

It is difficult for me to write a Haskamah for someone who is superior to me in Torah and Hashkafah.

Rather, I want to take this opportunity to share my thoughts regarding this Sefer.

Books on Chumash today are, for the most part, books with stories, gematriyos and short 'vertlach', which may be appropriate for children and those with little Torah background.

We, Bnei Torah who seek to grow in our studies, should be learning with greater depth as is appropriate for the study of our Holy Torah, the word of God.

This Sefer provides that opportunity; it provides insights of significant depth in Jewish thought. It belongs on the table of those who seek appreciation of the words of Torah.

The Gaon, Rabbi Immanuel Bernstein, as the name Immanuel suggests, is a man who walks with God, with thoughts that connect to God. It is wonderful that he shares these thoughts with us. His seforim are tools for growth and an appreciation of Torah.

With Appreciation,

Yisroel Reisman
Teves 5782

TABLE OF CONTENTS

CHUMASH BEREISHIS

Parshas Bereishis

Parshas Noach

Parshas Lech Lecha

Parshas Vayeira

ACKNOWLEDGMENTS

I would like to express my thanks to all those who reviewed the manuscript of this *sefer*. A special thank you to my dear *talmidim* Shmuel Levenson and Marc Osian for their extremely helpful and insightful comments.

My thanks to Zev and Rena Lewis for their continued encouragement and support in all my writing projects.

I would like to thank Rabbis Yaacov Haber and Doron Kornbluth of Mosaica Press for overseeing this project, Rabbi Robert Sussman for his expert editing of the manuscript, Mrs. Sherie Gross and her entire team for the copy editing and proofreading, and Mrs. Rayzel Broyde and the graphics team for designing the *sefer* and the cover.

This *sefer* was dedicated by my dear friend Mr. Avi Weinstock in memory of his father, R' Yisroel, *z"l*. It is my hope that the words of Torah contained within will be an *iluy* for his *neshamah* and an honor for his memory.

The discussions in this *sefer* are based on a weekly Monday evening parsha *shiur* given in the Rechavia neighborhood of Jerusalem for more than twenty years. I would like to express my profound appreciation to Jenny and Mel Shay, who were the driving force behind its inception and ongoing organization. May they both be blessed with many more years of good health and *nachas*.

A number of years after the *shiur* had begun, while talking to my brother, Jonathan, I mentioned to him my feeling that it might be of benefit if the *shiurim* were available to the wider public via technological means. It could not have been more than an hour or two later that I received a message from him telling me to check out the new website for the *shiur*. Through this new platform, people from all over the world were able to listen to a digital recording of the *shiur*. For the first few years, Jonathan managed the website, after which it was handed over to my dear *talmid* Jordan Gross, who uploaded the *shiurim* and, later on, the written *Dimensions in Torah* series. My boundless thanks to them for enabling the *divrei Torah* from the *shiur* to spread outward from Jerusalem across the world. Around the same time, Rabbi Jack Abramowitz, the Torah-content editor for the OU website, graciously agreed to host the *shiurim* and, in time, the *Dimensions* essays on the OU website. I would like to express my gratitude to him for his ongoing support and encouragement and wish him continued *hatzlachah* in spreading words of Torah to the wider community.

Lastly, to my dear wife, Judy, whose support and encouragement allow me to continue learning, writing, and teaching. The weekly parsha *shiur* has been an ongoing presence in our home over the years, so that my predictable first response when planning any family event is invariably, "Just not on a Monday evening." May we merit to have many more such *simchahs* together in good health and happiness.

INTRODUCTION

The Jewish People have been blessed with a treasury of commentaries on the Chumash over the centuries, each one with its own particular approach, methodology and flavor. The goal of this book is to draw on that heritage, taking ideas and insights from the spectrum of commentators—many of whom are well-known, as well as some who are less well-known—and crafting them into discussions of key topics and episodes in the Chumash. Some chapters will introduce the reader to questions of which he may not have been aware, while others will present new answers to questions with which he is already familiar. A number of the chapters are devoted to identifying and developing concepts that span numerous parshiyos of the Chumash and shed light on the various ways in which the Torah expresses itself.

The discussions take many forms and head in many directions, reflecting the numerous levels on which the Torah transmits its messages. Most of the discussions take place in the realms of *pshat*, some in the sphere of Midrash, and others, occasionally, in the world of *remez*. However, it is fair to say that the point of departure that characterizes all of these discussions is attentiveness to the words, phrases, and cadences of the verses. In this, I am mindful of a comment that my father, Rabbi Isaac Bernstein, *zt"l*, once mentioned to me in the name of the *Vilna Gaon*: The reason a word in Hebrew is called a *teivah*, which also means a box, is because, like a box, one needs to open up the words of the Chumash in order to access that which is contained inside.

A number of chapters in the book are devoted to *Rashi* and the principles that guide his commentary on the Chumash. Arguably, the entire book could have been devoted to *Rashi*, and indeed, many books have. However, I sufficed with a select number of discussions that present some fundamentals of the methodology of this seminal and quintessential commentator.

In addition to the discussions in the chapters themselves, at the end of each parsha there is a section called "From the Commentators," which contains a number of classic shorter ideas and interpretations from the various *mefarshim*.

In prefacing a work on the Chumash, I feel I must mention two figures who fundamentally impacted and shaped my learning of the Chumash. The first of these is my father, Rabbi Isaac Bernstein, *zt"l*. Although he was known for his breadth of knowledge in Torah generally, he had a particular love for the Chumash and its commentaries. His command of seemingly the entire corpus of Torah commentators from *Rashi* until his own time was all-encompassing and awe-inspiring. His weekly Chumash *shiur* in the Ner Yisrael shul in northwest London was a phenomenon in its time, and recordings of those *shiurim* continue to be heard throughout the world even now, some thirty years after they were given. Indeed, it is fair to say that his teachings impacted the study of the Chumash well beyond the setting of the *shiur* itself. First, the *divrei Torah* themselves have been repeated in countless *shiurim*, sermons, and at Shabbos tables throughout the world. Second, he introduced people to commentators they had never heard of, encouraging them to pursue those works and see what else they had to say. Finally, the structure and level of the *shiur* set a standard for what a high-level Chumash *shiur* should sound like, encouraging others to invest their energies in their *shiurim* accordingly.

Secondly, I would like to mention my uncle, Rav Yehuda Copperman, *zt"l*. His influence on me actually began before I was born, as he himself was a major influence on my father, his first cousin. Subsequently, when I arrived in Israel to study in yeshiva, we began a weekly *chavrusa* that was to last for twenty-five years. During that time, I received broad exposure to his system of understanding the concept of *pshat* and its role within the totality of Torah, an approach which finds expression in his monumental work *Pshuto Shel Mikra*. Although I only cite my father's and my uncle's words occasionally in this book, their influence pervades the way I look at the verses of the Chumash and the words of its commentaries. I pray that I am able to faithfully communicate the rigor and attentiveness of textual analysis, the joy of Torah discovery, and the love and reverence for its words that they instilled within me.

It is my hope that this book will inspire and encourage people to further and deepen their investigations into the Chumash, and avail themselves of the wealth of commentaries with which we have been graced—from the earliest to the most recent—finding therein ever-deepening levels of interpretation, illumination, and inspiration.

Immanuel Bernstein
Jerusalem, 5782

בְּרֵאשִׁית בָּרָא אֱלֹהִים אֵת הַשָּׁמַיִם וְאֵת הָאָרֶץ

CHUMASH
BEREISHIS

PARSHAS BEREISHIS

CONCERNING
CHUMASH BEREISHIS

INTRODUCTION: THE FIRST RASHI

Rashi's comments on the Torah are generally devoted to a word, or group of words, in the verse before him. His opening comment to our parsha, however, addresses the entire *Chumash Bereishis*, and some of *Chumash Shemos* as well. *Rashi* asks:

> *Why did the Torah not start with the first mitzvah, sanctifying the new moon, that was given to B'nei Yisrael when they were about to leave Egypt?*

He answers that the Torah starts with the account of Creation in order to establish our people's claim to the land of Israel. Should the nations of the world ever charge that we were bandits in taking possession of the land, we can respond that the entire world was created by and belongs to Hashem, Who is thus entitled to apportion it as He sees fit, and He gave us the land of Israel.

FURTHER RESPONSES: DERECH ERETZ KADMAH LATORAH

As later commentators point out, *Rashi*'s answer would seem to explain why the Torah began with the account of Hashem creating the world, but not why *Chumash Bereishis* describes the life of the

Patriarchs and Matriarchs in such great detail.[1] Moreover, the question itself seems to be based on the premise that the purpose of the Torah is purely to communicate the mitzvos to us. In this regard, others take a different approach.

R' Yaakov Kamenetsky explains that the role of *Chumash Bereishis* preceding the presentation of the mitzvos is reflected in the statement of the Sages in the Midrash: "*Derech eretz kadmah laTorah*—Correct behavior precedes the Torah."[2] The foundation of the laws of the Torah is an ethical outlook and moral disposition. It is to this foundation that the Torah's account of the events prior to *Matan Torah* is dedicated.[3] Indeed, the Gemara informs us that the reference found later in Tanach to "*Sefer HaYashar*—the Book of the Upright,"[4] is to *Sefer Bereishis*, which details the lives of the Avos and Imahos, who were upright.[5] We read, for example, of the kindness and respect that Avraham showed all wayfarers, praying even for the wicked people of Sodom in the hope that they may ultimately renounce their evil ways and attain goodness, as well as the grace and patience with which he conducted negotiations with the conniving Efron when seeking a place to bury Sarah. So too, we see that Yitzchak exhibited great forbearance as the Pelishtim repeatedly laid claim to his wells and then banished him from the region, while he was still prepared to reconcile with them shortly thereafter. Similarly, we learn of Yaakov's dedicated service to Lavan, even as the latter repeatedly tried to swindle him and change the terms of their working agreement.[6] All of these are lessons in *derech eretz* and are a necessary prerequisite to receiving the Torah, where they then attain higher form and definition through the mitzvos.

---

1   It is also worth considering how many of the nations of the world, who claim that we are bandits, have been convinced otherwise based on the Torah's account of Creation. In this regard, there is room to say that *Rashi's* explanation is more for us, the people of the Torah, to be confident in our claim to the Land.

2   See *Vayikra Rabbah* 9:3: "*Esrim v'shishah doros kadmah derech eretz es haTorah*—*Derech eretz* preceded Torah by twenty-six generations."

3   *Emes L'Yaakov, Bereishis* 14:14.

4   See *Yehoshua* 10:13 and *Shmuel II* 1:18.

5   *Avodah Zarah* 25a.

6   See *Haamek Davar*, Preface to *Chumash Bereishis*.

The extent to which the Avos were immersed in *derech eretz* is demonstrated by the fact that some of their moral and ethical decisions exceeded that which the halachah sanctions. For example, Avraham going to war against four massive armies with only a handful of his disciples in order to rescue Lot would certainly be considered a risk that he was halachically forbidden to take. However, in the formative *derech eretz* era, primacy was given to the moral sense of responsibility that he felt toward his nephew.

Indeed, it is arguably for this reason that the Torah was not given in that early stage, in order to allow *derech eretz* to establish itself firmly and soundly in the spiritual make-up of the Jewish People, giving them the necessary foundation upon which to receive the Torah. Thus, even though we have a tradition that the Avos kept the mitzvos of the Torah even without being commanded to do so, nevertheless, the voluntary nature of that fulfillment meant that should there be a clash between the future mitzvos and current *derech eretz* concerns, the former would need to make way for the latter. This is probably the most straightforward answer to the well-known question of how Yaakov could marry two sisters, something that the Torah would forbid in the future. He was not prepared to allow his voluntary fulfillment of the mitzvos to cause him to go back on his commitment toward marrying Rachel.[7]

"THE TORAH AND THE MITZVAH"

R' Kamenetsky explains that it is with this in mind that Hashem later told Moshe to ascend Mount Sinai where He would give him *"ha-Torah v'hamitzvah*—The Torah and the commandment."[8] What is the meaning of these two terms? Are the Torah and its commandments not one and the same? Rather, the first term, "Torah," which means instruction, refers to the moral instruction in the realm of *derech eretz*, which is then followed by the commandments themselves.

Indeed, the lessons from the Avos are crucial in terms of how to keep the mitzvos themselves. For while we may not learn many mitzvos

---

7   Heard from R' Yehudah Copperman, *zt"l.*
8   *Shemos* 24:12.

from the Avos, we learn how to perform them. Hashem's command to Avraham to offer up his son Yitzchak is not a mitzvah that applies to the Jewish People on an ongoing basis, but there is no better guide for the devotion, alacrity, and commitment with which one should perform a mitzvah.

Thus, we find that there is a tractate of Mishnah dealing with matters of piety that is called "*Pirkei Avos*—Chapters of the Fathers," for the purpose of this tractate is to enlighten and inspire us to emulate the ways of the Avos—their devotion both to Hashem and His mitzvos as well as to other people—as related in *Chumash Bereishis.*[9]

All this should hopefully serve to give both our appreciation and study of *Chumash Bereishis* an added dimension. It exists not just to inform us about our past, but also to elevate our present—and provide horizons for our future.

---

9   *Maharam Schick*, Introduction to commentary on *Pirkei Avos.*

THE SIN OF THE EITZ HADAAS

Behind Good and Evil

BACKGROUND: "KNOWING GOOD AND EVIL"

Without a doubt, one of the dominant episodes in *Parshas Bereishis* is the sin of the *Eitz Hadaas*. In order to attain some understanding of this sin, as well as its reverberations throughout history until our times, we first need to understand, on some level, what the *Eitz Hadaas* was and why it was forbidden to eat from it. We begin with a basic question:

Why is knowing the difference between good and evil a bad thing? It actually sounds like a good thing, for if one doesn't know the difference between them, how will he be able to choose the one over the other?

Clearly, Adam and Chavah had the wherewithal to make the right choices even without eating from the tree, and eating from it transitioned them to a drastically inferior way of choosing good over evil. But what other ways of choosing good over evil are there?

- The *Rambam* explains that prior to eating from the *Eitz Hadaas*, man's choices were not framed in terms of "good and evil" but rather in terms of "truth and falsehood."[1] Sin was recognized as being inherently false, and any of its supposed benefits were

---

1   *Rambam, Moreh Nevuchim* 1:2. See *Michtav Me'Eliyahu*, vol. 1, p. 139.

instantly seen through for the spurious vanities that they are. With that clarity of vision, choosing to sin would essentially involve choosing to do something that one knew was false, which most people don't do. Upon eating from the *Eitz Hadaas*, man came to see things differently. Evil became something whose benefits seemed quite real. The basis for avoiding sin was no longer because it was false, but rather because it was the morally wrong thing to do, beneficial though it might be. This type of choice is harder to make, as history and experience have shown.

- In a different vein, the *Ramban* explains that prior to eating from the *Eitz Hadaas*, although man had the capacity to sin, he had no inherent desire to do so; his nature was pure and upright, directed toward fulfilling Hashem's will. The temptation to do evil came from outside, in the form of the snake who resided by the tree. Upon eating from the *Eitz Hadaas*, the desire to sin entered man.[2]

UNDERSTANDING ADAM'S SIN

The above two approaches should suffice to illustrate the idea that eating from the *Eitz Hadaas* produced a negative outcome, which was the reason why it was prohibited in the first place. However, this begs the obvious question. How did Adam come to sin? What led him to make the wrong choice?

The question is accentuated when we remind ourselves that at this stage, Adam's nature was fundamentally attuned to doing the will of Hashem. So, how is that compatible with the idea of him sinning at all?

The Arizal explains: The way in which the snake was able to tempt man to sin was to persuade him to eat from the tree *for the purpose of*

---

2   *Ramban* to *Bereishis* 2:9. In this context, the *Ramban* translates the term *"daas"* as "will." See also *Nefesh Hachaim* (1:6) who explains the word *daas* as "connection." Upon eating from the tree, good and evil became fused together inside of man. From this stage on, the temptation to sin comes from within, making it harder to combat and, indeed, sometimes harder to even identify. If both impulses exist within the person, how does he know whether what "he" wants to do is good or evil?

better serving his Creator! The very fact that making the right choices would become harder once Adam ate from the tree was presented as the reason for him to do so. If he ate from the tree and, nonetheless, succeeded in choosing good over evil, the glory to God would be immeasurably greater than it would be in his current state. This brings us to a paradox: Adam violated Hashem's command in order to further the fulfillment of His will! This was how eating from the *Eitz Hadaas* was rationalized—the ends (future high-level mitzvos) would justify the means (a present sin).

We may ponder further and ask: What led Adam to this decision? After all, presumably he should have asked himself if, as the snake claimed, the post-*Eitz Hadaas* state was superior to his current state, why would Hashem Himself not have commanded Adam to eat from the tree, or simply have created him that way to begin with?

The answer to this question is that a significant element within the sin of the *Eitz Hadaas* was that of Adam subscribing to the idea that he had a better idea of how to succeed in life, better even than Hashem, in terms of fulfilling Hashem's will! Although this sounds delusional (and it is), this is testimony to the extent to which man's ego can inflate his perceived capacities. Although the notion of finite man out-thinking Infinite Intelligence is by definition ludicrous, he can still be tempted to try and do so. This essentially means that while man's intellect is limited, his ego-driven sense of self is potentially unlimited.

ROOTS: THE EARTH'S DECISION

If we wish to attain a deeper understanding of Adam's sin, we need to consider its background. To do so, let us consult what is probably one of the most baffling comments of *Rashi* in our parsha, indeed, perhaps in the entire Chumash. On the third day of Creation, Hashem commanded that the earth bring forth "*eitz pri.*"[3] Although this translates literally as "trees of fruit," i.e., trees that bear fruit, that is mentioned in the very next phrase: "*oseh pri*—which produce fruit." What, then, is the meaning of the first phrase? Based on the Midrash, *Rashi* explains:

---

3   *Bereishis* 1:11.

"Eitz pri"—*[means] that the taste of the tree itself should be like that of the fruit. However, the earth did not do so, rather, "The earth brought forth...trees that produce fruit," but the tree itself was not as fruit. Therefore, when man was cursed for his sin, [the earth] was likewise recalled for its sin and it was cursed.[4]*

Needless to say, these words require much elucidation:

- How are we meant to understand the idea of the earth disobeying Hashem's instructions? Does the earth have a *yetzer hara* which would cause it to sin?
- Even if the earth somehow has the capacity to "disobey," what would cause it to do so on this occasion?
- If, indeed, the earth sinned by deviating from Hashem's instructions, why was it not punished straight away, instead only being cursed later on when man sinned?

The commentators explain that the earth's act of disobedience was not a sin per se, but an expression of the earth as a distinct physical entity. In the same way that the earth is distant from Hashem in that it is physical in nature while He is absolute spirituality, likewise, it is distant from being in absolute accordance with His will.[5] To develop this point further, the *Chizkuni* explains that the reasoning behind the earth's decision was that if the trees would taste the same as their fruit, then people might not wait for the fruit to grow, instead eating the trees, leading to their depletion.[6] Now, while the earth itself does not possess the faculty of reason, every physical entity has a *sar* (spiritual overseer) that is responsible for its growth and well-being. Hence, although the *sar*, too, does not have free will in the moral sense,[7] nevertheless, in

---

4   This refers to Hashem's words to Adam after he ate from the *Eitz Hadaas* (3:17): "*Arurah haadamah baavurecha*—Cursed is the earth on your account."
5   See *Gur Aryeh*, *Bereishis* loc. cit.
6   Ibid.
7   Although we find instances of angels sinning and being punished, this is in situations where they have descended to earth and assumed human form, thereby also incorporating human

its capacity as overseeing an independent entity, the *sar* naturally sought to vouchsafe the preservation of its creation. Now, this itself was not a sin, nor, indeed, was the earth punished for it at the time. Subsequently, however, as we will see, it would lead to a sin on someone else's part.

Adam was created comprised of two parts: his spiritual soul, which was blown into him by Hashem, and his physical body, which was formed from the earth. As such, included in his physical makeup was the earth's property of asserting its independence. This was in contrast to the soul, which remained intimately connected to its spiritual Source. Indeed, the challenge of man was for his spiritual connectedness to assert itself over his physical disconnectedness, drawing them both toward his Creator. In the end, though, the opposite occurred, for his disconnected, physical sense of self ended up encroaching on his spiritual side, leading him to disobey Hashem's instruction based on what he felt was the better course of enhancing that spiritual connection itself!

In this light, we can understand why, although the earth was not originally cursed, nevertheless, when Adam was subsequently cursed, the earth was cursed with him. The destiny and well-being of all elements of Creation rise or fall based on man's usage of them. Hence, when the faculty of disconnectedness and "assertion of self" which existed naturally within the earth contributed to man's sin, it shared in the consequences of that sin.

The result of that first sin was that death was introduced into the world. This was not "only" as a punishment for disobeying Hashem's command, but also a natural consequence of the fact that in eating from the *Eitz Hadaas*, Adam had distanced himself from Hashem, the Source of Life.

To be sure, the point here is not that the intellect is the enemy. Rather, like every human faculty, it is a gift that can be used for good or for bad. We are all encouraged to use our intellect to the best of our abilities in a manner that is meaningful and productive. What is unacceptable,

characteristics. See, e.g., *Yoma* 67b with *Rashi* ibid., s.v. *Uza*, and *Rashi*, *Bereishis* 19:22, s.v. *ki* (*Maayan Beis Hashoevah*, *Parshas Vayeira*, c.f. *Rabbeinu Bachya*, *Bereishis* 3:6).

and the point at which things begin to go wrong, is when we take our intellect and use it vainly and destructively, insisting on trying to out-think the Infinite Wisdom regarding how best to lead our lives.

BRANCHES: THE CHEIT HAEIGEL

Approximately twenty-five hundred years after the sin of the *Eitz Hadaas*, the Jewish People committed the sin of the Golden Calf. This episode would alter the course of their history and continues to rever-berate until our times, as the Gemara states, "There is no generation that does not taste a portion from the punishment for that sin."[8] In describing that episode, we find an unusual expression in the words of the prophet Hoshea:[9]

וְהֵמָּה כְּאָדָם עָבְרוּ בְרִית.

And they, like Adam, transgressed a covenant.

This verse informs us that not only did the people violate their cov-enant with Hashem by making the *eigel*, but they did so "like Adam." Apparently, there is some essential commonality between these two sins. Likewise, the Gemara explains that Hashem's words, "אֲנִי אָמַרְתִּי אֱלֹהִים אַתֶּם...אָכֵן כְּאָדָם תְּמוּתוּן—I had said, 'You are as angels...however, like Adam you shall die,'"[10] refer to the state of the Jewish People before and after the *eigel*.[11] Here too, we see that the fall of the *eigel* is framed with reference to the *Eitz Hadaas*: "Like Adam."

In what way were the Jewish People "like Adam" when they made the *eigel*?

OUR FINEST HOUR

In order to appreciate the connection between these two episodes, let us consider a well-known statement in the Gemara:

---

8   *Sanhedrin* 102a.
9   6:7.
10   *Tehillim* 82:6–7.
11   *Avodah Zarah* 5a.

בשעה שאמרו ישראל נעשה ונשמע, יצאה בת קול ואמרה מי גילה רז זה
לבני שמלאכי השרת משתמשין בו?

At the time when Yisrael said, "We will do and we will hear,"
a Heavenly voice issued forth and said, "Who revealed this
secret to My children, the one used by the ministering angels?"

The commentators explain: The phrase "we will do and we will hear" appears backwards, for how can one do anything without first hearing it? Rather, with this phrase, the people indicated their preparedness to act even before hearing what Hashem would actually demand of them. This reflects an implicit and complete alignment of their will with that of Hashem, similar to the level of the angels, who exist purely to fulfill Hashem's will. In terms of our discussion, we can understand that the Jewish People at Har Sinai succeeded in reclaiming the level of Adam before the sin. Indeed, the Gemara states elsewhere that when the Jewish People stood at Har Sinai, the "impurity" that had entered humankind during the sin of the *Eitz Hadaas* left them.[12] Moreover, as was the case with Adam in his pre-sin state, they could have been free from death, as the verse states, "I had said, 'You are as angels.'"

Yet here, too, we must ask: With their will in total alignment with that of Hashem, how could the people then proceed to make the Golden Calf?

ECHOES OF THE EITZ HADAAS

The commentators explain that essentially, when the people built the Golden Calf, they were purely looking for a means through which to communicate with Hashem.[13] Until now, the conduit had been Moshe, yet he had not returned from the mountain. Such a desire is not in itself reprehensible; indeed, it is highly laudable. The problem, however, was the way in which this desire was expressed. Let us consider that in the absence of Moshe, the obvious conduit for Hashem's will was there in the form of Aharon. As such, the correct course should have

---

12 *Shabbos* 146a.
13 See at length *Beis Halevi, Parshas Ki Sisa* and *Ramban, Shemos* 32:1.

been to approach Aharon and ask, "What shall we do now?" Instead, they approached him and demanded, "Here is what you shall do now!" instructing him to make a calf for them. What was behind this reversal of the "flow of command"? The answer will be distressingly familiar: The people had a compulsion for *them* to arrange the way in which the Divine Presence would draw close to them. With this, they were giving in to the aspect which demands independence and control—even regarding fulfilling Hashem's will! Having given entry to this impulse, it was now possible for what may have originally been a well-intentioned enterprise to degenerate overnight into actual idol worship.

Looked at in this light, it is not hard to see how this was effectively a repeat of Adam's own sin. Thus, the verse says, "And they, like Adam, transgressed a covenant." Likewise, in distancing themselves from total identification with Hashem's will, they left themselves, once more, susceptible to death, as Adam himself had originally done; hence, "Like Adam, you will die."

CONCLUSION: REVERBERATIONS

Indeed, it is fair to say that once we understand the background to the sin of the *Eitz Hadaas*, we will appreciate that it not only echoed in the episode of the *eigel*, but continues to reverberate throughout the generations. It is still a challenge to use our God-given faculty of intellect in a productive and elevating manner and not allow it to be enlisted in the service of vanity and delusion. To this end, Hashem has granted us a gift of love, the *Eitz Hachaim* (Tree of Life) in the form of the Torah, which illuminates our path toward an ultimate connection with the Source of life.

FROM THE COMMENTATORS

EXITS AND ENTRIES: THE WORLD AND THE LETTER HEI

אֵלֶּה תוֹלְדוֹת הַשָּׁמַיִם וְהָאָרֶץ בְּהִבָּרְאָם.

*These are the products of the heaven and earth when they were
created.*[1]

Commenting on the word "בְּהִבָּרְאָם," *Rashi* cites the midrashic exposition that this world is analogous to the letter *hei*—"*b'hei beraam.*"
The Gemara elaborates that like the letter *hei*, the world is open at the
bottom and it is easy for someone to "slip out" and lose his meaningful
presence there.[2] However, the Gemara adds, just as a *hei* has another
opening between the leg of the *hei* and its roof, so too, a person seeking to do *teshuvah* can re-enter. The Gemara then asks, why should
a separate opening be required? Why not simply come back the way
through which one left? To this, the Gemara replies somewhat cryp-
tically, "That would not work." However, the Gemara does not specify
why exactly it would not work.

In a certain sense, *teshuvah* contains a paradox: On the one hand,
the more mistakes we make, the more we need to correct them through

---

1   *Bereishis* 2:4.
2   *Menachos* 29b.

teshuvah. However, at the same time, the more mistakes we make, the less likely it is that we will do *teshuvah*. When we do something wrong, aside from the wrongful act itself, we dull our sensitivity to that area. As the Gemara puts it, "Once a person has committed a sin and then repeated it, it becomes in his eyes like a permitted matter."[3] Yet, these are the very sensitivities which we need in order to prompt us to do *teshuvah*! In this respect, sins are not just mistakes, they also impede a solution. This is why the Gemara says that it "does not work" to come back the way you leave, for when one "exits the world" through his wrongful behavior, he coats that path with a numbing agent, thereby rendering it of little help as a potential way back.

How, then, can a person re-enter the world? The Gemara informs us that this must happen through a "higher opening." By way of analogy: A child defines "good" or "bad" situations based on whether or not he feels pleasure or pain, comfort or distress. If his arm hurts him, that is "bad" and he will cry for help; if it does not hurt him, he is fine. If he has no feeling whatsoever, that is also OK, for there is no pain. Yet a grown-up in that situation will respond to that very lack of feeling with infinitely more alarm than he would to pain, for he is fully aware of its implications: circulation may have been cut off from the limb and he could risk losing its function and going through life without it. The faculty that brought about the adult's complete opposite reaction to that of the child is his broader awareness of his situation and its implications for his effective existence. In other words, *the very state* our lower consciousness views as cause for reassurance (lack of feeling) is viewed by higher consciousness as cause for alarm.

Similarly, in our child-like world, which focuses on our own agenda and aggrandizement, the loss of certain sensitivities—to *lashon hara*, to focus during *tefillah*, to refusing to cave in to the *yetzer hara*, to emotional engagement in performing mitzvos—is of no cause for alarm. But, when we attain a higher view of the world, losing feeling to those spiritual "limbs" itself becomes the cause of profound concern and

---

3   *Kiddushin* 40a.

alarm, for with those limbs rendered useless, Heaven forbid, our true function in the world is catastrophically impaired. The process of "*te-shuvah*" is literally that of returning from our virtual world to the world of Hashem, and it always starts with a person re-entering the world from a higher viewpoint than he left it—the opening between the leg and the roof of the *hei*.

OBJECTS AND PEOPLE: A DIFFERENT TAKE

וַיִּקַּח ה' אֱלֹקִים אֶת הָאָדָם וַיַּנִּחֵהוּ בְגַן עֵדֶן.

Hashem-Elokim took Adam and placed him in the Garden of Eden.[4]

Commenting on the word "*Vayikach*—And He took," *Rashi* explains:

לקחו בדברים נאים ופיתהו ליכנס.

He took him with pleasant words and enticed him to enter.

This explanation seems somewhat elaborate. Why not simply explain that Hashem actually took Adam and placed him there, or, at the very least, told him to go there? Indeed, this idea of *Rashi* will repeat itself numerous times throughout his commentary as the Torah describes people taking other people.[5] But why is it necessary?

The *Gur Aryeh* explains: The essence of a human being is not his physical body, something that animals also have, but his mind and will. As such, if one would physically coerce a person to go somewhere that he does not wish to go, one cannot be said to have "taken the person," since the essence of the person does not concur. It is only through persuading the person that this is something that he would want to do, can one truly be said to have taken the person.[6]

---

4   *Bereishis* 2:15.

5   See, e.g., *Bereishis* 16:3, s.v. *va'tikach*, *Shemos* 14:6, s.v. *v'es* and *Vayikra* 8:2, s.v. *kach*.

6   It is interesting to note this distinction in *Onkelos's* translation as well. When a verse describes objects being taken, *Onkelos* translates it as "*nasav*," whereas when a person is being taken, he uses a different word, "*d'var*," which relates to the word "*dibbur*—speech," for that is how a person is taken!

SAYING MORE WITH LESS: THE LAST
CONVERSATION BETWEEN KAYIN AND HEVEL

וַיֹּאמֶר קַיִן אֶל הֶבֶל אָחִיו וַיְהִי בִּהְיוֹתָם בַּשָּׂדֶה וַיָּקָם קַיִן אֶל הֶבֶל אָחִיו וַיַּהַרְגֵהוּ.

Kayin said to his brother Hevel, and it happened when they
were in the field, Kayin rose up against his brother Hevel and
killed him.[7]

Commenting on the opening words of our verse, *Rashi* writes:

נכנס עמו בדברי ריב ומצה כדי להתעולל עליו להרגו.

He [Kayin] entered into an argument with him [Hevel] in order
to form a pretext on which to kill him.

This is a most fascinating insight. Kayin clearly wished to kill
Hevel—hence, the fabricated argument. However, if so, why did Kayin
need to enter into an argument in order to lead him to an act that he, in
any case, wanted to do? Why not simply do it? Rather, says *Rashi*, Kayin
could not bring himself to kill Hevel in cold blood, so the only way he
could commit the act was by arranging to "heat up his blood." In other
words, Kayin acted in a "pre-meditated heat of the moment," having
organized the heat himself.

Yet, we still need to understand why *Rashi* provides this insight—after all, *Rashi*'s job is to resolve *pshat* matters within the verse.
For this, we turn to the verse itself and notice that it states, "*Vayomer*
Kayin el Hevel—Kayin said to Hevel," but it does not say what he said!
That is indeed a worthy *pshat* issue. In response to this difficulty, *Rashi*
provides the background, explaining that Kayin entered into an argument with Hevel.

However, the question remains: *Why* did the verse not specify what
Kayin said? Upon reflection, we will appreciate that this is what *Rashi*
is coming to explain. The verse does not provide the contents of that
final conversation because, given Kayin's goal for that conversation,
whatever it is that they said is *completely irrelevant*. With the desired

---

7   *Bereishis* 4:8.

result of getting into an argument set from the beginning, they could have spoken about anything and the result would have been the same! Hence, says *Rashi*, the Torah leaves the actual details of the conversation out. And so, it turns out that we never really know what it was that Kayin said to Hevel before killing him—and still we know all we need to know; for by omitting the *contents* of that final conversation, the Torah provided us with *commentary* concerning it. Indeed, by omitting this phrase, the verse speaks volumes.

PARSHAS NOACH

ZECHER TZADDIK LIVERACHAH

Dimensions in Rashi

WHEN RASHI GIVES TWO EXPLANATIONS

אֵלֶּה תּוֹלְדֹת נֹחַ נֹחַ אִישׁ צַדִּיק תָּמִים הָיָה בְּדֹרֹתָיו.

These are the offspring of Noach; Noach was a perfect, righteous man in his generations.[1]

INTRODUCTION—AND DIGRESSION

Commenting on the words of our opening verse, *Rashi* says:

הוֹאִיל וְהִזְכִּירוֹ סִפֵּר בְּשִׁבְחוֹ שֶׁנֶּאֱמַר "זֵכֶר צַדִּיק לִבְרָכָה."
דָּבָר אַחֵר, לְלַמֶּדְךָ שֶׁעִקָּר תּוֹלְדוֹתֵיהֶם שֶׁל צַדִּיקִים מַעֲשֵׂיהֶם הַטּוֹבִים.

Having mentioned him, [the verse then] spoke in his praise, as it says, "The remembrance of the righteous shall be for a blessing."
Alternatively, it is to teach you that the primary offspring of the righteous are their good deeds.

---

1   *Bereishis* 6:9.

The issue to which *Rashi* is responding is quite clear: The verse begins with words that appear to introduce *Noach's children* and then immediately proceeds to veer from that topic, talking instead about *Noach himself*!

In response to this, *Rashi* cites the above two explanations from Chazal.[2] Indeed, having identified the issue, we can see that *Rashi's* two explanations actually relate to this issue in fundamentally different ways:

- The first approach concedes the notion that the verse interrupted its discussion to talk about Noach, explaining why it did so (*"zecher tzaddik liverachah"*).
- The second approach, in re-translating *"toldos"* as referring to good deeds, explains that there is actually no interruption in the verse.

WHEN ARE TWO BETTER THAN ONE?

It is an established rule among the classic commentators on *Rashi* that whenever *Rashi* presents two explanations of a certain matter, it is because each explanation contains some merit or advantage not found in the other in resolving the issue at hand. The commentators then proceed to discuss what it was about each explanation which still left the matter requiring resolution, resulting in *Rashi* presenting an alternative answer.

In our case, starting backwards, it is easy to understand why *Rashi* was not satisfied with presenting the second explanation alone, for it entails the dramatic step of redefining the word *"toldos"* as "good deeds," while the simple meaning of this term throughout the Torah relates to one's biological children. The other question, however, remains: Why was *Rashi* not content with the first explanation, which indeed understands *toldos* as children, and explains the interruption to talk about Noach himself as based on the principle of *"zecher tzaddik liverachah"*? In this regard, a number of straightforward explanations come to mind:

---

2   See *Bereishis Rabbah* 30:6.

- If the interruption is based on *"zecher tzaddik liverachah,"* why are there not similar interruptions when describing other *tzaddikim* in Chumash?
- This is not the first time Noach is mentioned in the Torah. He has already been introduced in the final section of *Parshas Bereishis*. Why did the Torah not interrupt there, when mentioning him, to speak of his praise?

Although one can certainly suggest answers to these questions, and the commentators do, at the same time, it is also easy to understand why *Rashi* saw fit to suggest an additional approach to this matter.

However, as we will see, it is possible that what lies behind the two explanations of *Rashi* is a question of a much more fundamental nature.

THE MEANING OF "BERACHAH"

In his classic work, *Nefesh Hachaim*,[3] R' Chaim of Volozhin discusses at length the meaning of the Hebrew word *"baruch."* He cites a widely held notion that the word *baruch* is a term of praise, belonging, therefore, to the family of words like *shevach* and *hallel*. In this light, another way of saying, "Blessed are You," would be, "Praised are You." R' Chaim strongly rejects this view. In his opinion, the word *baruch* is not an expression of praise, and he proceeds to demonstrate this from the following episode recounted in the Gemara:[4]

> Said R' Yishmael ben Elisha, "On one occasion I entered the Holy of Holies to offer the incense, and I beheld an apparition of Hashem sitting on a high and exalted throne, and He said to me, 'Yishmael, my son, bless Me.' I responded, 'May it be Your will that Your mercy should suppress Your anger, and that Your mercy should prevail over Your other attributes, and that You deal with Your children with the attribute of mercy, and that You enter with them within the letter of the law.'"

---

3   *Shaar* 2, chap. 2.
4   *Berachos* 7a.

How does this episode help shed light on the meaning of the word *baruch*? Explains R' Chaim, if *baruch* is an expression of praise, then having been asked by Hashem to bless Him, R' Yishmael should have responded with some words of praise! But he didn't; he responded by asking for things such as mercy and forbearance. We see clearly, says R' Chaim, that the word *baruch* does not mean "praised."

However, having established what the word *baruch* does not mean, we now need to find out what it does mean.

R' Chaim explains that the word *berachah* is an expression of increasing something. Thus, we find, for example, that the verse says, "He [Hashem] will bless your bread."[5] This doesn't mean that Hashem will praise our bread. It means that He will bring about an increase in our harvest.[6]

This understanding of *berachah* has profound implications for how *berachos* work. We must preface by saying that our knowledge of Hashem and our relationship with Him is specifically in terms of His connection to the world. His existence outside of that context is completely beyond our grasp. Therefore, when we say the words, *"Baruch atah Hashem,"* we are saying that our recognition of Him as the Ultimate Source should bring about an increase of His involvement with and Divine input into the world.

Similarly, says R' Chaim, when R' Yishmael was asked to bless Hashem, he responded by asking for *an increase* in Divine mercy and grace.

IN DEFENSE OF "BERACHAH" AS PRAISE

The *Nefesh Hachaim*'s understanding of "*berachah*" as increase, as well the accompanying proof from the episode with R' Yishmael, can be

---

5   *Shemos* 23:25.

6   The *Maharal* explains in a number of places that the nature of the Hebrew language is such that the root letters of a word can convey the message that the word represents. With regard to the word *baruch*, the *Maharal* (*Tiferes Yisrael* chap. 34) concurs with the definition of increase, and indeed notes that this connotation is embedded within the root letters of the word, which are ב-ר-ך. All of these letters represent the basic level of increase from one to two. The numerical value of ב is two, כ is twenty, and ר is two hundred. Hence, the very root of the word ברך is made up of letters which are a product of the type of increase that the word represents.

found in earlier works dating back to the Rishonim.[7] Having said that there are others among the Rishonim who, in fact, endorse the notion that *berachah* is an expression of praise.[8] Naturally, we must ask, how would they respond to the proof from R' Yishmael's "*berachah*"?

A disarmingly simple answer to this is found in the writing of one of the earliest Rishonim, Rabbeinu Chananel.[9] Commenting on Hashem's request of R' Yishmael, "Bless Me," Rabbeinu Chananel writes:

> *The meaning of this "blessing" is praise, as we find in the verse "Barchu Hashem malachav—Bless [i.e., praise] Hashem, O His angels"...And having offered blessing and praise before Hashem's glory, he [R' Yishmael] offered the following prayer, "May it be Your will, etc."*

In other words, according to Rabbeinu Chananel, R' Yishmael's prayer was not the response to the request, "Bless Me"; rather, it followed the praise which was said in response to that request. The Gemara does not specify what that praise was, but rather moves straight to the follow-up request which was the reason the Gemara cited this episode in the first place.

Perhaps we may add another suggestion. The Gemara states that one should not add requests in the first three blessings of the *Shemoneh Esreh* since they are dedicated for praise only.[10] However, the Geonim qualify this restriction as referring only to requests of the individual. Requests for the community, on the other hand, can be made even in these first three blessings.[11] The explanation for this distinction is offered by the *Tosafos HaRosh*: Petitions for the community are, in effect,

---

7   See *Rashba*, commentary to *Aggados Berachos* ibid., commentary of *Rabbeinu Bachya* to *Devarim* 8:10, and his work *Kad Hakemach*, s.v. *berachah*. See also *Rashi*, *Sotah* 10a, s.v. *bameh*, and *Sefer HaIkarim, maamar* 2, chap. 26.

8   See, e.g., *Chizkuni* to *Bereishis* 24:27 and *Abarbanel* to ibid., 27:1. (See also *Yaaros Devash*, vol. 2, *drush* 16.)

9   Commentary to *Maseches Berachos* loc. cit., cited in *Ohr Zarua, Hilchos K'rias Shema* sec. 8.

10   *Berachos* 34a.

11   Indeed, this is the basis of the insertion of the request, "*Zachreinu l'chaim*—Remember us for life," at the end of the first blessing of *Shemoneh Esreh* during the Ten Days of *Teshuvah*.

a praise of Hashem, for they indicate that the entire community needs Him. Here too, since R' Yishmael offered a prayer on behalf of the entire Jewish People, that too constitutes praise in response to Hashem's request, "Bless Me."

A SOURCE IN THE SAGES

So far, we have seen that the meaning of the word *"berachah"* is a matter whose discussion goes back as far as the early Rishonim. However, a bit more reflection will reveal that it goes back further still.

Let us return to our question regarding *Rashi*'s two explanations of our verse. The first explanation invokes the idea of *"zecher tzaddik liverachah,"* yet *Rashi* was not entirely satisfied by this and, therefore, added a second approach. Perhaps now we can understand why:

- The first approach can only work if one adopts the understanding of the word *"berachah"* as *praise*. If so, one can explain the verse's apparent interruption praising Noach based on this idea.
- However, if one understands *"berachah"* not as praise, but as *increase*, the concept of *"zecher tzaddik liverachah"* will be of no relevance or assistance here, since the verse's interruption did not bring about any "increase" within Noach. Hence, that understanding of *"berachah"* will require an alternative explanation of our verse, which *Rashi* provides with his second answer.[12]

---

12   From R' David Pardo, commentary *Maskil L'David* on *Rashi*. It should be noted that *Rashi* also invokes the concept of *"zecher tzaddik liverachah"* later on in *Bereishis* (18:18–19), where Hashem says, "Am I withholding from Avraham that which I am doing [regarding Sodom]?" and then states, "And Avraham will be a great and mighty nation." Here, too, there appears to be an interruption, which *Rashi* explains based on *"zecher tzaddik liverachah."* We note that in this second instance, the interruption was not speaking in praise of Avraham, but foretelling the greatness that would come from him, reflecting the understanding of *"berachah"* as increase. (See also *Yoma* 38b, where the Gemara identifies the source for the concept of *"zecher tzaddik liverachah"* as the verse dealing with Avraham. Although, as a rule, one normally cites the first instance where an idea is found in the Chumash, which in our case would seem to be Noach, that opinion in the Gemara clearly understands *"berachah"* as increase, in which case the first instance of this in the Chumash is not Noach, but Avraham.)

It is fascinating to consider how a basic question such as this, which is first expressed in the Rishonim and subsequently elaborated upon by the Acharonim, has its roots in the words of Chazal themselves when we ponder and contemplate their meaning.

In our own experience, this discussion has major ramifications for our understanding of the words, "*Baruch atah Hashem*," which we recite many times each day. Beyond this, when we use the term "*zecher tzaddik liverachah*" regarding a righteous person who has passed away, the meaning will depend on the above. If *berachah* means praise, then we are purely speaking in praise of them. However, if it means "increase," then we are also speaking about ourselves, for we are saying that bringing the *tzaddik* to mind should lead to an increase in our promoting and adhering to the values which they held dear.

WHO BY WATER

BACKGROUND

The first half of our parsha deals with the flood that destroyed the generation of Noach, which had descended into an abyss of evil and corruption, with only Noach and his family being saved in the ark. The present discussion begins with a simple question: Why, of all things, was the punishment Hashem chose for that wicked generation a flood of water? Surely there are other ways to punish the wicked which would be quicker, less dramatic—and less cataclysmic! We know that Hashem's punishments are *"middah k'neged middah*—measure for measure"; why was water deemed the appropriate response to their deeds?

Let us consider two approaches to this question.

FIRST APPROACH: OF FORM AND FORMLESSNESS

If we reflect on the appalling moral decline into which that generation had sunk, we could sum it up by saying that they had lost their *human form* and *moral distinction*; they had abandoned their Divinely-oriented qualities and characteristics known as *tzelem Elokim*—the Divine image. All the sins which are associated with that time—robbery, violence, being steeped in immorality and vice—depict a generation which acted no differently than animals.

Water represents formlessness. It has no form of its own and, moreover, can wear away the form of other things with which it comes into contact.[1] The most dramatic expression of this formless quality of water can be seen in the flood at the time of Noach. The Hebrew word for flood is "מבול." One of the interpretations offered by *Rashi* for this word is that it relates to the word "מבלה—to wear away."[2] Indeed, the waters of the flood wore away the form of everything that was in the world at that time. In other words, having abdicated their distinctly human form, that generation was punished by a flood of water which erased the form of the face of the entire world.

It is most interesting to note in this regard that one of the first things which Hashem communicated to Noach upon leaving the ark was the permission to eat from the meat of animals,[3] something that had been forbidden prior to the flood. What changed now? Apparently, the prohibition against eating the meat of animals had been misinterpreted as saying that animals are equal to human beings in every sense; an equation which, if stated backwards, means that human beings are no different than animals. This error contributed to the climate which enabled the Generation of the Flood to sink to the depths that it did. Moreover, that permission was followed by and contrasted with the prohibition against murdering another human being,[4] as that verse concludes: "for in God's image He created man." Hence, the first message they received upon leaving the ark to start anew was: Man is not an animal![5]

SECOND APPROACH: DILUTION VS. DEPRAVATION

After Noach and his family exited the ark and offered *korbanos* to Hashem, Hashem declared that He would never again bring a flood upon mankind. The verse reads:

וַיֹּאמֶר ה' אֶל לִבּוֹ לֹא אֹסִף לְקַלֵּל עוֹד אֶת הָאֲדָמָה בַּעֲבוּר הָאָדָם כִּי יֵצֶר לֵב הָאָדָם רַע מִנְּעֻרָיו וְלֹא אֹסִף עוֹד לְהַכּוֹת אֶת כָּל חַי כַּאֲשֶׁר עָשִׂיתִי.

---

1   See *Maharal, Gevuros Hashem*, chap. 18.
2   *Bereishis* 6:17.
3   Ibid., 9:3.
4   Verse 6.
5   See *Sefer HaIkarim, maamar* 3, chap. 15.

Hashem said in His heart, "I will never again curse the ground because of man, for the impulse of man's heart is evil from his youth, and I will never again smite all of life as I have done."[6]

Let us ask:

- What is the meaning of this declaration? The flood was brought upon mankind as a punishment for their corrupt ways. Given that man has free will, is it not conceivable that the world could become corrupt again, in which case a flood (or some similar punishment) would be likewise appropriate?
- The reason Hashem gives for this commitment is that "the impulse of man's heart is evil from his youth." How is that a reason not to bring another flood? The matter is all the more puzzling when we recall that it was the evil of man that was the reason for bringing the flood in the first place, as stated at the end of *Parshas Bereishis*: "וַיַּרְא ה' כִּי רַבָּה רָעַת הָאָדָם בָּאָרֶץ וְכָל יֵצֶר מַחְשְׁבֹת לִבּוֹ רַק רַע כָּל הַיּוֹם—Hashem saw that the evil of man was great upon the earth and every impulse of thought was continually turned solely to evil."[7] How can the reason for something happening then become the reason it will never happen again?

MIDRASH: FINDING A MATE FOR FALSEHOOD

There is a most astonishing account in the Midrash concerning Hashem's instructions that all should enter the ark in pairs:

Each kind entered with its mate. Then, Falsehood came and wanted to enter. Noach said to it, "You cannot enter unless you bring a mate in with you." Falsehood then went in search of a mate, whereupon it met Greed, who asked, "From where are you coming?" [Falsehood answered,] "From Noach. I went to ask him to admit me into the ark and he wouldn't let me enter without a mate. Would you like to be my mate?" Greed said,

---

6   Ibid., 8:21.
7   6:5.

"And what will you give me?" Falsehood replied, "I will arrange with you that everything that I amass you can then take." They arranged between them that everything that Falsehood would bring in, Greed would then take, and thus they entered the ark together.

It is actually difficult to even know where to begin when contemplating this Midrash—it is simply a riddle from beginning to end! Let us see if we can unravel it and access some of its message.

REINING IN EVIL

One of the classic works of *drash* of the eighteenth century, the *Afikei Yehudah*,[8] explains as follows. Hashem created evil for a purpose, as without evil man cannot exercise his free will. The problem with the Generation of the Flood was that evil had broken free of all boundaries and had become an ideology unto itself. Thus, the verse mentioned above says that "every impulse of thought was continually turned solely to evil," indicating that people became dedicated to evil *purely for the sake of doing evil*. This is illustrated by the fact that they cross-bred all the species of animals that existed, even though no conceivable benefit would come from it. Clearly, this pathologically corrupt system could not be allowed to endure. On the other hand, evil itself in some measure is a necessary component of Creation to allow for moral choices on the part of man. In addition, the urges of physicality are necessary for the continued existence of the physical world.

This brings us to Noach's ark.

With the world around it being destroyed, everything that was to exist in the world after the flood was brought into the ark. We now appreciate that this includes Evil, too, as a necessary component of the world. Hence, Evil, represented in the Midrash as "Falsehood"—as all evil is ultimately false—approached Noach and requested to be admitted into the ark. However, it could not be allowed to enter "without a mate," i.e., as evil alone with no context or constraints, as this was what led to

---

8   R' Yehudah Adel of Slonim, *drush* 5.

the flood in the first place. Thus, Evil set out in search of a "mate" that would define and contain it. The mate Evil found was Greed, meaning that evil would continue to exist, not for its own sake, but for some perceived gain, thus leaving it up to the individual to exert his free will, either succumbing to greed or overcoming it. This is the meaning of the arrangement described by the Midrash whereby "everything that Evil would bring in, Greed would then take." Having been limited to a specific context and thus allowing for a meaningful moral life after the flood, Evil, together with its mate Greed, were granted entry into the ark.

Thus, when the world was established anew after the flood, Hashem declared that He would not bring another flood, "for the impulse of man's heart is evil from his youth." In other words, unlike the evil which was initially pursued for its own sake, which led to the flood, the evil which exists now is purely that which derives from one's physical makeup and desires; while people will yet have their victories and defeats in dealing with this form of evil, it is not something that will lead to another flood.

OF TEACHERS AND STUDENTS

One question, however, remains: What measures were taken to ensure that the same form of unconstrained evil that brought about the flood would not itself resurface at some later stage?

The answer is: the flood.

When Hashem informed Noach of His intention to destroy mankind, He said: "Hineni mashchisam es haaretz." Rashi explains these words to mean, "And behold, I will destroy them *together with the earth*." The Midrash,[9] which is the source of Rashi's comment, elaborates upon the idea of the earth being "punished" together with man:

> This may be compared to a king's son who had a teacher. If the son sours, his teacher will [also] be punished...So too, said the Holy One, Blessed is He, "Behold, I will destroy them [mankind] together with the earth."

---

9   *Bereishis Rabbah* 31:7.

In what way is the earth considered the "teacher" of man, such that it bears some responsibility for his mistakes? The *Afikei Yehudah* explains that initially, the physicality of the earth was of extremely high potency, which then became imparted to man as he partook of the world. This was expressed, for example, in the much longer life spans people had before the flood. Ultimately, however, this level of physicality proved too much for man to control and ended up controlling him. In this light, we return to the verse where Hashem surveys the evil of man prior to the flood: It states, "The evil of man was great *on the earth [baaretz],*" i.e., his relationship with the earth had resulted in an uncontrollable level of evil.

The response to this situation was not only to punish man, but also to address the cause of his corruption. To this end, Hashem brought a flood upon the earth, which not only wiped out that generation, but also deluged and "watered down" the potency of the earth itself, thereby diminishing the level of physicality it would impart to man. Thus, Hashem said after the flood, "I will never again curse the ground because of man," i.e., the ground will never again be implicated as a cause of man's failings, for its potency had been tempered. Any evil that remains is "the impulse of man's heart [that] is evil from his youth," and is his responsibility alone to contend with.[10] Moreover, with evil having been modified in this way, although each person bears responsibility for his sins, mankind will never again incur the cataclysmic destruction of the flood: "and I will never again smite all of life as I have done."

---

10 Although it is still possible for a person to choose a path of "evil for evil's sake," for this too is within the range of his free will, nevertheless, given the diminished physicality of the world, such a choice became an anomaly.

ENVIRONMENTAL AWARENESS

INTRODUCTION: A MIDRASH TO MYSTIFY

In the fifth chapter of *Tehillim*, we read:

תְּאַבֵּד דֹּבְרֵי כָזָב...וַאֲנִי בְּרֹב חַסְדְּךָ אָבוֹא בֵיתֶךָ.

You shall destroy the speakers of falsehood...And I, through
Your abundant kindness, will enter Your house.[1]

The Midrash relates these verses to the events of the flood, with the "speakers of falsehood" in the first verse referring to the generation which was wiped out, while the second verse is Noach speaking about himself. In this light, how are we to translate the opening word "*vaani*"? On a *pshat* level, we would translate it as "as for me," with the letter *vav* setting Noach *apart* from those in the first verse. The Midrash, however, proceeds to translate the letter *vav* in accordance with its primary meaning—"and me"—which serves to *link* the two:

ואני: כאשר עשו כן עשיתי. ומה ביני לבינם? אלא שגמלתני חסד ואמרת לי
בא אתה וכל ביתך אל התיבה.

"And I": Just as they did, so did I. What, then, is the difference
between me and them? That you performed a kindness for me
and told me, "Come you and all of your household to the ark."

---

1   Verses 7–8.

A number of questions arise regarding this Midrash:

- How can Noach meaningfully equate himself with the wicked people of his generation to the extent that he sees no difference between them and him other than Hashem's kindness toward him? The Torah explicitly calls him a *tzaddik*! Is this simply Noach being humble and ignoring his righteousness?
- Assuming we accept Noach's indicting assessment of himself, his question still remains: Why was he spared from the flood? His answer was that Hashem performed a kindness for him and allowed him to enter the ark, but why did Hashem perform this kindness for him and not for anyone else?

An additional observation on this Midrash is that it adduces the verse, "And I, through Your abundant kindness, will enter Your house," regarding Noach entering the ark. This is most intriguing; we would naturally refer to the ark as "Noach's house" for that year, yet the Midrash is informing us that it was actually "Hashem's house." What is the meaning of this designation, and how does it relate to the Midrash's discussion of Noach?

THE LAWS OF NATURE—AND THEIR RULES

The *Beis Halevi* prefaces his explanation of the Midrash by asking another question. Chazal inform us that in the Generation of the Flood, the entire world was corrupt, with even animals mating with other species. How are we to understand the idea of animals acting in a corrupt manner? Animals do not possess free will, they are bound to follow their nature! The answer, says the *Beis Halevi*, is that when man chooses evil over good and corrupts his nature, this also has a corrupting effect on the nature of his surroundings and all the beings therein. It is true that an animal can only follow its nature, but, at that time, the nature of animals itself had been changed. In other words, when man became *corrupt*, the animals became *corrupted*.[2]

---

2   This may also give us insight into a curious group of animals at that time. *Rashi* informs us that the two of each species which were allowed to enter Noach's ark were those who had not

NOACH AND THE FIRST SUCCESSFUL
TRANSPLANT OPERATION

This brings us to Noach himself. Delicately, we ask: if the corruption of mankind's nature can affect the nature of animals, can it affect the nature of another person? The answer, says the *Beis Halevi*, is that it can, especially as each person has an animal part to his nature.[3] This is the meaning of the Midrash in which Noach equates his behavior with that of his generation. He was not saying that he was as wicked as them; after all, as the Torah states explicitly, he was a righteous person. However, he was conceding that he had not remained immune to the effect that their choices had on his nature, which made it harder for him to always do the right thing.[4]

This brings us to the ark. It was not just a place where it didn't rain that year. It was a place that allowed for the rehabilitation of Noach to his full, original spiritual capacity! If Noach's problem was that he had been adversely affected by what had become a bad environment, the obvious antidote was to place him in a good one. The best environment for that year was the ark, for it housed not only all the animals, but

---

acted in a corrupt manner. This idea is now even more perplexing. Having just established that the nature of animals at that time had changed, how can we then understand that there was a group of individual animals who were somehow immune to this change? Rav Gedalyah Schorr (*Ohr Gedalyahu, Parshas Noach*) explains that if the wicked behavior of mankind at that time affected the nature of animals in general, the specific moral stance of Noach and his family in refusing to choose evil over good likewise affected a sub-group of each species. These were the animals who found their way to Noach's ark. They were, in a sense, "his" animals.

3   The full implication of this idea is that it is possible for someone to sin to the extent that he makes it harder for another person to resist sinning. In this situation, although the second person bears primary responsibility for his actions, the first person will also bear some responsibility for having facilitated those sins. In this vein, the *Beis Halevi* explains the expression used by the Sages (see, e.g., *Pirkei Avos* 3:1) whereby a person will in the future need to give "*din v'cheshbon*—a judgment and a reckoning" for his actions. "Judgment" refers to him being judged for the deeds that he committed, while "reckoning" refers to the calculation of his share in the deeds of others.

4   The *Beis Halevi* explains that it is in this regard that certain Sages compare Noach negatively with Avraham. Avraham also lived in a generation whose deeds corrupted his surroundings. However, unlike Noach, Avraham did not allow this to affect his own behavior, even to a small degree.

also the Divine Presence itself. This is why it is referred to as Hashem's house, and that was the kindness which Hashem performed for Noach.

There is a parallel comment of the Midrash which bears out this theme, which applies the verse "*Shesulim b'veis Hashem*—planted in the house of Hashem" to Noach and his family. A tree derives its nutrition from the soil in which it is planted. When something is transplanted, its nutrition changes in accordance with its new setting. This was a crucial theme within Noach's time in the ark, transplanting him from a corrosive setting to a place where he would receive positive nutrition.

An idea of which we have become increasingly sensitive to in recent decades is that of environmental awareness, namely, the profound effect that a person's actions can have on his surroundings, even though the person might not be directly interacting with the things that he is potentially damaging. The Torah itself is alerting us to this idea in our parsha: a person's moral choices have moral reverberations, sometimes far-reaching ones. Together with this idea, the experiences of Noach also remind us of the effect that one's surroundings can have on himself. If Noach, whom the Torah itself calls a *tzaddik*, was not immune to his surroundings, we are hardly likely to be. This should encourage us to seek the most positive environment for ourselves and our families. This, too, is part of environmental awareness.

However, there is a third element to this discussion which can also be gleaned from Noach's ark.

THE ARK AS HASHEM'S NAMES

The verse in *Mishlei* reads:[5]

מִגְדַּל עֹז שֵׁם ה' בּוֹ יָרוּץ צַדִּיק וְנִשְׂגָּב.

Hashem's name is a tower of strength; the righteous shall run toward it and be saved.

The *Zohar* states that this verse refers to the ark built by Noach. The connection between Hashem's name and Noach's ark is demonstrated

---

5   18:10.

in a fascinating way by the *Malbim*.[6] As we know, the dimensions of the ark were: three hundred *amos* (cubits) long, fifty *amos* wide, and thirty *amos* high.[7] What is the significance of these dimensions? Lest we be inclined to respond simply that this is the size required in order to house all the animals and birds, the *Ramban* demonstrates conclusively that there is no way an ark of that size could naturally house a pair of every type of animal and bird.[8] Rather, says the *Ramban*, the ability of the ark to contain all the creatures within it was miraculous. Noach's job was to make an ark of a certain size, and Hashem would see to it that all the animals and birds would fit in. This being the case, we ask again, given that there was no way the ark was naturally big enough for its task, why these specific dimensions?

The *Malbim* explains: The name *Yud-Hei-Vav-Hei* represents Hashem as Creator of the world. The name *Aleph-Dalet-Nun-Yud* represents His ownership and control of the world. Since the ark was the vehicle through which Hashem would create the world anew and guide its destiny, these two names formed the dimensions of the ark. Both of these names have four letters. The product of multiplying the letter of one name with the corresponding letter of the second name will give us the dimensions of the ark, as follows:

- The first letters of each name are *yud* and *aleph*, which have the numerical value of ten and one respectively. Ten times one equals ten, which is the height of the top story of the ark, where Noach and his family lived.
- The second letters of the two names are *hei* and *dalet*, which have the numerical value of five and four. Five times four equals twenty, the height of the lower two floors.
- The third letters are *vav* and *nun*, which equal six and fifty, the product of which is three hundred, the length of the ark.

---

6   *Bereishis* 6:15.
7   Ibid.
8   Commentary ibid.

- The fourth letters are *hei* and *yud*, which equal five and ten; the product of which is fifty, the width of the ark.

We would like to suggest that by Hashem giving Noach an ark comprised of His names, He was essentially giving him two types of arks, each one capable of protecting him from a different type of flood. One's environment is not just limited to one's physical surroundings, for there are corrosive ideas which can permeate any physical wall that surrounds a person, a phenomenon to which we are witness in our times more than ever before. The only environment which can effectively protect a person against such toxins resides within him. This concept is expressed by R' Elazar Ezkari with the words: "*Bilevavi mishkan evneh*— In my heart, I will build a sanctuary."

This, therefore, is the lesson from Noach's ark(s):

- When the flood consists of water, an ark made of wood coated with pitch will protect you.
- When the flood consists of ideas that can penetrate wood—and any other material, for that matter—the only ark that will protect you is Hashem's name that resides within you, with all the ideals and values that it represents.

Even as we strive to choose the best physical environment for ourselves, we should at the same time be developing and nurturing the environment which "envelopes us from within"—the Sanctuary of Hashem's names inside our hearts.

FROM THE COMMENTATORS

BIRDS, CLOUDS, AND RAINBOWS

קִנִּים תַּעֲשֶׂה אֶת הַתֵּבָה.

You shall make the ark as booths.[1]

The word *"kinim"* (booths) refers to the cubicles in which each of the animals were to be housed. However, the Midrash presents an additional explanation of this term, associating it with the concept of *"kinim"* as a pair of birds brought as an offering:

אמר הקדוש ברוך הוא לנח: מה הקן הזה מטהר את המצורע, אף תיבתך מטהרתך.

Said the Holy One, blessed is He, to Noach, "In the same way a pair of birds purifies a metzora, so too your ark will purify you."[2]

Why does Noach need to be purified like a *metzora*? We know that *tzaraas* comes upon a person as a punishment for speaking *lashon hara* (slander). Where do we find Noach guilty of this sin?

---

1   *Bereishis* 6:14.
2   *Bereishis Rabbah* 31:9.

It would appear that Noach's sin of *lashon hara* lay not in something that he said but in what he didn't say. As is well-known, the Sages take note of the fact that upon being informed by Hashem that his generation was to be wiped out, Noach did not respond by praying on their behalf. Moreover, even though he administered rebuke to those around him over the course of the many years that he spent building the ark, we see that no one was moved to repent and join him. We can only conclude that his words of exhortation were not said with a great amount of conviction or passion. The question is, why?

It seems that Noach simply felt that the people in his generation had crossed the point where they could have been saved and that their situation was beyond repair. Indeed, upon reflection, it is not that hard to understand why Noach thought this way, surrounded as he was by the corruption and depravity to which his generation had sunk, with all traces of humanity seemingly eradicated. However, on his level, Noach was expected to harbor hope even for people such as these. In this regard, Noach's silence when he should have been praying for his generation, and his lack of enthusiasm while exhorting them, were effectively communicating a message: "There is no hope for them." This was the *lashon hara* for which Noach required purification in the form of the ark. Throughout the long months of taking care of every other form of life, Noach may have found himself wishing that there were other people who could have also joined him in the ark.

Indeed, in this regard, R' Meir Shapiro explains the choice of the rainbow as the sign of the covenant between Hashem and Noach. Primarily, the rainbow is a reassurance to Noach, but it also contains an element of rebuke. When Noach surveyed his generation, all he saw was grey clouds, with no hope of light ever penetrating the darkness of their souls. To this end, Hashem showed him that light can shine through clouds, and when it does, it produces the majestic prismatic effect of the rainbow.

We may wonder if there is any actual benefit in discussing Noach's failing regarding the people in his generation. It would appear that the answer lies in the goal of such a discussion. If it is in order to accompany our glass of wine and well-seasoned cholent, completing our Shabbos enjoyment with a discussion of Noach's flaws, then it is hardly likely to be productive or meaningful. However, if the discussion inspires us to ask whether there are people whom *we* know that we might have condemned as being beyond reach, then it is indeed most worthwhile.

WITH RESPECT TO FREEDOM

וַיֵּשְׁתְּ מִן הַיַּיִן וַיִּשְׁכָּר וַיִּתְגַּל בְּתוֹךְ אָהֳלֹה. וַיַּרְא חָם אֲבִי כְנַעַן אֵת עֶרְוַת אָבִיו
וַיַּגֵּד לִשְׁנֵי אֶחָיו בַּחוּץ. וַיִּקַּח שֵׁם וָיֶפֶת אֶת הַשִּׂמְלָה...וַיְכַסּוּ אֵת עֶרְוַת אֲבִיהֶם
וּפְנֵיהֶם אֲחֹרַנִּית וְעֶרְוַת אֲבִיהֶם לֹא רָאוּ.

[Noach] drank from the wine and became intoxicated, and lay uncovered in his tent. Cham, the father of Canaan, saw the nakedness of his father and told his two brothers outside. Shem and Yefes took a garment...and they covered over the nakedness of their father; their faces were turned away and they did not see the nakedness of their father.[3]

As the simple reading of the verse indicates, while Cham told his brothers about what he had seen, he did nothing to remedy the situation. R' Shimshon Raphael Hirsch explains that Cham was happy to see his father in this degraded state, for witnessing him in a moment of weakness and disgrace allowed him to free himself from the moral hold that his father held over him. His position was essentially, "My father can no longer presume to be the bearer of a moral message, condemning my lifestyle or anything I wish to do. I am finally free to do as I please."

For their part, Shem and Yefes understood that this momentary lapse did not define Noach and, therefore, took measures to preserve the regard and reverence they had for him by covering him up, facing away as they did so. Not only did they feel that it was dishonest to reframe their entire perception of their father based on a momentary failure, it was not even in their own interests to dismiss him as a moral voice in their lives, as he conveyed messages which they recognized were to their benefit to heed. Hence, they acted not only to restore his

---

3   *Bereishis* 9:21–23.

own dignity, but to maintain the position of honor that he enjoyed and commanded.

It is for this reason that Noach responded to Cham's behavior on that occasion by cursing his progeny with slavery. With this, Noach confirmed that not only were Cham's actions reprehensible in and of themselves, but they were also flawed in terms of the goal that they aimed to achieve. If a person has no moral guide exhorting and encouraging him to assert control over his life, the freedom with which he is left is none other than a form of ongoing slavery, with him at the mercy of his drives, habits, and weaknesses, lacking both the inclination and the ability to rise above them. Cham's curse may thus have been leveled toward him alone, but the crucial message contained therein is of relevance to all.

THE TOWER OF BAVEL

When considering the verses that describe the episode toward the end of our parsha, known as the Tower of Bavel, two points stand out:

- The verses are somewhat vague regarding what exactly the problem was, stating simply that the people wanted to build a tower "lest we become dispersed across the face of the earth."[4]
- It is not entirely clear that they had even *done anything wrong.* Indeed, Hashem's response was not phrased as *punishment* for something that they *had* done, but rather as a *prevention* against something that they *would* do: "And now, it will not be withheld from them all that they proposed to do. Come, let us descend and confuse their language."[5]

While the verses do not explicate where within this episode the sin lay, the Midrash provides more detail. For example, the *Midrash Tanchuma* explains that they said, "Let us build a tower so that we may ascend and do battle against Hashem with our shovels!" In truth, this

---

4   Ibid., 11:4.
5   Ibid., verses 6–7. See *Drashos HaRan, drush* 1, and commentaries of *Seforno* and *Akeidas Yitzchak* to our parsha.

Midrash itself requires explanation, for the notion of "doing battle against Hashem" sounds so ridiculous as to not even warrant a response from Hashem—aside from the fact that while a shovel may be a useful instrument in the building of the tower, it is hardly a weapon of choice with which to do battle once they had actually ascended! And yet, as ludicrous and pitiful as this idea sounds, we see that Hashem takes it very seriously, stating that if they were not prevented, they would, in time, succeed in their plans—requiring Him to respond, therefore, by dispersing them across the earth! Moreover, aside from the question of understanding what the Midrash is saying, we must contend with the fact that the Midrash seems to be supplying details of a sin to which, as we mentioned, there appears to be no reference in the verse itself!

A most profound and meaningful understanding of this episode is presented by R' Yosef Leib Bloch of Telz.[6] The key is the fear voiced by the people in verse 4: "lest we be dispersed." They understood that when individuals are isolated and alone, they are vulnerable to the elements and the hazards of life. However, by uniting together, they could pool their collective resources to fathom the secrets behind the forces of the world—both natural and metaphysical, thereby assuring themselves protection and prosperity. The rallying point for this enterprise was the tower, a symbol of their unity.

Now, on the face of it, seeking to protect themselves is not a sin in itself, and hence there is no negative treatment of this idea in the verses. However, what is explicitly stated tells us that something very negative indeed could come from this idea, and this is what the Midrash elaborates upon. Man was created in order to live a life that is both connected to Hashem and representative of His will. In seeking to unlock the secrets of the world, there was a subliminal element of seeking to detach themselves from Hashem by accessing and manipulating the laws of nature. This idea receives expression in another statement of the Midrash, whereby the people reasoned that once every 1,506 years, a flood descends on the world, so they sought to build a tower in order

---

6   *Shiurei Daas*, "*Dor Hapalagah*."

to plug the hole for the next time around! Here too, their aim was to move away from any notion of Divine accountability, seeking instead to protect themselves through their control of nature and taking their fate into their own hands.

This is the war that they sought to wage against Hashem "with their shovels." Through trying to gain control of the world, they were sending a message, saying, "We do not need to obey You in order to assure our success; we can do so on our own." This idea, however, was not stated openly, nor, perhaps, even fully recognized by the people themselves; rather, it was latent in the lower levels of their consciousness. To this end, it is explicated in the realm of *drash*, with the verses only indicating that something very negative could result from this enterprise, yielding the result that Hashem confused their language and dispersed them throughout the world.

What is most fascinating about this approach to the Tower of Bavel is that it takes the entire episode from being in the realm of ancient history to an issue of ongoing concern for all times. On the one hand, man has been charged by Hashem Himself to "subdue the earth." However, this Divine directive must be applied with a view to representing Hashem in this world and connecting it to His will. The idea that subduing the forces of nature is something which could detach a person from Hashem—be it in the area of earning a livelihood, pursuing medical treatment, or the like—is one that confronts us regularly. To this end, we would do well to learn the episode of the Tower of Bavel most carefully and ensure, as far as possible, that we do not fall prey to their ideology.

PARSHAS LECH LECHA

UNDERSTANDING RASHI'S COMMENT ON THE WORDS "LECH LECHA"

Dimensions in Rashi

Our parsha begins with the test of *lech lecha*—for Avram to leave everything behind and follow Hashem to a destination that He will make known. The words *"lech lecha"* translate literally as, "Go for yourself." *Rashi*'s comment on this double expression is very well known:

> לֶךְ לְךָ: לַהֲנָאָתְךָ וּלְטוֹבָתְךָ וְשָׁם "אֶעֶשְׂךָ לְגוֹי גָדוֹל", וְכָאן אִי אַתָּה זוֹכֶה לְבָנִים, וְעוֹד שֶׁאוֹדִיעַ טִבְעֲךָ בָּעוֹלָם.

> *Lech lecha: For your benefit and for your good; and there, "I will make you into a great nation," whereas here, you will not merit to have children. Furthermore, I will make your nature known to the world.*

IDENTIFYING RASHI'S ISSUE WITH THE VERSE

As always, before analyzing *Rashi*'s words themselves, we first need to establish what difficulty it is in the verse that *Rashi* is responding to. Here, the answer appears quite obviously to be one of redundancy: the word "*lecha*—for yourself" seems to be redundant. What does it add to the command itself of "*lech*—go"? To this, *Rashi* answers that Hashem is informing Avraham that the journey will be "*lecha*—for you," i.e., for your benefit.

Having said this, we note that *Rashi* seems to have responded to the issue of one extra word with four separate explanations:

- For your benefit.
- For your good.
- There you will have children.
- I will make your nature known to the world.

That is a lot of explanations!

However, upon closer inspection, we will realize that *Rashi* is, in fact, saying two things and then elaborating upon them. For let us ask: What is the difference between the two terms, "for your benefit" and "for your good"? Is not everything that is for one's benefit also for his good? Rather, the difference is that "for your benefit" denotes things that will be beneficial for Avraham, while "for your good" refers to the good that Avraham will be able to do for others. To these two terms, *Rashi* then adds elaboration and illustration:

- "For your benefit"—I will make you into a great nation.
- "For your good"—I will make your positive nature known to the world, so that people will be inspired to emulate you.

Having said that, even scaling *Rashi*'s comments down to two positive outcomes still leaves them in excess of the one redundant word "*lecha*."

THE RAMBAN'S OBJECTION: DERECH HAKASUV

Getting back to the matter of redundancy, the *Ramban* strongly objects to *Rashi*'s comment. The basis of his objection is that he claims that the word "*lecha*" is not redundant! The definition of redundancy is when something is "extra," i.e., beyond what would normally be used to express that idea. In our instance, however, we see throughout Tanach that it is the "*derech hakasuv*," the normal way of the verse, to attach the terms *"li, lo, lecha,"* denoting, "myself, himself, yourself" to a verb like *"lech."* For example, the verse says, *"Eilchah li*—I shall go myself."[1] Since this is not at all unusual, *Rashi* shouldn't have commented on it, citing the Midrash's explanation.

In other words, the *Ramban* has no issue with *Rashi's* midrashic comment in and of itself. Rather, the *Ramban's* issue is specifically with *Rashi* citing this explanation. Since *Rashi's* commentary is devoted to resolving *pshat* issues in the verse, he should not have given entry to an explanation of a word that does not need to be resolved on a *pshat* level. This is a truly remarkable situation, wherein the *Ramban* is not debating *Rashi* over the meaning of a word, but rather, over whether *Rashi*—in terms of his own methodology—even needed to explain its meaning in the first place!

GUR ARYEH: WHEN THE WORD "LECHA" NEEDS TO BE EXPLAINED

A classic explanation of *Rashi's* position is found in the commentary *Gur Aryeh* on *Rashi* by the *Maharal*. In truth, he explains, the word *"lecha"* is never just "there" as a matter of linguistic form. It always has a meaning, for it denotes that the decision regarding the enterprise comes from the person himself. In other words, the word *"lecha"* as "for you" means "it is your decision." If so, however, then we will appreciate that it cannot have this meaning when the person is *being commanded to go by someone else*—such as in our case. By definition, in commanding Avraham to go, Hashem was initiating the journey. As such, the word *"lecha"* regarding Avraham cannot assume its normal meaning of him being the one to decide. That is why, even though *Rashi* agrees that this kind of word is not always redundant, nevertheless, in our situation, it needs an explanation. Hence, he brings the midrashic interpretation of "for your benefit." For even though Avraham was not the one who decided to go, nevertheless, given that it was for his benefit, it was something that he would want to do, and thus in accord with his will.

---

1   *Yirmiyahu* 5:5.

A TALE OF TWO "LECH LECHA"S

A completely different perspective on *Rashi's* comment can be found in the commentary *Maskil L'David* by R' David Pardo. In truth, he says, this is not the only time Hashem addresses Avraham with the words "*lech lecha*"; rather, it is one of two places. At the end of the following parsha, *Vayeira*, in the episode of the *Akeidah*, Hashem appears to Avraham and says, "*Lech lecha el eretz HaMoriah*—go, yourself, to the land of Moriah."[2] Needless to say, if we wish to gain a full understanding of *Rashi's* approach to this phrase, we will need to consult his words on that second occasion as well. However, when we do, we will note that *Rashi* makes no comment there at all! We now have a most perplexing situation. On the one hand, when this phrase appears in the beginning of our parsha, *Rashi* responds with *four* comments, which we were then able to whittle down to two. By contrast, when the *very same phrase* appears at the end of the next parsha, *Rashi* makes no comment at all!

What are we to make of all this? Does the second word "*lecha*" require an explanation or not?

Says the *Maskil L'David*: In reality, as far as *Rashi* is concerned, the word "*lecha*" does not require any explanation. In this regard, *Rashi* agrees entirely with the *Ramban* that this is "*derech hakasuv.*" This is true even if the context is Hashem commanding someone, adding the extra word "*lecha*" or "*lachem.*" Indeed, we find that even regarding instances such as these in the Torah, *Rashi* makes no comment.[3] Rather, what causes *Rashi* to comment on the phrase "*lech lecha*" in our parsha is not the extra word "*lecha*," but something much more fundamental.

MASKIL L'DAVID: TWO TERMS FOR "GOING"

The Hebrew word for "go" is "*lech.*" However, as we go through the Chumash and Tanach we will notice something of great importance:

---

2   *Bereishis* 22:2.
3   E.g., *Devarim* 1:14: "*V'atem pnu lachem u'seu hamidbarah,*" and ibid., 2:13: "*Atah kumu v'ivru lachem es Nachal Zared.*"

- The term *"lech"* is always used with reference to the place *toward which* the person is going.
- If the verse is describing a person going *from* a certain place, the word it will use is *"tzei*—to leave."

A classic example of these two usages can be seen in the first verse of *Parshas Vayetzei*,[4] which reads:

וַיֵּצֵא יַעֲקֹב מִבְּאֵר שָׁבַע וַיֵּלֶךְ חָרָנָה.

Yaakov went out from Be'er Sheva and went toward Charan.

We see that when referring to the place Yaakov was going from (Charan), the Torah uses the term *"vayeitzei,"* while when describing where he was going to, it says *"vayeilech."* With this in mind, let us come back to the beginning of *Parshas Lech Lecha* and we will encounter a most unusual situation. The only places mentioned in the verse are those Avraham is going from: *"Me'artzecha u'mimoladetecha u'mibeis avicha*—From your land, from your birthplace, and from your father's house." If so, then the command should not have been *"lech lecha,"* but *"tzei lecha"*! This, says the *Maskil L'David*, is *Rashi's* issue with the verse: Not that the second word *"lecha"* seems to be *redundant*, but that the first word *"lech"* seems to be *inaccurate*!

Now we can understand why *Rashi* makes no comment at all on the second instance of *"lech lecha"* in *Parshas Vayeira*. Since Hashem's command there to Avraham is to go "to the land of Moriah," everything is in order: the first word *"lech"* is the appropriate term, and the second word *"lecha"* is *derech hakasuv*—a normal feature within the verse—and hence not redundant.

Yet, having identified *Rashi's* issue with the first *"lech lecha,"* how do we understand his response?

DRASH RESPONSES TO PSHAT QUESTIONS

As *Rashi* himself informs us, while his preferred method of resolving issues in the verse is through *pshat*, if necessary, i.e., if no *pshat* resolution

---

4   *Bereishis* 28:10.

seems forthcoming, he will invoke a *drash* approach. Similarly, in our instance, there does not appear to be a *pshat* explanation for the choice of the word "*lech*." Therefore, *Rashi* adopts a *drash* approach, namely, that the Torah chose to use the first word "*lech*" due to its affinity with the second word "*lecha*." In light of this, we now start to take notice of the second word "*lecha*," something we would not have done had the first word been the intuitive choice of "*tzei*," but which we now come to see as having been "highlighted" by the first word "*lech*." Accordingly, we note that the word "*lecha*" literally translates as "for yourself"; hence, *Rashi* explains that the message is that the journey would be for Avraham's benefit.

Indeed, there is more. The full impact of the Torah using "*lech*" as the opening word on account of its similarity with "*lecha*" is that now, it is as if the word "*lecha*" has been *written twice*. Therefore, *Rashi* comments that there will indeed be *two positive outcomes* from the journey: "*l'ha-naasecha u'l'tovasecha*—For your benefit and for your good.*"

Stunning!

FOLLOW-UP AND FURTHER INTRIGUE: RASHI'S SECOND SWEEP ON "LECH LECHA"

And there the matter rests. Until, that is, we get to a comment of *Rashi's* a little further on in our verse. The first place Hashem tells Avraham to leave is "*artzecha*—your land," which, according to *Rashi*, refers to Ur Kasdim. The problem is, at this stage, Avraham was already in Charan, having moved there from Ur Kasdim. Why is Hashem telling him to leave a place that he has already left? To this, *Rashi* responds by explaining that the meaning was, "*hisrachek od misham*—distance yourself further from there."

As we can appreciate, this comment of *Rashi's* could potentially re-open our entire discussion. If we now ask the question as to why Hashem used the word "*lech*" to tell Avraham to go, rather than "*tzei*," we would appear to have a very simple answer: Having already left his land, Avraham could not be told to "leave it," he could only be told to "go from it" and distance himself further. If this is so, then we would seem to have found a *pshat* answer to *Rashi's pshat* question! While this is, of course, good news, it forces us to look back to the opening *Rashi* and ask: Why did *Rashi* feel the need to provide a *drash* answer regarding the Torah's choice of the word *"lech,"* when a perfectly good *pshat* answer exists, as will be discussed ten lines later in *Rashi*?

The reason for this, says the *Maskil L'David*, is extremely nuanced. While it is true that *Rashi's* later comment would resolve the question of why Avraham was told to "go" from his land (Ur Kasdim), there are two other places from which he is also told to go: *"U'mimoladetecha u'mibeis avicha."* The final term, *"beis avicha,"* means "your father's house." However, as we know, Avraham's father was with him in Charan, which made his father's house something that he actually would be leaving now. Additionally, the term *"moladetecha,"* which some commentators translate as "your birthplace," is translated by others as "your family," again denoting people Avraham was currently with and whom he would need to leave.

It turns out that *Rashi* was faced with a fascinating *"pshat/drash* trade-off":

- On the one hand, there is a *pshat* answer to the use of *"lech,"* which is always preferable for *Rashi*. However, that answer does not satisfy the rest of the context in which the command to "go" was given.
- On the other hand, the *drash* answer explains the choice of *"lech"* for all three parts of the phrase, but it is a *drash* answer.

Rashi therefore includes both approaches, beginning with the *drash* answer that resolves the totality of the matter, and then sweeping back for a *pshat* approach. Thus does one of the master commentators guide us through the inner workings of *Rashi's* well-known comment on the words, *"lech lecha."*

THE DAY LOT LOST DIRECTION

וַיְהִי רִיב בֵּין רֹעֵי מִקְנֵה אַבְרָם וּבֵין רֹעֵי מִקְנֵה לוֹט...

וַיֹּאמֶר אַבְרָם אֶל לוֹט אַל נָא תְהִי מְרִיבָה בֵּינִי וּבֵינֶיךָ...

הֲלֹא כָל הָאָרֶץ לְפָנֶיךָ הִפָּרֶד נָא מֵעָלָי...

וַיִּשָּׂא לוֹט אֶת עֵינָיו וַיַּרְא אֶת כָּל כִּכַּר הַיַּרְדֵּן כִּי כֻלָּהּ מַשְׁקֶה...

וַיִּבְחַר לוֹ לוֹט אֵת כָּל כִּכַּר הַיַּרְדֵּן וַיִּסַּע לוֹט מִקֶּדֶם...

There was a quarrel between the shepherds of Avram's flock and the shepherds of Lot's flock...

Avram said to Lot: "Let there please be no strife between me and you...

Is not all the land before you? Please, part from me..."

And Lot raised his eyes and saw the entire plain of the Jordan that it was all fertile...

And Lot chose for himself the plain of the Jordan, and Lot journeyed from the east...[1]

BACKGROUND: A TIME TO PART

Although Lot, Avram's nephew, originally accompanies his uncle on his journey from Charan to the land of Canaan, at a certain point he seems to stray from Avram's program. Thus, we find him allowing his

---

1   *Bereishis* 13:7–11.

animals to graze in whichever fields they like, with the flimsy explanation that the land has been promised to Avram's descendants. Since Avram does not yet have any descendants, Lot, his nephew, stands to inherit him, in which case he is merely taking an advance on his inheritance.[2] Indeed, a few verses later, when Hashem speaks to Avram, the Torah emphasizes that this was "after Lot had separated from him," which the Sages explain to mean that as long as Lot was with Avram, Hashem was not prepared to communicate with him.

The matter finds its most acute expression in the concluding phrase of verse 11: "*Vayisa Lot mikedem.*" Although the straightforward translation of this phrase is, "And Lot journeyed from the east," the Sages explain that it alludes to a matter deeper than geography:

הסיע עצמו מקדמונו של עולם, אמר אי אפשי לא באברם ולא באלקיו.

He removed himself from the Ancient One of the world [Hashem], saying, "I have no interest in Avram nor in his God."

The reason the Sages do not leave this phrase at face value is very simple. When one travels "from the east," he is traveling west. Yet even a cursory look at a map of Israel will indicate that Sodom lies *to the east* of where Avram and Lot were, so that Lot was actually traveling from the west! Hence, the Sages conclude that there is more to this journey than one of physical location, rendering the word "east" not as indicating geographical direction, but rather spiritual direction—away from "the Ancient One of the World."

The question that we need to consider in all of this is: How did it happen? How did Lot go from being an adherent of Avram's path to becoming a citizen of the most immoral city in the region? After all, in the beginning of the parsha Hashem appears to Avram upon his arrival

---

2   *Rashi* to verse 7. The spurious nature of this argument is made worse by the fact that it contains a contradiction: If Lot believed Hashem's promise to Avram, he should also have believed the part which stated that Avram will have descendants, in which case they, not Lot, will inherit the land. If he did not believe Hashem's promise, then the land didn't belong to Avram at all! Either way, it didn't belong to Lot. Apparently, contradictions were no obstacle in the face of Lot justifying what he was doing (R' Yosef Salant, *Be'er Yosef*).

in Canaan, promising the land to his descendants, even though Lot was with him at that time! Clearly, Lot was not always an impediment to Hashem speaking with Avram.

What happened to Lot?

ANATOMY OF A FALL

The commentators explain that although Lot was originally an ardent follower of Avraham, events which took place in the early stages of their time in Canaan challenged his commitment, and his focus began to shift from Avraham's mission toward other, less noble goals.[3]

The journey to Canaan was accompanied by great expectations of success and prosperity, as promised by Hashem to Avraham. However, upon their arrival, there was a famine in the land, forcing them to move temporarily to Egypt. This was one of Avraham's famous ten tests, which he passed by being patient, forbearing, and not complaining that Hashem's promise had not been immediately fulfilled. Lot, who had accompanied Avraham on the journey from Charan, was not as gracious in accepting this setback. Where was the prosperity that Hashem had promised Avraham?

In Egypt, there was further trouble as Sarah, Avraham's wife—and Lot's sister[4]—was taken by Pharaoh against her will, another of Avraham's ten tests. By the time they returned to Canaan after the famine had abated, Lot's feelings of attachment and dedication had all but expired, leading him to retract his original commitment to Avraham's program and to develop ideas for a program of his own.

Indeed, if we lend a careful ear to the verses, we will see this shift reflected in the Torah's description of these events. After returning from their sojourn in Egypt, the verse says that Avraham came back to the place where he had originally built a *mizbeiach*, and concludes with the words: "*Vayikra sham Avram b'shem Hashem*—Avram called out there in the name of Hashem." It is interesting that in the earlier verse it simply says, "*vayikra b'shem Hashem*—he called out in the name of

---

3   See, e.g., *Hakesav V'hakabbalah* and *Malbim* to *Bereishis* 13:14.
4   Both Sarah and Lot were children of Avraham's brother, Haran.

Hashem," relying on us to understand that the pronoun "he" refers to Avraham. Why, then, is Avraham mentioned explicitly by name on this later occasion?

R' Eliezer Ashkenazi, in his classic commentary *Maaseh Hashem*,[5] explains that initially the verse uses the pronoun because, although Avraham was the primary force in spreading awareness of Hashem, he was accompanied and seconded in this endeavor by Lot. Sadly, however, since their return from Egypt, Lot had taken to "missing choir practice," and hence the verse emphasizes that it was "Avraham" alone who was now spreading Hashem's message—leaving out Lot.

THE PLACE WHERE PSHAT AND REMEZ MEET

The picture that emerges is one where Lot was prepared to follow Avraham's path on the understanding that it would lead him to prosperity and acclaim, but he was not prepared to follow him on a path leading purely toward truth and elevated, Godly living. When these two ideas ceased being synonymous in Lot's mind, it was time for him to leave.

Leaving Avraham, however, was not a simple thing; leaving him to go to Sodom was something Lot was extremely uncomfortable doing. It is important to realize that Lot had not openly expressed his antipathy toward Avraham's spiritual way of life. Indeed, in the verses, this is only alluded to, since, within Lot himself, it was not apparent on the outside. This instance is a good example of the fact that *pshat* (clearly stated) and *remez* (allusion) within the *words* of the Torah often reflect the "*pshat*" (clearly visible) and "*remez*" (not readily noticeable) of the *situation* that they are describing. Indeed, with this in mind, let us return to Lot's trip to Sodom.

We noted that the *pshat* of the words "*vayisa Lot mikedem*" seems to indicate that he traveled westward from the east. However, that is difficult, seeing as Sodom is to the east of where he was. Therefore, we probed these words further for their *remez* message, which is that Lot was moving away from Hashem and Avraham. But what about the *pshat*? Does it just disappear in favor of more hidden messages? One

---

5   *Bereishis* 13:4.

of the classic commentators on *Rashi*, the *Divrei David*, explains that not only does the *pshat* not become *replaced* by *remez*, it is actually *illuminated* through *remez*. If Sodom was to the east, why on earth would Lot journey toward the west? The answer is, since Lot could not bring himself to have his uncle Avraham see him leaving his house and making his way toward Sodom, he actually set off in the opposite direction! This would give the impression to Avraham that Lot was heading toward some city in the west. In due time, and having made some distance between himself and Avraham's house, he veered around until he arrived in Sodom.

Not only does this idea give us a deeper insight into Lot's journey, it is also a fascinating example of the synergy that exists between the different ways of looking at the verse.

CONCEALED FROM WHOM?

Taking this discussion one step further, we note that even when describing what Lot himself saw, the verse makes explicit reference to how fertile the plains were, implying that that is what drew him toward Sodom.

In light of this, R' Yaakov Kamenetsky explains that the full meaning of what the Sages mean to say is that Lot's underlying motivation was concealed *even from himself!*[6] In other words, the *pshat* reason given in the verse (fertile pasture) reflects Lot's conscious draw toward Sodom, while the allusion (moving away from Hashem toward a place of immorality) represents his unconscious motivation.

It is very interesting to note that the Hebrew word "*lot*" means "concealed." In this regard, we may say that Lot reflects a person whose true motives are often concealed, whether from others or from himself.

Taking this matter one stage deeper, it is possible that Lot's true underlying motivation was not entirely unknown to him to the point of being completely inaccessible. Rather, he was aware of it as something which existed in the deeper levels of his consciousness—and sought to keep it there! Given his origins as a follower of Avraham, Lot was not

---

6   *Emes L'Yaakov, Bereishis* loc. cit.

comfortable recognizing that he was now drawn by such base things as that which went on in Sodom, and so he "managed his awareness," suppressing his knowledge of this motivation and preventing it from coming to the surface. In other words, he *chose* not to know, making the conscious decision to remain unconscious about this matter. Indeed, in this regard, the charade of first traveling west and subsequently veering around toward Sodom was potentially as much for Lot himself as it was for Avraham.

TO KNOW AND NOT KNOW

We encounter this idea again with Lot after Sodom is destroyed, and his daughters, fearing that no one is left alive in the world, decide that they need to intoxicate their father and bear children from him. On the first night, when the older daughter implements this plan, the verse concludes:

וְלֹא יָדַע בְּשִׁכְבָהּ וּבְקוּמָהּ.

And he [Lot] was not aware of her lying down or getting up.

Rashi comments on the fact that in a *Sefer Torah*, the word "*u'v'ku-mah*" has a dot on top of it. In general, dots accompanying a word tend to diminish its meaning. In our case, *Rashi* explains:

This teaches us that when she got up, he did know, and still he did not guard himself from drinking again on the second night.

Let us ask: How can the dot inform us that he *knew* by the time she got up, when the words explicitly state that he *did not know* at any stage? How could he both know and not know the same thing? Here too, we see that Lot was aware on some level of what had happened, yet he chose to repress that awareness, keeping it in the realms of the concealed and the unknown.

This fascinating idea may be one that is personified by Lot, but it is one that can potentially be exhibited by anyone, so that the study of Lot can be of great benefit to us in our own lives. Indeed, it may be to this that we refer in the *viduy* (confession) on Yom Kippur, when we mention sins that we have committed before Hashem *"b'yod'im u'v'lo yod'im."* This phrase is commonly taken as referring to the victims, i.e., whether they were aware of our sins against them or not. However, perhaps it also refers to the ones who committed the sins, i.e., to situations where we know there might be a problem, yet respond by choosing not to know.

CONCEPT:
HOW VOWELS REVEAL
THE CHARACTER OF
A WORD IN TORAH

Our parsha relates how Sarah, after being childless for many years, suggests to Avraham that he take her maidservant, Hagar, as a wife, which he proceeds to do. The verse then states:

וַיָּבֹא אֶל הָגָר וַתַּהַר וַתֵּרֶא כִּי הָרָתָה וַתֵּקַל גְּבִרְתָּהּ בְּעֵינֶיהָ.

He came unto Hagar and she conceived; she saw that she had conceived, and her mistress [Sarah] became light in her eyes.

BACKGROUND: NOTES WHICH GIVE US PAUSE

There is actually something very unusual about this verse, although, admittedly, it is not something we would automatically notice. As we know, there are times when the *nikkud* (vowelization) of a word changes. This will happen when the word appears either

- at the end of a verse, or
- at the strongest pause within the verse.

This is known as the pausal form. Frequently in such case, a *patach* will change to a *kamatz*. A simple illustration of this idea can be seen in a verse at the beginning of our parsha,[1] which reads:

וַיֵּצְאוּ לָלֶכֶת אַרְצָה כְּנַעַן וַיָּבֹאוּ אַרְצָה כְּנָעַן.

They set out to go to the land of Canaan, and they came to the land of Canaan.

The word "Canaan" in the middle of the verse has a *patach* under the letter *nun*, while the same word at the end of the verse has a *kamatz*.

In light of the above, let us consider our verse. The strongest pause is the *esnachta* under the word "*vatahar*," which is roughly equivalent to a semicolon. In keeping with the idea of the pausal form, this word should have had a *kamatz* under the letter *tav*, but instead it remains with a *patach*. How can we explain this?

Before we allow ourselves to get too upset over this anomaly, we should note that the problem is actually compounded, for there is, in fact, a word in the verse whose *nikkud* changes. This is the word "*ha-rasah*," which has a *kamatz* under the *reish*, while it should really have a *sh'va*. The problem is that the note consisting of two dots on top of this word, known as a *zakef-katan*, is roughly equivalent to a comma, and signifies a weaker pause than an *esnachta*.

Thus, the full problem in our verse is one of *complete reversal*, whereby the stronger pause (*esnachta*) does not receive the pausal form, while the weaker pause (*zakef*) does!

Now we can be upset.

Having noted the grammatical upheaval within the verse, to where can we turn for insight into its meaning?

RABBEINU BACHYA'S PRINCIPLE: AN INNER LOOK AT THE VOWELS

I believe the answer to this question can be found in a fascinating comment of Rabbeinu Bachya, where he discusses the significance of

---

1   13:5.

the vowels in the Torah.[2] The purpose of the vowels, says Rabbeinu Bachya, is not merely to instruct us how to pronounce the words; rather, *the vowels give us insight into the character of the words*. To this end, he quotes one of the early kabbalistic works, the *Sefer Habahir*, which states that the relationship of the letters to the vowels is parallel to that of the relationship between the body and the soul.

Indeed, says Rabbeinu Bachya, this is the real reason behind the change of *nikkud* in the pausal form. As surely as a *kamatz* is physically more elevated than a *patach*, so too, it reflects an elevated quality within the word. An "ordinary" *patach* word that appears at the end of a phrase or sentence brings with it a measure of "completion" to that idea, attaining greater significance. As such, it becomes elevated or "upgraded" from a *patach* to a *kamatz*!

Moreover, this concept can also explain a situation where the opposite occurs and a *kamatz* changes to a *patach*. This happens when the word is "of" something or someone, known as the construct form. For example, the Hebrew word for "hand" is "יָד" with a *kamatz*. However, if we wish to say, for example, "the hand of Moshe," we will say "יַד מֹשֶׁה" with a *patach*. Why the change? Because in such a situation the word does not fully communicate its meaning; it relies on the word that follows. Since it has lost its independence, it becomes "downgraded" from a *kamatz* to a *patach*.

THE DAY THE RULES OF GRAMMAR WERE BROKEN

Once we appreciate that the vowels reflect the character and quality of the word, which can help us *explain* the rules of grammar, we can now consider a case where this principle *overrides* the rules of grammar.

The beginning of *Shmuel II* recounts how David and his camp anxiously await news of Shaul HaMelech, who had gone to war against the Philistines but had not returned. They are approached by someone whom the verse refers to as a *Ger Amaleki*, who was with Shaul in the battle and who claimed that he killed him. This was not true, as Shaul had in fact taken his own life. However, the *Ger Amaleki* thought that by

---

2   Commentary to *Bereishis* 18:3.

claiming to have killed Shaul, he would curry favor with David, whom he presumed would rejoice over the death of his enemy. The *Ger's* description of his act is presented in the verse with the following words:[3]

וָאֶעֱמֹד עָלָיו וַאֲמֹתְתֵהוּ...

I stood over him and I killed him...

Without going into too much detail, there is a grammatical anomaly in these words: When the letter *vav* acts as a *vav hahipuch*[4] and precedes the letter *aleph*, it always takes a *kamatz* (as indeed is the case with the word "וָאֶעֱמֹד"). As such, the *vav* in the follow-up word "וַאֲמֹתְתֵהוּ" should likewise have been accompanied by a *kamatz*, yet it is written with a *patach*. Rabbeinu Bachya explains that since this word expressed a lie—as the *Ger Amaleki* did not actually kill Shaul—it is inherently deficient; hence, it does not receive the elevated *kamatz* vowel; rather, *it is demoted on moral grounds* to a *patach*!

It is truly fascinating to see a situation where the inner meaning of the vowels "takes over" and asserts itself over the rules of grammar themselves.

HAGAR'S PREGNANCY: OBJECTIVE AND PERCEIVED REALITY

With all this in mind, let us return to Hagar's pregnancy, which, as the verse indicates, occurred very soon after marrying Avraham. This is in stark contrast to Sarah, who had been married to him for many years and had not yet conceived. The Midrash has the following to say about this imbalanced situation:[5]

> *Thorns and thistles are neither tended nor sown; they sprout up by themselves. When it comes to wheat, however, how much effort and investment is required until it grows!*

---

3   *Shmuel II* 1:10.

4   Known as the conversive form, where the *vav* at the beginning of the word changes it from future to past tense (e.g., changing "*yedaber*—he will speak," to "*vayedaber*—he spoke").

5   *Bereishis Rabbah* sec. 45.

The Midrash informs us that the speed with which Hagar conceived was actually a reflection of the lack of quality of her offspring. This is in contrast to Yitzchak, a product of the highest quality, the emergence of whom required much more time and investment. Now we can understand why the word *"vatahar"* describing Hagar's pregnancy, which according to the rules of grammar should have a *kamatz*, instead features a *patach*. Since her speedy conception was due to her offspring's lack of quality, the word which describes it cannot have a *kamatz*—a vowel which represents significance and elevation! Once again, the rules of grammar are overridden, with the character assessment of Hagar's progeny reflected by a *"dis*-honorary" *patach*, telling us all we need to know.

On the other hand, Hagar herself naturally does not interpret the situation in this way, for she sees her speedy conception as a sign of her worth, as is evidenced by the flippant and disrespectful way in which she proceeds to treat Sarah. This brings us to the second grammatical upheaval in the verse, for in describing *what* Hagar saw, the Torah presents it *in the way that she saw it*. Therefore, the word *"harasah"* is written with a *kamatz*, denoting the elevated significance that she ascribed to these events.

And so, through a deep appreciation of the meaning of the vowels, we come to see that our verse effectively presents Hagar's situation on two diametrically opposing planes: one of the reality and the other of her distortion thereof—and all this by moving the leg of a *kamatz* a mere few centimeters to the left!

THE COVENANT OF MILAH

INTRODUCTION: WHO WAS THE FIRST JEW?

With the mitzvah of *milah* (circumcision), Avraham entered into a covenant with Hashem, as outlined in the verses of chapter 17 of the parsha. However, as we will see, it is possible that the ramifications of *milah* for Avraham went beyond this and affected his fundamental status and identity.

A most interesting—and somewhat disarming—question is raised by the early commentators: Were our Patriarchs and Matriarchs Jewish? Of course, they were the forebears of the Jewish People, but did they themselves attain the status that would come to define the people of Israel? This question has been discussed and debated over the generations, with proofs being adduced for either side from throughout the Chumash and the literature of Chazal.[1] The opinion of numerous commentators is that Avraham, although obviously not born Jewish, indeed converted in the full sense of the word.[2] Moreover, the stage when this happened was at the time of the covenant of *milah*, for at that point, Avraham relinquished the status of a *ben Noach* (gentile)

---

1   This question is famously discussed at length by R' Yehudah Rosannes, author of the commentary *Mishneh Lamelech* on the *Rambam's Mishneh Torah*, in his treatise on the Chumash known as *Parashas Derachim*, *drush* 1.

2   See *Chagigah* 3a, where Avraham is referred to as "the first of the converts."

and attained *kedushas Yisrael* (the sanctity of Israel).[3] It was truly a transformational moment for Avraham.

AVRAHAM AND YISHMAEL

This idea might shed some light on an episode in the next parsha that also has far-reaching implications. When Sarah insists that Hagar and Yishmael be sent away from the home on account of Yishmael's behavior around and toward Yitzchak, the verse tells us that Avraham was "greatly distressed regarding his son." In response to this, Hashem tells him not to be distressed, and to listen to Sarah in this matter, "for it is through Yitzchak that you will be considered to have offspring."[4] The implication of these words is that Yitzchak alone, not Yishmael, is considered to be Avraham's progeny. While it is true that in the very next verse, Hashem assures Avraham that Yishmael will also become a nation "for he is your offspring"—seemingly contradicting the previous statement!—nevertheless, this is purely in recognition of the fact that Yishmael is Avraham's biological son. In any other sense of continuing Avraham's line and legacy, however, Hashem is informing Avraham that Yishmael is not included.[5]

How did Yishmael come to be excluded from the category of Avraham's progeny? We might reply simply that it is due to him being born of Hagar. Alternatively, it may have been Yishmael's own corrupt actions, as noticed by Sarah, that excluded him, actions which the Midrash informs us included some of the gravest sins.[6] However, in light of the view of the commentators mentioned above that Avraham's *milah* also constituted his conversion to *kedushas Yisrael*, perhaps Yishmael's exclusion came through a different route. It is known that when a person converts to Judaism, he is considered "as a newborn," i.e., from the point of view of halachah, all prior family relationships are discontinued. As such, although Yishmael may have originally been

---

3   See the *Ramban* to *Bereishis* 17:4 and *Vayikra* 24:10, *Chiddushei Aggados Maharsha* to *Yevamos* 100b, and *Parashas Derachim* ibid., citing R' Shmuel Ashkenazi.
4   *Bereishis* 21:11–12.
5   *Yad Ramah* (Rabbeinu Meir Halevi Abulafiah) to *Sanhedrin* 59b.
6   Cited in *Rashi* to *Bereishis* 21:9, s.v. *metzachek*.

considered Avraham's son, from the time of the *milah* this was no longer the case. Thus, Hashem informs Avraham: "For it is through Yitzchak that you will be considered to have offspring."

YISHMAEL AND MILAH

Let us take this discussion one step further. The notion of Yishmael not being fully considered Avraham's son is communicated to him at the time Yitzchak is weaned—over a year after Avraham performed the *milah*. As such, why did Avraham need to be told this here? Surely, he is aware that they have not been considered related for some time now, ever since he became a convert and assumed *kedushas Yisrael*!

Perhaps we may suggest the following: As the Torah describes in chapter 17, *milah* was performed not just by Avraham, but by all the males in his household, including Yishmael. It is noteworthy that in that section, Yishmael's *milah* is mentioned three times: first as part of Avraham's household,[7] then as describing only him,[8] and finally together with that of Avraham.[9] Each of these times he is referred to as "Avraham's son." Another development at the time of the *milah* was that Avraham was now considered to be "the father of all converts." The halachic implications of this idea are spelled out by the *Rambam*,[10] who states that any mitzvah which requires referring to the Avos as "our fathers" can also be fulfilled by a convert. Upon reflection, this puts Yishmael in a potentially unique situation. If the *milah* was an opportunity for Avraham to convert to *kedushas Yisrael*, it was likewise an opportunity for Yishmael to do so. If he should convert at the time of his *milah*, he would conceivably remain Avraham's son in every sense of the word: On the one hand, he was Avraham's biological son, while as a convert, he would also enjoy Avraham's fatherhood in the halachic sense!

---

7   Ibid., verse 23.
8   Verse 25.
9   Verse 26, with Avraham's household being mentioned separately in the following verse.
10   *Hilchos Bikkurim* 4:3. See also *Tur, Yoreh Deah* 217 who rules that one who takes a vow regarding "the descendants of Avraham" is bound by that vow also regarding converts.

This, then, was Avraham's hope for Yishmael. However, we now appreciate the full impact of Avraham discovering the truth about Yishmael's behavior. His involvement in sinful behavior indicated that he had not actually assumed *kedushas Yisrael* at the time of his *milah*. As such, when Sarah tells Avraham to send Yishmael away, she refers to him as Hagar's son. The verse then states that Avraham was very distressed about *his son*, namely, the notion that Yishmael may no longer be considered his son as a genuine convert! To this, Hashem responds by telling Avraham to heed Sarah's voice, which the Midrash explains to mean to defer to her level of prophecy. What form of prophecy is needed to see that Yishmael is being a bad influence on Yitzchak? Perhaps, the need for prophetic powers was in order to establish that Yishmael's behavior was not a recent development, but was part of his way of life from earlier on, reaching back to the time of his *milah*. As such, Hashem informed Avraham at that time that Yishmael had not proven himself worthy of remaining his son in the complete sense. That status would accrue to Yitzchak alone, with Yishmael being given consideration only as Avraham's biological son, as the next verse proceeds to state.

FROM THE COMMENTATORS

AVRAHAM'S ACQUISITION OF THE LAND OF ISRAEL

וַה' אָמַר אֶל אַבְרָם...שָׂא נָא עֵינֶיךָ וּרְאֵה...כִּי אֶת כָּל הָאָרֶץ אֲשֶׁר אַתָּה רֹאֶה לְךָ
אֶתְּנֶנָּה וּלְזַרְעֲךָ עַד עוֹלָם.
קוּם הִתְהַלֵּךְ בָּאָרֶץ לְאָרְכָּהּ וּלְרָחְבָּהּ כִּי לְךָ אֶתְּנֶנָּה.

*Hashem said to Avram...raise now your eyes and look...for all
the land that you see, to you I will give it, and to your descendants forever.[1]*

*Arise, walk through the land, through its length and breadth,
for to you I will give it.[2]*

The verses relate that Hashem told Avram to do two things: to look
upon the land and to walk its length and breadth. The Gemara informs
us that according to R' Eliezer,[3] by walking the length and breadth
of Eretz Yisrael, Avraham effected an acquisition of the land. This act
constitutes a form of acquisition known as *chazakah*—demonstrating
a proprietorial relationship with the land. But what of the first instruction, to "look upon the land"? What did that accomplish?

---

1   *Bereishis* 13:13–14.
2   Ibid., verse 17.
3   *Bava Basra* 100a.

Additionally, it is interesting to note a discrepancy between these two verses:

- When Hashem tells Avraham to look upon the land, He states that He will give the land to Avraham "to you *and to your descendants forever.*"
- When He subsequently tells Avraham to walk through the land, He states only that "to *you* I will give it."

What is behind this shift in terminology between the two verses?

The *Meshech Chochmah* adds an entirely new dimension to our understanding of Avraham viewing the land. He explains that through this, Avraham was doing more than merely "previewing" it. The halachah states that although acquisition normally requires some form of act, there are times when something can be acquired just by looking at it, namely, when the object is *hefker* (ownerless).[4] Our relationship with the land exists on two levels:

- On a basic, temporal level, it is ours in the physical sense, to dwell there as a nation with all that that entails.
- However, beyond that, as we know, Eretz Yisrael has unique, elevated spiritual properties, which are available to those who dwell there.

The question for us to consider is: which of these aspects had been taken ownership of prior to Avraham's arrival in the land?

- In physical/temporal terms: the people of Canaan populated the land before Avraham arrived. In this respect, they enjoyed an element of ownership of the land, one which would need to be transferred to Avraham.
- In spiritual terms: *no one* had hitherto accessed the higher qualities of Eretz Yisrael. In this respect, the land was *hefker*!

---

4   See *Bava Metzia* 118a.

Therefore, since Hashem wanted to grant Avraham full ownership over the land, He instructed him to do two things. First, He told Avraham to look at the land, thereby acquiring the *spiritual* connection to and ownership of Eretz Yisrael. Since this aspect of the land was ownerless, Avraham could acquire it through *looking* at it. Second, Hashem wished to grant Avraham ownership of the *physical* aspect of the land. Since the Canaanites were currently living there, it was not considered ownerless in this respect; taking ownership of this aspect required an actual *act* of acquisition—to walk the length and breadth of the land.

Moreover, since the spiritual aspect of the land can never be owned by anyone other than the Jewish People, the first verse, which describes Avraham's spiritual acquisition of the land, states that the land would be given to Avraham and his descendants, forever. However, since the Jewish People would not always enjoy temporal control of the land, the second verse, which describes the acquisition of that element, states that it will be given "to you," but does not mention Avraham's descendants, for there was no guarantee the Jewish People would necessarily enjoy uninterrupted control of the land from that point onwards.[5]

TO BE AN IVRI

וַיָּבֹא הַפָּלִיט וַיַּגֵּד לְאַבְרָם הָעִבְרִי.

The fugitive came and told Avram, the Ivri.[6]

---

5   Based on this idea, the *Meshech Chochmah* provides a deeper level of understanding of Hashem's opening words to Avraham in the beginning of verse 14: "Raise up your eyes." On a straightforward level, these words refer to Avraham physically raising his head so as to allow him to look around in all directions. However, the *Meshech Chochmah* explains that these words are actually describing an *elevated way of seeing*. In physical terms, Avraham did not immediately see the effects of his acquisition of the land: the Canaanites, who then populated the land, did not recognize him as its owner. Additionally, as we know, when the time came that he needed a plot to bury Sarah, he was forced to pay an exorbitant amount for it. Nevertheless, in a more elevated sense, reflected in the words "raise up your eyes," Avraham fully acquired the land—immediately and permanently—by fulfilling Hashem's instructions in that verse, "and look upon the land."

6   *Bereishis* 14:13.

There are a number of interpretations of the term *"Ivri"* as applied to Avram. According to the Midrash,[7] this term either signifies Avram as being a descendant and spiritual heir of the righteous Ever, or alternatively, it denotes Avram's moral stance, whereby he was on one side (*eiver*) while the rest of the world was on the other.

It is most interesting to note that in the entire Torah, Avram is only referred to as an *Ivri* on one occasion, and that is in our verse, which describes the arrival of the fugitive who came from the war between the four kings and the five. What is behind this particular choice of context to highlight Avram's *"Ivri"* status?

The commentary *Hakesav V'hakabbalah* explains that the refugee came to Avram seeking to enlist his support in freeing the region from the reign of terror introduced by the four kings. The problem he faced was how to do so. After all, most people do not want to get involved in any war, and certainly not in one where the odds of victory are minimal at best! To this end, the verse states that he came to "Avram the *Ivri*," that is to say, he appealed to Avram as an *Ivri*. The Midrash informs us that Amrafel, the first of the four conquering kings, was none other than Nimrod, who declared a war of rebellion against Hashem. Thus, the fugitive's message was, "Avram, as an *Ivri*, you cannot stand idly by while Nimrod and his cohorts spread their anti-God message. You must get involved!"

This is indeed a most fascinating explanation; however, there appears to be room to raise a very simple question. The very next verse says:

וַיִּשְׁמַע אַבְרָם כִּי נִשְׁבָּה אָחִיו וַיָּרֶק אֶת חֲנִיכָיו...וַיִּרְדֹּף וְגו'.

Avram heard that his relative had been taken captive, he galvanized his disciples...and he pursued them.

This verse states that Avram going out to war was in response to hearing that his relative, Lot, had been captured. How then, can the *Hakesav V'hakabbalah* state that he was being appealed to here as an *Ivri* who was opposed to idolatry?

---

7   *Bereishis Rabbah* 42:8.

Yet, it appears that this is exactly the point Avram was making. Avram's theological contribution did not just relate to the question of whether there is one deity or many. It also addressed the scope of what is included in Godly living. In Avram's time, the general notion of religion was that it was purely a matter of one's relationship with the Divine. It did not leave room for other people, who were tolerated at best and generally considered a distraction in the pursuit of spiritual attainments. Avram introduced the radical idea that part of one's relationship with the Divine includes taking care of His creations. Thus, he engaged in hospitality, much to the bemusement of the onlookers whose religious views allowed them no time for such pursuits.

In this regard, there is a classic comment from the *Chiddushei HaRim*. After Avram's stunning victory, the verse states that Malkitzedek, a priest to God on high, brought out bread and wine for him and his army.[8] Up until this point, Malkitzedek saw religion as a purely theological involvement, as the verse itself describes him, "a priest to God on high." Like others, he looked askance at Avram's worldly involvements in the name of religion. However, after Avram's stunning victory against four world powers with just a miniscule number of his disciples, Malkitzedek was forced to reconsider, for clearly Someone on High felt that Avram was going about things the right way! Therefore, Malkitzedek decided to try Avram's way of Godly living himself, beginning with bringing out refreshments for Avram and his army.

This is what Avram was saying to the fugitive: "It is true, I am an *Ivri*. However, you did not need to focus on the spread of idolatry in order to get me involved in this cause. It is sufficient for me to hear that a relative of mine is danger, and that alone will lead me to action—as an *Ivri*!"

WHEN WAS THE BRIS BEIN HABESARIM?

Verses 7–21 of chapter 15 are known as the *Bris Bein Habesarim*— The Covenant Between the Pieces, where Hashem informs Avraham concerning the future subjugation of his descendants in a foreign land. Although this section is written toward the end of our parsha, the *Seder*

---

8   Verse 18.

Olam states that it actually took place a number of years prior, when Avraham was seventy years old. This means that Avraham visited the land of Israel at the age of seventy, then returned to Charan and came back for good at the age of seventy-five, as recorded in the beginning of our parsha.

According to this approach, we have before us an example of the concept of, *"Ein mukdam u'meuchar baTorah*—the Torah does not always present events in the chronological order in which they took place," since this earlier event is written in the Torah later than subsequent events. Indeed, *Tosafos*[9] prove that the two sections in our chapter are not in chronological sequence from the fact that in verse 5, Hashem tells Avraham to count the stars, indicating that it was nighttime, while verse 12 states that the sun was setting! This indicates clearly that these two sections took place at different times and are not describing one long episode.

Rashi, however, does not appear to adopt this approach, as he provides two answers to resolve the apparent contradiction between verse 6, which states that Avraham believed Hashem's word, and verse 8, where he seems to question it.[10] This contradiction only exists if one sees these verses as sequential.[11]

Why does *Rashi* not invoke the principle of *"ein mukdam u'meuchar"*? After all, he uses this principle several times in his commentary on the Torah! Now, we may reply simply that he feels no compelling need to do so here.[12] However, it is possible that in our instance, *Rashi* actually sees active reason *not* to invoke this principle.

The episode of the *Bris Bein Habesarim* begins with the words: *"Vayomer eilav*—He said to him."[13] The use of the pronouns "He" and "him"

---

9   *Berachos* 7b, s.v. *lo.*

10   Verse 6, s.v. *v'he'emin.*

11   See also *Rashi* to *Bereishis* 21:1, s.v. *kaasher,* where he refers to verses 1–4 of our chapter as taking place "during the *Bris Bein Habesarim.*" (It should be noted that *Rashi,* later on in *Shemos* 12:40, does mention the *Seder Olam.* However, in our parsha, he does not seem to be adopting that approach.)

12   See glosses of *Rashash* to *Berachos,* loc. cit., regarding *Tosafos'* proof from the sun setting after Avraham was told to count the stars.

13   Verse 7.

obviously relate them back to Hashem and Avraham respectively, who are mentioned in the previous verse. And now let us ask a simple, but fascinating question regarding the principle of *ein mukdam u'meuchar*:

When we say that the Torah will sometimes insert a chronologically earlier section at a later point, does it maintain its distinct integrity *as a separate section*, or is it rather now "naturalized" and integrated syntactically into the section where it is written?

Rashi, taking the first approach, understands that if verse 7 was in fact describing an earlier historical event, it would not draw on verses that described later events—even if written right before it in the Torah—to give it context! Rather, if verse 7 is prepared to use terms such as "He" and "him," referring back to the parties mentioned in earlier verses, it must mean that these verses are all part of one chronological sequence. For this reason, *Rashi* is not prepared to invoke the principle of *ein mukdam u'meuchar* in our verse.[14]

---

14   In fact, it is possible to demonstrate that this is *Rashi's* approach. The Gemara in *Gittin* 88b states that when the verse in the beginning of *parshas Mishpatim* (*Shemos* 21:1) says, "*V'eileh hamishpatim asher tasim lifneihem*—And these are the laws that you shall place before them," it is referring to expert judges. *Rashi* (*Gittin* ibid.) explains that the phrase "before them" refers to the seventy elders who are mentioned later, in *Shemos* 24:1. *Rashi* adds that although this verse is written at the *end* of *parshas Mishpatim*, it describes events which took place *beforehand* during *Matan Torah*; hence, the phrase "before them" can refer to those mentioned in this verse. Here we see the converse situation to the one in our parsha, which demonstrates very clearly that pronouns will take their cue from earlier chronological events and not from the order that they are written in the Torah if those two diverge. *Tosafos*, by implication, lay contextual emphasis on *where* the verses are written, regardless of *when* they happened (*Tosafos* in *Gittin*, loc. cit., explain the Gemara's exposition that "before them" refers to expert judges differently than *Rashi*. In terms of our discussion, we can understand that they dispute *Rashi's* premise that the term "them" could refer to people mentioned in a later chapter, even if the events described therein happened earlier).

PARSHAS VAYEIRA

SARAH'S LAUGHTER

BACKGROUND: A MIRACLE BLESSING

In the beginning of our parsha, Avraham is visited by three angels in the form of wayfarers, to whom he extends his legendary hospitality. After the meal, one of the guests informs Avraham that at this time next year, Sarah will have a son. Sarah, who is currently eighty-nine years old and has never had children, overhears this blessing. Verse 12 describes her reaction:

וַתִּצְחַק שָׂרָה בְּקִרְבָּהּ לֵאמֹר אַחֲרֵי בְלֹתִי הָיְתָה לִּי עֶדְנָה וַאדֹנִי זָקֵן.

Sarah laughed inside saying, "After having become withered will I then become young? And [besides,] my husband [too] is old!"

Sarah's laughter is met with rebuke from Hashem, as stated in the following verse:

וַיֹּאמֶר ה' אֶל אַבְרָהָם לָמָּה זֶּה צָחֲקָה שָׂרָה...הֲיִפָּלֵא מֵה' דָּבָר.

Hashem said to Avraham, "Why did Sarah laugh?...Is anything beyond Hashem?"

This situation, which is already somewhat uncomfortable, becomes infinitely more so in the verse which follows:

וַתְּכַחֵשׁ שָׂרָה לֵאמֹר לֹא צָחַקְתִּי כִּי יָרֵאָה וַיֹּאמֶר לֹא כִּי צָחָקְתְּ.

Sarah denied it, saying, "I did not laugh," for she was afraid.
And He [Hashem] said, "No, for you did laugh."

Amazingly, the Torah leaves it at that, immediately moving on to other matters, leaving us confounded and perplexed. How could Sarah, upon being confronted by Hashem over her laughter, hope to deny it out of fear?

UNDERSTANDING SARAH

To understand this situation, we need to return to Sarah's laughter itself. Here too, we ask, how could she laugh in incredulity upon receiving a blessing from an angel? In this matter, however, we are failing to see things from Sarah's perspective. We are aware that the guest who issued the blessing was, in fact, an angel. Avraham and Sarah, however, were not. As far as they knew, these were three random strangers who had been wandering around in the midday sun, probably for a little too long![1] When someone enjoys hospitality in a stranger's home, it is customary to express his appreciation to the hostess, to which end

---

1   One of the first things that Avraham does upon approaching his guests is to request that they wash their feet. *Rashi* explains that Avraham suspected them of being idolaters who bow down to the dust on their feet, and he did not wish for items of idolatry to enter his home. We may ask: How prevalent was dust-worship at that time that this should be a standing concern for Avraham? Moreover, even within the misguided worldview of idolatry, how does the concept of dust-worship even exist? Idolatry tends to isolate things that are powerful and ascribe to them independent power. Nothing reflects insignificance more than dust. How would even an idolater subscribe to such a practice?
The *Shelah Hakadosh* says that in fact, no one worships dust. If someone bows down to dust, it is because he worships the sun—for dust represents the power of the sun, which beats down on things, crumbling them, and reducing them to dust. Thus, we understand that Avraham actually suspected that these men were sun-worshippers. Should we then proceed to ask why he would specifically suspect them of worshipping the sun, we need only to remind ourselves of what the weather was like on that day. We are informed that in order not to trouble Avraham with guests while he was recovering from his *milah*, Hashem made it so hot that no normal person would be outdoors. Avraham, however persisted in looking for guests, at which point Hashem sent him the three angels in the guise of men. This is why Avraham, who thought they were people, naturally assumed that they were sun-worshippers, for the only people who would venture outdoors on a day like this would be those who were celebrating the hottest day in history!

a simple "thank you" tends to suffice. It is *not* customary to inform the hostess that she will have a son next year, by which time she will be ninety years old! Looked at in this light, we can well understand Sarah's reaction—for who *wouldn't* laugh in such a situation?

The *Ramban* explains that the reason Sarah was nonetheless rebuked for her laughter was that regardless of who says it will happen, someone on Sarah's spiritual level can never reject *the possibility itself* that she may yet have a child. This is the *madreigah* of the Avos and Imahos!

BLESSING, LAUGHTER—AND DIVINE INTERVENTION

What form did Sarah's laughter take? The simple reading of the word "*b'kirbah*—inside of her" indicates that Sarah did not express her thoughts verbally. Indeed, this understanding is corroborated by the fact that the rebuke for this laughter came from Hashem Himself, as the verse states, "Hashem said to Avraham, 'Why did Sarah laugh?'" Let us remind ourselves that Avraham had taken leave of Hashem in order to tend to his three guests, and the entire conversation had been conducted between them, including the blessing that Sarah would have a child. Why does Hashem have to enter the conversation at this stage to rebuke Sarah? Is this, too, not something that the angel could have done? However, once we realize that Sarah's laughter took place solely in the realm of thought, we understand that the angel could not have responded to it, for angels do not know what a person is thinking. That knowledge is restricted to Hashem alone, as the verse states in *Tehillim*,[2] "ה' יֹדֵעַ מַחְשְׁבוֹת אָדָם"—Hashem knows man's thoughts," implying that this is something only Hashem knows, not even an angel can know.

A TOSAFOS THAT THICKENS THE PLOT

This matter becomes somewhat more intriguing, however, when we consider a most interesting comment of *Tosafos*. The Gemara states that an individual should not pray in Aramaic, since the angels who are involved in conveying his prayers do not relate to that language.[3]

---

2   94:11.
3   *Shabbos* 12b.

Tosafos ask: why do angels not relate to Aramaic? It cannot be because they do not understand Aramaic, for angels even know what a person is thinking![4]

Tosafos clearly are of the understanding that angels, too, know a person's thoughts. In terms of our discussion, we now have the following two questions:

- If an angel knows a person's thoughts, the question returns as to why it was necessary for Hashem to intervene regarding Sarah's laughter.
- *Tosafos'* position seems to be directly contradicted by the verse quoted from *Tehillim*, which implies that only Hashem knows a person's thoughts!

WHEN THOUGHTS ARE HEVEL

One of the great Sephardic commentators, R' Moshe Chagiz,[5] explains *Tosafos'* position in the following way. Every thought actually begins as a feeling, which then becomes developed and formulated into a finished thought. This transition generally happens very rapidly, although sometimes it occurs quite slowly. For example, sometimes there is something about a situation which bothers us, but we cannot immediately put our finger on it and say what it is. After pondering the matter, we can hopefully identify what the problem was, formulating the feeling into a thought.

With this in mind, R' Chagiz takes us back to the verse in *Tehillim* which states: "ה' יֹדֵעַ מַחְשְׁבוֹת אָדָם כִּי הֵמָּה הָבֶל." The standard translation of this verse is based on the understanding of the word "*hevel*" as "vanity," thus reading, "Hashem knows the thoughts of man, for they are vanity." However, the word "*hevel*" has another meaning, that of something which is formless and lacking in substance. Additionally, the word "*ki*,"

---

4   Ibid., s.v. *she'ein*. See commentary of *Vilna Gaon* to *Shulchan Aruch*, *Orach Chaim* 101 sec. 12 for a discussion of the source of *Tosafos'* position.

5   *Mishnas Chachamim* sec. 92, cited by R' David Pardo in his commentary on *Rashi*, *Maskil L'David* (to verse 2), who, in turn, is cited by R' Akiva Eiger in his glosses to *Maseches Shabbos* loc. cit.

as we know, has a number of meanings. It can mean "for," but it also means "when." This brings us to the difference between Hashem's knowledge of a person's thoughts and an angel's knowledge. Even an angel only knows a person's thought when it actually attains the status of a formulated thought. As long as the person himself is not aware of what he is thinking, an angel cannot know either. Hashem, however, knows the person's thought even at the initial primordial stage when it has no form and is nothing more than a feeling. This, then, is the meaning of the verse. It is not to be translated as "Hashem knows man's thoughts, for they are vanity," but rather, "Hashem knows man's thoughts when they are [still] formless"!

Wow!

BETWEEN THE "HEART" AND THE "INSIDE"

Now let us return once more to Sarah's laughter, which, we established, took place in the realm of thought, and ask: *What* realm of thought?

Throughout the Torah, when a verse presents a person's thoughts, it describes him as "speaking in his heart,"[6] for the heart is the realm of formulated thought. When it comes to Sarah's laughter, however, the Torah does not say that "she laughed in her heart (*b'libah*);" rather, "she laughed *in her inside* (*b'kirbah*)"! What this means is that Sarah's laughter took place entirely within her, never rising to the level of a formulated thought. Indeed, it is very easy to understand why this was so. Since she did not take the "guest's" blessing seriously, she did not invest any significant thought to how impossible its fulfillment would be. Rather, it was a fleeting and formless laugh whose contents Sarah herself did not develop, even internally. In terms of our discussion, Sarah's laughter never went past the *hevel* stage. This is why, even according to *Tosafos*, Hashem had to intervene and enter the conversation, for even the angels were not aware of what Sarah had thought. In fact, what is fascinating to consider is that from a certain point of view—neither was Sarah!

---

6   See, e.g., *Bereishis* 17:17 and 27:41.

FEAR AND DENIAL

This brings us to the question of Sarah's denial of her having laughed. Often, it is possible to "revisit" a feeling that one had earlier which was not developed at the time and access its contents in hindsight. However, this requires peace of mind, and cannot happen if a person is in a state of constricted consciousness. This is what lay behind Sarah's denial of her laughter, which the verse explains by saying, "Because she was afraid." The meaning is not that she consciously denied having laughed because she was afraid to admit it, but rather that she was *unable to recognize* that she had laughed, since she was in a state of fear![7] In this light, when Hashem then said, "No, for you laughed," it was not in the form of admonition, but of information.

REINSTATING THE BLESSING

It remains for us to ponder the purpose of Hashem's intervention. We may ask, if it was purely in order to rebuke Sarah, why did He not rebuke her directly, rather than through speaking to Avraham?[8] After all, Sarah was also a prophetess! Additionally, why was it necessary to conclude by restating the blessing that they would have a child, something which had already been said earlier and heard by both Avraham and Sarah?

It seems the answer is that in order for the miracle of Avraham and Sarah having a child to occur, it required their complete belief that this was possible. Once Sarah registered a sliver of disbelief, even on the most subliminal of levels, this had the effect of frustrating and even negating the blessing. Therefore, Hashem apprised them of this situation, and then proceeded to restate the blessing for purposes of reinstating it! All this was done through addressing Avraham, as had been done with the original blessing.

---

7   R' Shimon Schwab, *Maayan Beis Hasho'evah*.

8   As is well-known, by rebuking Sarah through speaking to Avraham, Hashem was then "required" to change her words from saying "my husband is old" to "I (Sarah) am old," for purposes of maintaining harmony between them (*Yevamos* 65b), something which would not have been necessary had He rebuked her directly.

THE LAST NIGHT OF SODOM

וַיָּבֹאוּ שְׁנֵי הַמַּלְאָכִים סְדֹמָה בָּעֶרֶב.

And the two angels came to Sodom in the evening.[1]

INTRODUCTION: ANGELS IN SODOM

Chapter 19 of our parsha describes the destruction of Sodom. The events surrounding this episode are well known, which is all the more reason to raise a couple of basic questions:

- As the verses later describe, the destruction itself did not take place until daybreak. If so, why did the angels already come to Sodom in the evening, where they would have spent the night in the street had Lot not persuaded them to come to his house—which only led to further commotion? Given that they had been with Avraham earlier that day, wouldn't it have been preferable to spend the night at *his* house, only making their way to Sodom the following morning?
- When Lot first approaches them and invites them to his house, they refuse and say that they will lodge in the street instead, relenting only after he persists in his invitation.[2] What was

---

1   *Bereishis* 19:1.
2   Verses 2–3.

behind their initial refusal of his hospitality, and what changed when he persisted?

- When the people of Sodom surround Lot's house and demand that he turn over his guests, he implores them not to harm them, concluding his plea by saying, "כִּי עַל כֵּן בָּאוּ בְּצֵל קֹרָתִי."[3] These words are somewhat elusive.[4] The simple translation is, "for it is on account of this that they came under the shelter of my roof." What does Lot mean by this? On account of *what*, precisely, did these men enter his house, and whatever it was, how would this feasibly dissuade the people of Sodom from molesting his guests?

WHEN WAS SODOM'S FATE SEALED?

To gain deeper insight into these events, let us go back to the point where Hashem informs Avraham of His intentions regarding Sodom. He begins by describing the extent of their wickedness:

זַעֲקַת סְדֹם וַעֲמֹרָה כִּי רָבָּה וְחַטָּאתָם כִּי כָבְדָה מְאֹד.

The outcry of Sodom and Amorah has become great, and their sin has become exceedingly heavy.

The following verse then reads:

אֵרְדָה נָּא וְאֶרְאֶה הַכְּצַעֲקָתָהּ הַבָּאָה אֵלַי עָשׂוּ כָּלָה וְאִם לֹא אֵדָעָה.

I will descend and see: If they act in accordance with the outcry that has come to me—then destruction; and, if not—I will know.

The concluding words of this verse require clarification:

- To what is Hashem referring by saying, "and if not"?
- What will He "know" in that case?

The simple understanding of the words "and if not" would seem to be: if Sodom's actions are not as bad as the outcry depicts them. However,

---

3   Verse 8.
4   See *Rashi* ibid.

Onkelos translates these words as saying, *"and if they repent*, I will not destroy them." With these words, *Onkelos* is informing us that the fate of Sodom had not yet been sealed! Even at this stage, if they would do *teshuvah*, Hashem would "know" how to dispense judgment for their wrongdoings, but it would not be in the form of complete destruction.

Sodom and the Ir Hanidachas

Amazingly, the notion that *teshuvah* could have helped avert the destruction of Sodom actually has halachic ramifications. In *Sefer Devarim*, the Torah discusses the *ir hanidachas*—a city whose population has been led astray toward idol worship.[5] In addition to punishing those who committed idolatry, the Torah commands that the city and all that is in it be destroyed. The *Tosefta* states that even the property of a righteous person that remains in the city is to be destroyed, citing as a proof the fact that although Lot himself was saved from Sodom, all his property there was destroyed with the rest of the city.[6]

These words of the *Tosefta* reveal a fascinating element within Sodom's destruction; namely, Sodom is seen as a prototype for the *ir hanidachas* later in the Torah! This is notwithstanding the fact that its corruption lay primarily in its cruelty to outsiders and not to idolatry per se.[7]

In the course of his discussion of *ir hanidachas*, the *Rambam* writes that if the citizens of the city do *teshuvah*, it is not destroyed.[8] Many commentators wonder as to the *Rambam*'s source for this ruling, as no such statement is to be found in the Talmud or Midrash. R' Yosef Rosen, the Rogatchover Gaon, explains that the *Rambam*'s source is in fact *Onkelos*'s words on our verse, where he informs us that had the city of Sodom done *teshuvah*, it would not have been destroyed. This, too, then became codified by the *Rambam* regarding an *ir hanidachas* itself![9]

---

5 See *Devarim* 13:13–18.
6 *Sanhedrin* 14:1. See also *Yerushalmi Sanhedrin* 10:8.
7 See, in this regard, *Rambam* in *Moreh Nevuchim* 3:41, where he states that a city that formally rebels against any mitzvah is treated as an *ir hanidachas*.
8 *Hilchos Avodah Zarah* 4:6.
9 *Tzofnas Paaneach, Bereishis* 18:21.

This idea, that *teshuvah* could have averted the destruction of Sodom, is a truly amazing one. However, it is also very problematic, since no one in Sodom appears to be even slightly aware of their impending fate, and certainly no one sees any need to consider changing his ways. Accordingly, if things continue as usual from now until their destruction, of what use is it to know that *teshuvah could have* helped? What do we imagine might happen that could conceivably cause the people of Sodom to consider doing *teshuvah*?

This brings us back to the angels.

"NO, FOR WE SHALL LODGE IN THE STREET"

As we mentioned above, when Lot initially approaches the angels and invites them to stay with him, they refuse, stating, "No, for we will lodge in the street."

What is behind this refusal of Lot's hospitality? The *Chizkuni* explains: "In order that the people of the city shall see us, that we have come to overturn it; perhaps they will repent."

In other words, the *Chizkuni* is informing us that the reason the angels came to Sodom the night before its destruction is because their mission was not simply to go and destroy it! Rather, it was first to tell its residents about their impending fate, in the hope that they would do *teshuvah*.[10] Should the people fail to do so, *then* the angels were tasked with destroying the city. Hence, for purposes of issuing their warning, the angels expressed their desire to remain in the street where people would encounter them.

LOT'S COUNTERPLAN

In light of this, however, it now becomes difficult to understand what happens next. As the following verse relates, Lot pleads with them to come to his home and they accede to his request. We have to wonder:

---

10   Indeed, the *Rambam* loc. cit. explicitly states that the *beis din* dispatches two *talmidei chachamim* to the *Ir Hanidachas* to exhort the inhabitants to do *teshuvah*. The commentators discuss what the *Rambam's* source for this idea might be. According to the Rogatchover Gaon (ibid.), the precedent for this, too, is in the two angels who went to Sodom for that very purpose!

Why is Lot insisting that they come with him? Given their reason for wanting to stay in the street, if they will follow Lot to his home instead, the people of the city will not hear their message and will not be given the chance to do *teshuvah*, effectively sealing their fate! Equally puzzling is the fact that the angels *accept* Lot's offer of hospitality. How could they leave their post in the street, failing thereby to relay the message which would effectively be Sodom's last hope to avert destruction?

It would seem that Lot's intention here was not to seal the city's fate, but to save it. Lot was well acquainted with the citizens of Sodom and knew full well that they would not respond to any message calling for them to repent. As such, if these visitors were to stay in the street and issue their warning, the city would be doomed for sure. Therefore, Lot saw that the only positive outcome would be if he were to invite the guests to *his* home. In this way, he would, so to speak, represent the people of Sodom in extending hospitality. (Indeed, the Midrash informs us that Lot had recently been appointed as a judge in Sodom,[11] perhaps thereby officially entitling him to act on the people's behalf.) For their part, the city's residents simply had to not interfere with his act, thereby signaling their tacit acquiescence. Since it was nighttime, this should have been simple enough—all they needed to do was simply stay home and do nothing!

OUTRAGE IN SODOM

Sadly, however, Lot underestimated the people of Sodom and the lengths to which they would go in order to uphold their constitution and cruelty. After all, how could they sleep at night knowing that somewhere in the city there were guests in someone's home? No sooner had word gotten out that Lot was harboring visitors, the citizens of Sodom were galvanized into action. Verse 4 reads:

טֶרֶם יִשְׁכָּבוּ וְאַנְשֵׁי הָעִיר אַנְשֵׁי סְדֹם נָסַבּוּ עַל הַבַּיִת מִנַּעַר וְעַד זָקֵן.

They had not yet lain down when the people of the city, the people of Sodom, surrounded the house, from young to old.

---

11   *Bereishis Rabbah* 50:3, cited in *Rashi* to *Bereishis* 19:1, s.v. *yoshev*.

There is a seeming redundancy here. It is clear that the city we are talking about is Sodom; isn't it obvious that "the people of the city" are none other than "the people of Sodom"? Rather, the point is that the people of the city *as the people of Sodom*, committed to its "values," converged upon the house, seeking to protect their constitution against such a "terrible crime."[12]

LOT'S PLEA

Against this background, we can now appreciate that when Lot exits his house to plead with the mob that had surrounded it, he has in mind not just protecting his guests, but also the entire city. Thus, he says, "רַק לָאֲנָשִׁים הָאֵל אַל תַּעֲשׂוּ דָבָר—but to these men do nothing." The normal word for "these" is "*ha'eileh*," yet here Lot says "*ha'eil*," which also means "strong." Through this, Lot was trying to reason with the people of Sodom even in terms of their own policy. In effect, he was saying, "The entire policy of banning guests from Sodom is specifically in order to protect our assets from being depleted by strangers. These, however, are powerful people, to whom extending hospitality and establishing ties could only be to our benefit! Does it not make sense that our constitution should allow for an exception?" Beyond this, Lot concludes "כִּי עַל כֵּן בָּאוּ בְּצֵל קֹרָתִי—for it is on account of this that they came under the shelter of my roof." We now understand that "on account of this" means that it was specifically in order *that you stay at home and do nothing* that I invited them to my house, since this was the only thing that could save you from condemnation.

For their part, the people of Sodom were incensed that Lot was trying to tamper with their laws, regardless of whether his reasoning was sound; for as protectors of "The Sodom Way," they felt that if an exception was allowed to be made, who knows where it would end. Thus, they exclaimed, "הָאֶחָד בָּא לָגוּר וַיִּשְׁפֹּט שָׁפוֹט—*This one comes to sojourn and he yet judges?*" This sounds like an unusual objection, given that they had appointed him as a judge! What did they expect him to do? However, the double expression "*vayishpot shafot*" means that he is *judging our*

---

12 *Malbim.*

judgments, and not merely implementing them as he should be doing.[13] This was too much for them, and they proceeded to try and break down the door, standing up thereby for all that was "right" in Sodom.

The full extent of their investment in Sodom's laws is tragically and frighteningly depicted in verse 11, which states that after they had been stricken with blindness by Lot's guests, "וַיִּלְאוּ לִמְצֹא הַפָּתַח." We normally take these words to mean that they were now unable to find the entrance to Lot's house, which is, of course, true. However, the word "*vayil'u*" comes from the word "*nil'ah*," which means weariness, so that the verse is relating that they *grew weary* trying to find the entrance. In other words, being struck by blindness did nothing to deter them from trying to break down the door! They continued to fumble in their blindness, trying to find the entrance, until they simply had no more energy left.[14] As far as the notion of them doing *teshuvah* was concerned, there was nothing left to say. They literally expended the last of their energies sealing their fate, which came at daybreak, as described in the ensuing verses.

---

13   *Kli Yakar.*
14   *Seforno.*

CONCEPT:
THE USE OF A GRAMMATICAL
TOOL (THE DAGESH) FOR
NON-GRAMMATICAL PURPOSES

BACKGROUND: THE DAGESH IN A NUTSHELL

One of the prominent grammatical features in *lashon hakodesh* is the *dagesh*—the dot which appears in certain letters, giving them a "harder" sound. Although the full discussion of the criteria that require a *dagesh* can become quite involved, three rules will account for most of them:

- The letters בג"ד כפ"ת when they appear at the beginning of a word, e.g., בָּרָד, גָּמָל.
- The letter following a *hei* that denotes the definite article, e.g., הַמַּלְאָךְ, הַשָּׂדֶה.
- The middle root letter of a word when it appears in the *pi'el* (intensive) form, e.g., שִׁבֵּר, מִלֵּא.

However, there are times when a word has a *dagesh* that cannot be explained by any of the grammatical rules. In these instances, the commentaries explain that the *dagesh* has been employed for *extragrammatical purposes*, to lend emphasis of a narrative nature or otherwise. Let us consider some fascinating examples of this idea.

Our parsha relates how, as the city of Sodom was about to be destroyed, Lot goes to his sons-in law and pleads with them to leave. The verse reads:

וַיֹּאמֶר קוּמוּ צְּאוּ מִן הַמָּקוֹם הַזֶּה כִּי מַשְׁחִית ה' אֶת הָעִיר.

He said, "Get up and leave this place, for Hashem is about to destroy the city!"[1]

We note that the letter *tzaddi* in the word "צְּאוּ—leave" has a *dagesh*, even though it is not one of the six letters mentioned above to which this rule applies. Why, then, is it there? The *Netziv* in the *Haamek Davar* explains that in this case, the *dagesh* expresses the urgency with which he urged his sons-in-law to leave; he was not just telling them to leave, he was saying, "Get out!"[2]

A similar comment is made by the *Maharal* in a later context. In *Parshas Shemos*, we are told how, when Moshe was born, his mother, Yocheved, hid him from the Egyptians. However, the Torah relates that at a certain point she could not hide him any longer. The verse reads:

וְלֹא יָכְלָה עוֹד הַצְּפִינוֹ וַתִּקַּח לוֹ תֵּבַת גֹּמֶא...וַתָּשֶׂם בָּהּ אֶת הַיֶּלֶד וַתָּשֶׂם בַּסּוּף עַל שְׂפַת הַיְאֹר.

She could not hide him any longer, and she took for him a wicker basket...she placed the child into it and placed [it] among the reeds at the bank of the Nile.[3]

Here too, we note that the letter *tzaddi* in the word "הַצְּפִינוֹ—to hide him" has a *dagesh* whose presence cannot be explained by any of the rules. The *Maharal* explains that this *dagesh* is there to express the

---

1   *Bereishis* 19:14.

2   See also *Haamek Davar* to *Shemos* 12:31 and *Vayikra* 10:19. In his Introduction *Kidmas Ha'emek* to *Bereishis* (sec. 7) the *Netziv* further explains that an "extra" *dagesh* in a word can sometimes indicate that it has two meanings, referring the reader to his commentary on *Bereishis* 2:25 and *Shemos* 16:12 for examples of this idea.

3   *Shemos* 2:3.

intensity with which she tried to hide him, until the point that it became absolutely impossible to do so any longer.[4]

IN THE REALM OF HALACHAH: BRINGING THE SH'TEI HALECHEM

Taking this discussion further, we will see that the *dagesh* can be present in a word not only for narrative emphasis, but also for halachic emphasis. In *Parshas Emor*, the Torah discusses the festivals of the year and their various obligations. With regards to the festival of Shavuos, a special *minchah* (meal-offering) is brought consisting of two loaves of bread, known as the *Sh'tei Halechem*. The verse reads:

מִמּוֹשְׁבֹתֵיכֶם תָּבִיאּוּ לֶחֶם תְּנוּפָה שְׁתַּיִם שְׁנֵי עֶשְׂרֹנִים.

From your dwelling places you shall bring bread that is to be waved, two loaves from two tenths of an eiphah.[5]

Once again, there is an "extra" *dagesh*, this time, in the letter *aleph* of the word "תָּבִיאּוּ—you shall bring." Rav Hirsch explains that although there are numerous types of *minchah* offerings that are brought in the Beis Hamikdash, the *Sh'tei Halechem* is unique. In all other cases, when a *minchah* is brought together with an animal, the animal is considered the primary offering and the *minchah* is secondary, with numerous halachic ramifications. When it comes to the *Sh'tei Halechem*, the relationship is reversed: It is the loaves that are considered the primary offering, while the animals which accompany them, as described in the following verse, are secondary to them, again with attendant halachic ramifications.[6] It is in order to emphasize this primary halachic status that the word with which the Torah commands us to bring the *Sh'tei Halechem* has an extra *dagesh*!

---

4   *Gevuros Hashem* chap. 17. See, similarly, *Haamek Davar* to *Bereishis* 43:26.
5   *Vayikra* 23:17.
6   Commentary to *Vayikra* ibid.

CONVERSE SITUATIONS: WHEN DOTS GO MISSING

Having seen some examples where a *dagesh* is *added* for other purposes, let us conclude this discussion by noting the converse situation, where a *dagesh* that should have been there is *missing!*

In *Parshas Matos*, we are told of how two and a half tribes settled on the east side of the Jordan River, which they had conquered from the Amorites. As they settled these territories, some of the families renamed them. The final verse of *Parshas Matos* describes such a renaming on the part of Novach, from the tribe of Menasheh:[7]

וְנֹבַח הָלַךְ וַיִּלְכֹּד אֶת קְנָת וְאֶת בְּנֹתֶיהָ וַיִּקְרָא לָה נֹבַח בִּשְׁמוֹ.

And Novach went and conquered Kenas and its surrounding areas, and he called it "Novach" like his name.

Rashi notes a grammatical anomaly here. The words "וַיִּקְרָא לָה—and he called it" should have a dot inside the *hei* of the word *lah*, called a *mapik hei*, denoting the preposition for a feminine noun. *Rashi* explains why this dot is absent in this case:

וראיתי ביסודו של רבי משה הדרשן לפי שלא נתקיים לה שם זה לפיכך הוא רפה, שמשמע מדרשו כמו לא.

I have seen in the writings of R' Moshe HaDarshan that the reason is because the name did not last; therefore, the letter has a weak sound, so that it can be expounded to be read as [the Hebrew word for] "no."

In other words, while the dot should be there in terms of the rules of grammar, it is missing in order to teach us that although he called it Novach, it did not remain with that name.[8]

---

7   *Bamidbar* 32:42.

8   For a discussion of the significance of Novach's name not enduring, see "From the Commentators" section in *Parshas Matos*. For alternative explanations regarding the absence of the *mapik*, see *Haamek Davar* and *Emes L'Yaakov* to *Bamidbar* ibid.

FURTHER EXAMPLES: BOAZ AND RUS

A similar comment can be found in the Midrash regarding Rus.[9] In verse 13 of chapter 2, when Boaz approaches Rus, telling her that he has heard of her kindness toward Naomi and instructing her not to glean in anyone else's field, she replies, "כִּי נִחַמְתָּנִי וְכִי דִבַּרְתָּ עַל לֵב שִׁפְחָתֶךָ וְאָנֹכִי לֹא אֶהְיֶה כְּאַחַת שִׁפְחֹתֶיךָ—For you have comforted me and you have spoken to the heart of your maidservant, though I am not even as worthy as one of your maidservants." The following verse reads:

וַיֹּאמֶר לָה בֹעַז לְעֵת הָאֹכֶל גֹּשִׁי הֲלֹם וְאָכַלְתְּ מִן הַלֶּחֶם.

At mealtime, Boaz said to her, "Come over and partake of the bread."

Here too, the word "*lah*," which means "to her," should have had a *mapik* in the *hei*, but does not. The Midrash explains:

אמר לה, חס ושלום אין את מן האמהות אלא מן האמהות.

He said to her, "Heaven forbid, you are not as one of the maid-servants, but as one of the matriarchs!"

In this case, also, we see that the *mapik*, which should have been present in terms of the rules of grammar, is omitted in order to allow for an additional message by reading the reading the word "*lah*" as "no."

It is quite fascinating to see how, alongside the rules of grammar themselves, the Torah will enlist certain grammatical tools for purposes of communicating other messages—be they halachic, hashkafic, or narrative.

---

9   *Rus Rabbah* 5:5, cited by the *Ramban* to *Bamidbar* loc. cit. See also *Meshech Chochmah* to *Devarim* 33:23.

THE AKEIDAH

Its Uniqueness, Impact, and Legacy

The final section of our parsha deals with the *Akeidah*—the Binding of Yitzchak. According to most commentators, it is the last of the Ten Trials of Avraham, and, from a certain point of view, it is in a category all unto its own, whose enduring significance is reflected clearly in the focal place that it occupies in our prayers to this day. This idea receives ultimate expression in the blessing of *Zichronos* (remembrances) in *Mussaf* of Rosh Hashanah, which culminates with the single plea: "*V'akeidas Yitzchak l'zar'o hayom b'rachamim tizkor*—Remember the binding of Yitzchak on this day for his descendants with mercy."

REFLECTION AND CONNECTION

Although the events of the *Akeidah* are well known, a moment's reflection on the elements involved will allow us to appreciate the magnitude of this trial. At the outset, we will appreciate that much of the *Akeidah* can be lost on us, since we approach and discuss the *Akeidah* with the knowledge that it didn't happen in the end. To this end, putting ourselves back for a moment in "real time," when Avraham had no notion that it would not occur, will also contribute most meaningfully to appreciating this test.

And what was the test? Avraham and Sarah had been childless for decades. Finally, when Avraham was one hundred years old, and Sarah ninety, they are given a son, the answer to all those years of longing and in whom all their hopes for the future are invested. Now, Avraham is being told to offer him up, with no notion of being left with any other child to replace him, leaving any hope for continuation devastated. Moreover, the act itself of offering one's child as a sacrifice was one against whose fundamental immorality Avraham had preached for all these years. To do so now, himself, would be the complete undoing of his life's work. There was to be, essentially, no future to speak of after the *Akeidah*. Additionally, the command to offer up his son is directly contradicted by an earlier promise he had received from Hashem Himself stating that Yitzchak would continue his line. Finally, it is clear that Avraham understood that he could tell no one about this, including his wife, Sarah. This means he had to embark on this task without her knowledge or support, utterly alone.

Bearing all of these points in mind, we will begin to get a sense of the magnitude of this test of Avraham's absolute devotion to Hashem's word. Nor can this be a spur-of-the-moment decision, made in haste or without adequate forethought. It was three days of journeying before Avraham reached the site where the *Akeidah* was to take place.

NAMING THE MOUNTAIN

In the present discussion, however, we would like to focus not only on the event of the *Akeidah* as the ultimate test that Avraham passed, but also on the impact and reverberations of the test beyond that point. To this end, we note that having passed the test, Avraham proceeds to name the place where it occurred. Verse 14 states:

וַיִּקְרָא אַבְרָהָם שֵׁם הַמָּקוֹם הַהוּא ה' יִרְאֶה אֲשֶׁר יֵאָמֵר הַיּוֹם בְּהַר ה' יֵרָאֶה.

Avraham called the name of that place "Hashem will see," as it is said this day, "On the mountain Hashem will be seen."

None of the earlier tests resulted in the place where they were passed receiving a new name. What is the significance of this occurrence after the *Akeidah*?

In truth, the words that describe the renaming are themselves some-what enigmatic. Let us ask:

- What, specifically, is Avraham saying that "Hashem will see"?
- Why does the sentence begin referring to Hashem "seeing" and then conclude with "being seen"?
- What day is being referred to by the words "this day"?
- How is all of this connected to the *Akeidah*?

Not surprisingly, the commentators from *Rashi* onwards discuss and deal with these basic questions. Let us consider a most fascinating explanation which is offered by the *Vilna Gaon*. The basis of his comment is a Midrash which states that initially, the Divine Presence resided in this world. However, as a result of Adam's sin, it distanced itself from this world and ascended Heavenward, residing in the first and lowest level of Heaven. The major wrongdoings of six notable subsequent generations[1] resulted in the Divine Presence ascending six levels higher, until it was at the seventh and highest level of Heaven, the nth degree removed from this world. However, Avraham brought about a turning point, bringing the Divine Presence one level closer, and the next six generations[2] bringing it closer still, until, in the days of Moshe, the Divine Presence had returned to reside in the world below.[3] It turns out that the process of returning the Divine Presence to this world was one which began with Avraham and culminated with Moshe. Both of these initial and final stages are described in verse 14, as follows:

- The verse begins by saying that Avraham called the place "Hashem will see," reflecting his achievement in bringing the Divine Presence closer to the world, so that all may know that Hashem sees and supervises the events of this world. At this point, the verse has finished quoting Avraham's words at that time.

---

1   Kayin, Enosh, the Generation of the Flood, the Generation of the Tower of Bavel, and in Avraham's own time, the wrongdoings of Egypt and of Sodom.

2   Yitzchak, Yaakov, Levi, Kehas, Amram, and Moshe.

3   *Bereishis Rabbah* 19:7.

- The concluding words of the verse are *those of the Torah itself*, as it proceeds to describe how that process, initiated by Avraham, was concluded six generations later, in Moshe's days. Thus, it says, "which today may be said as 'Hashem can be seen on the mountain.'" In other words, "today" is the Torah referring to when the Torah had been given on Mount Sinai, where the people apprehended a vision of Hashem's glory, in the culmination of the process which began as "Hashem seeing" in Avraham's time.

Truly amazing.

Through this, we can see that the *Akeidah* went beyond being an event; rather, it began a process which ended in the giving of the Torah. Still, we persist and ask, what was it about the *Akeidah* which marked it as the beginning of this process? To answer this question, let us consider another fascinating understanding of Avraham's words in renaming the mountain—"Hashem will see."

ESTABLISHING THE NATURE OF THE JEWISH PEOPLE

There are a number of statements from Chazal which reflect something unique about the nature of the Jewish People. For example, the Gemara states that if a Jew wanted to perform a mitzvah but was unable to do so, it is nonetheless considered as if he performed the mitzvah.[4] The reason is that since his inner will desires the performance of mitzvos, any external impediment to its performance does not detract from his intention as a true expression of his will. Indeed, this idea even has implications in the realm of halachah. The Gemara elsewhere states that if a person is halachically required to perform a mitzvah that requires his consent (e.g., offer a *korban* or give his wife a "*get*—bill of divorce"), yet he does not consent, we coerce him until he says that he consents.[5] The *Rambam* explains that since his inner will is to fulfill the mitzvos, it is actually his *yetzer hara* (evil inclination) that is interfering.

---

4   *Kiddushin* 39b.
5   Ibid., 50a.

Coercion serves to subdue his *yetzer hara*, at which point the consent he expresses reflects his actual will![6]

Both of these statements reflect the idea that the innermost will of the Jew is aligned with that of Hashem. Where does this nature come from?

The answer, says the *Meshech Chochmah*, is that it comes from the *Akeidah*.[7]

When Yitzchak allowed himself to be brought as an offering and was prepared to nullify his entire existence in response to Hashem's command, this yielded within his nature the absolute alignment of his will with that of Hashem, and became an inherent quality which he bequeathed to his descendants. The fascinating idea here is that this alignment was, by definition, already latent within Yitzchak before he was called upon to act on it. However, by responding to Hashem's word and expressing this quality outwards, it then became further embedded as a fundamental part of his essential makeup to the extent that it now could be passed down to his descendants.

This idea has ramifications not only for when the Jewish People seek to do—or are coerced to do—that which is right, but also when they do that which is not. An incorrect act will be judged very differently if it represents the essential will of the perpetrator, or, perhaps, some outside influence. Jewish nature, as established through the *Akeidah*, is such that no wrongdoing ever expresses a Jew's true will, which is ultimately aligned with that of Hashem. This core nature, which lies beneath every other layer of consciousness and will, is something that can only be perceived by Hashem Himself. Thus, the *Yerushalmi* states that while Hashem initially judges in conjunction with the Heavenly court, He concludes the judgment alone, basing it on the innermost nature of Israel that He alone can see.[8]

This, says the *Meshech Chochmah*, is the meaning of the name that Avraham gave to the mountain upon completing the *Akeidah*: "Hashem

---

6   *Hilchos Geirushin* 2:20.
7   *Bereishis* 22:14.
8   *Sanhedrin* 1:1.

will see." With this, Avraham was praying that He should always see the essential nature of the Jewish People which was set during the *Akeidah*, and judge them accordingly.

Indeed, perhaps, it is with this in mind that we conclude the blessing of *Zichronos* by asking Hashem to remember the *Akeidah* for us with compassion. We are not simply asking Him to recall the great merit of that event, for why limit the merits of our forefathers that might help us? Rather, we are asking Him to recall the *Akeidah* for what it says about our essential nature and judge our deeds—both the positive and the negative—in that light.

WHAT BRINGS THE DIVINE PRESENCE CLOSER?

Putting the above two ideas together, we will appreciate that they are essentially two expressions of the same concept. The extent to which the Divine Presence is close to the world is a product of the extent to which people are connected with the Divine will. The initial distancing of the Divine Presence came about through Adam choosing a path which diverged from that which Hashem had prescribed for him. This distancing process continued until it was reversed by Avraham and Yitzchak through their total embracing of Hashem's will. Thus, the personal (the level of Avraham and Yitzchak), national (instilling that nature within their descendants), and global (bringing the Divine Presence closer to the world) reverberations were all emanations of the same idea.

Moreover, the completion of this process six generations later likewise took place not only in the world, but also in the Jewish People. The link between these two events is expressed by the Sages, who state that the shofar which sounded at the giving of the Torah was one of the horns of the ram which Avraham offered in Yitzchak's stead. In fact, the Mishnah in *Pirkei Avos* informs us that this ram was part of a special list of items that were created at twilight on the sixth day of Creation.[9] The *Alshich* explains that the significance of this timing—for clearly Hashem had the capacity to create these things earlier on that day—is

---

9   5:8.

that they came into the world after Adam had sinned. This means that these items were created *as a response to that sin* and in order to facilitate its rectification.[10] Hence, the ram was offered up on the occasion which marked the beginning of mankind's recovery and re-connection with the Divine will. This re-connection found national expression when we stood at Har Sinai and proclaimed, "*Naaseh v'nishma*—We will do and we will hear!" By first stating that "we will do," even before "hearing," we were indicating a total acceptance of the Torah, whatever it may say. This complete alignment of our goals with those of Hashem was, in national terms, an *Akeidah* event and hence, it was only fitting for the shofar which sounded at that time to come from the ram which Avraham had offered at the time of the *Akeidah* itself.

And indeed, the Midrash further states that the second shofar from that ram will be the one that sounds to herald the arrival of Mashiach. That time will represent the full and final connection between the world and Hashem and will reflect the full realization of the idea which began with the *Akeidah* all those centuries ago.

All this can serve to give us deeper insight into our connection with the *Akeidah* and its meaning for us. When we read of it, we are not only recalling a great episode in our early history, but we are reminding ourselves of the capacity that it instilled within us, from where the ability to realize our highest aspirations can come. The full legacy and message of the *Akeidah* is: Look *forward* to the final redemption of Israel and the world—by looking *inward* for the wherewithal to bring it about!

THE AKEIDAH AND THE LAND OF ISRAEL

After successfully completing the *Akeidah*, Avraham receives a blessing from an angel in Hashem's name, part of which says:

וְיִרַשׁ זַרְעֲךָ אֵת שַׁעַר אֹיְבָיו.

And your descendants shall inherit the gate of their enemy.[11]

---

10   *Bereishis* 22:13.
11   Verse 17.

One of the great Chassidic masters, the *Be'er Mayim Chaim*,[12] explains the connection between the *Akeidah* and meriting the land of Israel as follows. The land of Israel is intimately bound up with the performance of the mitzvah of *milah* (circumcision). Thus, we find that as part of commanding Avraham with this mitzvah, Hashem says:[13]

וְנָתַתִּי לְךָ וּלְזַרְעֲךָ אַחֲרֶיךָ אֵת אֶרֶץ מְגֻרֶיךָ אֵת כָּל אֶרֶץ כְּנַעַן לַאֲחֻזַּת עוֹלָם.

I will give to you and to your descendants after you the land of your sojourns, the whole of the land of Canaan, as an everlasting possession.

Indeed, in recognition of this, we make special mention of the mitzvah of *milah* in the second blessing of *Birkas Hamazon*—known as *Birkas Haaretz*, which focuses on the land of Israel.

However, Yishmael and his descendants were also included, to a degree, in the mitzvah of *milah*, for which reason the *Zohar* states that they, too, have a certain hold on the land. What is our response to their claim?

Actually, according to Chazal, the *milah* of Yishmael instigated the *Akeidah*. The Gemara relates that Yishmael was boasting to Yitzchak that his mitzvah was more complete, seeing as he had consented to undergo *milah* at the age of thirteen, an age when he could have protested, while Yitzchak's *milah* took place when he was only eight days old. To this, Yitzchak responded that even if Hashem would tell him to offer his entire life, he would do so without hesitation.[14] This formed the backdrop to Hashem actually calling on him to do so in the form of the *Akeidah*. In this regard, the *Akeidah* serves as the refutation of Yishmael's *milah*-based claim to the land.

Rabbeinu Bachya informs us that the term "*oyev*" used for "enemy" in the Chumash[15] refers specifically to the descendants of Yishmael.[16]

---

12   R' Chaim Tirar of Tchernovitz (1760–1816).

13   *Bereishis* 17:8; see *Rashi* there.

14   *Sanhedrin* 89b, cited in *Rashi* to *Bereishis* 22:1, s.v. *achar*.

15   This is in contrast to the term "*soneh*," which refers to the descendants of Eisav.

16   Commentary to *Devarim* 30:7.

Therefore, having completed the *Akeidah*, Avraham was told that in its merit, his descendants would be able to inherit the "gate" of their enemy, Yishmael, overcoming any holding he may have had in the land of Israel.

THE COMPLETION OF THE AKEIDAH

When did the *Akeidah* finish? There are a number of points within this episode that could be identified: when Avraham was stopped from killing Yitzchak, when he offered the ram in his stead, etc. However, an entirely new dimension in this matter was revealed by R' Klonimus Kalman of Piaseczno, *Hy"d*, in his *drashah* on the first yahrzeit of his son, R' Elimelech, *Hy"d*, delivered on the second day of Sukkos, 5701 (1940).[17] There, he addresses the uniqueness of the martyrdom in his times. Throughout history, the martyrdom of the Jewish People was a result of their choice not to relinquish their Judaism. Here, however, Jews were being killed without being given a choice in the matter. R' Klonimus Kalman explained:

> The Akeidah was not a trial for Yitzchak alone; rather, it was the beginning of a Divine service of the Jewish People offering their souls for Hashem and His people. Since the trial of Avraham and Yitzchak took place solely within the realm of will and thought that were not realized in action, therefore, any Jew who is killed in the opposite manner, with action and without thought, represents the completion of the Akeidah of Yitzchak. For what began there with thought is completed here with action, thereby constituting one unified act.

These harrowing words, which could probably not have been said by anyone else, cast the *Akeidah* in a completely new light as a composite historical process, culminating in the decimation of European Jewry. In light of the idea mentioned earlier from the *Be'er Mayim Chaim*, it is left for us to contemplate the miraculous return of the Jewish People

---

17   *Aish Kodesh*, p. 72.

to their land three short years afterwards, overcoming the "gates" of their enemy against all odds, as a fulfillment of the blessing, "And your descendants shall inherit the gate of their enemy."[18] May we merit to see the completion of this process, too, speedily in our days!

---

18   Rav Mordechai David Neugershal, *Galut Yishmael*, pp. 62–63.

FROM THE COMMENTATORS

"AFAR" AND "EIFER"

Over the course of the festival of Sukkos, seventy bulls are brought as part of the *Mussaf* offerings. On the eighth day, Shemini Atzeres, a single bull is offered. The Midrash explains that the seventy bulls are brought on behalf of the seventy nations of the world, with their well-being in mind, while the single bull brought on the final day reflects the unique and special relationship between Hashem and the Jewish People.[1] Effectively, what these offerings represent is the goodwill that the Jewish People have for the nations of the world generally, alongside—and as part of—their special status as Hashem's people.

According to the *Vilna Gaon*,[2] this idea is alluded to in our parsha, in which Avraham steps forward to pray for the people of Sodom. For even though they are not members of his fledgling group and represent, moreover, the complete opposite of his moral principles and teachings, nevertheless he is prepared to ask for mercy for them. As a preamble to his pleas on their behalf, he states, "וְאָנֹכִי עָפָר וָאֵפֶר—And I am dust and ashes."[3] On a straightforward level, these are words of self-deprecation, whereby Avraham is saying, "I wish to pray for them, *although* I am dust

---

1   Cited in *Rashi* to *Bamidbar* 29:18.
2   Cited by R' Avraham Korman, *Haparashah L'doroteha*.
3   *Bereishis* 18:27.

and ashes." However, there is also an allusion in these words, whereby Avraham is saying, "I wish to pray for them *because* I am dust and ashes."

- The word "עפר" comprises the letters "ע-פר," denoting "seventy cows," as *par* means cow and the letter *ayin* has the numerical value of seventy.
- The word "אפר" comprises the letters "א-פר," denoting one cow, as the numerical value of *aleph* is one.

Thus Avraham is saying, "Since I embody the message of the seventy bulls (ע-פר) along with the one bull (א-פר), I wish to pray even for the people of Sodom."

A TALE OF TWO (MISSING) CITIES: WHAT HAPPENED TO ADMAH AND TZ'VOYIM?

וַה' הִמְטִיר עַל סְדֹם וְעַל עֲמֹרָה גָּפְרִית וָאֵשׁ מֵאֵת ה' מִן הַשָּׁמָיִם.

Hashem rained down sulfur and fire upon Sodom and Amorah, from Hashem, out of Heaven.[4]

Our verse mentions only the two cities of Sodom and Amorah. However, as we know, there were two other cities—Admah and Tz'voyim—that were also destroyed.[5] The only city of the plains that was spared was the fifth city, Tzo'ar, as described in verses 21–24. Why, then, does our verse mention only two of the four cities that were destroyed?[6]

It is also noteworthy that our verse begins by stating that "Hashem rained down...," and then mentions again, "from Hashem." What is the meaning behind this repetition?

---

4   *Bereishis* 19:24.

5   These four cities are referred to as *"the cities of the plain"* in verse 29, and listed explicitly in *Devarim* 29:22: "כְּמַהְפֵּכַת סְדֹם וַעֲמֹרָה אַדְמָה וּצְבוֹיִם אֲשֶׁר הָפַךְ ה' בְּאַפּוֹ וּבַחֲמָתוֹ"—Like the upheaval of Sodom and Amorah, Admah and Tz'voyim, which Hashem overturned in His anger and wrath."

6   See *Tzofnas Paaneach* of the Rogatchover Gaon to our verse.

The nature of the wickedness of the four cities is outlined by the Midrash (cited by *Rashi*), commenting on the names of the kings of those cities:

- Bera, king of Sodom: He was wicked in two areas (ב' רע), between man and God and between man and man.
- Birsha, king of Amorah: He rose in wickedness (ברשע).
- Shin'av, king of Admah: He hated his Father in Heaven (שנא אב).
- Shemever, king of Tz'voyim: He wanted to attach wings (שם אבר) to fly up and rebel against the Holy One, Blessed is He.[7]

The Lubavitcher Rebbe points out that these four cities can now be categorized into two groups of two: the first two cities were wicked both between man and man and between man and God, while the wickedness of the second two cities was focused between man and God.[8]

What is the significance of such a distinction? At the end of the first chapter of *Megillas Rus*, when Naomi returns to Beis Lechem after the famine, she tells the inhabitants, "אַל תִּקְרֶאנָה לִי נָעֳמִי קְרֶאןָ לִי מָרָא...וַה' עָנָה בִי—Do not call me Naomi [pleasantness], call me Marah [bitterness]...for Hashem has testified against me."[9] The *Vilna Gaon* explains that changing one's name represents accepting a new situation without any expectation of it changing back. Naomi was resigned to her bitter state and did not expect that Hashem would be merciful toward her, since she had accompanied her husband when he abandoned their people at a time of need and did not show compassion toward them. As such, she felt she could not hope for mercy from Heaven, since the Divine attribute of mercy would itself now be a source of indictment

---

7   What is the basis of the Sages expounding these four names as descriptions of wickedness and evil? The *Maaseh Hashem* explains that it comes from the verse's reference to the fifth king, whom it simply calls, "the king of Bela, that is, Tzo'ar." This is most unusual! Does the king of Tzo'ar not also have a name, as do the first four kings? If so, why is it not mentioned? From here we see that the names are depictions of wickedness and, hence, seeing as the city of Tzo'ar was (relatively) free of these crimes, no name is given for its king. However, this moves us to return to the kings whose names were given, and to expound on the messages within those names.

8   *Likutei Sichos* 5752.

9   1:20–21.

against her, due to her not showing mercy to others in need! The name of Hashem that represents the attribute of Mercy is the *Shem Havayah*.[10] Thus, Naomi says "*Hashem anah vi*"—Hashem's attribute of mercy itself is testifying against me over my lack of mercy toward my people; hence, I might as well change my name to Marah.[11] In other words, when a person acts without mercy toward another person, the resulting sin is distinct from a sin against Hashem; in such a case, even Hashem's attribute of mercy serves to indict him, rather than protect him.

Putting the above two ideas together, we return to our verse, which singles out Sodom and Amorah for mention. Even though all four cities of the plain were destroyed, these two cities were punished not only for their sins between man and God, but also between man and man. Moreover, this will explain to us why the *Shem Havayah* is repeated in the verse, as it emphasizes the fact that for these two cities, even the attribute of mercy represented by that name was a source of indictment and retribution, making their punishment all the greater. In contrast, the destruction of "all the cities of the plain," including Admah and Tz'voyim, is mentioned in verse 29. There, the name "Elokim" is used, denoting the attribute of justice; for in this respect, all four cities were the same.

YITZCHAK, YISHMAEL, AND THE PRICE OF LAUGHTER

וַתֵּרֶא שָׂרָה אֶת בֶּן הָגָר הַמִּצְרִית אֲשֶׁר יָלְדָה לְאַבְרָהָם מְצַחֵק. וַתֹּאמֶר לְאַבְרָהָם גָּרֵשׁ הָאָמָה הַזֹּאת וְאֶת בְּנָהּ כִּי לֹא יִירַשׁ בֶּן הָאָמָה הַזֹּאת עִם בְּנִי עִם יִצְחָק.

Sarah saw the son of Hagar, the Egyptian, whom she had borne to Avraham, mocking. And she said to Avraham, "Banish this maidservant and her son, for the son of this maidservant will not inherit with my son, with Yitzchak."[12]

The simple understanding of these verses is that Sarah saw that Yishmael was being a harmful influence on Yitzchak and therefore

---

10   The name spelled *Yud-Hei-Vav-Hei*.

11   Commentary to *Rus*, loc. cit.

12   21:9–10.

insisted that he be banished from the household, stating further that she would not allow him to inherit together with Yitzchak.

A very different approach is found in the writings of R' Yaakov Ettlinger.[13] The verse informs us that Sarah's request came as a result of her seeing Yishmael laughing or mocking. What was he laughing about? The verse doesn't specify. However, according to the *Seforno*, the laughter related to that which was mentioned in verse 8, namely, that Avraham made a celebratory feast on the day Yitzchak was weaned. Why was that cause for laughter?

Chazal inform us that when Yitzchak was born, the scoffers of the generation joked that he was not the son of Avraham, but of Avimelech, by whom Sarah had recently been held captive.[14] This, too, was the cause of laughter for Yishmael, saying, "Why is Avraham making a feast to celebrate the weaning of a child who is not his?"

Now, while for the scoffers in general this represented mockery at its most nefarious and reprehensible level, for Yishmael the implications were much more sinister. For if Yitzchak was not Avraham's son, then it would emerge that his only son and heir was Yishmael! In other words, Yishmael was seeking through this mockery to *completely delegitimize Yitzchak's status* as a rightful heir of Avraham.

This was Sarah's concern, in response to which she felt the only course was to remove Yishmael completely from the picture, before he ended up doing that to Yitzchak! Thus, when Sarah said, "for the son of this maidservant will not inherit with Yitzchak," she was not expressing what would happen from *her* point of view, but rather, from *Yishmael's* point of view. Sarah was informing Avraham that if Yishmael was allowed to remain, then he would maintain and promote his narrative to the point where, when the time came to inherit Avraham, he, Yishmael, would claim that he was the only true heir. Faced with such a prospect, there was no choice but to send him away.

Moreover, this understanding gives us further insight into a later episode regarding Yitzchak and Yishmael. When Avraham passed away,

---

13   *Drashos Minchas Ani, Parshas Vayeira.*
14   *Midrash Tanchuma, Toldos* sec. 1, cited in *Rashi* ibid., 25:19, s.v. *Avraham.*

the verse states, "וַיִּקְבְּרוּ אֹתוֹ יִצְחָק וְיִשְׁמָעֵאל בָּנָיו"—Yitzchak and Yishmael, his sons, buried him."[15] Chazal note that the verse mentions Yitzchak first, implying that Yishmael allowed him to go first in the burial procedure.[16] This indicates, say Chazal, that Yishmael subsequently did *teshuvah*. How is this gesture an act of *teshuvah*? The *Meshech Chochmah*[17] explains that once we understand that Yishmael's primary sin was the delegitimization of Yitzchak as Avraham's son, his *teshuvah* took the form of his renouncing any such claim, which was expressed most unambiguously in his allowing Yitzchak to precede him in performing a son's duty to bury his father.

Chazal inform us that "the deeds of the fathers are a foretelling for their children." In this matter, too, we await the *teshuvah* of Yishmael's descendants in renouncing the reprehensible claims which take their cues from those of their patriarch. May it happen speedily in our days!

---

15   *Bereishis* 25:9.
16   *Bava Basra* 16b, cited in *Rashi* ibid., s.v. *Yitzchak*.
17   *Bereishis* ibid.

PARSHAS CHAYEI SARAH

THE NATIONAL SIGNIFICANCE OF THE PURCHASE OF ME'ARAS HAMACHPEILAH

INTRODUCTION: ELABORATION—AND REITERATION

The opening section of our parsha devotes a full twenty verses to Avraham's purchase of Me'aras Hamachpeilah from Ephron and the B'nei Cheis, describing each stage of the negotiations in detail. What is behind this extensive description?

Beyond this, it is noteworthy that every subsequent time Me'aras Hamachpeilah is mentioned in *Chumash Bereishis*, the Torah sees fit to add how it was purchased from Ephron:

- This begins in the end of this parsha, in the verses that describe the burial of Avraham: "וַיִּקְבְּרוּ אֹתוֹ יִצְחָק וְיִשְׁמָעֵאל בָּנָיו אֶל מְעָרַת הַמַּכְפֵּלָה אֶל שְׂדֵה עֶפְרֹן...הַשָּׂדֶה אֲשֶׁר קָנָה אַבְרָהָם מֵאֵת בְּנֵי חֵת—Yitzchak and Yishmael, his sons, buried him in the Cave of Machpeilah, in the field of Ephron...The field that Avraham bought from B'nei Cheis."[1]
- Similarly, in *Parshas Vayechi*, in Yaakov's final words to his sons where he asks them to bury him in Me'aras Hamachpeilah, he

---

1   *Bereishis* 25:9–10.

adds: "אֲשֶׁר קָנָה אַבְרָהָם אֶת הַשָּׂדֶה מֵאֵת עֶפְרֹן הַחִתִּי לַאֲחֻזַּת קָבֶר...מִקְנֵה הַשָּׂדֶה וְהַמְּעָרָה אֲשֶׁר בּוֹ מֵאֵת בְּנֵי חֵת—Which Avraham bought together with the field from Ephron the Chiti as a burial estate...the purchase of the field, and the cave that is in it, from the B'nei Cheis."[2]

- This is again reiterated in the following chapter, when the Torah describes the burial itself: "וַיִּקְבְּרוּ אֹתוֹ בְּמְעָרַת שְׂדֵה הַמַּכְפֵּלָה אֲשֶׁר קָנָה אַבְרָהָם אֶת הַשָּׂדֶה לַאֲחֻזַּת קֶבֶר מֵאֵת עֶפְרֹן הַחִתִּי עַל פְּנֵי מַמְרֵא—They buried him in the cave of the field of Machpeilah, the field which Avraham purchased as a burial plot from Ephron the Chiti, on the plains of Mamrei."[3]

Why is every mention of this location accompanied by a recalling of how and from whom it was purchased?

NOTICEABLY SILENT

Interestingly, a curious contrast to the above exists in the case of Yitzchak. After his passing, the verse simply says, "וַיִּקְבְּרוּ אֹתוֹ עֵשָׂו וְיַעֲקֹב בָּנָיו—Eisav and Yaakov, his sons, buried him."[4] And that's it! In this case, not only does the Torah not mention the background to the purchase of Me'aras Hamachpeilah, it does not even tell us he was buried there! Why would the Torah completely omit in Yitzchak's case what it went out of its way to mention with the other two Patriarchs?

TWO ELEMENTS OF PURCHASE

The key to understanding this matter lies in the fact that on this occasion, Avraham was looking to not only buy a single burial plot for Sarah, but rather, as he expresses it, an "achuzas kever—a burial estate" for his entire family.[5] This basic idea will enable us to understand the different elements and stages in Avraham's negotiations, as described at length in the verses. He first approaches the B'nei Cheis, who represent the local populace, to secure their permission for purchasing

---

2   Ibid., 49:30–32.
3   Ibid., 50:13.
4   Ibid., 25:39.
5   See *Ramban* to verse 4.

a burial estate in their jurisdiction.[6] Only after having done that does he make contact with Ephron for purposes of purchasing the specific property of the field of the Machpeilah.[7] All of this is done, as the verses emphasize, in full view of the local populace, so that no one can later object to his purchase.

Indeed, this will explain to us something else. After having described Avraham handing over the money for the field to Ephron, the concluding verses then record Avraham's purchase twice![8] Additionally, there is a discrepancy between these two descriptions. The first verse states that the purchase took place "*l'einei B'nei Cheis—in the view of* B'nei Cheis,"[9] while the second verse states that it took place "*me'eis B'nei Cheis—from* the B'nei Cheis."[10] What is behind these two descriptions?

One of the classic commentators among the Rishonim, Rabbeinu Yosef Bechor Shor, explains that these two concluding verses reflect the two things that Avraham acquired on that occasion:

- First, the verse describes Avraham's acquisition of the field of Machpeilah itself from Ephron, through the means of the money that he paid him. This acquisition from Ephron took place "*in the view of* B'nei Cheis."
- Subsequently, the Torah relates how, through the act of burying Sarah, Avraham secured his right to use that property as a burial plot. This right is one that he acquired "*from* the B'nei Cheis" themselves.

FIRST STEPS

In light of all this, R' Leib Mintzberg explains that although the opening section of the parsha is about the burial of Sarah, it also involves something whose significance goes beyond that event. Avraham was

---

6   Verses 3–7.
7   Verses 8–16. See, e.g., the *Alshich* and *Malbim* for detailed discussion of these verses in this light.
8   Verses 17–20.
9   Verse 18.
10   Verse 20.

promised the Land of Israel for his descendants. This episode contains the first act of Avraham actually taking legal possession of a portion of the Land, establishing his roots there by purchasing a burial plot in one of its cities. In so doing, it represents the concretization of his presence in and acquisition of the land generally. For this reason, Avraham does not wish to accept the plot as a gift from Ephron, so as not to have any residual "fingerprints" left on this land from its donor.[11]

This will explain an additional nuance in the concluding verses which, as we saw, describe Avraham's dual acquisition of the field:

- In verse 17, dealing with the purchase of the property itself from Ephron, it mentions only that the cave was *"lifnei Mamrei—*near [the territory of] Mamrei."
- In verse 19, it elaborates further on the location of the field, stating that it was *"hi Chevron b'eretz Canaan—*in Chevron, in the land of Canaan."

Why is this broader setting mentioned only in the second verse? Indeed, why is it mentioned at all? We already know that the field is in Chevron, and we certainly know that it is in the land of Canaan! Rather, the matter being dealt with in that verse specifically—the securing of a burial plot—represents an act of acquisition that had implications for Avraham's ownership of the land of Canaan as a whole!

BELOVED MOMENTS

With this in mind, let us return to the numerous repetitions throughout *Chumash Bereishis* of the fact that Avraham purchased Me'aras Hamachpeilah from Ephron. Our parsha is famous for its repetition of the story of Eliezer finding a wife for Yitzchak, which the Sages explain by saying that the Torah repeats things to show how beloved they are. Likewise, the acquisition of Me'aras Hamachpeilah is repeated at every opportunity, for it reflects the beloved moment when our people's acquisition of the Land of Israel began.

---

11   *Ben Melech, Parshas Chayei Sarah.*

NO MENTION NECESSARY

Moreover, with this in mind, we may now understand why, as we noted, there is no mention of Me'aras Hamachpeilah at all regarding the burial of Yitzchak. Yitzchak was unique among all the Avos, in that his entire life was lived in Eretz Yisrael. Since the totality of his existence was in that land, this made it unnecessary for our connection with it through the acquisition of Me'aras Hamachpeilah to be mentioned in the context of his burial.

A SERVANT'S MISSION

Much of this parsha is devoted to the Torah's description of Eliezer's quest to find a wife for Yitzchak. Notably, not only does the Torah recount this episode itself in detail, it also includes Eliezer's retelling of it in full. Commenting on this phenomenon, the Midrash states:[1]

יפה שיחתן של עבדי אבות לפני המקום מתורתן של בנים, שהרי פרשה של אליעזר כפולה בתורה, והרבה גופי תורה לא ניתנו אלא ברמיזה.

The conversations of the servants of the Patriarchs are more beautiful before the Omnipresent than the Torah of the descendants; for the section dealing with Eliezer is presented twice, while many primary Torah laws are only imparted through allusion.

This itself is a very beautiful statement, but it does require some contemplation on our part. *Why* are the Patriarchs' servants' conversations more beautiful than the laws of the Torah itself?

SOME DIFFERENCES BETWEEN THE TWO ACCOUNTS

To understand this matter, we first note that upon inspection, Eliezer's account of the story is not a verbatim repetition of the Torah's

---

1   *Bereishis Rabbah* 60:8, cited in *Rashi* to verse 42.

"own" account, for there are numerous aspects which differ between the two presentations. A couple of notable examples:

- Avraham tells Eliezer that he must go *"el artzi v'el moladeti—To my land and to my birthplace."*[2] When Eliezer tells the story, he quotes Avraham as telling him to go *"el beis avi v'el mishpachti—To my father's household and to my family."*[3]
- As soon as Rivkah has given both Eliezer and his camels to drink, he gives her the jewelry and then asks her who she is.[4] When he recounts the story, he first mentions that he asked who she was and only then says that he gave her the jewelry.[5]

These discrepancies certainly require our attention, for why would Eliezer see it as either necessary or appropriate to depart even slightly from the events as they actually happened?

AVRAHAM'S INSTRUCTIONS— AND HASHEM'S ORCHESTRATIONS

The key to this matter lies in understanding Avraham's original instructions to Eliezer, and then noting how the entire mission underwent a complete transformation approximately halfway through. We might be inclined to formulate Avraham's instructions as telling Eliezer to find a wife for Yitzchak in his hometown, Charan, specifically among his family who still lived there. However, the *Malbim* explains that in actual fact, Avraham's family *did not feature in his original plan at all.* Rather, Avraham simply felt that in general, the inhabitants of Charan were the type of people from whom a suitable girl could be found for Yitzchak. Thus, he stipulates only that she come from "my land and my birthplace," but makes no mention of his family. What, then, will determine who is the right girl? The answer is simply that anyone who

---

2   Verse 4.
3   Verse 38.
4   Verses 22 and 23.
5   Verse 47.

exhibits exemplary character traits and generosity of spirit is, *by definition*, a good choice for Yitzchak.

It is for this reason that when he arrives at Charan, Eliezer makes his way, not to Besuel's house, but rather to the well in order to conduct his test and find a wife for Yitzchak. That test will tell him all he needs to know about the prospective bride—whoever she may be! Indeed, not only does Eliezer not make his way to Avraham's family, he *doesn't even enter the city*; as verse 11 relates, the well was outside the city limits. Eliezer reasoned that a family which was prepared to send its daughter outside of the city to draw water would hopefully be agreeable to her leaving the city for purposes of a good marriage. Throughout all this planning, Avraham's family could not be further from Eliezer's mind. It is fascinating to consider that the way he envisages his mission going, they will never even need to know that he was there.

This explains why, as soon as the girl Eliezer approaches has passed his test with flying colors, he gives her the jewelry before even asking her name. By passing the test, she has already demonstrated that she is a suitable match for Yitzchak, regardless of who she is. Needless to say, Eliezer needs to ask her name at some stage, but that is only to find out who this anonymous, wonderful girl actually is, and what name to put for "Bride's Family" on the wedding invitation. With this background in mind, we will appreciate that nothing could have prepared Eliezer for what was about to happen next.

Although Avraham's family were not part of Eliezer's original plan, they were part of Hashem's plan, Who arranged that the girl who Eliezer approached and who passed the test was Rivkah, Avraham's great-niece. Indeed, we can only imagine Eliezer's utter astonishment upon hearing that the girl who had passed his test was none other than the granddaughter of Nachor, Avraham's brother!

REVISING THE SCRIPT

At this stage, it is clear beyond any doubt that Rivkah is the one for Yitzchak. However, it is equally clear that if Eliezer tells her family the story exactly the way it occurred, he will practically guarantee the failure of his mission. If they hear that they were *completely incidental* to Avraham's plan, it will not bring out their most agreeable side, to say the least. Therefore, Eliezer realizes that in order for this to work, he will need to retell the entire story—with them as the focus from the beginning! This will require a number of adjustments, the first among them being tailoring Avraham's original instructions telling him to go "to my land and to my birthplace," stating instead that he was told to go "to my father's house and to my family."

Fine-Tuning

In this regard, there is a fascinating accompanying shift in nuance between the two accounts. Avraham's words were "*Ki el artzi v'el mo-ladeti*—Except to my land and to my birthplace," Eliezer retells this as "*Im lo el beis avi v'el mishpachti*—If not to my family and my father's house." Why does he shift the pivotal term from "except" to "if not"?

The difference between the two versions is that Avraham was absolutely insistent that the girl come from Charan, hence he used the term "except." The reason he could be so insistent is because he was not particular as to who exactly the girl should be. From the pool of prospects in the entire city, surely someone suitable could be found. When Eliezer retold those instructions, with his version centering on Avraham's family specifically, he also needed to back away and "tone down" that level of insistence. For if they knew that they were Avraham's only choice, they could become unreasonably demanding; after all, what other alternative did he have? To this end, he modified Avraham's words as saying: "Do not consider anyone from Canaan unless ("if not") it doesn't work out with my family." In this way, Eliezer is communicating a nuanced message to her family, saying, "You are certainly Avraham's *first* choice, but you are by no means his *only* choice. I sincerely hope it works out and I don't have to consider other options."

Of course, a major piece in Eliezer's retelling of the story will be the test at the well. After all, if he was only ever meant to come to Avraham's family, what is the purpose of stopping off at the communal well outside the city to conduct a test that anyone could pass? For this, Eliezer resourcefully weaves this element of the story into his presentation, making it, in fact, even more ambitious than it originally was. In blessed hindsight, he can claim that in order to seek absolute Divine approval for the match, he set up a test whereby the one who passed would be from Avraham's family—and so she was!

For this reason, in retelling the part where she had passed the test, Eliezer reversed the order of his actions, stating first that he asked her name and only then that he gave her the gifts. According to his version of events, he could not have given her the gifts prior to finding out who she was; after all, what if she was not from Avraham's family? Wasn't that what the test was all about? Therefore, he says that first he asked her for her name, and when she turned out to be from his master's family—representing the success of his test—he then gave her the gifts.

Understanding Eliezer's retelling in this manner illuminates this entire chapter, as well as serving as encouragement to look at Eliezer's account vis-à-vis that of the Torah with much more alertness than we otherwise might have done.

ELIEZER'S FAITHFULNESS

There is yet another element in this story which reveals a whole new dimension to Eliezer's actions. The Sages inform us that Eliezer had his own ideas for a match for Yitzchak—his own daughter! When he communicated this wish to Avraham, the latter rejected his proposal, and instructed him instead to find a girl from Charan.[6] Set against this background, we can fully appreciate that throughout his mission, Eliezer is working against his own self-interest.

This brings us to the changes in Eliezer's story. No one could have faulted him for telling the episode exactly as it occurred. If that should lead to the match breaking down, that would be regrettable, but it would also bring a glimmer of hope for Eliezer himself. However, his faithfulness to his master overcame such an inclination, and expressed itself not only in carrying out his instructions to the letter, but also in then enlisting his resourcefulness and ingenuity to see that the outcome would be the optimum for his master. Such selflessness and

---

6   *Bereishis Rabbah* 59:9, cited in *Rashi* to verse 39.

dedication to a higher ideal in the face of one's own preferred outcome is indeed a very beautiful thing to behold. It is this quality that the Sages have in mind when they refer to "the beauty of the conversations of the Patriarchs' servants."

In this regard, there is an overarching lesson contained in this story that relates to the Jewish People themselves. Our relationship with Hashem is, likewise, that of servants to a Master, and, in this, our role model is the quintessential servant of *Chumash Bereishis*—Eliezer. Moreover, the particular laws of the Torah can be effectively derived from a mere allusion in a verse, using the principles of halachic exposition. In contrast, the lesson of what it means to be a servant specifically emerges from the Torah recounting in full not only the episode itself, but also in replaying it, this time set to the beautiful melody of a servant's faithfulness. It is a song presented not only for our appreciation and admiration, but also for our emulation and application.

PESUKIM AND PERCEPTION

PART I: ELIEZER—EVED OR ISH?

A noteworthy feature of this parsha is the fact that although Eliezer is the prime protagonist in the search for a wife for Yitzchak, the Torah does not refer to him by name even once throughout the entire parsha. Instead, he is referred to either as *"ha'eved*—the servant" or *"ha'ish*—the man." Specifically, the allocation of these two terms within the parsha can be broken down as follows:

- From the beginning of the chapter until he meets Rivkah, he is called *"eved"* (verses 2–20).
- From the time Rivkah begins watering his camels until he finishes talking to her family, he is called *"ish"* (verses 21–51).
- From that point until the end of the chapter, he is again called *"eved"* (verses 52–66).

Naturally, we are moved to ask: Given that Eliezer is both an *eved* and an *ish*, what is behind the variations in the way in which the Torah refers to him?

"HE WILL SEND HIS ANGEL BEFORE YOU"
A classic explanation of this matter is found in the commentary of

Rabbeinu Bachya.[1] He draws our attention to a verse early on in the chapter that is very easy to read and then to forget about. When Eliezer asks Avraham what he should do if the girl he finds does not wish to come back with him to the land of Canaan, Avraham responds:

ה' אֱלֹקֵי הַשָּׁמַיִם אֲשֶׁר לְקָחַנִי מִבֵּית אָבִי וּמֵאֶרֶץ מוֹלַדְתִּי...הוּא יִשְׁלַח מַלְאָכוֹ לְפָנֶיךָ וְלָקַחְתָּ אִשָּׁה לִבְנִי מִשָּׁם.

Hashem, God of Heaven, Who took me from the house of my father and the land of my birth...He will send his angel before you, and you will take a wife for my son from there.[2]

When we read this verse, we likely summarize Avraham's words as basically saying, "Don't worry, Hashem will help you and everything will work out." However, Avraham said more than this. He said Hashem would *send an angel* before Eliezer to help him. We tend to gloss over that point because we never actually see or hear from an angel as the episode unfolds. However, perhaps this is because we are not looking in the right place.

As the verses relate, no sooner had Eliezer finished formulating his test for Yitzchak's prospective bride than Rivkah, the one intended by Hashem to marry Yitzchak, appeared at the well. We will appreciate that Eliezer could probably not have conducted his test more than once before being either shooed away from the well, or simply being unable to drink any more! And yet, the first girl was Rivkah, who turned up exactly at that moment. This was the angel at work, taking the form of arranging for everyone to be where they needed to be at the right time.

As Eliezer contemplates Rivkah responding to his demanding test with alacrity and graciousness, he recalls Avraham's assurance and realizes that it was Hashem's angel who brought her to the well. And it is for this reason that from this point on, he is now called "the *ish*." We find the term "*ish*" in Tanach referring to an angel.[3] Likewise, Eliezer's awareness of the angel's input in his situation is reflected by the way

---

1   Commentary to verse 15. See also the *Shelah Hakadosh* to this parsha, *Torah Ohr* sec. 5.
2   Verse 7.
3   See *Daniel* 9:21. See also *Rashi* to *Bereishis* 37:15.

in which the Torah refers to him—as "the *ish*." This title remains until he has met Rivkah's family and secured their consent. At that point, with his mission successfully concluded, the angel departs, whereupon Eliezer reverts to his original title, "the *eved*," for the rest of the chapter.

What is most fascinating to ponder about this approach is that the Torah's choice regarding how to refer to Eliezer is based, not on the *reality itself* of the angel's input—which was in play from the outset—but on Eliezer's *recognition of* that reality. And indeed, this is most appropriate. Since the two terms in question are referring to Eliezer himself, it is only fitting for them to be determined by his realization of what is happening, for his enhanced awareness represents a change within himself.

PART II: FROM "MAYBE" TO "TO ME"

When Avraham initially charges Eliezer with finding a wife for his son Yitzchak, he tells him to go to Haran to find a suitable young woman and bring her back to the land of Canaan. At a certain point, Eliezer asks, "Perhaps the woman will not wish to come back with me; shall I bring your son over there?"[4] *Rashi* comments:

> The word "perhaps" [אולי] is written without a vav [אלי], which means it can be read as "to me." This is because Eliezer had a daughter and wanted Yitzchak to marry her. To this Avraham replied, "My son is blessed, and you are [descended from Canaan who is] cursed, so there can be no match."

There is something very intriguing about this comment of *Rashi*'s. The story of Eliezer finding a wife for Yitzchak is actually told twice in this chapter: once as it actually happens, and then again in Eliezer's words, as he retells it to Rivkah's family. If we look at *Rashi*'s commentary

---

4   Verse 5.

on the verse which originally presents Eliezer's question, we will see that he makes no comment! It is only when Eliezer retells the story and reaches this point[5] that *Rashi* tells us about his hopes for his daughter. Why would *Rashi* not make this comment when the question was originally asked—which is when this exchange between Eliezer and Avraham must have taken place? Surely something new cannot become part of the actual story when it is being retold!

In truth, this question should not really be addressed toward *Rashi* for, as he stated, his comment is a response to the fact that the Torah writes the word *ulai* without a *vav*, spelling it like *eilai*. If we look at the earlier verse when Eliezer asked the question, we will see that there, the word is written with a *vav*. It is only the second time around when he retells the story that the *vav* is absent. Essentially, therefore, the question is not on *Rashi*, but on the verse itself: Why is this part of the conversation only alluded to (through the missing *vav*) in the retelling of the story?

The Kotzker Rebbe gives a fascinating answer to this question: In reality, the underlying motivation for Eliezer's question was, indeed, his desire for Yitzchak to marry his daughter. However, at the time, specifically because Eliezer was so emotionally invested in the situation, he could not bring himself to recognize his personal agenda. Eliezer honestly felt that his question was motivated by the practical considerations of how to react to the contingency of the girl not wanting to travel to Canaan. We should appreciate that this also means that when Avraham responded and said that Yitzchak would never marry his daughter, Eliezer felt that he had been misjudged by his master!

All of this had changed by the time Eliezer comes to tell the story to Rivkah's family. By that stage, Rivkah has demonstrated beyond any doubt that she is the one for Yitzchak. Once this is established, Eliezer is "free" of any plans he may have had about his own daughter. To his great credit, he thinks back over the episode from the beginning and realizes that Avraham was right. When he was asking, "What if she says no?" it

---

5   Verse 39, based on *Midrash Yalkut Shimoni, Hoshea* sec. 12, cf. *Bereishis Rabbah* 59:9.

really *was* rooted in his hope that Yitzchak would marry his daughter. The reason there is no *vav* missing from the word when Eliezer first asks his question is because it was not apparent at that time—even to him—that this is what he meant. Only when he perceives his true intent later on does the Torah reflect this by removing the *vav*, and that is where *Rashi* comments. In other words, at the point in the story where this idea actually registered with Eliezer, only then does it also register in the verse.

We may say that this is an added benefit of the Torah relating the story twice, with the second time being in Eliezer's own words, for it was thus able to communicate this additional lesson by choosing where to relate this element of the story.

FROM THE COMMENTATORS

THE DEATH OF SARAH AND AKEIDAS YITZCHAK

The parsha opens with the death of Sarah and Avraham's negotiations with Ephron to procure a burial plot for her. In a well-known comment, *Rashi* provides the context to this episode:

נסמכה מיתת שרה לעקידת יצחק, לפי שעל ידי בשורת העקידה שנזדמן
בנה לשחיטה וכמעט שלא נשחט, פרחה נשמתה ממנה ומתה.

The death of Sarah was juxtaposed with Akeidas Yitzchak, since through hearing news of the Akeidah, that her son had been prepared for slaughter and was almost indeed slaughtered, her soul flew up from her and she died.[1]

On the face of it, *Rashi* appears to be referencing the concept of *semichus parshiyos*—juxtaposition of sections in the Torah, something which he discusses numerous times throughout his commentary. However, upon closer inspection of this comment, as well as of the parshiyos themselves, we will see that this is not a discussion of *semichus parshiyos* at all.

- First, *Rashi's* discussions of *semichus parshiyos* always constitute his first comment in the parsha, addressing the general issue

---

1   *Bereishis* 23:2, s.v. *lispod.*

of the parsha as a whole before dealing with specific words and phrases in the verses. Here, *Rashi's* comment isn't even in the opening verse; it is toward the end of the second verse, on the words "*lispod l'Sarah v'livkosah*—to eulogize Sarah and to cry for her."

- Moreover, it doesn't even appear that these two sections are actually juxtaposed. The concluding section in the previous parsha deals with an event that occurred after the *Akeidah* and before the Torah's mention of Sarah's death, namely, Avraham receiving news of the children born to his brother, Nachor.[2] In light of this, not only is the juxtaposition of Sarah's death with the *Akeidah* not something that needs to be explained—it is not something that even exists!

Rabbeinu Eliyahu Mizrachi, the foremost commentator on *Rashi*, explains that *Rashi's* intent here is not to explain the Torah's juxtaposition of *the parshiyos* of the *Akeidah* and Sarah's death, but rather, he is noting the juxtaposition of *the events themselves*. And the reason he does so is in order to explain the words in the end of the second verse: "to eulogize Sarah and to cry for her." Crying is an emotional reaction, while eulogizing is an intellectual appraisal. As such, in a situation of bereavement, the reaction of crying would naturally come first, yet our verse put it second!

It is this reversal that *Rashi* is coming to explain: the background to Sarah's death was responsible for the order of Avraham's reactions. The Gemara states that if a person does a mitzvah and then subsequently regrets having done it, he loses the merit of that mitzvah.[3] Here, Avraham had just attained the outstanding merit of the *Akeidah*, one which would stand by his descendants for generations to come until our time. For this reason, he was acutely conscious of the fact that if he was not careful, his mourning over the loss of Sarah could turn into regret for ever having embarked on the *Akeidah* that led to her passing,

---

2   See ibid., 22:20–24.
3   *Kiddushin* 40b.

thereby compounding the tragedy immeasurably by losing the merit of the *Akeidah* as well! To this end, Avraham took great measures to keep his mourning in check, deferring any weeping until after the eulogizing, so that it would be framed by an appreciation of Sarah and what she stood for, rather than purely his feelings of loss.[4]

And so, a deeper look at what seemed to be the first *"semichus par-shiyos Rashi"* revealed it to be something else entirely. At the same time, the process itself which led us to that conclusion shed much light on the parameters within which *Rashi* will involve himself in the question of *semichus parshiyos*, many instances of which are yet to come.

AVRAHAM'S COINS? THOSE WILL DO NICELY!

וַיִּשְׁקֹל אַבְרָהָם לְעֶפְרֹן...אַרְבַּע מֵאוֹת שֶׁקֶל כֶּסֶף עֹבֵר לַסֹּחֵר.

Avraham weighed out to Efron...four hundred silver shekels, [of a quality] acceptable in all locations.[5]

Our verse informs us that not only did Avraham agree to pay the exorbitant sum of four hundred silver shekels for the cave of Machpeilah, but that he did so with currency that would be accepted anywhere. Interestingly, not only does the verse state this, but it also indicates what particular currency met those standards.

The Gemara relates that upon the birth of Yitzchak, Avraham minted coins to publicize the miracle of him and Sarah having a child at their advanced age. Indeed, to this end, the coins actually had the words *"zakein—old man"* and *"zekeinah—old woman"* minted on them.[6]

We note that the final word in our verse, "סֹחֵר," is written without a *vav*, although it is pronounced as if it had a *vav*—"סוֹחֵר." The penultimate word in the verse, *"over,"* means to pass through, but it also derives from the word *"avar,"* which means to precede. If we take the three letters of the word ס-ח-ר and then see what precedes them in the Hebrew alphabet, we will find the letters נ-ז-ק, which spell the word "זקן."

---

4   R' Binyamin Zev Hartman, commentary *Ohr Yashar* on *Rashi*.
5   *Bereishis* 23:16.
6   *Bava Kama* 92b.

Furthermore, as we noted, the word is written without the letter *vav*, but is pronounced as if it contains that letter. The letter that precedes *vav* is *hei*. If we add that to the other preceding letters, we get ‎נ-ה-ו-ק‎, which spell the word "‎זקנה‎." Thus, by going "‎עֵבֶר לַסֹּחֵר‎—preceding the letters of the word *socher*" both in terms of how the word is written as well as how it is pronounced, we discover exactly which currency it was that was *"over la'socher*—acceptable in all locations": Avraham's own coins![7]

TWO TYPES OF KINDNESS

On two occasions in our parsha, Eliezer makes a request for kindness. The first is from Hashem, before embarking on the test at the well, while the second is from Rivkah's family, after the test, when he asks them to send her with him to marry Yitzchak. There is a subtle difference in the phraseology of these two requests. When Eliezer asks for kindness from Hashem toward Avraham, he says, *"Vaaseh chessed im adoni Avraham*—And perform kindness with my master, Avraham."[8] When he later addresses Rivkah's family, he says, *"Im yeshchem osim chessed v'emes es adoni*—If you will do kindness and truth with my master."[9] The word for "with" has changed from *"im"* in the first case to *"es"* in the second. What is behind this change?

The *Vilna Gaon* states that the reason that there are two words for "with" in *lashon hakodesh* is because there are two ways people can be with each other:

- The term *es* denotes people who may be traveling or collaborating together, but not for the same reason or purpose. Their togetherness is purely external and functional.
- The term *im* denotes people who are united not only in action, but also in purpose.[10]

---

7   R' Avraham Korman, *Haparashah L'doroteha*, citing R' Shimon Mellior.

8   *Bereishis* 24:12.

9   Ibid., verse 49.

10   Cited in *Kol Eliyahu, Parshas Balak*.

With this distinction in mind, let us likewise consider that there are two ways to perform an act of kindness. It is possible to bestow kindness on someone with their interests at heart, but it is also possible to bestow kindness with other, more selfish or ulterior motives. In the first case, the giver and receiver are fully aligned (*im*), while in the second, they remain distinct from one another. Therefore, when asking Hashem for kindness, Eliezer uses the term "*im adoni*," as Hashem's kindness will have the recipient's best interests at heart. By contrast, when talking with Rivkah's family, he has no expectation that they will do kindness with him for his sake; if they decide to agree, it will only be for something they perceive that they will gain. As such, the Torah expresses his request with the term "*es adoni*."

PARSHAS TOLDOS

EISAV'S DECEPTION: A DEEPER LOOK

INTRODUCTION: THE TRAPPINGS OF A GOOD RELATIONSHIP

In the beginning of our parsha, the Torah relates how the love of Yitzchak and Rivkah was divided significantly—though by no means entirely—between Eisav and Yaakov respectively.[1] This was something which would come to a head later in the parsha when the question arose as to which son should receive the blessings. The verse does not mention any particular basis for Rivkah's love of Yaakov, stating simply that she loved him; indeed, no explanation for this is required! Yitzchak's love for Eisav, on the other hand, is explained with the words *"ki tzayid b'fiv."* What is the meaning of this phrase? The word *"tzayid"* is quite straightforward: it means hunting or trapping. However, the word *"b'fiv*—in his mouth"* is somewhat open-ended, as the verse does not specify to *whose* mouth it refers. Let us consult the sources.

Onkelos translates this phrase as saying that Yitzchak would eat from Eisav's hunting. In other words, according to *Onkelos*, the phrase *"tzayid b'fiv"* means: "[Eisav's] trapping was in his—Yitzchak's—mouth." Needless to say, this approach requires much explanation, for, on the face of it, it is completely dumbfounding. How can Yitzchak favor Eisav

---

1   *Bereishis* 25:28.

over Yaakov on the basis of something so mundane as eating from his hunting to the extent that ultimately, he judges Eisav as being the one who deserves the blessings?

The Sages provide a very different rendition of our phrase, whereby the word "*b'fiv*" translates not as "*in* his, [i.e., *Yitzchak's*] mouth," but rather, "*with* his, [i.e., *Eisav's*] mouth," for Eisav trapped his father with his words. As the Midrash describes:

וְשׁוֹאֲלוֹ: "אבא, היאך מעשׂרין את המלח ואת התבן?" כסבור אביו שהוא מדקדק במצוות.

He would ask, "Father, how does one take maaser [tithes] from salt and straw?" His father [therefore] thought that he was particular regarding mitzvos.[2]

Actually, this rather impressive sounding question itself requires our examination, for, in reality, one does *not* take *maaser* from those items at all. As such, this question sounds not so much like an expression of punctiliousness in mitzvah observance as one coming from a place of total ignorance! The commentators explain that Eisav was asking how, even though these items are exempt from *maaser*, one could nevertheless perform the mitzvah with them as a matter of added stringency, beyond that which the basic law requires. Yitzchak was very taken by this expression of extra piety and reserved a special love for Eisav.

BROADENING THE PICTURE

Still, the question remains. Eisav's pietistic questions notwithstanding (and we can assume he had a few more), how could they cause Yitzchak to believe that Eisav was the *more deserving* of his two sons? He had to have known that Yaakov's quality and his way of life far surpassed that of Eisav!

Moreover, a comment of *Rashi's* later in the parsha seems to contradict the idea that Yitzchak viewed Eisav as someone who was particular in performing mitzvos. In chapter 27, as a prelude to giving Eisav the

---

2   *Bereishis Rabbah* 63:10, cited in *Rashi* to *Bereishis* loc. cit.

blessings, Yitzchak tells him to sharpen his knives, go out to the field, and bring back some of his hunting.[3] Commenting on these words, *Rashi* explains:

- Sharpen your utensils—and slaughter correctly, so that you do not feed me non-kosher food.
- And trap for me—from ownerless animals, and not from stolen ones.

These comments are quite astounding. It seems that even after all these years, Yitzchak did not have such a high regard for Eisav's mitzvah performance at all, suspecting rather that unless told otherwise, he would feed him food that is either not kosher, stolen—or both! How does this fit with the earlier comment of *Rashi*'s, according to which Yitzchak was completely taken in by Eisav's questions? More importantly, in light of these later comments, how can he nonetheless proceed to choose Eisav as the one on whom to bestow the blessings?

TWO TYPES OF GODLY LIVING

R' Yosef Tzvi Salant, in his commentary *Be'er Yosef* on this parsha, reveals a deeper level to Eisav's deception of Yitzchak. He prefaces by noting that living one's life in service of Hashem can take one of two forms, depending on the nature of the person:

- For someone who has naturally positive tendencies, it takes the form of continually developing and perfecting them.
- For someone who has naturally negative tendencies, it takes the form of striving to overcome and elevate them.

Indeed, in some respects, there is room to argue that the second person is more worthy than the first, as he has to battle and overcome his tendencies to do the right thing. In this regard, the Gemara states that a person who has a tendency toward shedding blood can still choose his path in terms of how he enlists it:[4]

---

3   Verse 3.
4   *Shabbos* 156a.

- If he is a *tzaddik*, he can become a *mohel* or a doctor, channeling his nature toward the performance of mitzvos.
- If he is a regular person, he can become a butcher, using his nature to secure a livelihood.
- If he is a wicked person, he can become a murderer.

Yitzchak knows that Eisav is no Yaakov. Yaakov is a naturally spiritual person, while Eisav emerged from the womb literally the color of blood, giving a clear indication of where his tendencies would lie. Eisav's deception of Yitzchak lies not in his pretending to be a Yaakov, but in pretending to work on himself as Eisav. This is why *Onkelos* explains the basis of Yitzchak's love for Eisav as the fact that he would bring him his hunting. This represented Eisav's seeking to elevate and sublimate his tendency for bloodshed into the mitzvah of honoring his father!

OF SALT AND STRAW

With this in mind, we return to the question that Eisav is famous for asking, "How does one take *maaser* from salt and straw?" The *Pardes Yosef* explains that this question so came to characterize Eisav because it was actually about him! As we noted, one does not take *maaser* from salt and straw. The reason for this is that the elevation achieved through *maaser* applies only to actual food, while salt and straw are merely accessories to food. Thus, Eisav was asking, "Father, I have no doubt that Yaakov will achieve his perfection; after all, he is "the food"—the real article. But what about someone like me, who is merely an accessory, like salt and straw? Is there any hope for me?"[5]

Eisav's portrayal of himself to his father was thus not as a finished article, but as a work in progress. We can now understand how there is no contradiction between Eisav's halachic questions and Yitzchak feeling that he needed to remind his son to sharpen his knife and to make sure that the animals he trapped were not owned by others. Eisav did not balk at such reminders. On the contrary, his response to all this

---

5   R' Yosef Potzonovsky, *Pardes Yosef, Parshas Toldos.*

was, "Thank you for reminding me, Father; you know I try, and that I forget sometimes. Thank you for not giving up on me!"

FOR WHOM THE BLESSINGS?

And so, Yitzchak's heart goes out to Eisav, feeling that there is room for him in the future of the Jewish People. And indeed, the nation will need both those who are involved in material pursuits as well as the spiritual, not unlike the Yissachar-Zevulun partnership which would later exist within Yaakov's own children. As such, he decides to give Eisav the blessings, which are primarily material in nature: "the dew of the heavens and the fat of the earth."[6] Rivkah, however, judges otherwise. She recognizes the charade in Eisav's questions and is convinced that he has forfeited his place in the program of Avraham and Yitzchak.

How does Rivkah see what Yitzchak does not? There are two classical answers to this question:

- Rivkah has a keener eye for deception, having grown up with Lavan, a master deceiver, whose schemes and manipulations we will encounter in the following parsha.
- As related in the beginning of our parsha, upon experiencing severe turbulence during her pregnancy, Rivkah received a prophecy informing her that her two sons would be heading in opposite directions.[7] Although this could mean many things, and by no means consigns Eisav to a life of wickedness, it does alert her to the notion that his path may be decidedly different than that of Yaakov's. Yitzchak received no such message, and it seems quite clear that Rivkah never informed him of the prophecy that she received.[8]

---

6   *Bereishis* 28:1.
7   Ibid., 25:23.
8   This idea will help us resolve a seemingly simple question. When Rivkah experiences trouble with her pregnancy, she travels to the yeshiva of Shem, who is a prophet, in order to receive an explanation as to her situation. Upon reflection, this trip seems entirely unnecessary, seeing as both her husband Yitzchak and her father-in-law Avraham were prophets. This means that in terms of seeking an answer from a prophet, she could not have been better placed at home! Why, then, did she travel to Shem? However, Rivkah understood that the

AN AKEIDAH MOMENT

However, there is an additional consideration, whereby Yitzchak had active reason to expect that both of his sons would be part of the future of the Jewish People. This idea dated back to the very moment that they were born.

The Torah relates how Yaakov emerged from the womb with his hand holding on to Eisav's heel. Seeing this, Yitzchak named him Yaakov, deriving from the word "*ekev*—heel."[9] Upon reflection, this choice of name requires some explanation. After all, why should the fact— curious though it may be—that the second son was holding on to the heel of the first become the basis of his name?

R' Leib Heyman[10] offers a stunning suggestion. Undoubtedly, one of the outstanding spiritual highlights of Yitzchak's life was when he was prepared to allow his father to bring him as a sacrifice, as described in the end of *Parshas Vayeira*.[11] We refer to this event as "*Akeidas Yitzchak*," which means "The Binding of Yitzchak," referring to the Torah's description of Avraham tying Yitzchak down before placing him on the altar.[12] Actually, the term "*akeidah*" refers specifically to a form of binding whereby the hands are tied to the heels, so that this term encapsulates the state of absolute submission that Yitzchak attained toward Hashem's will. In this light, let us imagine Yitzchak's reaction when he saw two sons emerge in a most unusual manner, with *the hand of one attached to the heel of the other*! For him, this was a clear evocation of the *Akeidah*, indicating that both sons were destined to be worthy heirs to that event. Indeed, so great was his excitement over this portent that he called the second son Yaakov after this event! Yitzchak thus lived in

---

answer to her question would likely have implications for the future of her family, and, hence, it may have been withheld from the family members themselves. As such, she had no choice but to "outsource" the question to someone who was a prophet, but who was also not part of her family, and, thus, she travelled to Shem. In the end, her concerns were borne out, as it seems Yitzchak was not meant to know about the diverging nature of his two sons (R' David Pardo, *Maskil L'David*).

9   Ibid., verse 26.

10   *Chikrei Lev, Parshas Toldos.*

11   *Bereishis*, chap. 22.

12   Verse 9.

expectation of both his sons continuing his legacy, and, therefore, had a greater inclination to judge Eisav favorably.

In truth, Yitzchak's hopes for Eisav were not entirely unfounded, for, as mentioned, Eisav's natural tendencies toward bloodshed did not mean that he was condemned to lead a life of wickedness. His challenge was to deal with these tendencies, channeling them toward positive goals. What Rivkah saw more clearly than Yitzchak was that Eisav had abdicated this challenge, and hence, she set in motion the means through which the only worthy son, Yaakov, would receive the blessings and continue single-handedly the legacy of Avraham and Yitzchak.

YAAKOV AND EISAV

INTRODUCTION: DESTINY FOR SALE

The divergence between Eisav and Yaakov doesn't even wait for "day one" to express itself. Already in the womb, Eisav clamors to get out when Rivkah walks by a place of idol worship. He comes out of the womb blood-red and grows up to pursue a path of violence and vice. His antagonism and enmity toward Yaakov ultimately become formulated in a "halachah" which states: "Eisav hates Yaakov."[1] This is a halachah that Eisav's descendants and spiritual heirs have fulfilled punctiliously throughout the ages, often adding their own embellishments.

It is very easy to survey all this and never ask if things could have been any different for Eisav; in other words, to consider whether or not he was effectively doomed from the start to become the wicked person that he became. It should only take a moment's reflection to recognize that if everyone has free will, then Eisav must have, too. Indeed, were this not the case and he had no choice but to follow a path of wickedness, he could not then be faulted, indicted, or punished for his wicked deeds. Apart from this, we consider the fact that not only was he the son of both Yitzchak and Rivkah, he was at least part of the answer to years of heartfelt prayer on their part. Additionally, numerous lofty

---

1   *Sifri, Behaalosecha* sec. 69, cited in *Rashi* to *Bereishis* 33:4.

individuals were counted among his progeny, including the righteous Antoninus and the Tanna R' Meir.

What all this means is that although Eisav undoubtedly had deeply embedded tendencies toward violence and wrongdoing, he also had the capacity to overcome and control them, channeling them toward productive purposes. As the Sages point out, a later personality in Tanach who received exactly the same appellation as Eisav, "*admoni*" (ruddy), was David HaMelech,[2] but he used those very same qualities to wage war against the enemies of Israel. In other words, while there is no question that Eisav's character was vastly different from that of Yaakov, this only means that his challenges and possibilities were, likewise, very different, but no less noble or praiseworthy.

YITZCHAK'S BLESSINGS

Indeed, it was with this in mind that Yitzchak desired to give the blessings to Eisav. If we look at the contents of the blessings, they appear to be simply an abundance of material prosperity: "*Mital hashamayim u'mishmanei haaretz*—From the dew of the heavens and the fat of the land, etc."[3] How do these things form the contents of the coveted blessing of Yitzchak? What is even more puzzling is that at the end of the parsha, even after Yaakov has received the blessings and Eisav asks his father if there is any blessing left for him, Yitzchak responds by essentially blessing him with exactly the same things—"*Mishmanei haaretz yihiyeh moshavecha u'mital hashamayim me'al*—Of the fat of the land shall be your dwelling and of the dew of the heavens from above!" Were those not the very things with which he had already blessed Yaakov?[4]

The key difference between these two blessings is the way the original blessing begins: "*V'yiten lecha haElokim mital hashamayim*—And **God shall give you** from the dew of the heavens, etc." The blessing lies not in the material assets themselves, but in the way that they come to the person—directly from Hashem. With the recipient of these things

---

2   *Shmuel I* 16:12.
3   *Bereishis* 27:28.
4   Ibid., verse 39.

mindful of Hashem as their Bestower, the sense of connection that ensues will remind and exhort him toward using them in the service of Godly pursuits.[5]

This was Yitzchak's plan to provide Eisav with the basis for channeling his physical tendencies toward moral and spiritual living. Unfortunately, what Eisav had been concealing from Yitzchak over the course of all those years was the fact that he had long since abdicated any notion of doing so, instead embracing a life of temporal and material enjoyment. This was something that Rivkah saw much more clearly than Yitzchak, leading her to conclude that if Eisav received the blessings, he would only squander and abuse them. Therefore, it was Yaakov who should be the one who received them.

More specifically, Rivkah saw not only the lifestyle that Eisav had chosen, but that he had adopted an attitude which effectively guaranteed that he would never develop any of the good that was inside of him…

GROOMED TO PERFECTION

As a prelude to the chapter which deals with the blessings, the Torah relates the following:

וַיְהִי עֵשָׂו בֶּן אַרְבָּעִים שָׁנָה וַיִּקַּח אִשָּׁה אֶת יְהוּדִית בַּת בְּאֵרִי הַחִתִּי וְאֶת בָּשְׂמַת בַּת אֵילֹן הַחִתִּי.

And Eisav was forty years old, he took a wife Yehudis the daughter of Be'eri the Hittite, and Bosmas the daughter of Elon the Hittite.[6]

It is noteworthy that the verse sees fit to inform us of exactly how old Eisav was when he got married. *Rashi* comments:

Eisav was compared to a pig…when the pig crouches down, it stretches out its hooves to say, "See, I am pure!"…For forty years, Eisav had been snatching women from their husbands

---

5   R' Dovid Cohen, *shlita, Mizmor L'Dovid, Parshas Toldos.*
6   *Bereishis* 26:34.

*and violating them. Now, when he became forty, he said, "My
father married at forty, I will do likewise."*

We see that the only area of kosherness in which Eisav invests is
that of *appearing* kosher, something we have witnessed in his ongoing
charade before his father. Not only does this emphasis divert all of
his spiritual energy away from actually being or becoming kosher, it
effectively blocks the path which would allow him to do so. There is
only so long Eisav can grant exclusive focus to convincing people that
he is a moral person before he himself comes to believe it. In this regard,
Eisav is both the perpetrator and the victim of his deceit. Once he fully
believes that he is as kosher as he looks, any introspection with a view
to self-improvement becomes practically impossible—for why spend
time developing a product that is already perfect?

Rivkah notes this fatal flaw because she has seen it before. It was
a trademark of the master of appearances with whom she grew up—her
brother, Lavan. Time and again, we see that Lavan can perpetrate any
crime and then not only defend it, but assume the moral high ground
when doing so. After agreeing to give Rachel to Yaakov for seven years of
work and then substituting Leah at the last moment, when confronted
by Yaakov the next day, Lavan simply answers, "We do not act that way
in this place, to give the younger [sister] before the older one."[7] Just
like that! Lavan is saying to Yaakov, "I know you specified Rachel in
your terms, but that is immoral and insensitive. I was sure you were not
actually asking me to be involved in an immoral enterprise. Were you?
Yaakov, I will say that I am disappointed in you. I hope you won't let me
down again. You may now marry Rachel—for another seven years of
work, naturally. Please try and be a good husband, and I hope we never
have to speak of this business again."

Likewise, when Lavan chases after Yaakov to kill him at the end
of *Parshas Vayeitzei*, which he is ultimately prevented from doing, he
explains the background to his pursuit as the fact that Yaakov ran away

---

7   Ibid., 29:26.

and did not give him a chance to kiss his daughters and grandchildren goodbye![8]

For people like Lavan and his spiritual heir, Eisav, introspection and self-improvement are simply unfathomable. Recognizing this quality in Eisav only too well, Rivkah realizes that for him to receive the blessings will not have a good outcome and will only lead to more wickedness on his part.

WEDDED TO FAILURE

This disposition of Eisav receives tragic expression in another of his weddings, this one at the very end of the parsha. After Yaakov succeeded in receiving the blessings from Yitzchak, the Torah recounts:

וַיַּרְא עֵשָׂו כִּי רָעוֹת בְּנוֹת כְּנָעַן בְּעֵינֵי יִצְחָק אָבִיו. וַיֵּלֶךְ עֵשָׂו אֶל יִשְׁמָעֵאל וַיִּקַּח אֶת מָחֲלַת בַּת יִשְׁמָעֵאל...לוֹ לְאִשָּׁה.

And Eisav saw that the daughters of Canaan were evil in the eyes of Yitzchak, his father. So Eisav went to Yishmael and took Machlas, the daughter of Yishmael...as a wife for himself.[9]

Another wedding! This is a very interesting way to conclude this section of the Torah. After all the events of that day, whose repercussions would echo and reverberate throughout history, the final event we are told about is Eisav marrying again.

Why does Eisav keep getting married?

The *Shem MiShmuel*[10] explains that Yaakov receiving the blessings from Yitzchak was a bitter disappointment for Eisav. In spite of his best efforts over the course of many years to win his father over, Yaakov had still outdone him. What followed was a moment of reflection for Eisav. What was wrong with him that Yaakov kept on getting the better of him? He thought and thought, and finally he found the answer: *nothing* was wrong with him! The answer, therefore, must be that he is being held back by someone else, i.e., that he is married to the wrong woman.

---

8   Ibid., 31:28.
9   Ibid., 28:8–9.
10 *Parshas Toldos* 5672, s.v. *vayar Eisav.*

If only he had the right wife, everything would work out for him. It is a very sad moment indeed, and one which encapsulates the path Eisav had chosen for himself. Upon being presented with a rare opportunity to finally consider what was wrong with his life, he could only use it to focus instead on what was wrong with his wife.

POSSIBILITY OF PARTNERSHIP?

Taking this discussion one stage further, numerous commentators explain that not only did Eisav have the potential to live a good and moral life, he moreover had the capacity, together with Yaakov, to be *part of the legacy of Avraham and Yitzchak.*[11] What this means is that while Yaakov would devote himself to spiritual pursuits, Eisav would oversee the more practical and temporal aspects of maintaining the nation.

Support for this approach would appear to be forthcoming from a comment of the *Midrash Yalkut Shimoni* in *Sefer Yehoshua.*[12] The Midrash states that the term *gedulah* (greatness) is mentioned in conjunction with each of the Avos. When it comes to Yaakov, the Midrash cites the verse *"Vayigdelu hane'arim—*The lads grew up."[13] The Midrash then notes that this verse refers to both Yaakov and Eisav, commenting:

ועשיו היה בכלל, אלא שקלקל במעשיו.

Even Eisav was [originally] included, except he corrupted his ways.

The Midrash is informing us that Eisav was originally part of the greatness associated with Avraham and Yitzchak, but subsequently abdicated and forfeited this role.

In this regard, Yitzchak's blessings were intended not only to help Eisav live a meaningful life, but to allow him to fulfill his role in maintaining the material prosperity and security of the future Jewish People. The full implications of this idea are that when Rivkah sees that Eisav has neither interest in nor prospects for being part of that future, and

---

11   See *Ohr Gedalyahu, Asufos Maarachos, Sifsei Chaim* and *Ben Melech* to our parsha.
12   Sec. 23.
13   *Bereishis* 25:27.

therefore arranges for Yaakov to receive the blessings, Yaakov thereby *assumes both roles*. Indeed, from that day on, he is forced to leave the spiritual environs of the study hall and travel to an alien and hostile location where he must deal with the likes of Lavan.

This will also explain an additional matter. The Sages inform us that Leah was originally intended to marry Eisav, except that she prayed and wept incessantly that this outcome be averted, which it ultimately was.[14] The meaning behind this is, had Eisav assumed his role in the building of the Jewish People, Leah would have been his wife and partner in this venture. In the end, with Eisav rejecting that path and Yaakov assuming both roles, Yaakov then came to marry Leah as well as Rachel.

TRADING ROLES IN EXILE

The full extent of the reversal that took place with Eisav is brought home when contemplating a comment of the Midrash,[15] whereby Yitzchak's words to Eisav when sending him out to hunt for food before receiving the blessings contain an allusion to the four exiles the Jewish People would endure:

- "Your utensils"—this is Bavel.
- "Your sword"—this is Persia.
- "And your bow"—this is Greece.
- "And go out to the field"—this is Edom.

Why are these four exiles being alluded to at this stage? Because the blessings Yitzchak was planning on bestowing upon Eisav were for purposes of assisting him in fulfilling his role within the temporal arena of the Jewish experience, including waging war against the enemies of Israel, as represented by the four exiles. And now let us consider: Eisav was by this stage so estranged from such noble pursuits that not only did he not play his role in warring *against* the four exiles, he actually ended up *spearheading* the fourth and most bitter of them all—the exile of Edom.

---

14   *Bereishis Rabbah* 70:16.
15   Ibid., 65:13.

Although the full extent of blind anti-Semitism remains a source of heartbreaking bafflement that defies comprehension, a significant part of its core is understood as the exception people take to the Godly message that our people bear in the world. Perhaps, the deepest animosity thus emerges from the corner of Eisav, for whom the rejection is not only of the message itself, but also of the role which he himself could have played in promoting it. This places Eisav as our final and most bitter antagonist, whose ultimate downfall will mark the final redemption itself, as we say in our prayers, citing the prophet Ovadiah:[16]

וְעָלוּ מוֹשִׁעִים בְּהַר צִיּוֹן לִשְׁפֹּט אֶת הַר עֵשָׂו וְהָיְתָה לַה' הַמְּלוּכָה.

The saviors will ascend Mount Zion to judge the mountain of Eisav, and the kingdom will be Hashem's.

May it happen speedily in our days!

---

16   1:21.

FROM THE COMMENTATORS

THE SIMPLEST RASHI IN CHUMASH BEREISHIS

וְאֵלֶּה תּוֹלְדֹת יִצְחָק בֶּן אַבְרָהָם.

And these are the offspring of Yitzchak, son of Avraham.[1]

Commenting on the words, "And these are the offspring," *Rashi* writes:

יעקב ועשו האמורים בפרשה.

Yaakov and Eisav, who are spoken of in this section.

This comment of *Rashi*'s seems pretty straightforward; so much so, that it is very easy to gloss over it and move on to the next *Rashi*. However, it isn't too long before the very simplicity of this comment actually becomes extremely puzzling—and somewhat unsettling:

1. The simple meaning of the word *"toldos"* throughout the Torah is that it refers to the person's offspring. Why does *Rashi* feel the need to reassure us that this is what it means here as well? What else might we think it means?

---

1   *Bereishis* 25:19.

2. Why does *Rashi* feel it necessary to add the words "who are spoken of in this section"? What other Yaakov and Eisav might we think the verse is referring to?

In brief: Why does *Rashi* feel the need to make this comment? What issue in the verse is he addressing, and how is he doing so?

It seems quite clear that *Rashi* is addressing a concern very similar to that in the beginning of *Parshas Noach*.[2] There, the opening verse stated, "*Eileh toldos Noach*—These are the offspring of Noach," but then digressed to talk about Noach himself, only enumerating his sons in the following verse. *Rashi* there presents two approaches to resolving this interruption. Here, we seem to have exactly the same situation—if not worse—for although the opening verse seems to introduce Yitzchak's children, they are not mentioned by name until six verses later! To this, *Rashi* responds by reassuring us that although they will only be mentioned in a few verses' time, the reference to "Yitzchak's offspring" in our opening verse is nevertheless directed toward Yaakov and Eisav.

The question that remains, however, is: What is the difference between the two cases? Why did *Rashi* feel the need to explain a minor delay in *Parshas Noach*, but in our parsha, he seems much more easygoing, saying simply, "Be patient, they will be mentioned before too long"?

The answer to this is in *Rashi's* concluding words, "*haamurim baparsha*—who are spoken of in the parsha." And herein lies the difference between the two cases:

- The central figure in *Parshas Noach* is undoubtedly Noach himself, not his children. As such, a verse which introduces his offspring is not an introduction to the parsha, but only to his offspring. Therefore, we will expect them to be mentioned immediately in that verse, and if there is any delay, we will demand an explanation.
- By contrast, Yaakov and Eisav, the "offspring of Yitzchak," are figures no less central in our parsha than Yitzchak himself.

---

2   Ibid., 6:9.

As such, the introductory words, "These are the offspring of Yitzchak," are introducing the parsha generally and therefore, it is entirely acceptable for the verse to digress to give us the background of Yitzchak's marriage to Rivkah, etc.

It is most interesting to note in this regard that although the parshiyos of Noach and Toldos both begin with the words, "V'eileh toldos," nevertheless, the first parsha is called "Noach" while the second is called "Toldos"! This highlights the idea that Parshas Noach is essentially about Noach, while Toldos is equally about Yitzchak's children—his Toldos.

The above brief discussion should hopefully encourage and remind us that the "simple Rashis" require equal—if not more—vigilance and attentiveness to try and fathom what issue Rashi has identified in the verse, and how he is addressing it with his seemingly simple comment.

YITZCHAK AVINU

וְאֵלֶּה תּוֹלְדֹת יִצְחָק בֶּן אַבְרָהָם אַבְרָהָם הוֹלִיד אֶת יִצְחָק.

And these are the offspring of Yitzchak, son of Avraham; Avraham gave birth to Yitzchak.[3]

When reading this verse, we note what appears to be a clear redundancy, for if Yitzchak is the son of Avraham, then surely it is understood that Avraham gave birth to Yitzchak!

Of all the Avos, Yitzchak is surely the most enigmatic. There is very little in the Chumash devoted to him compared to what is recorded about Avraham and Yaakov. The commentators explain that Yitzchak's contribution was that of containing and preserving the way of Avraham. Avraham represents inspiration, love, and kindness, attributes which could easily exceed their appropriate boundaries, or alternatively, simply dissipate over time. Yitzchak introduced the elements of discipline and consistency. This is the significance of the events described further on in our parsha, of Yitzchak re-digging the wells that had originally been dug by Avraham and were then filled in by the Pelishtim, representing

---

3   *Bereishis* 25:19.

all the forces which can bring a venture of Avraham to a halt. Yitzchak's characteristics of commitment and perseverance enabled him to overcome all such setbacks, reclaiming the wells and returning to them the names Avraham had originally given them.[4]

We are told that Avraham and Sarah attracted many converts while still in Charan, and more still when they arrived in the Land of Israel. Curiously, we do not hear much from these converts, nor do we know who their descendants are. They seem to have just faded away. Once Avraham passed away and Yitzchak assumed the helm, these converts observed his reserved and contained manner and concluded that it was antithetical to Avraham's way, leading them to either simply abdicate and return to their former ways, or, alternatively, to try and maintain Avraham's path on their own as they remembered it. Either way, without Yitzchak's contribution, nothing remained of them.[5]

This is the deeper understanding of *Rashi*'s comment to our verse that when Yitzchak was born, the scoffers of the generation said he was fathered by Avimelech, whereupon Hashem changed his facial features to look like those of Avraham, thereby silencing the slander. This means that people looked at Yitzchak and could not see how his path was a continuation of that of Avraham, concluding, therefore, that his message drew from a completely different source. In the fullness of time, however, all came to understand that if one is seeking the face of Avraham, it will only be found with Yitzchak.[6]

This, then, is the message of our opening verse, which emphasizes Yitzchak as Avraham's son. This idea is of crucial value, not only for our understanding this figure in our formative history, but also in our own personal experience. Often, we begin a venture with enthusiasm and zeal, only to find those feelings dissipating within a matter of days, if not sooner, leaving us disoriented and discouraged. The message of Yitzchak is that at this stage, the idealism which gave us that initial inspiration now needs to be translated into commitment and consistency,

---

4   *Shem MiShmuel.*

5   R' Leib Gurwitz, *Me'orei She'arim.*

6   *Pachad Yitzchak, Sukkos, maamar 4.*

which will allow us to attain long-lasting and meaningful results, bringing back the face of Avraham to wells that stay open for good.

THE AVOS AND TARYAG MITZVOS

עֵקֶב אֲשֶׁר שָׁמַע אַבְרָהָם בְּקֹלִי וַיִּשְׁמֹר מִשְׁמַרְתִּי מִצְוֹתַי חֻקּוֹתַי וְתוֹרֹתָי.

Because Avraham heeded My voice, he observed My safeguards, My commandments, My decrees and My laws.[7]

Rashi, based on Chazal,[8] explains the different phrases in this verse as comprising the various components of the Torah's mitzvos, reflecting the idea that Avraham kept the mitzvos of the Torah even prior to them being given at Har Sinai to the Jewish People. This tradition is likewise assumed by the Rishonim to pertain also to Yitzchak and Yaakov, as well as their children. The understanding behind this idea is that even without being formally commanded regarding the mitzvos, the heightened spiritual sensitivity of the Avos enabled them to independently intuit what acts would be spiritually beneficial for them, as well as those which would be spiritually detrimental.[9]

The commentators discuss the fact that understandably, there are many mitzvos whose practical performance would not seem to have been relevant to the Avos. Additionally, they raise the specific question of Yaakov marrying Rachel and Leah, seeing as marrying two sisters is something that the Torah would in time prohibit. Nevertheless, as a matter of general principle—to whatever degree and in whatever way feasible—the Avos kept the mitzvos of the Torah.[10]

A well-known position regarding this tradition is that of the *Ramban*,[11] who states that this applied only when they were in the Land of Israel. They perceived and recognized that life in Hashem's land intrinsically

---

7   *Bereishis* 26:5.
8   See *Yoma* 28b and *Bereishis Rabbah* 64:4.
9   R' Yehoshua Heller, *Beis Tefillah*, chap. 17.
10   For a discussion of these questions, see, e.g., *Daas Zekeinim MiBaalei HaTosafos*, *Bereishis* 37:35, *Maharsha Yoma* loc. cit., *Gur Aryeh*, *Bereishis* 46:10, *Ohr Hachaim* ibid., 49:3 and *Nefesh Hachaim* 1:21.
11   *Bereishis* 26:5.

entails keeping the mitzvos of the Torah—regardless of whether they have been commanded yet or not. Outside of Israel, however, the Avos did not adopt this practice. With this, the *Ramban* offers his answer to the question of how Yaakov could marry two sisters, since he did so while he was living outside of Israel, in the land of Aram.

The *Ramban* proceeds to cite one statement of Chazal that appears to contradict his position: The Midrash states that Yosef kept Shabbos even while he was in Egypt![12] To this, the *Ramban* responds that this practice of Yosef's was an exception, which he deemed necessary in order to instill the fundamentals of faith and monotheism within his children who were surrounded by the pagan society of Egypt. With regards to the other mitzvos, however, there was no notion of electing to keep them outside of the Land of Israel.

However, there is another statement of Chazal that the *Ramban* does not mention, which would appear to pose a much greater challenge to his approach. Commenting on Yaakov's words to Eisav upon his return to the land, "*Im Lavan garti*—I sojourned with Lavan,"[13] the Midrash notes that the letters of the word "גַּרְתִּי" are identical with those of "תרי"ג," the numerical value of the six hundred and thirteen mitzvos of the Torah, indicating that Yaakov kept them all even while with Lavan.[14] Once again, with the above-mentioned proviso that many of the *taryag mitzvos* could not be kept on a practical level, the Midrash nevertheless indicates that at least as a matter of principle, Yaakov was keeping the *taryag mitzvos* in *chutz la'aretz*. This seems to directly contradict the *Ramban*'s position!

Perhaps we may suggest the following. The word "*garti*" itself actually means "I sojourned," indicating a short-term or transient stay. Let us ask: is there any connection between the *pshat* meaning of the word "*garti*" itself and the *gematria* that Chazal attached to it denoting Yaakov's fulfillment of the mitzvos? Perhaps it is revealing

---

12   See *Bereishis Rabbah* 92:4.

13   *Bereishis* 32:5.

14   Cited in *Rashi* ibid., s.v. *garti*. See *Torah Sheleimah* ibid., sec. 31, who cites various sources in the Midrash where this comment appears.

the reason why Yaakov kept the mitzvos while staying with Lavan. In reality, seeing as he was in *chutz la'aretz*, there was no *actual* need to keep the mitzvos. However, *since he regarded his stay with Lavan as temporary*—as indicated by the word *"garti"*—with the notion of his return to Eretz Yisrael firmly entrenched in his vision, he thus saw it as appropriate to continue his fulfillment of the *taryag mitzvos* even while outside the land, in order to maintain his familiarity and fluency with them for when he would ultimately return. It thus emerges that the allusion within the word *"garti"* is in fact a product of its meaning on a *pshat* level![15]

Indeed, looked at this way, not only can the above comment of the Midrash be *reconciled* with the *Ramban's* approach, but it actually emerges as a *support* for it, since it specifically frames Yaakov's observance of *taryag mitzvos* within the context of the temporary nature of his stay in *chutz la'aretz*. Without the *"garti"* element in Charan, there may not have been *"taryag"* there either!

---

15   In this regard, this is a "pre-echo" of the words of the *Sifri* in *Parshas Ekev* (sec. 43, cited in *Rashi, Devarim* 11:18, s.v. *ve'samtem*, and discussed at length by the *Ramban* in *Vayikra* 18:25) which state that the fulfillment of the mitzvos while in exile is in order that they not be new when we return to Eretz Yisrael. Of course, we will understand that once the fulfillment of the *taryag mitzvos* in *chutz la'aretz* is not essential but "provisional," it could be overridden by other concerns, such as those which led Yaakov to marry two sisters, something which would not have occurred in Eretz Yisrael itself, as the *Ramban* states.

PARSHAS VAYEITZEI

CONCEPT:
THE TORAH'S USE OF SPACE
TO COMMUNICATE MESSAGES

PART I: REMOVING SPACES

NO BREAKS IN PARSHAS VAYEITZEI

By definition, the medium through which the Torah communicates is that of words. However, there are times when the Torah imparts an idea without adding any extra words, but simply by the way it arranges them.

The way the Torah breaks up sections is into paragraphs, known as *parshiyos* (not to be confused with the term "parsha" we commonly use to refer to the weekly Torah portion). These *parshiyos* come in two forms:

- The new paragraph begins on a different line than the previous one. This is called a *pesuchah*—an open paragraph.
- The new paragraph begins at the end of the same line in which the previous one ended. This is called a *s'tumah*—a sealed paragraph.

Virtually every Torah portion contains paragraphs of this kind. Our parsha, however, is an exception, for there is not a single break in it from beginning to end! What are we to learn from this?

R' Gedaliah Schorr explains that our parsha, which details Yaakov's forced journey from his home and his sojourn with Lavan, with all the difficulties that that entailed, is the prototype parsha of exile. Exile is a time when Hashem's connection with us is not so open, nor is our understanding of events so clear. As such, this blockage of the manifestation of the Divine Presence among us is communicated by the Torah reading itself having no openings, as it describes Yaakov's travails and ordeals in Lavan's house.[1]

R' Chaim Shmuelevitz expounds on this idea by referring to the Midrash[2] that states that the purpose of the breaks provided by the paragraphs was to allow Moshe—and us—to pause and reflect on what had just been taught.[3] It is symptomatic of the exile that one can never expect to be able to pause halfway to reflect and find enlightenment. For while the exile is still in progress, events often do not make sense. Things we were convinced would take us forward throw us backwards, strategies which were guaranteed to bring us success leave us in failure, and contemplating all this may lead only to bewilderment, confusion, and frustration. It is only when the exile is over that one can finally look back with hindsight on the entire process and attain understanding of how things led to their ultimate outcome. This is the lesson that is communicated by the lack of breaks in our parsha.[4]

THE BEGINNING OF PARSHAS VAYECHI

A similar observation of the above-mentioned phenomenon has already been made by Chazal themselves regarding the beginning of *Parshas Vayechi*.[5] Although there are numerous breaks in the course of the parsha itself, nevertheless, it does not start with a new paragraph,

---

1   *Ohr Gedalyahu, Parshas Vayeitzei.* See also *Baal Haturim, Bereishis* 28:10.

2   *Toras Kohanim, Parshas Vayikra* sec. 1, cited in *Rashi* ibid., 1:1, s.v. *vayedaber.*

3   *Sichos Mussar, maamar* 13.

4   The same idea could be applied to the other parsha in *Chumash Bereishis* that has no breaks—*Mikeitz.* Here too, Yosef is isolated from his family, alone in exile in Egypt. Likewise, the events of the parsha are a source of bafflement for the brothers, who cannot fathom why things are happening the way they are. This situation persists until everything is revealed in *Parshas Vayigash.*

5   *Bereishis Rabbah* 96:1, cited in *Rashi* to *Bereishis* 47:28, s.v. *vayechi.*

but is rather a continuation of the previous paragraph. Commenting on this unusual situation, the Midrash states:

למה פרשה זו סתומה, לפי שכיון שנפטר יעקב אבינו נסתמו עיניהם ולבם של ישראל מצרת השיעבוד שהתחילו לשעבדם.

Why is this section blocked up? For once Yaakov died, the eyes and hearts of Israel were blocked up from the distress of the subjugation that [the Egyptians] began to subjugate them.

Here too, a certain mood or attitude is communicated by the Torah, not by anything it says, but by the way in which it arranges the relevant verses. Through blocking up the opening of the parsha, the Torah reflects the emotional blockage which was brought on by the onset of the oppression. Alternatively, it reflects blocking out on the people's part—their refusal to recognize that things were changing and that the climate for oppression was being set.[6]

PARSHAS BALAK

The final example of a parsha that has no breaks is *Parshas Balak*. There too, the Chafetz Chaim explains that although Bilaam clearly possessed great wisdom and, moreover, was the beneficiary of Divine revelations concerning the Jewish People, he never stopped to reflect on the path that he was taking to consider whether it might need adjusting—or replacing.[7] Rather, having chosen a life of greed and depravity, he continued upon it without allowing anything that he experienced to give him pause for thought. This attitude then becomes reflected in the parsha which is presented in the way that reflects Bilaam's life, with no breaks.

---

6   R' Shimon Schwab, *Maayan Beis Hasho'evah, Parsha Vayechi.*
7   *Sefer Chafetz Chaim Al HaTorah, Parshas Balak (Maasai Lamelech, sec. 2).*

PART II: ADDING SPACES

B'NEI GAD AND B'NEI REUVEN

Having discussed a number of cases where the Torah does not provide a break where we would have expected it, let us now consider the converse situation, where there is a space in a place we would not have expected it.

In chapter 32 of *Chumash Bamidbar*, we are told of the tribes of Reuven and Gad who were blessed with an abundance of livestock, and who, therefore, approached Moshe with the idea of settling on the east side of the Jordan river, where pasture was plentiful. In verses 4 and 5, they enumerate the territories that have already been conquered which are rich in pasture and explain that they have much livestock. Then there is a paragraph break, after which verse 6 presents their request to stay on the east side of the river. This is a most unusual situation. Surely, all these verses are essentially one communication, with the first two serving as the introduction to the request in the third! Why, then, are they placed in different paragraphs?

The *Abarbanel* explains that in reality, the people of Gad and Reuven did not feel entirely comfortable requesting of Moshe that they be allowed to reside on the east side.[8] They were aware that all the tribes should, in principle, be crossing the Jordan to the land of Canaan proper. Therefore, they decided that the best way for things to proceed would be just for them to put their situation before Moshe as if they were not sure what to do about it, and then *let him suggest to them* that perhaps, they may wish to stay on the east side, an offer to which they would then agree. Moshe, for his part, was not prepared to suggest this to them, as he wanted to hear from them exactly what they had in mind and on what terms. This is what is indicated by the paragraph break after the first two verses, for that was all they initially said, hoping that Moshe would respond. What followed, however, was probably the longest

---

8   Commentary to *Bamidbar*, loc. cit.

and most awkward silence in the entire Chumash, as Moshe indicated that any suggestion concerning the matter would have to come from them. For this reason, although verse 2 had already introduced their words with the word "*vayomru*—they said," verse 5 starts with a second "*vayomru*," as they found themselves having to initiate the conversation a second time, as indicated by the Torah through placing this verse in a new paragraph.

MEI MERIVAH

One of the most unusual approaches to the episode with Moshe and the rock, known as *Mei Merivah*, as recorded in *Bamidbar*, chapter 20, is found in the *Sefer HaIkarim* of R' Yosef Albo.[9] He explains that the sin occurred long before Moshe hit the rock, for it lay in the fact that when the people needed water, Moshe had the opportunity to take the initiative and call upon Hashem to bring forth water, thereby strengthening the people's faith in the power of a *tzaddik* who has bound himself completely to Hashem. Instead, however, Moshe and Aharon approached the *Mishkan*, awaiting instructions from Hashem, thereby forfeiting the opportunity to impart the above lesson. At that point, the only way to redeem the situation was to follow Hashem's instructions to the letter—i.e., to speak to the rock—which, for various reasons, they did not do.

Here too, it is very interesting to note that verse 7, which describes Moshe and Aharon approaching the *Mishkan*, ends a paragraph, while Hashem's instructions appear in a new paragraph. Why would the flow of events be broken up in this way? This would appear to lend support to the *Ikarim*'s approach, namely, that essentially, the sin *had already occurred* by that stage, with the ensuing instructions being aimed at undoing it; hence, they appear in a new paragraph!

All this should encourage us to pay close attention not only to what the Torah says, but also to how it says it—even down to the spacing of the verses!

---

9   *Maamar* 4, chap. 22.

CONCEPT:
PSHAT AND DRASH ISSUES

Stones around Yaakov's Head

BACKGROUND: STONES THAT BECAME A STONE

The beginning of our parsha relates how Yaakov, before embarking on his journey toward Charan, arrived at the site of the future Beis Hamikdash. Before going to sleep, he took a number of stones and placed them around his head. *Rashi* explains that he did so as protection from wild animals. *Rashi* then cites a well-known tradition from the Sages that the stones began to quarrel among themselves, each one wanting to be the one upon which the *tzaddik* would rest his head. A miracle then occurred whereby all the stones merged into one stone.

Understandably, there are a number of questions that can be raised on this occurrence from a purely content point of view, among them:

- If Yaakov placed the stones "*around* his head" for protection, what is the meaning of each stone then wanting to be the "one *upon which* he placed his head"?
- How are we meant to understand the idea of inanimate objects such as stones expressing their desire that a *tzaddik* rest his head on them?
- What is the significance of all the stones becoming one?

In the present discussion, however, we would like to focus on the basis in the words of the Torah for these events. The source for this tradition is the Gemara in *Maseches Chullin* that points to a contradiction between two verses:

כתיב "ויקח מאבני המקום" וכתיב "ויקח את האבן"! אמר ר' יצחק מלמד שנתקבצו כל אותן אבנים למקום אחד וכל אחת אומרת עלי יניח צדיק זה ראשו. תנא וכולן נבלעו באחד.

*It [first] states, "He took from **the stones** of the place,"[1] and [subsequently] it states, "He took **the stone**"![2] Said R' Yitzchak, this teaches that all the stones gathered together, to one place, with each one saying, "Let the tzaddik rest his head on me." It was taught in a Beraisa that they all became absorbed as one stone.[3]*

To summarize: The basis of the Gemara's discussion lies in noting a simple contradiction between two verses, with the Sages' tradition of "the quarrel among the stones" coming as the resolution to that contradiction.

TOSAFOS CONFOUND US

Tosafos, in their commentary to the above-mentioned Gemara,[4] make a most interesting—and somewhat alarming—comment. Here are their words:

לפי פשוטו יש לפרש שלקח אבן אחת מאבני המקום.

On a straightforward level, one can explain [the verse as saying] that he took one stone from among the stones of the place.

Tosafos are alerting us to the fact that the first verse does not state that Yaakov took "*avnei hamakom*—stones of the place," but rather, "*me'avnei hamakom*—from the stones of the place"! How many stones of

---

1   Verse 11, implying many stones (*Rashi, Chullin* ibid.).
2   Verse 18.
3   91b.
4   S.v. *kesiv*.

the place did Yaakov take? The verse doesn't say—it could be one, or it could be more. As such, when the second verse states that he took "the stone," now we know that initially, he only took one of the stones that were there. In this sense, the second verse does not *contradict* the first one, it *clarifies* it!

Needless to say, this is a most unusual situation. On the one hand, *Tosafos'* point about the two verses not having to contradict each other is quite clear. On the other hand, what exactly do they mean to say by this, given that the Gemara *does* pose them as a contradiction? *Tosafos* are a commentary on the Gemara. How do their words here add to our understanding of the Gemara when all they seem to be doing is undermining it?

PSHAT AND DRASH QUESTIONS

The answer to the above question lies in *Tosafos'* opening words: *"l'fi peshuto."* To understand the significance of these words, let us consider two concepts which run throughout the entire Torah, known as *pshat* and *drash*. We normally encounter these two terms when considering different ways of interpreting a verse:

- *Pshat*: Explains the verse in terms of what can be derived from the words using the disciplines of language, syntax, and grammar.
- *Drash*: Explains—and expounds—the verse using a broader spectrum of meaning, including allusions to further ideas, as well as further information relating to that situation known to the Sages through tradition.

However, it is important to note that *pshat* and *drash* differ, not only in terms of the *interpretations they provide*, but also in terms of the *issues that they raise* that require interpretation:

- The word *pshat* derives from the word *pashut*, which means simple or straightforward. The goal of *pshat* is to read the verse in a way whereby the straightforward meaning of the words emerges.

- The word *drash* derives from the word *lidrosh*, which means to seek. *Drash* seeks a resolution of aspects of the verse beyond that which the *pshat* requires. It pays attention to details which do not present an impediment to a straightforward understanding, but which, upon closer inspection, require resolution nonetheless.

Or, to put it slightly differently: the difference between *pshat* and *drash* is that *pshat analyzes* the verse, while *drash scrutinizes* it.

An example of these two approaches is in our verse. As *Tosafos* point out, on a *pshat* level, the verse does not necessarily indicate that Yaakov took more than one stone. With this observation, *Tosafos* do not mean to negate the Gemara's contradiction; they purely mean to establish that it is a product not of *pshat*, but of *drash*. What does this mean? Rabbeinu Eliyahu Mizrachi explains that the Gemara is bothered by the Torah mentioning that what Yaakov took was "from the stones of the place." If, indeed, Yaakov only took one of those stones, why is this detail mentioned? Would we have thought that he took it from somewhere else? The verse should have stated simply, "*vayikach even*—he took a stone"! This would be similar to what we find in the verse at the end of *Parshas Beshalach*[5] describing the war with Amalek, which states that when Moshe began to tire from raising his arms, "*vayikchu even*—they took a stone" from nearby for him to sit on. If our verse does add that there were other stones there, it is to indicate that he took a number of them; but, if so, then this leads to a contradiction with the later verse which refers only to one stone. This is a classic *drash* approach to the words of the Torah, and, indeed, it is the approach taken throughout the Talmud, not only in the halachic sections of the Torah, but also in its narrative sections.

And so, *Tosafos'* comment has led us to a deeper appreciation of the Gemara's discussion. However, it now leads us to a new question: How did a discussion of this nature gain entry into *Rashi's* commentary on the Torah?

---

5   *Shemos* 17:12.

THE GOAL OF RASHI'S COMMENTARY ON THE TORAH

The background to this question is best presented by referring to the words of *Rashi* himself describing the purpose of his commentary:[6]

ואני לא באתי אלא לפשוטו של מקרא, ולאגדה המיישבת דברי המקרא.

I have come only to address the pshat of the verse, and to Aggadah which resolves the words of the verse.

In other words, *Rashi's* relationship with *pshat* and *drash* in his commentary depends on whether we are dealing with questions or answers:

- In terms of the *answers* that he gives, *Rashi* is prepared to use both *pshat* (ideally) and *drash* (if need be).
- However, in terms of the *questions* that he addresses, *Rashi* will only deal with issues that arise in *pshat*.

In light of this, we ask: Given that the Gemara's discussion is generated by a *drash* question, not a *pshat* one, why does *Rashi* give it entry in his commentary?

A MEETING OF METHODS

To understand *Rashi's* position, we need to read his words from the beginning. By "the beginning," we refer not to *Rashi's* own opening words, but to the part of the verse which he quotes as the headline for his comment. As we noted, the Gemara perceives a contradiction based on the tension between the plural *"me'avnei"* and the singular *"even."* Let us consider: Which of these two terms does *Rashi* quote as the headline for his comment?

The answer is: Neither of them.

Rashi's headline for his comment is the phrase in our verse, *"vayasem meraashosav*—and he placed [them]about his head." In so doing, *Rashi* indicates that the notion that Yaakov initially took numerous stones emerges from reading this phrase *on a pshat level*! How so?

---

6   *Bereishis* 3:8, s.v. *vayishmeu.*

First, the word *"meraashosav"* is written in the plural. Certain commentators of *Rashi*[7] put the question somewhat bluntly: How many heads does Yaakov have? Given that he has only one, why is the plural used? It is clearly to indicate that he placed whatever he took at *different sides* of his head. If this is so, then it means he took more than one stone.

Even if we take a milder approach and say that the plural form doesn't necessarily denote different sides of his head, but simply means "by his head,"[8] this alone will lead us to the conclusion that he took numerous stones. Presumably, whatever he put by his head was for protection, which would not be afforded to him by one stone, but rather, by numerous stones surrounding his head.[9]

This is a rare situation, indeed! While we generally do not expect that an issue raised by *drash* will be the same as one raised by *pshat*, in our case it is; with the difference being that, whereas for the Gemara a *drash* flag was raised as soon as we encounter the phrase *"me'avnei hamakom,"* Rashi notes that a *pshat* flag will in any case be raised very soon after when we meet the phrase *"vayasem meraashosav."* And so, our verse emerges as a setting for unity, not only for the merging of different stones into one stone, but also for the merging of the two worlds of *pshat* and *drash* into one discussion.

---

7   See *Levush Ha'orah* and *To'afos Re'em.*
8   See *Shmuel I*, 26:7.
9   *Nachalas Yaakov* on *Rashi.*

FROM THE COMMENTATORS

BEIS EL: DEFINING IMMORTALITY

וַיִּקְרָא אֶת שֵׁם הַמָּקוֹם הַהוּא בֵּית אֵל וְאוּלָם לוּז שֵׁם הָעִיר לָרִאשֹׁנָה.

He named that place "Beis El;" however, Luz [was] the name of the city originally.[1]

Several times throughout the Chumash we find places that are re-named to mark significant events. In this instance, though, the Torah makes a point of also mentioning what the place was called before it was renamed. But why is that relevant, given that its original name has now been replaced?

The Midrash informs us that the city of Luz had a most unusual property: its inhabitants were beyond the reach of the angel of death.[2] Those who stayed in the city lived forever. It was at this place that Yaakov arrived and had his famous dream with the ladder whose legs were embedded in the earth and whose top reached Heavenward. That dream gave him not only an assurance of Divine guidance and protection, but also a vision of the type of life that can be led by man—"embedded in the earth" while at the same time, "its top reaching Heavenward." As

---

1   *Bereishis* 28:19.
2   *Bereishis Rabbah* 59:8.

such, upon awakening from his dream, Yaakov bestowed a new name upon that place, "Beis El," introducing, thereby, a new definition of immortality to the world. Yaakov was teaching us that immortality is not defined by the quantity of one's years, but by the quality of one's days—whatever their span—living them in the way through which one reaches out from within the temporal and touches the Infinite and Eternal.[3]

WATCHWORD FOR REDEMPTION

וְשַׁבְתִּי בְשָׁלוֹם אֶל בֵּית אָבִי וְהָיָה ה' לִי לֵאלֹקִים.

And I will return in peace to my father's house and Hashem will be for me as a God.[4]

נְטַל הַקָּדוֹשׁ בָּרוּךְ הוּא שִׂיחָתָן שֶׁל אָבוֹת וְעָשָׂאָן מַפְתֵּחַ לִגְאוּלָתָן שֶׁל בָּנִים. אָמַר לוֹ הַקָּדוֹשׁ בָּרוּךְ הוּא, אַתָּה אָמַרְתָּ "וְהָיָה ה' לִי לֵאלֹקִים," חַיֶּיךָ כָּל טוֹבוֹת וּבְרָכוֹת וְנֶחָמוֹת שֶׁאֲנִי נוֹתֵן לְבָנֶיךָ אֵינִי נוֹתֵן אֶלָּא בַּלָּשׁוֹן הַזֶּה, שֶׁנֶּאֱמַר "וְהָיָה בַּיּוֹם הַהוּא יֵצְאוּ מַיִם חַיִּים מִירוּשָׁלַם," "וְהָיָה בַּיּוֹם הַהוּא יוֹסִיף ה' שֵׁנִית יָדוֹ לִקְנוֹת אֶת שְׁאָר עַמּוֹ," "וְהָיָה בַּיּוֹם הַהוּא יִתָּקַע בְּשׁוֹפָר גָּדוֹל."

The Holy One, Blessed is He, took the conversation of the fathers and made it the key for the redemption of the sons. Said the Holy One, Blessed is He, to [Yaakov], "You said 'Hashem will be [v'hayah] for me as a God,' by your life, all the goodness, blessings, and consolations that I give to your descendants, I will only give with this expression [v'hayah], 'It shall be on that day, living waters shall flow out of Yerushalayim,'[5] 'It shall be on that day, Hashem will once again show His hand to acquire the remnant of his people,'[6] 'It shall be on that day, a great shofar will be blown.'"[7]

---

3   Heard from my father, Rabbi Isaac Bernstein, *zt"l.*
4   *Bereishis* 28:21.
5   *Zechariah* 14:8.
6   *Yeshayahu* 11:11.
7   Ibid., 27:13; *Bereishis Rabbah* 70:6.

This comment of the Midrash is quite perplexing, for it seems to highlight the word *"v'hayah"* as a motif word for redemption. Yet the word *"v'hayah"* does not seem to be that distinctive at all; all it means is "it will be." How then, does it come to be the term that will herald all the goodness that the future will bring?

Rav Shlomo Yosef Zevin explains that every nation has a past, and none more than the Jewish People. However, we cannot live in the past, for then we are doomed to remain there. In order to progress, the Jewish People needs to lift its eyes toward the future. However, should we make the mistake of heading toward the future while forgetting our past, cutting ties with our history and unique relationship with Hashem embedded therein, we will never achieve our national destiny, in which case what future is there to speak of? The formula to success is to take our past and turn it into the basis for our future.[8]

This concept is contained within the word "והיה," which consists of the word "היה" in the past tense that is turned into the future tense via the letter *vav*, which in Hebrew means a hook. This is why this word is chosen to herald the future redemption: for it contains the secret as to how to bring it about.

YAAKOV'S CONVERSATION WITH THE SHEPHERDS

When Yaakov arrives at Charan, he encounters some shepherds at the well on the city's outskirts. The Torah records the following conversation between them:

וַיֹּאמֶר לָהֶם יַעֲקֹב אַחַי מֵאַיִן אַתֶּם וַיֹּאמְרוּ מֵחָרָן אֲנָחְנוּ. וַיֹּאמֶר לָהֶם הַיְדַעְתֶּם אֶת לָבָן בֶּן נָחוֹר וַיֹּאמְרוּ יָדָעְנוּ. וַיֹּאמֶר לָהֶם הֲשָׁלוֹם לוֹ וַיֹּאמְרוּ שָׁלוֹם וְהִנֵּה רָחֵל בִּתּוֹ בָּאָה עִם הַצֹּאן.

Yaakov said to them, "My brothers, where are you from?" And they said, "We are from Charan."
He said to them, "Do you know Lavan, the son of Nachor?" And they said, "We know [him]."

---

8   *LaTorah V'lamoadim, Parshas Vayeitzei.*

He said to them, "Is it well with him?" And they said, "It is well, and behold, his daughter Rachel is coming with the flock."[9]

Yaakov's final question here, "Is it well with him?" is most intriguing. Having been instructed by his parents to make his way to Lavan, that is what he should have been doing, so that his third question really should have been, "Can you please tell me how to get to his house?" What does he mean by asking the shepherds about how Lavan is doing? Let him get to Lavan's house and then he can see for himself!

It is possible to approach this whole conversation with an entirely new perspective; namely, Yaakov is trying to use it as an opportunity to find out about Lavan. Yaakov will likely be at Lavan's house for a significant duration, so the more he knows from the outset about the type of person Lavan is, the better equipped he will be in terms of knowing how to deal with him. Rivkah's memories of Lavan from their shared childhood were of a somewhat crafty and devious personality. However, many decades have passed since then. Perhaps, in the interim he has become more honest and honorable—or perhaps he is now craftier than ever!

How can Yaakov attain clarity on this issue? Needless to say, he cannot just approach the shepherds and ask them if Lavan is morally deficient. However, he might be able to get some sort of picture by asking them an innocent, but leading, question, such as, "Is all well with him?" Their response to this question could well reveal something about Lavan's character, whether they say as much in words ("Yes, he is much loved in this town for his upright ways," or "Why shouldn't all be well with a trickster like him?") or alternatively, perhaps through intonation and intimation.[10] This, then, is what lies behind Yaakov's question of, "Is it well with him?"

Developing this idea further, this might help explain Yaakov's follow-up comment, which is even harder to understand. Verse 7 reads:

וַיֹּאמֶר הֵן עוֹד הַיּוֹם גָּדוֹל לֹא עֵת הֵאָסֵף הַמִּקְנֶה הַשְׁקוּ הַצֹּאן וּלְכוּ רְעוּ.

---

9   *Bereishis* 29:4–6.
10   Based on *Kli Yakar*.

He said, "Behold, the day is still long, it is not yet time to gather
in the flock; water the flock and continue grazing!"

If Yaakov asking how Lavan was doing was somewhat mystifying, him telling a group of total strangers how to do their job is completely baffling! Perhaps, however, this was still part of Yaakov trying to find out about Lavan. The shepherds had answered his question about Lavan by briefly stating, "It is well with him." This alone does not reveal much about Lavan. However, if indeed everyone gets on well with him, then finding out more about *their* moral character will yet reveal something about Lavan, since they are unlikely to be on good terms with someone whose moral standing they clash with. The question is: How is it possible to find out what type of people they are? The answer is to rebuke them, for the way a person reacts to rebuke reveals a lot about that person. If their reaction betrays low moral standing, then Yaakov can yet learn about the type of people with whom Lavan gets on well, which will reflect on Lavan himself. Hence, Yaakov rebukes and upbraids them about not watering the flock.

In fact, their response to this also did not reveal much, as, amazingly, they were quite amenable to his words of rebuke, explaining simply that they could not water the flock until all the shepherds had arrived. Having showed themselves to be morally upright people, this too failed to confirm for Yaakov anything about Lavan's devious character. Thus, even after the exchange with the shepherds, the matter remained inconclusive. By this stage, and with Rachel having arrived at the well, Yaakov sees that he is significantly more likely to find out about his uncle from her, which he then proceeds to do.

LAVAN'S BROTHER AND RIVKAH'S SON

וַיַּגֵּד יַעֲקֹב לְרָחֵל כִּי אֲחִי אָבִיהָ הוּא וְכִי בֶן רִבְקָה הוּא.

Yaakov told Rachel that he was her father's brother and that he was Rivkah's son.[11]

---

11   *Bereishis* 29:12.

There appears to be an obvious redundancy in this verse, for surely being Lavan's relative and Rivkah's son are not two different things; was Yaakov not Lavan's relative purely *because he was* Rivkah's son? For this reason, the Midrash explains that these two phrases reflect two specific characteristics: If Lavan wants to be tricky, then I am "his brother" in trickery, while, if he wants to be upright and honest, then I am also "Rivkah's son" and am certainly capable of acting in that way.[12]

The *Ohr Hachaim Hakadosh* explains that Yaakov did not mean to mention these as two alternative paths of behavior, either of which he could adopt. After all, is it even at all desirable that Yaakov should assume the devious behavior of Lavan in order to counter him? Rather, Yaakov was saying the following: "Tell your father that as resourceful as he is in deviousness, I am likewise resourceful in protecting myself. However, do not think that I mean that he can expect me to act toward him in the same underhanded manner that he might act toward me, for that is something I cannot allow myself to do. For at the same time that I am "his brother" in trickery, I am also "Rivkah's son," and that is a status that I am not prepared to compromise by stooping to his level or employing his methods.

Indeed, it may be said that the challenge of the Jewish People throughout the ages has been to be the "brothers of Lavan," anticipating and protecting themselves against his schemes and devices, while at the same time maintaining their moral status as "sons of Rivkah," eschewing any methods that would taint or compromise that exalted calling.

---

12 *Bereishis Rabbah* 70:13, cited in *Rashi* loc. cit.

PARSHAS VAYISHLACH

YAAKOV'S MESSAGE TO EISAV

וַיִּשְׁלַח יַעֲקֹב מַלְאָכִים לְפָנָיו אֶל עֵשָׂו אָחִיו.

Yaakov sent malachim ahead of him to Eisav his brother.[1]

INTRODUCTION: THE MEANING OF THE WORD "MALACH"

The beginning of our parsha relates how Yaakov, after being away for twenty years, sends a message of peace and reconciliation to Eisav. The means which he employs to deliver this message is that of "*malachim.*" We commonly translate the word *malach* as "angel," and, indeed, *Rashi* states that Yaakov sent angels to Eisav. However, the word *malach* can also simply mean messenger, referring to a person.[2] Indeed, this is how *Onkelos* in our verse translates the word "*malachim.*" Of course, this then raises the question as to why *Rashi* chose not to translate the word in this seemingly more straightforward way.[3] Interestingly, both

---

1   *Bereishis* 32:4.

2   The term מלאך derives from the word מלאכה, and thus refers to any being that is dedicated to performing a specific task (*Hakesav V'hakabbalah*).

3   A beautiful explanation of this matter is provided in the commentary *Biurei Maharai* by R' Yisrael Isserlin (author of Responsa *Terumas Hadeshen*). At the very end of the previous parsha, Yaakov is met by angels, who *Rashi* explains are the angels of Eretz Yisrael. These angels, together with the angels of *chutz la'aretz*, make up two camps, as indeed Yaakov proceeds to name the place—"*Machanayim.*" On the face of it, this would seem to mirror Yaakov's dream at the beginning of that parsha, in which he saw angels of Eretz Yisrael going

of the above explanations are presented in the *Midrash Rabbah* to our verse.[4]

UNDERSTANDING YAAKOV'S INTENTIONS

Yaakov begins his message to Eisav by saying, "*Im Lavan garti*—I have sojourned with Lavan." *Rashi* explains these words as follows:

לא נעשיתי שר וחשוב אלא גר. אינך כדאי לשנוא אותי על ברכת אביך שבירכני "הוי גביר לאחיך" שהרי לא נתקיימה בי.

I did not become a dignitary or a notable, but [only] a sojourner. There is [thus] no need for you to hate me over the blessing of your father who blessed me, "You shall be a master to your brothers" for it has not been fulfilled in me.[5]

The basis of *Rashi's* comment is the fact that the word "*garti*" denotes a short-term stay, whereas Yaakov was at Lavan's home for twenty years, so that the appropriate term should have been "*yashavti*," denoting a stay of lengthy duration. Therefore, *Rashi* explains that Yaakov was referring not to the duration of his stay, but to his lack of prominence there, as he was always regarded as an outsider of no significant standing.

---

up a ladder and those of *chutz la'aretz* coming down. The difference, however, is that in the earlier case, the two groups of angels simply changed places without coinciding, while, in this later case, they *overlapped*. Why would Yaakov need both sets at the same time? From here *Rashi* learned that although Yaakov was already being escorted by the angels of Eretz Yisrael, he still had need of those of *chutz la'aretz*, namely, in order to send them with a message to Eisav, who was outside Israel in the land of Edom.

4 *Bereishis Rabbah* 75:4.

5 The commentators note that Yaakov was not belittling the efficacy of Yitzchak's blessings in and of themselves; rather, he was noting that they had not been fulfilled through him due to his own unworthiness. Alternatively, he was indicating that the blessing had actually been fulfilled through Eisav, who had indeed risen to prominence during those years. Yaakov was saying that since Yitzchak thought it was Eisav who was before him and intended the blessings to go to him, he actually ended up being the recipient of the blessings after all, with Yaakov's attempts to receive them being of no avail (*Malbim*).

Rashi then proceeds to offer a second explanation:

דבר אחר, "גרתי" בגימטריא תרי"ג, כלומר עם לבן הרשע גרתי ותרי"ג מצוות
שמרתי ולא למדתי ממעשיו הרעים.

*Alternatively, the numerical value of "גרתי" is six hundred and
thirteen, as if to say, "I lived with the wicked Lavan, yet I kept
the six hundred and thirteen (תרי"ג) mitzvos, and I did not
learn from his evil deeds."*

One cannot help but note the difference in tone between these two
interpretations. They seem to be sending almost opposite messages.
The first approach sees Yaakov's words as conciliatory in nature, as if to
say, "Please make friends with me," while the second approach is much
more confrontational, saying, "Don't start up with me!"

One may respond to the above by saying that Yaakov was actually
sending a blended or layered message to Eisav, as if to say, "What
I would like is to make peace, but if you choose a path of war, then be
aware that I have the merit of the six hundred and thirteen mitzvos on
my side." Indeed, in this regard, by alerting Eisav to the fact that he was
fully prepared for war, Yaakov was, thereby, further encouraging him to
consider taking the more peaceful path.

WAR, PEACE, AND GEMATRIAS

In truth, however, we need to ask a more basic question:

What is the likelihood that Eisav got the *gematria*?

Of course, it is not inconceivable that Eisav would catch that part
of Yaakov's message. However, it is somewhat perplexing that Yaakov
would rely on Eisav's *gematria* powers at a time like this. Eisav, as we
know, was prone to allowing anger and emotion to cloud his judgment,
surely no more so than upon discovering that Yaakov was alive and well
and coming to meet him. This was no time for *gematrias*!

The matter becomes more baffling still when we consider Yaakov's
words in the next verse, "*Vayehi li shor vachamor*—I have acquired
ox[en] and donkey[s]." Here too, *Rashi* explains on a straightforward
level that Yaakov was demonstrating that he had only achieved success
in the area of livestock, as opposed to that of agriculture, which had

been the subject of Yitzchak's blessing—the "dew of the heavens and the fat of the land." This, then, was further reason for Eisav not to bear resentment over the episode with the blessings. The Midrash,[6] however, explains that the "ox" and the "donkey" refer to the personalities of Yosef and Yissachar, citing verses from later on in Chumash which characterize them as such.[7] Through this, too, Yaakov was informing Eisav of the people of caliber whom he had with him. But again we ask, even if Eisav was somehow able to decipher the earlier *gematria* message, when it comes to this Midrash, he never had a chance! He is not even aware of Yaakov's children by their own names, let alone by the beasts to which they may be likened—one in a verse at the end of *Bereishis* which had not yet been said, and the other in the end of *Devarim* by someone who had not yet even been born!

All of this requires our attention.

TWO PLANES OF CONFRONTATION

The key to this matter lies in the fact that Yaakov's confrontation with Eisav, as described in the parsha, took place on two levels. There was the physical meeting with Eisav himself, but the night beforehand, there was also a struggle with Eisav's ministering angel, which was spiritual in nature. The difference between these two struggles lies not only in their form, but also in Yaakov's approach toward them. It is often true in exile that one must act in a conciliatory way toward Eisav, with the goal of appeasing and mollifying him. However, in terms of the spiritual forces that Eisav represents, the approach is very different. We do not have as a value the idea of appeasing evil; rather, we seek to confront it, struggle with it, and conquer it. Indeed, we see that when Yaakov encountered Eisav's angel, he did not bow down to him, as he later did to Eisav, but rather wrestled with him throughout the night.

Once we remind ourselves that Yaakov was preparing for two confrontations, we can appreciate that his opening message was directed toward *both aspects* of his adversary. This means that his words were

---

6   *Tanchuma Vayishlach*, sec. 1.
7   See *Bereishis* 49:14 and *Devarim* 33:17.

invested with two levels of meaning. There was the plain meaning of the words, but they also functioned as "capsules" conveying deeper and more hidden messages, each one intended for its relevant recipient.

- With regards to Eisav himself, Yaakov's message was the plain meaning of his words, which were purely conciliatory in nature. Any deeper or hidden messages—such as *gematrias* and midrashic allusions—were not meant for him; in this instance, they literally flew over his head.
- With regards to Eisav's angel, Yaakov sent the message that he was ready to do battle, fortified by his performance of the mitzvos while in Lavan's house, as well as the prominent spiritual personalities he had accompanying him. For a spiritual entity such as an angel, these messages were able to be communicated through the medium of allusion, such as *gematria* and references to concepts that have yet to formally appear in verses in the Chumash.

Indeed, with this in mind, we can go back to the word that the Torah uses for Yaakov's messengers—"*malachim*"—which we noted was the subject of two opinions as to its meaning here: angels or human emissaries. We can now understand that it is possible that the Torah uses this word because both types were used, each one for its intended recipients:

- For the aspect of the message intended to reach Eisav himself, Yaakov was able to send human emissaries.
- For the aspect intended for Eisav's angel, Yaakov used emissaries who were angels themselves—*malachim mamash!*

DIVIDING THE CAMP

A New Perspective

In the beginning of our parsha, Yaakov sends a message of peace to Eisav. The messengers return to Yaakov, telling him that Eisav is coming toward him with four hundred men. Verses 8 and 9 record Yaakov's response to this news:

וַיִּירָא יַעֲקֹב מְאֹד וַיֵּצֶר לוֹ וַיַּחַץ אֶת הָעָם אֲשֶׁר אִתּוֹ...לִשְׁנֵי מַחֲנוֹת. וַיֹּאמֶר אִם יָבוֹא עֵשָׂו אֶל הַמַּחֲנֶה הָאַחַת וְהִכָּהוּ וְהָיָה הַמַּחֲנֶה הַנִּשְׁאָר לִפְלֵיטָה.

Yaakov was very afraid and it distressed him; he divided the people with him...into two camps. He said, "If Eisav will come to the one camp and will strike it, then the remaining camp will escape."

THREE QUESTIONS

Of the many questions which are raised on these verses, we will mention three at this opening stage:

- Numerous commentators note the seeming double expression concerning Yaakov's reaction: "(1) [He] was very afraid (2) and it distressed him." To what does this "distress" refer beyond what was the cause of his fear—Eisav's imminent attack?

- *Rashi* addresses another unusual feature in these verses: The word *"machaneh*—camp" is initially referred to in the feminine form—*"haachas,"* yet subsequently referred to in the masculine—*"v'hikahu...hanish'ar."* He responds by demonstrating that the word *machaneh* is one which is treated both as masculine and feminine, citing other examples of such words (e.g., *"shemesh"* and *"ruach"*). However, a question nonetheless persists: even if this word can be referred to in *either* form, our verse combines *both*—switching from one to the other! What are we to make of this?

- What was Yaakov's thinking in dividing the camps? If Eisav struck one, why would he not then strike the other? Wouldn't they stand more of a chance against him if they were united? Alternatively, why do they both not try and escape already?

UNDERSTANDING EISAV'S MESSAGE

One of the great commentators among the early Acharonim, the *Maaseh Hashem*,[1] explains this episode in the following way. First, to understand Yaakov's reaction to Eisav's message, we need to take another look at the message itself: namely, that he is coming toward Yaakov with four hundred men. The common understanding is that this was a declaration of war. However, certain Rishonim explain that it was in fact a message of peace.[2] The messengers open by saying, "We came to your brother, Eisav." They emphasize Eisav's identity as Yaakov's brother because he received them in a brotherly manner.[3] Accordingly, the four hundred men with whom he is coming are an honor escort for Yaakov![4]

---

1   Rabbi Eliezer Ashkenazi (1513–1585).
2   See, e.g., commentary of *Rashbam* to this verse.
3   This is in contrast to *Rashi's* explanation of those words; see s.v. *el achicha*.
4   This might explain the phrase "V'gam holeich likrasecha—And also he is coming to meet you." What is the meaning of the word "v'gam—and also"? This is the first and only piece of news they are bringing back! However, according to the *Rashbam*, the meaning is that in the same way that you seek peace with him, he also wishes to reconcile with you.

This changes everything, for it emerges that Eisav has stated only peaceful intentions toward Yaakov. This is wonderful news, which then leads us to the question: If so, why was Yaakov so afraid upon hearing this message?

The answer is: because it was a message from Eisav! Yaakov doesn't know if he can believe Eisav's brotherly words. While it is possible that the message is genuine, it is also quite possible that Eisav is fully intending to attack Yaakov, and has sent him this message of peace as a ruse. This is the source of Yaakov's fear. Moreover, not only is this prospect a cause for great fear, it is also a cause for distress.

In a sense, it would have been easier for Yaakov if the messengers had returned with an open declaration of war. Knowing what to expect, he could prepare himself accordingly. However, now that they have brought back a message of peace, the whole situation is much more complicated. On the one hand, it may be a lie, in which case Yaakov would need to arm his camp. On the other hand, there is always the chance that it is actually true, and that Eisav is coming to make peace. If this is the case, then, if Yaakov were to receive Eisav in a camp ready for war, this would itself precipitate a conflict which otherwise would not have occurred! This is Yaakov's dilemma, and this is why his reaction is twofold:

- On the one hand, "he was afraid" over the prospect that Eisav may actually be coming to attack him.
- On the other hand, "he was distressed" on account of the fact that he could not make adequate preparations to defend himself against such an attack, just in case Eisav really did want peace.

Given this complex situation, was there any way for Yaakov to effectively prepare for both eventualities?

The answer is, yes—to split the camps.

THE ROLE OF THE SECOND CAMP

Yaakov's reasoning in splitting the camp in two, as stated in the verse, was that if Eisav should come and strike the first camp—"v'hayah hamachaneh hanish'ar lif'leitah." What is the meaning of this concluding phrase? The word "p'leitah" can mean escape or rescue.

We normally assume that Yaakov meant that if the first camp is attacked, then the second camp could escape and could itself be "lif'leitah—spared." However, the Maaseh Hashem explains that Yaakov meant that if the first camp is attacked, the second camp will come to its rescue and be "lif'leitah" for the first camp!

The reason for the splitting of the camp in this way is based on the above. Yaakov cannot meet Eisav with a fully armed camp, just in case Eisav really wants to reconcile. Rather, he will need to receive Eisav with a camp of peace. However, if Eisav should enter that camp and then attack it,[5] there will be another camp nearby, fully prepared for war, that will be able to come to their defense and rescue.

MASCULINE AND FEMININE CAMPS

With the above in mind, we return to the question of the way Yaakov refers to the two camps. We noted that the verse begins by using the feminine form ("haachas") and then shifts midway to use the masculine form "(v'hikahu...hanish'ar")—a most unusual situation! Let us suggest that this shift reflects the differing nature of the two camps as we have come to understand them. The idea of war is primarily associated with men, while peace is more associated with women.[6] As such, the first camp, which is the camp of peace that will receive Eisav, is referred to with the feminine form—"haachas." However, in the event that Eisav will enter that camp and then turn it into a battle-ground—reflected by the shift to the masculine form—"v'hikahu," then there will be another camp of war nearby—"hanish'ar," likewise referred to in the masculine, to come to do battle with him.

---

5   The Maaseh Hashem adds that this is the meaning behind Yaakov's describing this scenario in two stages: "If Eisav should (1) come to the first camp and (2) strike it." Why does he not simply say, "If Eisav should strike the first camp"? Rather, the worry is that Eisav will first "come to the camp," i.e., he will be admitted entry in keeping with his declaration of peace, and then "strike it" once he is already inside.

6   See Kiddushin 2b, where it explains that although the word "derech—way" can also take either the masculine or feminine from, nevertheless, when it is used within the context of war, the masculine form is used, since: "Derech ha'ish laasos milchamah v'ein derech ha'ishah laasos milchamah—It is the way of men to wage war and not the way of women."

YAAKOV'S GIFT OF DISCOVERY

This approach may give us further insight into another of Yaakov's preparations before meeting Eisav. Let us ask: Given Yaakov's uncertainty regarding Eisav's intentions, is there any way that he might be able to gauge them ahead of the actual meeting? This brings us to the animals which Yaakov sends to Eisav as gifts. The common understanding is that the role of these gifts was to appease Eisav. However, it is possible that there was an accompanying goal: to discover Eisav's real intentions.

As the verses describe, Yaakov sent the gifts in numerous installments, with large breaks between each group of animals. Additionally, he instructed those leading each group to say that "this is from Yaakov and he is coming soon." What is behind this mode of presentation? Yaakov feels that by sending the gifts in this protracted way, as well as by placing Eisav in a state of suspense by repeatedly telling him that Yaakov will be here soon, he will be able to see if Eisav's declarations of peace are genuine or a ploy.

If Eisav's feelings toward Yaakov are ones of friendship and reconciliation, then the longer he has to wait until finally seeing Yaakov, the more excited he will be. However, if his display of friendship is a façade, he will become increasingly frustrated at Yaakov not turning up already, and by the fifth or sixth message that "Yaakov is coming soon," his friendly face will wear away and his true colors will be revealed.

In other words, Yaakov's goal in sending gifts to Eisav was not only to *appease* him, but also to *assess* him.

This idea might also give us new insight into Yaakov's explanation for sending these gifts, as expressed in verse 21: "כִּי אָמַר אֲכַפְּרָה פָנָיו בַּמִּנְחָה הַהֹלֶכֶת לְפָנָי וְאַחֲרֵי כֵן אֶרְאֶה פָנָיו אוּלַי יִשָּׂא פָנָי—For he said, 'I will appease him with the gift that goes before me and after that I will meet him; perhaps he will forgive me.'" What is the meaning of the first phrase: "*achaprah panav*"? The word "*kapparah*" is normally translated as "atonement." Here, though, *Rashi* explains that this phrase means "to nullify Eisav's face of anger," i.e., to appease him.

How does "atonement" come to mean "nullification"? *Rashi* explains that essentially, the word "*l'chaper*" means to wipe away and remove.

Hence, if it wipes away sin, then it brings atonement, and if it wipes away anger, then it brings appeasement. Based on this idea, let us suggest that with this gift, Yaakov was seeking to "wipe away" at *Eisav's face itself*, i.e., the face of friendship he was presenting, seeking to discover whether or not it was his real face, "and, after that, I will see his [true] face; perhaps, he will [indeed] forgive me."

In fact, as the Torah relates, Eisav did show compassion toward Yaakov on this occasion, in keeping with the message he sent back. Nevertheless, as the ensuing verses indicate, Yaakov did not see this as the beginning of any ongoing positive relationship with his brother, and proceeded to part ways peacefully with Eisav as soon as he could. And, indeed, history has shown not only that such compassionate moments on Eisav's part are few and far between, but also that his brotherly embrace brings with it its own challenges that are equally threatening, if not more so, for Jewish destiny and continuity.

YAAKOV'S STRUGGLE
WITH THE ANGEL

וַיִּוָּתֵר יַעֲקֹב לְבַדּוֹ וַיֵּאָבֵק אִישׁ עִמּוֹ עַד עֲלוֹת הַשָּׁחַר.

And Yaakov was left alone and a man wrestled with him until the break of dawn.[1]

INTRODUCTION: A DUEL WITH NO DETAILS

The Torah's account of Yaakov's struggle with the angel is extremely cryptic. Not only are we not informed who this "man" is, we are also not told what the struggle was about. All the verse tells us as a prelude to this episode is that "Yaakov was left alone," and then, abruptly, someone is wrestling with him.

The word the Torah uses to describe the struggle—"וַיֵּאָבֵק"—also requires our attention; how does this word come to denote a struggle? *Rashi* explains that it is derived from the word "אבק," dust, for it is the way of people who wrestle to kick up dust. Understandably, this explanation itself needs to be explained. Why refer to the struggle in terms of what is essentially a secondary effect, and, even then, is only relevant when the struggle is taking place where there is dust? The Gemara takes this matter even further, stating:[2]

שהעלו אבק עד לכסא הכבוד.

They raised dust until the Heavenly Throne of Glory.

---

1 *Bereishis* 32:25.
2 *Chullin* 91a.

These words, too, require our contemplation. Dust cannot naturally rise up that high; what is the meaning of it doing so here, especially considering that Hashem's Throne of Glory is not a physical entity to which dust could rise in any event?

FORGOTTEN VESSELS

The Sages inform us that the reason Yaakov was left alone is that he went back for some small jars that he had forgotten. The next thing we know, someone is wrestling with him. R' Yosef Salant explains that the reason we are provided with this background to the fight is because the fight was actually about those jars![3] The reason Yaakov went back for some small vessels of seemingly insignificant value is because his sense of Divine providence was so strong and all-pervasive that it was clear to him that if he owned them, they must have some purpose in his pursuit of higher spiritual living.

Eisav's angel, representing his ideology, rejects the notion of Divine supervision over man's affairs, a stance that allows him to act as he pleases without any sense of accountability. Whenever a force of evil wishes to attack a righteous person, it will do so at the farthest extreme of that person's spiritual level. For a person who prays three times a day without fail, the *yetzer hara* will not attempt to lower him to two times; he will, instead encourage him to pray a bit quicker or in a more distracted way. Here too, when the angel wishes to wrestle with Yaakov over his sense of connectedness to the Divine, he begins with the most trivial of items, as if to say, "Even if you subscribe to a connection with Hashem in a *general way*, does that really have to extend to these small jars?" As we can appreciate, a conversation that begins about small jars can graduate to a discussion about larger jars and from there to matters of greater and greater significance. In a sense, therefore, we could say that Yaakov's struggle throughout that night was to remain firm on the extent of his connection with Hashem and not waiver even on those small jars.

---

3   *Be'er Yosef, Parshas Vayishlach.*

The concept of insignificance is epitomized by the most insignificant entity that exists—dust. By contrast, the idea of Hashem's Throne of Glory represents His supervision over all of man's affairs, as mundane as they may be.[4] We can now return to the Gemara's statement that they "raised dust until the Throne of Glory" and appreciate that this is not a description of the *effects* of that struggle, but of *the struggle itself.* Yaakov's task was to remain firm in his insistence that even matters that one might term "dust" are also under the supervision of Hashem's Throne of Glory.

TEN TO SIX: FROM "PENIEL" TO "PENUEL"

The conflict between Yaakov and the angel, while spiritual and ideological in nature, had its ramifications on Yaakov's physical state and left him limping the following morning. The transition from the spiritual plane of conflict to the physical plane afterwards can be seen in the following fascinating way. The Torah relates that Yaakov named the place where the struggle took place in order to express his gratitude for having survived the ordeal. Verse 31 reads:

וַיִּקְרָא יַעֲקֹב שֵׁם הַמָּקוֹם פְּנִיאֵל כִּי רָאִיתִי אֱלֹהִים פָּנִים אֶל פָּנִים וַתִּנָּצֵל נַפְשִׁי.

*Yaakov called the name of the place **Peniel**—"For I have seen the Divine face to face, yet my life was spared."*

Most interestingly, in the very next verse, the name of the place shifts slightly from the one Yaakov bestowed upon it:

וַיִּזְרַח לוֹ הַשֶּׁמֶשׁ כַּאֲשֶׁר עָבַר אֶת פְּנוּאֵל.

*The sun rose for him as he passed by **Penuel**.*

Why does the first verse call it Peniel, and the second call it Penuel?

---

4   This idea finds expression in the *Asher Yatzar* blessing, which we recite after performing the most mundane of bodily functions, in which we say, "It is known and revealed before Your Throne of Glory" that if any part of the body that should be open would close up or vice versa, we could not endure. This is to emphasize that even such basic matters are subject to ongoing Divine supervision, represented by the Throne of Glory (*Vilna Gaon* in *Imrei Noam* to *Maseches Berachos* 60b).

Rabbeinu Bachya explains that these two names reflect the two different planes Yaakov was on at those respective times. To understand how, let us preface by considering the different connotations of the letters *yud* and *vav*:

- The letter *yud* represents spirituality. It is the letter with the smallest physical presence, and the only one which does not rest on the surface of the line, but rather floats above it. Moreover, *yud* represents the realm of thought, reflected in the fact that verbs in the future tense—which denote things that a person is thinking of, but which do not yet physically exist—begin with the letter *yud*.

- The letter *vav* represents physicality. In a sense, it is a *yud* with its leg extended so that it reaches the ground. The numerical value of *vav* is six, corresponding to the six days of physical Creation. Additionally, the word "*vav*" itself means a hook or link, denoting the sequential cause-and-effect of physical actions.

The first verse describes Yaakov when he was yet on the spiritual plane on which he had wrestled with the angel. As such, the name he gave to the place was פניאל with a *yud*, representing that sphere. The second verse describes the transition from the spiritual plane to the physical, which then left him limping. This transition is marked by the change in the name of the place itself from פניאל with a *yud* to פנואל with a *vav*!

GID HANASHEH: HALACHIC REMOVAL
AND HASHKAFIC TAKEAWAY

As we know, the injury that Yaakov sustained on that occasion translates into one of the mitzvos of the Torah, namely, that of not eating the *gid hanasheh* (sciatic nerve) of the animal. Practically, for those of us who do not prepare our own meat, this mitzvah is one we routinely fulfill without ever having to think about it, as the *gid hanasheh* is removed long before the meat becomes available to the kosher consumer. However, perhaps studying *Parshas Vayishlach* can provide us with an opportunity to contemplate this mitzvah—one of the first that we ever received.

The commentators explain that the blow that the angel was able to inflict on Yaakov's thigh, with its proximity to his reproductive organ, represents the fact that his descendants would not all be on his level in terms of his sense of connection with Hashem. By placing the *gid hanasheh* off-limits for consumption by Yaakov's children, the Torah is providing us with a reminder of the gap that we should be looking to close, developing the connection between our lives and the Throne of Glory. Indeed, the verse later on informs us that Yaakov's limp healed at a certain stage, allowing him to walk fully upright. This reflects the idea—and provides the inspiration—toward a time when Yaakov's descendants will free themselves of their "limp," arise to reclaim their heritage of connectedness with the Divine, and stride steadily and confidently toward redemption.

FROM THE COMMENTATORS

A BLESSING FROM EISAV'S ANGEL

After successfully prevailing in his struggle against Eisav's spiritual overseer, Yaakov demands that the latter confer a blessing upon him. The angel accedes, saying:

לֹא יַעֲקֹב יֵאָמֵר עוֹד שִׁמְךָ כִּי אִם יִשְׂרָאֵל.

No longer will it be said that your name is Yaakov, but Yisrael.[1]

This is truly an amazing moment, with Eisav's own overseer recognizing Yaakov's elevated status. Indeed, later in our parsha, Hashem Himself appears to Yaakov and says:

שִׁמְךָ יַעֲקֹב לֹא יִקָּרֵא שִׁמְךָ עוֹד יַעֲקֹב כִּי אִם יִשְׂרָאֵל יִהְיֶה שְׁמֶךָ וַיִּקְרָא אֶת שְׁמוֹ יִשְׂרָאֵל.

"Your name is [presently] Yaakov; no longer shall your name be called Yaakov, for Yisrael shall be your name." And He called his name Yisrael.[2]

Although the angel had already bestowed this blessing, we can understand how there is certainly room for Hashem to subsequently

---

1   *Bereishis* 32:29.
2   Ibid., 35:10.

endorse and ratify the angel's words. However, upon closer inspection, we will discover that not only was Hashem not endorsing the angel's words, he was actually reversing them.

The key lies in the verb used in both blessings. The angel says *"lo ye'amer*—it shall not be said," while Hashem says *"lo yikarei*—it shall not be called." What is behind this shift in phraseology?

R' Yaakov Ettlinger explains that one typically *calls* someone who is at a distance, who will then come closer, at which point one is able to *say* whatever he wishes to say to him. "Calling" thus denotes distance, while "saying" denotes proximity. Within the context of referring to a future event, this means that "calling" refers to the distant future, while "saying" refers to the near future. In this distinction lies the difference between Eisav's angel's "blessing" and Hashem's blessing.[3]

The transition from Yaakov to Yisrael is certainly a positive one for Yaakov himself. However, as the third and final Patriarch of the Jewish People, it could be potentially disastrous. The Jewish People themselves comprise different levels, with the higher level attaining the status of "Yisrael," while the lower level assumes the status of "Yaakov." As long as this imperfect division applies, both groups need a patriarch whose merit they can invoke and whose patronage they can enjoy. This means that as long as there is a group among the Jewish People called "Yaakov," there needs to be a patriarch called "Yaakov."

Eisav's angel sought to capitalize on Yaakov's personal success and say, "Now that you have graduated to the status of 'Yisrael,' may you soon transition into that name, leaving your earlier name 'Yaakov' behind—as well all those among your descendants who will need it. From this point on, only those who qualify as 'Yisrael' can claim a connection with you." It is not for nothing that he is Eisav's angel! Hence, he uses the term "will not be *said*," i.e., may this change happen in the near future.

When Hashem later appeared to Yaakov to make the actual change, He undid any such notion. With His blessing, He informed Yaakov,

---

3   *Drashos Minchas Ani, Parshas Vayishlach.*

"As long as there are those among your descendants who also need you to be Yaakov, you shall retain that name." Indeed, for this reason Hashem's words regarding the change began by emphasizing, "Your name is Yaakov"—and will remain so as long as necessary! The full transition will take place in the more distant future, when all your descendants will have reached a level where they only need "Yisrael" as their patriarch. Hence, Hashem described the switch with the term "will not be called," denoting the distant future.

In a beautiful concluding comment, Rav Ettlinger draws our attention to a verse in *Malachi*, chapter 3, which we read as part of the *haftarah* for Shabbos HaGadol:

כִּי אֲנִי ה' לֹא שָׁנִיתִי וְאַתֶּם בְּנֵי יַעֲקֹב לֹא כְלִיתֶם.

For I, Hashem, have not changed; and you, the sons of Yaakov, have not perished.[4]

As we know from the Pesach Haggadah, when the verse emphasizes, "I, Hashem," it means to exclude the activity or involvement of an angel. Here too, Hashem says that as opposed to Eisav's angel's plan, "I did not change," i.e., Yaakov's name to Yisrael. The second half of the verse describes the result of this, namely, that "you, the sons of Yaakov, have not perished"; for as long as there is a group called "the sons of Yaakov," there will be a father called Yaakov.

Thus was Eisav's angel denied any measure of victory in his defeat. We look forward to the time when conditions among the Jewish People allow for Hashem's blessing to be ultimately fulfilled!

MAKING SUKKOS

וְיַעֲקֹב נָסַע סֻכֹּתָה וַיִּבֶן לוֹ בָּיִת וּלְמִקְנֵהוּ עָשָׂה סֻכֹּת.

Yaakov journeyed to Sukkos and built for himself a house, and for his livestock he made shelters [sukkos].[5]

---

4   Verse 6.
5   *Bereishis* 33:17.

Our verse contains the first mention in the Torah of sukkos, and although it is not formally connected to the festival of Sukkos, it nevertheless teaches us a basic idea in terms of what a sukkah actually is. One of the basic halachos regarding a sukkah is that it is specifically a *diras arai*—a temporary dwelling. What is the source for this requirement?

According to the *sefer Revid Hazahav*,[6] the answer comes from our verse. If we look closely at the verbs used by the verse in describing Yaakov's actions, we see that it says he *built* a house for himself and *made* sukkos. This teaches us that unlike a house which is "built," on account of it being a permanent structure, a sukkah is simply "made," for it is temporary in nature.

It is amazing to see this fundamental idea regarding the structure of a sukkah emerging from *peshuto shel mikra* in our verse in *Chumash Bereishis*.[7]

PROTECTING THE HOUSE OF YAAKOV

וַיֹּאמֶר יַעֲקֹב אֶל שִׁמְעוֹן וְאֶל לֵוִי עֲכַרְתֶּם אֹתִי...וַאֲנִי מְתֵי מִסְפָּר וְנֶאֶסְפוּ עָלַי וְהִכּוּנִי וְנִשְׁמַדְתִּי אֲנִי וּבֵיתִי. וַיֹּאמְרוּ הַכְזוֹנָה יַעֲשֶׂה אֶת אֲחוֹתֵנוּ.

Yaakov said to Shimon and Levi, "You have compromised me...I am few in number and should they gather together and smite me, I will be destroyed, I and my household." They [Shimon and Levi] said, "Shall he treat our sister like a harlot?"[8]

It is very interesting that we never hear Yaakov's response to his sons' words, for here the chapter ends. What is more intriguing, however, is that Yaakov and his sons appear to be approaching the issue from different perspectives. Yaakov's concerns are practical; through their actions, they placed his family in danger. On the other hand, Shimon and Levi's point is more one of principle: such a deed could not go unanswered. Seemingly, both points are valid, with the sons nevertheless

---

6   *Parshas Vayishlach.*
7   Heard from my father, Rabbi Isaac Bernstein, *zt"l.*
8   *Bereishis* 34:30–31.

maintaining that the matter of their sister's honor overrode any other considerations.

However, the *Ohr Hachaim Hakadosh* explains that Shimon and Levi were actually addressing Yaakov's concern. Yaakov claimed that through their act of aggression, they were provoking the surrounding nations, who would then take action against them. To this, Shimon and Levi responded by arguing that the exact opposite is true. If the nations would see that a villain could lay his hands on a daughter of Yaakov without any fear of a response, that is what would encourage them to engage in similar acts. If we wish for this never to happen again, it has to be known that any such act will be met with a decisive response; only then will our enemies think long and hard before doing something like this again.

PARSHAS VAYEISHEV

YOSEF'S DREAMS

Their Meaning and Fulfillment

It is often the case in Chumash that big ideas are contained within small details, with a seemingly redundant word revealing an entirely new dimension to the situation being discussed. Yosef's two dreams in the beginning of our parsha, with the sheaves of wheat and with the sun, moon, and stars, are well known. However, let us direct our attention to the Torah's introduction to the second dream, where we will notice something very interesting. The verse reads:[1]

וַיַּחֲלֹם עוֹד חֲלוֹם אַחֵר וַיְסַפֵּר אֹתוֹ לְאֶחָיו וַיֹּאמֶר...וְהִנֵּה הַשֶּׁמֶשׁ וְהַיָּרֵחַ וְאַחַד עָשָׂר כּוֹכָבִים מִשְׁתַּחֲוִים לִי.

He dreamt another dream and related it to his brothers, and said..."And behold, the sun, the moon, and eleven stars were bowing down to me."

The opening phrase *"od chalom acher"* is a little puzzling. The word *"od"* means further, while the word *"acher"* means different. As such, one of these terms seems redundant, for if he dreamt "a further dream,"

---

1   *Bereishis* 37:9.

then, by definition, it was also "a different dream." Why does it need to say that he dreamt "a *further different* dream"?

I would like to suggest two answers to this question, each of which will open up key questions regarding these dreams.

FIRST APPROACH: HOW MANY DREAMS DID YOSEF HAVE?

Let us begin by asking a disarmingly simple question: How many dreams did Yosef have?

Of course, we naturally assume that the answer is two. However, a closer look at the verses will reveal that the matter might not be that simple. Verse 5 states:

וַיַּחֲלֹם יוֹסֵף חֲלוֹם וַיַּגֵּד לְאֶחָיו וַיּוֹסִפוּ עוֹד שְׂנֹא אֹתוֹ.

Yosef dreamt a dream and he told it to his brothers, and they hated him even more.

To which dream is this verse referring? If it is merely introducing the dream with the sheaves of wheat that Yosef relates in the following verse, why does this verse already describe the brothers' reaction *after* hearing the dream—something that will be stated explicitly at the end of verse 8? Additionally, the words in that second verse that describe their reaction are:

וַיּוֹסִפוּ עוֹד שְׂנֹא אֹתוֹ עַל חֲלֹמֹתָיו וְעַל דְּבָרָיו.

And they hated him even more, because of his dreams and because of his words.

Why does the verse which describes the brothers' reaction to the dream with the wheat refer to their feelings about "his dreams"? At this stage, he has only had one!

For this reason, there are some commentators who understand that Yosef did not have two dreams, but three. Verse 5 refers to the first of these dreams. It does not specify what this dream was about. Presumably, it was of less significance than the latter two, and is thus mentioned only in terms of the reaction it elicited from the brothers. He then had the dream with the sheaves of wheat, following which we hear of the brothers' reaction to what are now two dreams. Finally, he had the dream with the sun, moon, and stars, bringing the dreams to a total of three.[2]

With this in mind, we can understand why the final dream is introduced with the words, "and he dreamt a further different dream." According to this approach, the dream in verse 6 with the wheat was already a "different dream" to that mentioned in verse 5. As such, our verse states that Yosef proceeded to dream a "further different dream," in which the sun, moon, and stars were bowing down to him.

SECOND APPROACH: WHO WAS IN THE SECOND DREAM?

Let us now consider another approach, which we will preface by asking: To whom do the symbols in the second dream refer? At least part of the answer to this question is quite straightforward—the eleven stars clearly refer to Yosef's eleven brothers. But what about the sun and the moon? Seemingly, they refer to Yosef's father and mother. This creates a difficulty, as Yaakov himself pointed out, for Yosef's mother, Rachel, was no longer alive when Yosef had these dreams. Who, then, is the moon? One approach is that it referred to Bilhah, who raised Yosef as her son, while others say that this element represents part of a dream which is not fulfilled.

Additionally, let us ask: When were the contents of this second dream fulfilled? Here too, the eleven stars, represented by the eleven brothers, bowed down to Yosef when they came to Egypt. But what about the sun and the moon? Did Yaakov—the sun—ever bow down to Yosef? We do find that the Torah refers to Yaakov bowing down in Yosef's presence in the beginning of *Parshas Vayechi*.[3] If he was bowing down to Yosef,[4] then this could indeed be seen as a fulfillment of this part of the dream.

---

2   *Bartenura, Amar Nakeh* to verse 5. See *Ohr Hachaim Hakadosh* for an explanation of these verses according to the understanding that Yosef actually only had two dreams.
3   Ibid., 48:31.
4   See *Rashi* ibid.

However, when we consult the following Midrash, we will discover quite a different answer to the above questions.

THE DAY THE SUN AND MOON STOOD STILL

In one of Yehoshua's battles in conquering the land of Canaan, he saw that evening was approaching and his enemies would soon be able to flee under cover of nightfall. He thus issued his famous call: "*Shemesh b'Givon dom, v'yare'ach b'Emek Ayalon*—Sun, stand still at Givon, and the moon, in the valley of Ayalon!"[5] whereupon the sun and moon were both still, giving him time to finish the battle. Amazingly, the Midrash informs us that the sun and moon were not that inclined to follow Yehoshua's instructions, reflecting the fact that their natural path represents Hashem's Will and Wisdom as instilled within them. Upon encountering this resistance, Yehoshua said:

עבדיה בישא, לאו זבינת כספיה דאבא את, לא כך ראה אותך אבא בחלום "והנה השמש והירח...משתחווים לי." מיה, "וַיִּדֹּם הַשֶּׁמֶשׁ וְיָרֵחַ עָמָד."

You are a bad servant! Are you not the property of my father? Did my father not see you in a dream, where, "Behold, the sun and the moon...were bowing down to me"? Immediately, "the sun was silent and the moon stood still."[67]

According to the Midrash, the part of Yosef's second dream where the sun and the moon bowed down to him was fulfilled hundreds of years later when they stood still in response to the command of his descendant, Yehoshua. In other words, the interpretation of the dream is as follows:

- Eleven stars—refer to Yosef's eleven brothers.
- The sun and the moon—refer to *the actual sun and the moon*!

This comment of the Midrash is simply incredible. For it turns out that the second dream had two aspects to it, which differed from each other not only in terms of the time frame when they were fulfilled, but

---

5   *Yehoshua* 10:12.
6   Ibid., 10:13.
7   *Bereishis Rabbah* 84:11.

also regarding the basic question of whether they symbolized people or simply depicted themselves! Understandably, according to this approach, we do not need to look for an instance where Yosef's father or mother bowed down to him, as they were not actually part of the dream at all.[8]

We may ask: Where does the Midrash see that part of this second dream related to a different time entirely, while another part of it related to the brothers themselves?

I believe the answer is in the words that introduce this dream: "*Vayachalom od chalom acher*—And he dreamt a further different dream." With these words, the Torah is indicating that there are two aspects to the dream:

- *Od*—on the one hand, it is a "further" dream regarding Yosef and the brothers.
- *Acher*—however, it is also a "different" dream, with aspects of it relating to a different context in history entirely.

Indeed, we see that the very same verse that introduces this dream as "a further different dream" proceeds to quote Yosef's own words to his brothers, where he says, "*Hinei chalamti chalom od*—Behold, I have dreamt a further dream." Yosef does not refer to it as "different," the way the verse did, only as "further." This is because Yosef's interest in telling the dream to his brothers only related to the aspects of the dream which had a "further" message, relating to themselves. Indeed, it is quite possible that no one at that time even knew that, in addition to being a "further" dream about the brothers, it was also a "different" dream relating to events in centuries to come.[9]

---

8   *Nezer Hakodesh* to *Bereishis Rabbah*.

9   R' Yehudah Edel of Slonim (*Drashos Afikei Yehudah, drush* 29) suggests that Yaakov actually sensed that the sun and the moon did not refer to him or any of his wives. Thus, his words of rebuttal to Yosef in verse 10, "Shall I, your mother, and your brothers indeed come to bow down to you?" were genuine. He did not accept that all those things would happen, for he understood that not every element within the dream referred to someone in the family. Nevertheless, the next verse states that he "kept the matter in mind," for he knew that the elements of the sun and the moon, while not referring to him, would be fulfilled in some other way.

YOSEF'S ENCOUNTER WITH THE ANGEL

"And Behold, He Was Lost in the Field"

וַיִּמְצָאֵהוּ אִישׁ וְהִנֵּה תֹעֶה בַּשָּׂדֶה וַיִּשְׁאָלֵהוּ הָאִישׁ לֵאמֹר מַה תְּבַקֵּשׁ.
וַיֹּאמֶר אֶת אַחַי אָנֹכִי מְבַקֵּשׁ הַגִּידָה נָּא לִי אֵיפֹה הֵם רֹעִים.
וַיֹּאמֶר הָאִישׁ נָסְעוּ מִזֶּה כִּי שָׁמַעְתִּי אֹמְרִים נֵלְכָה דֹּתָיְנָה וַיֵּלֶךְ יוֹסֵף אַחַר אֶחָיו
וַיִּמְצָאֵם בְּדֹתָן.

A man found him, and behold, he was lost in the field. The man asked him, saying, "What do you seek?"

He [Yosef] said, "I seek my brothers; tell me, please, where they are shepherding."

The man said, "They have journeyed on from here, for I heard them saying, 'Let us go to Dosan.' And Yosef went after his brothers and found them in Dosan."[1]

BACKGROUND

Within the Torah's relating the events leading up to the sale of Yosef, we find a couple of verses that are seemingly purely practical or logistical

---

1   *Bereishis* 37:15–17.

in nature: Yosef arrived in Shechem, didn't find his brothers there and someone—whom the Torah refers to as *"ish"* (a man)—told him where they had gone. Yet, as we will see, this brief meeting contains a great deal, and touches on deep and profound concepts that were at play in this episode.

MESSAGES FOR YOSEF

Our Sages inform us that this *"ish"* was actually the angel Gavriel. Indeed, the Midrash further states that each mention of the word *"ish"* in the verse denotes a separate message to Yosef.[2] According to this, the very first thing the angel told Yosef—as reflected by the first mention of the word *"ish"*—was that "he was lost in the field." Understandably, Yosef did not need an angel to appear in order to tell him this, nor was the angel informing him that he was lost of any assistance in directing him toward his brothers! What, then, was the meaning of that first "message"?

Before addressing this question, let us consult some of *Rashi*'s comments to these verses.

נסעו מזה: הסיעו עצמן מן האחוה.

נלכה דותינה: לבקש לך נכלי דתות שימיתוך בהם.

They journeyed on from here—They have moved themselves away from brotherhood.

Let us go to Dosan—to seek concerning you legal pretexts by which they may put you to death.

The background to these comments is quite clear: The words *"nas'u mizeh"* literally translate as "they have journeyed on from *this.*" While it is true that one can explain it to mean "this place," nevertheless, the Torah did not simply use the word for "here," which is *"kan."* Therefore, *Rashi* explains that it means they have moved away from *this concept* that you just mentioned—"my brothers." Likewise, the Hebrew word for "to Dosan" is *"Dosanah,"* while this *ish* added the letter *yud*—"*Dosaynah*"!

2   *Bereishis Rabbah* 75:4.

Hence, *Rashi* explains that they were looking not only to change location, but to find a legal pretext to kill Yosef.

In light of this, let us ask some simple questions:

- According to *Rashi*, the angel was seeking to inform Yosef that his life was in danger. Presumably, that information would be urgent enough to warrant being stated explicitly, not merely alluded to with a nuanced word-change or extra letter. This is especially so in light of the fact that Yosef clearly did not get the message of danger at all, simply continuing on his way and very nearly getting himself killed in the process! Had that happened, could the angel meaningfully have said, "Don't say I didn't warn you"?
- If the angel was tasked with removing Yosef from potential danger to his life, there was a far easier way to accomplish this than by means of various allusions—namely, simply to not turn up! Yosef, as the verse states, did not know where the brothers were, and he would not have found them had the angel not told him where they were. In other words, but for the angel's appearance, Yosef would have returned home. It turns out that instead of *saving* him from danger, the angel actually ended up *leading* him to it, by directing him to the brothers, while, at the same time, failing to effectively warn him of their intentions!

BETWEEN DESTINY AND FREE WILL

The *Alshich Hakadosh* explains that this conversation between Yosef and the angel was intended to address a very fine balance, namely, between that which is ordained from Heaven and the decisions that people make through the Divinely bestowed faculty of free will. On the one hand, the time had come for the implementation of the next stage of the *Bris Bein Habesarim*, whereby B'nei Yisrael would undergo slavery in a foreign land. The way this was to occur was by Yosef being sold down to Egypt, with the ensuing events in the years that followed paving the way for his family to join him.[3] On the other hand, tensions between

---

3   See *Rashi* to verse 14, s.v. *me'emek*.

Yosef and the brothers had reached the point where there was a very real concern that they would actually decide to kill him. The *Alshich* is of the view that had the brothers indeed wanted to kill Yosef, the principle of free will states that they could have done so, notwithstanding the fact that Heaven had ordained him for greatness.[4]

In light of all this, we can appreciate that Yosef is in a very delicate situation: he needs to meet up with the brothers in order that he be sold down to Egypt, but he also needs to do so in a way that does not get him killed! Indeed, says the *Alshich*, the danger to Yosef was infinitely more pronounced when we consider that he was going out to meet his brothers in a field...

FIELD THEORY AND YOSEF'S DREAMS

When Yaakov summons Yosef to go and check on his brothers, Yosef responds by saying "*Hineni*—Here I am." This term denotes one who is prepared for what is to come. In this instance, Yosef was expressing his preparedness, not only for meeting his brothers, but for a great deal more.

Yosef had recently had two dreams in which the brothers accepted his dominion over them. As we see later in *Chumash Bereishis*,[5] the repetition or reiteration of a dream is generally an indication that the realization of its contents will come to pass shortly thereafter. In fact, we can see that this turned out to be true, as the sale of Yosef to Egypt began the process which led to those dreams ultimately being fulfilled. We can appreciate, however, that Yosef was probably anticipating a fulfillment of a more direct and immediate nature. Add to this the fact that the first dream involved *the brothers bowing down to him in a field*, and we will realize that Yosef was now heading out with the expectation of that first dream being fulfilled this very day!

The gaping disparity between Yosef's expectations regarding what was waiting for him in the field and the reality of the brothers'

---

4   See, regarding this, the comments of the *Ohr Hachaim Hakadosh* to verse 21 and of the *Netziv* in *Harchev Davar* ibid. See also, concerning this question, *Sefer Hachinuch*, mitzvah 241 and *Rabbeinu Bachya* to *Shemos* 21:13.

5   41:32.

disposition could only escalate the danger he was in. If he was, on top of everything else, to approach them in a field far from home and demand that they all bow down to him, those could very well be the final words he would ever utter—with what may have started as him going to meet his destiny ending with him simply meeting an "accident"! On the other hand, notwithstanding the potential danger that he was in, the solution could not be anything that might cause him to head back home; after all, he needed to get to the brothers so as to bring about his journey down to Egypt. For this reason, he could not simply be informed of the reality of how dangerous his situation was. Yosef, too, had free will, so that if he would choose, in light of this information, to avoid all danger and return home as quickly as he could, Heaven could not force him to choose otherwise! This, then, is the question: How could it be arranged for Yosef to be delivered to the brothers without placing him in certain danger at their hands?

Enter the angel Gavriel.

ANGELIC DISSONANCE

The delicate mission of the angel was to guide Yosef toward the brothers while, at the same time, modifying his attitude from one that might get him killed to one that would allow him to be sold down to Egypt. To this end, while the angel is telling Yosef where the brothers are, although he is not explicitly telling him he is in danger, he is nonetheless feeding him messages of a more subtle nature to that effect.

This begins with the very first message which, as we have noted from the Midrash, was to inform Yosef that he was "blundering in the field." As previously noted, this information seems entirely redundant, for did Yosef not already know that he was lost? However, once we appreciate that Yosef was harboring notions of dominion over his brothers based on the field in his dream, the angel's opening words, "You are blundering in the field," had the effect of beginning to sow doubt in his mind as to whether his expectations from that field were accurate.

Likewise, when informing Yosef about the brothers' change of location, the angel employed phrases such as "they have moved on *from this*" and "let us go to *Dosaynah*." These phrases, while not actually wrong per se, nonetheless were also not phrased entirely accurately. The goal of these curious anomalies was specifically not for Yosef to *decipher* them, but for him to *carry* them. For while officially he had not been told of any danger, in the back of his mind he would be mulling over these words which did not sound exactly right; and while he did not consciously decipher those messages of danger, he unconsciously responded to them. The result of all this was that by the time he arrived at his brothers in Dosan, for reasons he could not fully account, his mood was somewhat more subdued and he was no longer thinking of telling them to bow down to him. And, thus, was the angel's mission accomplished.

"BEHOLD, THE DREAMER IS COMING"

What is most fascinating in this regard is to follow through and see Yosef's arrival at Dosan from the brothers' perspective. Verses 18–19 describe their reaction upon seeing him from afar:

בְּטֶרֶם יִקְרַב אֲלֵיהֶם וַיִּתְנַכְּלוּ אֹתוֹ לַהֲמִיתוֹ. וַיֹּאמְרוּ אִישׁ אֶל אָחִיו הִנֵּה בַּעַל הַחֲלֹמוֹת הַלָּזֶה בָּא.

When he had not yet approached them, they conspired against him to kill him. They said one to the other, "Behold, the dreamer is coming."

The brothers here refer to Yosef as "the dreamer," because they are convinced that it is on account of his dreams that he has come. Of particular interest is the word "*halazeh*," which although it contains the letter *lamed*, is nonetheless commonly translated as "this." However, the *Alshich* sees the *lamed* as denoting "for," with the *hei* at the beginning of the word signaling a question, translating "*halazeh ba*" as saying: "Is it *for this* that he has come," i.e., to fulfill his first dream? As we have seen, this was in fact Yosef's expectation when he set out.

All this, however, was the brothers' appraisal when seeing him from afar, before they could detect any mannerisms indicating the contrary. As he approached, however, they saw that his demeanor somehow did not express such expectations. It is amazing to consider this situation, where everyone present expected Yosef to demand that the brothers bow down to him, and yet, for reasons that no one could really explain—including Yosef himself!—he did not do so. As the Torah informs us, this was the result of his meeting with the angel, and it set the climate for a potential recalibration of the brothers' plan to kill him, with it ultimately ending up being replaced by him being sold to Egypt, as Divine providence had ordained.

CONCEPT: THE WAY
THE TORAH DESCRIBES
PEOPLE SEEING THINGS

וַיִּשְׂאוּ עֵינֵיהֶם וַיִּרְאוּ וְהִנֵּה אֹרְחַת יִשְׁמְעֵאלִים בָּאָה מִגִּלְעָד...וַיִּמְכְּרוּ אֶת יוֹסֵף
לַיִּשְׁמְעֵאלִים.

They raised their eyes and saw, and behold, a caravan of Ishmaelites was coming from Gilead...and they sold Yosef to the Ishmaelites.[1]

INTRODUCTION: A CARAVAN OF ISHMAELITES

In these verses, the Torah states that Yosef was sold to the Ishmaelites. The final verse in our chapter, however, relates that "the Medanites brought him to Egypt and sold him to Potiphar."[2] *Rashi* explains that Yosef was sold in stages: (1) The brothers first sold him to the Ishmaelites, (2) who then sold him to the Midianite traders mentioned in verse 28,[3] (3) who subsequently sold him to Egypt. The problem resurfaces, however, in the opening verse of chapter 39, which states that

---

1   *Bereishis* 37:28.
2   Verse 36.
3   In this, *Rashi* apparently concurs with the commentaries who see the Midianites and Medanites (who were cousins) as the same group.

Potiphar bought Yosef from *the Ishmaelites*! Having already sold Yosef to the Midianites, why were the Ishmaelites still in the picture?

Interestingly, the *Maharal* in the *Gur Aryeh* cites with approval the approach that the Ishmaelites and Midianites were actually the same group. The reason they are called by different names in the various verses is because the Ishmaelites were the dominant tribe in the region, with all smaller tribes accepting their mode of dress, etc. Therefore, when our verse says that the brothers "saw a caravan of Ishmaelites," it is because that is how they appeared to them. By contrast, the Torah itself refers to them as they actually were—Midianites.

This explanation of the *Maharal* is truly fascinating, for it reveals an important idea regarding situations where the Torah describes people seeing things. In these instances, it is possible that what the Torah describes them seeing is not necessarily *the thing as it actually was*, but rather, *as they saw it*! Here too, The Torah itself presents the actual reality—that these were Midianites, while regarding the brothers it describes the perceived reality—that they were Ishmaelites.

FURTHER EXAMPLES: YOSEF— FAVORED AMONG SONS OR BROTHERS?

Another example of this idea can be found in the later commentators, relating to the opening verses of our parsha, where the Torah states:

וְיִשְׂרָאֵל אָהַב אֶת יוֹסֵף מִכָּל בָּנָיו כִּי בֶן זְקֻנִים הוּא לוֹ...

וַיִּרְאוּ אֶחָיו כִּי אֹתוֹ אָהַב אֲבִיהֶם מִכָּל אֶחָיו וַיִּשְׂנְאוּ אֹתוֹ.

And Yisrael loved Yosef from all his sons, since he was a child of his old age...[4]

---

4   This is the straightforward understanding of this phrase and the first explanation offered by *Rashi*. *Rashi* then cites *Onkelos*, who translates this phrase as *"bar chakim*—a wise son." According to this approach, the word *"zekunim"* refers not to Yaakov's age but to Yosef's wisdom. As always, the commentators discuss why *Rashi* felt it necessary to bring a second explanation when the first one seems entirely satisfactory on a *pshat* level. It would appear that the answer lies in the beginning of *Parshas Vayigash*, where Yehudah describes Binyamin as a *"yeled zekunim"* (44:20). Why does Yehudah use the word *"yeled"* while our verse uses *"ben"*? The word *yeled* normally denotes a young child; however, Binyamin at that stage was already much older than Yosef was when the Torah calls him *"ben"* in our parsha! Apparently,

His brothers saw that it was he whom their father loved most of all his brothers and they hated him.[5]

We note that the second verse seems to merely repeat what was stated in the first one, adding only the brothers' negative reaction. However, Rav Chanoch HaKohen Ehrentrau,[6] in his sefer *Kometz Haminchah*, explains that the descriptions in these two verses regarding Yaakov's relationship with Yosef are not the same.

- The first verse states that Yaakov loved Yosef "from all his *sons*." This reflects a special bond that can sometimes exist between a parent and a child who, as the verse explains, was "born in his old age." This is not a statement about the essential worth or merit of that child vis-à-vis his siblings.
- The second verse, however, describes "what the brothers saw." They saw the favoring of Yosef as singling him out "from among his *brothers*," seeing him as more worthy than they to continue the legacy of Avraham, Yitzchak, and Yaakov. This elicited their negative feelings toward him.

Once again, we see that the Torah's description of what people saw reflects the way they saw it, even though that might not have reflected the reality as it actually was.[7]

FLIGHT IN FOUR MOVEMENTS: YOSEF'S EXIT FROM POTIPHAR'S HOUSE

An additional fascinating illustration of this idea can be seen toward the end of the parsha, which describes how, when Potiphar's wife grabs

---

the appropriate term when referring to "the child of one's old age" is in fact "*yeled zekunim*," relating to the term "*nolad*," when the child was born. Indeed, *Onkelos* translates that later phrase as "*yeled savtin*—the child of his old age"! If so, then coming back to our parsha where the term used is "*ben zekunim*," *Rashi* explains that the use of the word "*ben*" is in order to reflect a characteristic of Yosef himself, i.e., his wisdom.

5   *Bereishis* 37:3–4.

6   Rav of Munich, grandfather of *yblcht"a* Dayan Chanoch Ehrentrau of London. See also *Malbim* to *Bereishis* loc. cit.

7   See also, regarding this, *Meshech Chochmah* to *Bamidbar* 12:10.

Yosef's garment and tries to seduce him, he flees the house, leaving the garment with her. Yosef's exit is mentioned no fewer than four times in the space of just a few verses:

1. When the verse itself describes him leaving[8]
2. When it describes Potiphar's wife seeing him leave[9]
3. When she tells the story to her household members[10]
4. When she later tells the story to her husband[11]

Interestingly, the description of Yosef leaving goes through a subtle shift between these four mentions:

- On the first and third occasions, the verse states: "*Vayanas vayeitzei hachutzah*—he fled, and went outside."
- On the second and fourth occasions, it states: "*Vayanas hachutzah*—he fled outside."

What is the difference in connotation between these two phrases? Specifically, what does the word "*vayeitzei*—he went" add to the description? Presumably, if he fled outside, then that is where he went!

The *Seforno* explains that these two phrases actually denote two different descriptions of what happened:

1. *The Event*: When Yosef left the house, he did so in a hurry to get away as quickly as he could. This is communicated by the word "*vayanas*—he fled." However, once he had exited the house, he slowed his pace and proceeded to make his way to the street in an unhurried manner, so as not to attract attention that might cause trouble. This change is described by the words "*vayeitzei hachutzah*—he went outside," at a walking pace.
2. *Potiphar's Wife*: The verse then proceeds to describe what Potiphar's wife saw. For her part, having only seen him rush

---

8   *Bereishis* 39:12.
9   Ibid., verse 13.
10   Ibid., verse 15.
11   Ibid., verse 18.

from the house, she naturally assumed that he continued to run even after having gone outside. Hence, the verse writes only "*vayanas hachutzah*—he fled outside," i.e., he continued fleeing all the way outside. As such, she assumed people had seen this and were already beginning to wonder what had happened, and were possibly even asking Yosef about it.

3. *Telling the Servants*: For this reason, Potiphar's wife felt impelled to summon all the members of her household as quickly as possible to "set the record straight" and provide her counter-narrative, in which it was he who attacked her. Under normal circumstances, she would never involve the servants in matters of such a personal nature, but given what she assumed they had already seen and heard from Yosef, she felt that she had no choice. However, in the course of telling her side of things, she perceived that the servants had no idea what she was talking about, from which she surmised that after Yosef fled, he must have slowed down. Accordingly, she concluded her narrative by saying, "*vayanas vayeitzei hachutzah*," as in fact happened.

4. *Telling Potiphar*: In spite of all this, when later retelling the event to her husband, Potiphar's wife described it as she had assumed it was, that Yosef had kept on running. This better fit her depiction of Yosef as the one who had attacked her and was running scared, and therefore she said, "*vayanas hachutzah*."

From these words of the *Seforno*, we see another example of the idea that when the Torah refers to someone seeing something, it describes that thing as how they saw it, not necessarily as it actually was.

RASHI'S APPROACH

Returning to the question of the Ishmaelites and Midianites, we note that *Rashi* does not adopt the approach that they are the same people, seeing them rather as two distinct groups. It would seem that the reason for this is that unlike the *Maharal*, *Rashi* understands that even when the Torah describes people seeing something, its depiction of that thing will be faithful to what it is, regardless of how they perceived it. Hence, if the Torah says that the brothers "saw a caravan of Ishmaelites," it must mean that that is what they were; it cannot be that they are referred to that way simply because that is how they appeared to the brothers. As such, *Rashi* understands that both Ishmaelites and Midianites were involved in the sale.

Indeed, it is possible to demonstrate *Rashi's* approach to this matter from his comments later on in the Chumash. In the end of *Parshas Shoftim*, the Torah says:

כִּי תֵצֵא לַמִּלְחָמָה עַל אֹיְבֶךָ וְרָאִיתָ סוּס וָרֶכֶב עַם רַב מִמְּךָ לֹא תִירָא מֵהֶם.

When you go out to war against your enemy, and you see horse and chariot, a people more numerous than you, you shall not fear them.[12]

Rashi on that verse comments as follows:

סוּס וָרֶכֶב—בעיני חשובים כולם כסוס אחד.
עַם רַב מִמְּךָ—בעיניך הוא רב אבל בעיני אינו רב.

Horse and chariot—In My eyes they are all considered as but a single horse.

A people more numerous than you—in your eyes they are numerous, but in My eyes they are not numerous.

We note that regarding the first phrase, which describes what the people "will see," *Rashi* still explains in terms of how Hashem sees them. It is only when we get to the word "*mimecha*—than you," that *Rashi* explains it to mean "from you," i.e., how they appear from your perspective. Thus, *Rashi's* position clearly emerges as one whereby, even when the Torah describes someone as seeing something, it will nonetheless describe that thing as it is, and not as the person himself might see it.

As we will appreciate, this is a most fascinating question which can potentially affect our understanding of many such verses in the Torah.

---

12   *Devarim* 20:1.

THE SALE OF YOSEF

וַיֹּאמֶר יְהוּדָה אֶל אֶחָיו מַה בֶּצַע כִּי נַהֲרֹג אֶת אָחִינוּ וְכִסִּינוּ אֶת דָּמוֹ. לְכוּ וְנִמְכְּרֶנּוּ לַיִּשְׁמְעֵאלִים וְיָדֵנוּ אַל תְּהִי בוֹ כִּי אָחִינוּ בְשָׂרֵנוּ הוּא וַיִּשְׁמְעוּ אֶחָיו. וַיַּעַבְרוּ אֲנָשִׁים מִדְיָנִים סֹחֲרִים וַיִּמְשְׁכוּ וַיַּעֲלוּ אֶת יוֹסֵף מִן הַבּוֹר וַיִּמְכְּרוּ אֶת יוֹסֵף לַיִּשְׁמְעֵאלִים בְּעֶשְׂרִים כָּסֶף וַיָּבִיאוּ אֶת יוֹסֵף מִצְרָיְמָה.

Yehudah said to his brothers, "What gain will there be if we kill our brother and cover up his blood? Come, let us sell him to the Ishmaelites, and let our hand not be upon him, for he is our brother and our flesh," and his brothers listened [to him]. Midianite traders passed by; they drew Yosef up and lifted him out of the pit and sold Yosef to the Ishmaelites for twenty pieces of silver, and they [the Ishmaelites] brought Yosef to Egypt.[1]

With these words, the Torah presents the sale of Yosef down to Egypt—both its plan and its execution. And, indeed, this fateful deed dominated the events of the decades that followed, finding blunt expression in Yosef's words, as he revealed his identity to his brothers, "*Ani Yosef achichem asher mechartem osi Mitzraymah*—I am your brother Yosef, whom you sold to Egypt."[2]

---

1 *Bereishis* 37:26–28.
2 Ibid., 45:4.

DEFINING "THEM"

It is most interesting to note, however, that the identity of the brothers as those behind the sale finds less clear expression in the verses that describe the sale itself. The Torah's words in verse 28 are: "**They** drew Yosef up and lifted him out of the pit and sold Yosef to the Ishmaelites."

The question is: Who are "they"?

Of course, the first place we look for guidance is *Rashi*'s commentary. And indeed, *Rashi* explains: "*They drew*—Yaakov's sons drew Yosef up from the pit and sold him to the Ishmaelites." We see that *Rashi* clearly identifies Yosef's brothers as the ones who drew him up and sold him. It is very easy to understand why *Rashi* explains the verse in this way, seeing as the previous verse describes the brothers planning to sell him to the Ishmaelites.

However, there is an issue that arises with this explanation. Generally, when a pronoun such as "he," "it," or "they" is used, it refers back to the most recently mentioned noun. Verse 28 begins by saying, "Midianite traders passed by." If so, then it sounds as if they are the "they" who drew Yosef up and sold him! Moreover, if we say that it was the brothers who drew him up and sold him to the Ishmaelites, then it is entirely unclear why the verse opens by mentioning the Midianite traders at all, as they are neither the sellers nor the buyers mentioned later in the verse.

For this reason, there are some early commentators who understand that the ones who sold Yosef were not the brothers, but the Midianites.

OF PLANS AND DEEDS

Although such an approach works well grammatically in terms of the pronoun "they" in verse 28, it is somewhat difficult in terms of the broader context. After all, verse 27 describes the brothers' plan to sell Yosef and then the next verse says that a completely different group of people actually did the sale. Why did the brothers not go through with their plan, and why does the Torah even mention it if other people ended up selling Yosef?

The answer, says R' Azaryah Fego, is: that was the plan.[3]

_____

3   One of the great Italian rabbis of the sixteenth century, *Drashos Binah La'itim, drush* 57. This

The key to this understanding is the opening word of verse 27, "lechu," which literally means "let us go." Where are they meant to go, and how does this relate to the words that follow, "and let us sell him to the Ishmaelites"? R' Fego explains. When Yehudah saw the Ishmaelite caravan approaching, he reasoned that there was now an effective way of removing Yosef and the threat he posed to the brothers without killing him, instead by selling him. Moreover, even the sale was not to be done directly by the brothers. Rather, Yehudah said "let us go," i.e., let us move away from here, for no one will approach Yosef in the pit as long as we are next to it. However, once we move away, someone will come across him and sell him to the Ishmaelites. In other words, according to this approach, when Yehudah says, "and let our hand not be upon him," it does not only relate to not killing him, but also to not selling him directly, but rather allowing others to do so. The next verse describes that this is exactly what happened, as Midianite traders came across Yosef, drew him up from the pit and sold him to the Ishmaelites. Where were the brothers at that time? Possibly watching from a safe distance, but certainly not directly involved.

Another approach, perhaps even more radical in its own way, is that of the *Rashbam*, who suggests that the brothers were far away when they developed the plan of selling him to the Ishmaelites, while, in the meantime, Midianite traders approached the pit where Yosef was and did just that, without the brothers knowing about it![4] This means that when verse 29 states that Reuven returned to the pit, only to find that Yosef was no longer there, this was not merely a surprise for him, but for all the brothers![5]

---

approach of the *Binah La'itim* is cited in his name by the *Malbim* in his commentary to our verse, who endorses and adopts it as the correct understanding of the sale.

4   Commentary to *Bereishis* 37:28. See also *Chizkuni* to *Bereishis* ibid., and *Hakesav V'hakabbalah* to ibid., 45:4.

5   The *Rashbam* adds that even if we adopt the view that it was the brothers who sold him, we will still need to explain the phrase "they drew Yosef out" as referring to the Midianite traders, which will then mean that the Midianites took him out on the brothers' instructions.

YOSEF'S WORDS

The *Tur* points out that the notion that the brothers did not sell Yosef is borne out by the simple reading of a verse toward the end of our parsha. When Yosef interprets the chief butler's dream and then asks him to remember him to Pharaoh when he is released, he says: "*Ki gunov gunavti me'eretz haIvrim.*"[6] The word "*lignov*" means "to steal," such that Yosef was saying "For I was kidnapped from the land of the Hebrews." This description would fit the understanding that it was not the brothers who took him out and sold him.[7]

Having said that, we need to come back to Yosef's statement to his brothers, mentioned earlier, "I am Yosef, your brother, whom you sold to Egypt." Here, Yosef is stating explicitly that it was the brothers who sold him!

This question is raised by the *Rashbam* himself, who says that since the brothers throwing Yosef into a pit and leaving him there was the cause of his being sold, he refers to them as selling him.

Further implications of this idea are discussed by Rabbeinu Bachya, who concurs with the approach of the *Rashbam*. We know that many generations after the sale, it came back to haunt Klal Yisrael in the form of the decree of the *Asarah Harugei Malchus*, the ten martyrs, whose account we read on Yom Kippur and Tishah B'Av. That later episode likewise needs to be assessed in light of the idea that Yosef's brothers did not actually sell him. There too, Rabbeinu Bachya explains that the fact that they enabled him to be sold was sufficient for this to be considered an outstanding sin that needed to be expiated, which then expressed itself with the *Asarah Harugei Malchus*.

CONCLUSION: WHAT THE TORAH CHOOSES TO SPECIFY

Regardless of one's understanding of who it was that sold Yosef, the fact remains that the Torah does not explicitly state that the brothers

---

6   *Bereishis* 40:15.
7   Commentary to *Bereishis* 7:28. In addition to the commentary known as the *Baal Haturim*, which deals mainly with the realm of *remez* (allusion), the *Tur* also wrote a comprehensive *pshat* commentary on the Torah which synopsizes the positions of numerous Rishonim who preceded him, as well offering his own commentary.

sold him. As the *Ohr Hachaim* states elsewhere,[8] there are major ramifications regarding what the Torah chooses to state explicitly, for whether something happened is one thing, but to have it recorded in the Torah is an entirely different matter. There are times when the Torah chooses to be more vague and circumspect in its presentation of events, so that even when someone acts wrongly, they do not necessarily deserve the further disgrace of this being enshrined in the Torah's text. Here too, the Torah phrases things vaguely, perhaps due to the enormity of the crime, or maybe in recognition of the fact that the brothers genuinely felt that they were acting correctly.

---

8   See, e.g., in his commentary to *Vayikra* 24:10 and *Bamidbar* 25:14.

WHAT HAPPENED
TO YOSEF'S COAT?

After selling Yosef to Egypt, the Torah describes how the brothers took his coat and dipped it in goat's blood to make it look as if he had been attacked by a wild beast.[1] The verse then relates:[2]

וַיְשַׁלְּחוּ אֶת כְּתֹנֶת הַפַּסִּים וַיָּבִיאוּ אֶל אֲבִיהֶם וַיֹּאמְרוּ זֹאת מָצָאנוּ הַכֶּר נָא הַכְּתֹנֶת בִּנְךָ הִוא אִם לֹא.

They sent the fine woolen coat and they brought it to their father and said, "We found this; identify it, please, is this your son's coat or not?"

There is a basic difficulty with the simple reading of this verse. It first states that they "sent" the coat, and then says that "they brought it to their father." The question is: Having already sent it, how could they then bring it?

The *Ramban* offers two answers to this question:

- The brothers sent the coat to their father via messengers, with the second phrase, "they brought it," referring to the messengers.

---

1   The word *kesones* is translated variously as coat, shirt, or tunic. We have used the word coat for simplicity's sake.
2   *Bereishis* 37:32.

The presumption is that the brothers were reluctant to bring the coat to their father themselves, and so had others do it.

- The word "*vayeshalechu*" is not related to the idea of *sending*, but of *tearing*, as we find this term used in *Iyov*.[3] The brothers first tore the coat to make it look as if Yosef had been attacked, and then they brought it to their father.

LISHLOACH AND LESHALACH: SENDING AND SENDING AWAY

With regards to the first explanation of the *Ramban*, namely, that the brothers sent the coat with messengers, it is worthwhile noting that the Torah has two terms for "sending": *Lishloach* (לשלוח) and *Leshalach* (לשלח).

Lishloach denotes sending something or someone to a destination with a mission in mind. An example of this is Yaakov's sending messengers to Eisav with a message of peace, where it states: "*Vayishlach Yaakov malachim.*"[4]

Leshalach denotes sending something *away*. An example of this term is the goat which is sent away to the wilderness on Yom Kippur, where it says "*Leshalach oso laAzazel.*"[5]

With this in mind, we return to our verse, where it says "*Vayeshalechu es kesones hapasim.*" If the brothers sent the coat with messengers to their father, the verb should have been "*vayishlechu*," as per the first type of sending. However, given that the verse uses the term "*vayeshalechu*," the implication is that they *threw his coat away*! This, of course, cannot be, for how could they—or anyone else—bring it to their father if they had thrown it away? Clearly, the verse is to be understood as describing them sending it to Yaakov, which then leaves us having to explain why the verb for "sending away" is used.

---

3   36:12.
4   *Bereishis* 32:4.
5   *Vayikra* 16:10. See *Rashi* to *Bereishis* 8:8 where he discusses the difference between these two terms.

HOW MANY COATS DID YOSEF HAVE?

According to one of the great Italian commentators of the seventeenth century, Rav Moshe Chefetz,[6] the key to this matter lies in an earlier verse, describing the brothers' actions when Yosef first approached them. Verse 23 reads:

וַיְהִי כַּאֲשֶׁר בָּא יוֹסֵף אֶל אֶחָיו וַיַּפְשִׁיטוּ אֶת יוֹסֵף אֶת כֻּתָּנְתּוֹ אֶת כְּתֹנֶת הַפַּסִּים
אֲשֶׁר עָלָיו.

And it was, when Yosef came to his brothers, they stripped Yosef of his coat, the passim coat that was on him.

We note that the verse contains two references to Yosef's coat. *Rashi* explains:

His coat—*this is a tunic.*
The passim coat—*this is the one his father added for him above and beyond his brothers.*

What is the meaning of these comments? Specifically, how many coats are we to understand that Yosef had?

R' Eliyahu Mizrachi, one of the foremost commentators on *Rashi*, insists that the verse cannot be relating that Yosef had more than one coat.[7] According to him, the second phrase—"the *passim* coat"—is there for emphatic purposes, specifying that "his coat" was the special *passim* coat which was the source of such contention.[8] However, he concedes that if this is true, the final two words of the verse, "*asher alav*," present a difficulty, for what do these words come to add? Surely, the idea that Yosef's coat was "on him" is not one that is in need of explication?

Other commentators, however, do understand the verse as indicating that Yosef wore two coats: His regular one, which was like the

---

6   *Meleches Machsheves, Parshas Vayeitzei.*
7   This is based on his assertion that the term *"kesones"* refers specifically to a garment that is worn directly on the body, of which there can be only one.
8   See commentary of *Tur* to this verse.

coats of the other brothers, and his additional *passim* one.[9] Moreover, according to them, this itself is the meaning of the concluding words "*asher alav*"; for the word "*alav*" here is not to be translated as "on *him*," i.e., on Yosef, but rather "on *it*"—i.e., that the second *passim* coat was *on top of the regular coat!*

MATERIAL CONSIDERATIONS

However, there is a basic issue to be raised with this explanation: The word "*kesones*" is a feminine noun. As such, had the Torah meant to say that the *passim* coat was on top of his regular coat, it would not have referred to it as "*asher alav*," but rather, "*asher aleha*"! Clearly, the words "*asher alav*" indicate that the coat was directly on Yosef, and, hence, as the *Mizrachi* pointed out, they appear entirely redundant.

All the above leads Rav Chefetz to a rather different conclusion. He concurs with those who understand that the verse is referring to two separate coats. However, it is also telling us something else, namely, that on this occasion, Yosef wore the two coats *in reverse order!*

Yosef is well aware that his *passim* coat is a point of contention between himself and the brothers. In this particular situation, far from home and on his way to the brothers, Yosef wishes to avoid unnecessarily agitating them any further and hence decides to wear his *passim* coat *underneath* his regular coat. For this reason, when the verse describes the brothers stripping him of his two coats, it first mentions his regular coat, which he was wearing on top, and then mentions his *passim* coat which, on this occasion, was "*alav*"—directly on his body!

DIPPING THE COAT IN BLOOD

This brings us back to our opening question. The verse states that the brothers "sent the coat, and brought it to their father." We asked: Having already sent it to their father, how could they then bring it to him? The answer, says Rav Chefetz, is that the coat that they sent was not the coat that they then brought.

How is this so?

---

9   See, e.g., *Gur Aryeh.*

The verse which describes the dipping of Yosef's coat in blood reads as follows:

וַיִּקְחוּ אֶת כְּתֹנֶת יוֹסֵף וַיִּשְׁחֲטוּ שְׂעִיר עִזִּים וַיִּטְבְּלוּ אֶת הַכֻּתֹּנֶת בַּדָּם.

They took Yosef's coat, slaughtered a goat and dipped the coat in blood.

We note that both references in this verse are to "Yosef's coat." His *passim* coat is not mentioned until the next verse, where it says that they "sent it." As we have seen, where not otherwise qualified, the term "Yosef's coat" refers to his regular coat. It was *that one* which they dipped in blood to bring to their father. Why did they choose to dip his regular coat and not his *passim* coat? Perhaps, they had such an aversion to that coat that they wished to have no further involvement with it. Alternatively, given the special love that their father attached to this coat, perhaps they could not bring themselves to bring it to him stained with blood. Therefore, they chose the regular coat as the medium through which to imply that Yosef had been devoured by a wild beast.

What then became of the *passim* coat? If it was not brought to Yaakov, where did it go? The answer is provided in the beginning of the following verse: "*vayeshalechu es kesones hapassim.*" As we noted, the word "*vayeshalechu*" indicates throwing something away, which is what the brothers did to the *passim* coat, discarding it in a nearby field. Then, as the verse proceeds to describe: "*vayaviu el avihem*—they brought to their father" Yosef's regular coat, which they had dipped in blood, which they then asked him to identify.[10]

---

10 While this phrase ("they brought") follows the opening phrase ("they sent") and would seem to also refer to the *passim* coat, we note that the pronoun which would connect the two—"*vayivi'eha*—they brought it"—is missing, allowing us to understand that what they brought was not the *passim* coat that they had "sent," i.e., sent away. Moreover, the fact that the brothers asked Yaakov to identify the coat indicates that it was not the *passim* coat, which would have been so distinct as to have been immediately recognizable to all. Yosef's regular coat, however, would have been less distinct from others like it and would have required identifying on Yaakov's part.

YOSEF, THE BUTLER, AND THE BAKER

A Deeper Look

BACKGROUND

The final section of our parsha deals with Yosef's encounter with Pharaoh's butler and baker. A brief synopsis of this episode would likely go as follows: Both the butler and the baker incurred Pharaoh's wrath, who threw them in jail, where they met Yosef. While there, they both had dreams, which Yosef interpreted—positively for the butler and negatively for the baker. In time, his interpretations were borne out, with the butler being restored to his post and the baker being executed, thereby setting the stage for Yosef's abilities to be recalled by the butler when Pharaoh had his dreams two years later.

However, a closer look at the verses in this chapter indicates that the matter might not be quite that simple...

THE BUTLER, THE BAKER—AND THE CHIEF BUTLER AND CHIEF BAKER

The key point to note at the outset is that reference to these two individuals seems to shift over the course of the chapter:

- Verse 1 states that "חָטְאוּ מַשְׁקֵה מֶלֶךְ מִצְרַיִם וְהָאֹפֶה לַאֲדֹנֵיהֶם לְמֶלֶךְ מִצְרָיִם—the **butler** and **baker** of the king of Egypt sinned against their master, the king of Egypt."
- Verse 2 then states: "וַיִּקְצֹף פַּרְעֹה עַל שְׁנֵי סָרִיסָיו עַל שַׂר הַמַּשְׁקִים וְעַל שַׂר הָאוֹפִים וַיִּתֵּן אֹתָם בְּמִשְׁמַר—Pharaoh became angry at his two stewards, the **chief butler** and the **chief baker**; and he placed them in jail."
- Verse 5 says "וַיַּחַלְמוּ חֲלוֹם שְׁנֵיהֶם...הַמַּשְׁקֶה וְהָאֹפֶה אֲשֶׁר לְמֶלֶךְ מִצְרַיִם אֲשֶׁר אֲסוּרִים בְּבֵית הַסֹּהַר—They both had a dream...the **butler** and the **baker** of the king of Egypt, who were incarcerated in jail."
- From that point on until the end of the chapter they are referred to, once again, as "the **chief butler**" and the "**chief baker**."

What is behind this shift in reference?

The *Malbim* explains that these are not two ways of referring to the same two people, but are actually *two sets of two people*.[1] It all began with one of the king's butlers and bakers mishandling his bread and wine. Chazal inform us that this took the form of a stone that was baked into Pharaoh's bread and a fly that found its way into Pharaoh's cup of wine. Pharaoh was incensed at this disgraceful lack of service. However, he did not take out his anger on the butler and baker, who themselves prepared the wine and bread, but on their overseers, the chief butler and chief baker, whom he held accountable for not ensuring that those under them were performing up to par. After all, with great prestige comes great responsibility, and, hence, the chief butler and chief baker were thrown into jail. Indeed, this will give us a more nuanced reading of the concluding words of verse 1, which state that the butler and baker sinned "*laadoneihem l'melech Mitzrayim.*" Although the word "*adoneihem*" in the plural form can be used even when referring to one master, in this instance, it is actually meant in the plural, as these two workers sinned both against "their masters"—the chief butler and chief baker—and against "the king of Egypt."

---

[1] The basis of the approach developed by the *Malbim* is found in the *Seforno* in this chapter. See also *Haamek Davar*.

Whatever became of the actual butler and baker who made the actual mistakes? This we do not know. Perhaps, they were dispatched forthwith; perhaps, they were thrown in some other jail; or, perhaps, they were simply ignored. Being insignificant does have its advantages. At any rate, the ones who became Yosef's cell-mates were their bosses, the chief butler and chief baker, as stated in verse 2.

WERE THE DREAMS INTUITIVE?

This brings us to the two dreams. On the one hand, the interpretations Yosef gave do not seem to indicate such great expertise. After all, the chief butler dreamt that he was giving a cup of wine to Pharaoh, while the chief baker dreamt that he wasn't doing anything, not even enough to stop birds from eating all the food in his baskets. What was it, then, about Yosef's interpretation that so impressed the chief butler that he would, in time, recommend Yosef to interpret Pharaoh's dreams?

The answer is that although the message of the dreams was quite straightforward, it was also entirely counterintuitive.

To understand why this is so, we must ask a simple question: Which of these two individuals should have more likely been restored to his former position?

Clearly, the one whose sin against Pharaoh was milder would be more expected to be restored, while the one whose sin was greater would be more likely to be punished. And so we proceed to ask: Which infraction was greater, that with the bread or with the wine? Interestingly, the answer to this question depends on whether we are looking at it from the point of view of the original butler and baker who prepared those items, or from that of their overseers who presented them to Pharaoh:

- Regarding the Bread—the problem really lay with the one who baked it, for it was only during the baking process that a stone could have gotten into the dough. After that stage, the chief baker could not really have done anything to remove or even detect the problem. If he was punished, it was only because he was ultimately in charge of the offending baker.

- Regarding the Wine—the opposite is true. The one who squeezed the grapes and made the wine was not necessarily at fault, for who knows when the fly actually entered the wine; perhaps, it was only after the butler had finished making the wine! By contrast, the chief butler, who was the one who actually handed the cup to Pharaoh, should have been able to notice the fly in it before doing so.

It turns out that while in terms of the original butler and baker themselves, it was **the baker** who was more at fault, but in terms of their overseers, it was **the chief butler** who was more at fault than the chief baker.

However, this leads us to a problem—for their dreams indicated exactly the opposite. It was specifically the chief butler who dreamt he would be restored while the chief baker dreamt he would killed. In fact, as we have seen, these dreams would have been more appropriate for the actual butler and baker, not for their respective overseers. It is for this reason that verse 5, which describes the two overseers dreaming, refers to them as "the butler and the baker." Although those two individuals were not actually in jail and did not have these dreams, nevertheless, the messages of their overseers' dreams were actually more appropriate for them.

In brief, although the message of each dream seems quite straightforward, the connection with each of the dreamers themselves was completely inverted.

A very perplexing situation indeed!

"IT IS ONLY THAT YOU SHOULD REMEMBER ME"

Upon hearing the dreams, Yosef informs his companions that the message of the dreams will be fulfilled through each of them. Each will undergo a reversal of fortune, contrary to all expectation. In three days' time, not only will the chief butler be pardoned and allowed to work in the palace again, but he will immediately be restored to his former post, placing the cup in Pharaoh's hand. Indeed, the reversal itself is part of the dream, for initially, there are no grapes on the vine, reflecting the total lack of prospects for the chief butler's future, yet they subsequently budded and ripened very rapidly, representing the rapid turnabout of events which would result in his reinstatement as Pharaoh's cup-bearer.

Likewise, the chief baker too would experience a reversal, indicated by the initial presence of all manner of baked goods which were subsequently consumed, leaving the basket empty.

As to the reason *why* these reversals were about to take place, which were completely contrary to all expectation and defied all comprehension, Yosef proceeds to inform the chief butler:

כִּי אִם זְכַרְתַּנִי אִתְּךָ כַּאֲשֶׁר יִיטַב לָךְ...וְהִזְכַּרְתַּנִי אֶל פַּרְעֹה.

It is only that you should remember me, when things go well for you...and mention me to Pharaoh.

In other words, Yosef is stating that when you consider all that you experienced here: both of you being placed in jail, thereby bringing you into contact with me, and then having your dreams, which I am informing you to mean that you, the chief butler, the one who would surely never be allowed to leave, will be presently reinstated as if nothing had happened; you will come to realize that all this can only be in order for you to remember me and mention me to Pharaoh.

In actuality, as we know, Yosef's interpretations of the two dreams were borne out, but it would be another two years before his accompanying message to the chief butler was recalled and acted upon. In the meanwhile, "The chief butler did not remember Yosef, and he forgot him."

FROM THE COMMENTATORS

WINDOWS OF THE SOUL

וַיְהִי כְּדַבְּרָהּ אֶל יוֹסֵף יוֹם יוֹם וְלֹא שָׁמַע אֵלֶיהָ.

And so it was, as she spoke to Yosef every day, and he would not listen to her.[1]

The Gemara relates that in the final day of the year spent in Potiphar's house, Yosef's resistance to Potiphar's wife was waning and he was in danger of succumbing:[2]

> *At that moment, his father's image appeared to him in the window and said, "At some point in the future, your brothers' names will be engraved in the stones worn by the Kohen Gadol. Do you want your name to be missing from among them?"*

Upon hearing these words, Yosef's resolved was strengthened, and he was able to resist temptation on that final occasion.

There are a number of observations regarding this appearance of Yaakov to Yosef in the window:

---

1   *Bereishis* 39:10.
2   *Sotah* 36b.

- First, we may ask, was it "cheating" for Yosef to receive this visit from his father? Most people would similarly refrain from sinning after such a visit, and yet they are left to work it out themselves! Why was Yosef able to receive this extra help?
- Second, on what level was Yaakov able to give this message to Yosef when in fact he had no idea where Yosef was—or even if he was alive?

The commentators explain that when Yosef saw "the appearance of Yaakov in the window," it was because he had absorbed and internalized his father's message and values. Even though they were separated by time and distance, Yaakov remained the primary influence on Yosef. This vision was a tribute to the extent to which Yosef had absorbed Yaakov's lessons. It was not "cheating" for him to receive the vision; rather, it was the product of Yosef's efforts to remain connected to Yaakov wherever he went.

SHARING DREAMS

A survey of Yosef's experiences in our parsha reveals him going from favorite son in the beginning of the parsha to the bottom of a pit in the end. By contrast, the following parsha begins with him in the pit and then charts his meteoric rise to become the viceroy of Egypt.

My father Rabbi Isaac Bernstein, zt"l, suggested that what lies behind this is the following. In the beginning of our parsha, Yosef says to his family, "Listen to my dreams."[3] Yosef wants everyone to be aware of his ambitions, his aspirations, his hopes. A person who is anxious only for others to know what he wants out of life is "on the way down." At the end of our parsha, however, Yosef says to the chief butler and baker, "Tell me your dreams"[4]—I am anxious to hear what your ambitions are, what you hope for. When one is ready to listen to the dreams of others, then the future is bright, and that person is "on the way up."

---

3   *Bereishis* 37:6.
4   Ibid., 40:8.

PARSHAS MIKEITZ

YOSEF'S ADVICE TO PHARAOH

BACKGROUND: FROM DREAM
INTERPRETER TO ROYAL ADVISOR

The beginning of our parsha describes how Yosef was able to accurately interpret Pharaoh's dreams as forecasting seven years of plenty and a further seven years of famine, something that had eluded the wisest of Egypt's men. What is quite astounding is that having successfully interpreted the dreams, Yosef does not stop there, but rather proceeds to offer Pharaoh advice as to how to deal with the impending situation:[1]

וְעַתָּה יֵרֶא פַרְעֹה אִישׁ נָבוֹן וְחָכָם וִישִׁיתֵהוּ עַל אֶרֶץ מִצְרָיִם...וְחִמֵּשׁ אֶת אֶרֶץ
מִצְרַיִם בְּשֶׁבַע שְׁנֵי הַשָּׂבָע.

And now, let Pharaoh choose a discerning and wise man, and appoint him over the land of Egypt...and he shall prepare the land of Egypt during the seven years of plenty.

These words of Yosef are simply dumbfounding. Let us remember: he is a young and unimportant slave who has been brought out of prison for one purpose only—to interpret Pharaoh's dreams, which he has just finished doing. On what basis does he then feel authorized to offer Pharaoh unsolicited guidance as to how to run his country? Many

---

1   *Bereishis* 41:33.

commentators over the ages have discussed this question.[2] A most interesting approach taken by a number of them is that Yosef's advice was in fact not extraneous to his role as interpreter; rather, the ideas he expressed were *also contained within the dreams*. Let us consider the words of two Acharonim who follow this approach.

FIRST EXPLANATION: STANDING OVER THE NILE

The Torah introduces Pharaoh's first dream by stating:

וּפַרְעֹה חֹלֵם וְהִנֵּה עֹמֵד עַל הַיְאֹר.

Pharaoh was dreaming, and, behold, he was standing over the Nile.[3]

What is the significance within this dream of Pharaoh standing over the Nile? We can appreciate the appearance of the Nile itself in the dream, as the years of plenty in Egypt predicted therein were connected to the water that comes from the Nile. However, the idea of Pharaoh standing over it seems somewhat extraneous.[4]

The *B'nei Yissaschar* explains as follows.[5] As we mentioned, the agricultural well-being of Egypt is provided by the Nile in the form of the water that flows therein. By introducing the dreams with showing Pharaoh that he was standing over the Nile, Heaven was indicating to him that in the years ahead, he would need to take over and assume the role of the Nile in providing for Egypt! In the years when the Nile would no longer be providing water, it would be Pharaoh who would need to arrange for providing food for his country. Thus, when Yosef proceeded

---

2   See, e.g., *Ramban* to ibid., verse 4, and *Abarbanel* and *Ohr Hachaim* to our verse.

3   Verse 1.

4   Indeed, in Pharaoh's retelling of the dream, he actually edits this opening part, stating instead that he saw himself standing "*al sefas hayeor*—on the banks of the Nile." As the commentators explain, the Nile was worshipped as a deity by the Egyptians, and as such, Pharaoh was uncomfortable informing Yosef that he had seen himself standing over his god. However, Chazal inform us (*Zohar* 1:196a) that Yosef was aware, not only of the version of the dreams as told to him by Pharaoh, but also of the original version, including the fact that Pharaoh was in fact standing over the Nile.

5   Tishrei, *maamar* 2, sec. 24.

to advise Pharaoh to take action to provide for Egypt's well-being, it was in his role of interpreter regarding this part of the dream!

In fact, there is a further point here. We see that Yosef does not advise that Pharaoh himself oversee the organization of the crops during the coming years, but rather, that he appoint someone else to do so. This, too, says the *B'nei Yissaschar*, was part of his interpreting Pharaoh standing over the Nile. The contribution of the Nile to Egypt's agriculture is not detailed or ongoing in nature. It consists of a single decisive gesture—water overflowing its banks—which then needs to be handled by others in order to provide for the country. Likewise, in placing Pharaoh over the Nile, the dream was indicating that his contribution, too, was to take the form of a one-time "Nile-like" gesture—in this instance, the appointment of someone who would then take over the ongoing management of the crops in the coming years.

SECOND EXPLANATION: WAKING UP IN A DREAM

A different approach to this discussion begins by asking a seemingly simple question: How many dreams did Pharaoh have? This question relates to the Torah's words after Pharaoh's second dream, which state: "וַיִּיקַץ פַּרְעֹה וְהִנֵּה חֲלוֹם"—Pharaoh awoke and behold, it was a dream."[6] These words are somewhat mystifying:

- Having prefaced the episode by stating that "Pharaoh was dreaming," it seems redundant to state that when he finally awoke, everything beforehand was a dream!
- Moreover, as the verses describe, Pharaoh had two dreams that night, in between which he woke up. This now makes it somewhat inaccurate to describe what he had seen that night as "a dream"!

These questions led certain commentators to conclude that in fact, Pharaoh had only one dream that night. When the verse states that he woke up after the first dream and then went to sleep again before the

---
6   Verse 7.

second, this too was all part of the dream: he dreamt that he woke up from the first dream and went back to sleep again. While he was dreaming, it felt as if he really had woken up in the middle; however, when he finally did actually wake up, he realized that *"v'hinei chalom"*—the whole thing had been one dream![7]

Indeed, this was one of the reasons Pharaoh rejected the interpretations of the Egyptian wise men. Verse 8 states: "וַיְסַפֵּר פַּרְעֹה לָהֶם אֶת חֲלֹמוֹ וְאֵין פּוֹתֵר אוֹתָם לְפַרְעֹה—Pharaoh related his dream to them, but none could interpret them for Pharaoh." We note that the verse describes him relating "his dream"—implying one dream, but then states that none could interpret "them"—implying more than one. For this was a significant part of his dissatisfaction with their interpretations: they all insisted on relating to them as two separate dreams, not realizing that they were all one dream.

This is true even though Pharaoh himself indicated this in his description of the dreams. After relating the first dream, he said that he woke up,[8] but did not then say that he went to sleep again before the second dream, stating rather, "I saw in my dream."[9] No one picked up on this nuance. No one, that is, except for Yosef. The first thing Yosef says upon hearing the dreams is: *"Chalom Pharaoh echad hu*—Pharaoh's dream is one."[10] With these words, Yosef indicated that he understood that both dreams of Pharaoh were really part of one big dream. We can now appreciate that already from this stage, Yosef had Pharaoh's attention!

This brings us back to Yosef's advice. If Pharaoh's two dreams were in fact one big dream, in the middle of which he dreamt that he woke up, that means that *Pharaoh waking up was part of the dream.* It was to this part Yosef was responding when he advised Pharaoh to take action, for part of the message in the dream was for Pharaoh to wake up and make provisions for the years of famine![11]

---

7   *Maaseh Hashem, Parshas Mikeitz.*
8   Verse 21.
9   Verse 22.
10   Verse 25.
11   *Chida, Nachal Kedumim, Parshas Mikeitz.*

Here too, there is a further point, for as we noted, Yosef did not advise that Pharaoh should deal with the logistics of the coming years himself, but that he should appoint someone else to do it. The *Be'er Yosef* explains that this, too, was part of the dream. As the verses describe, after dreaming that he woke up, Pharaoh dreamt that he went back to sleep again. The full message of the dream is therefore that Pharaoh does indeed need to wake up, but only to the extent that he can then go back to sleep! In practical terms, this means that Pharaoh needs to take action in the form of appointing someone who will take charge of the planning for the years ahead, allowing Pharaoh to return to a dormant state and let events take their course.

THE EARLIEST COMMENTARY ON THE TORAH

Concept: The Relationship of Chumash with Neviim and Kesuvim

וַיִּפְתַּח הָאֶחָד אֶת שַׂקּוֹ...בַּמָּלוֹן וַיַּרְא אֶת כַּסְפּוֹ וְהִנֵּה הוּא בְּפִי אַמְתַּחְתּוֹ...וַיֵּצֵא
לִבָּם וַיֶּחֶרְדוּ אִישׁ אֶל אָחִיו לֵאמֹר מַה זֹּאת עָשָׂה אֱלֹקִים לָנוּ.

One [of the brothers] opened his sack...at the inn, he saw his money, and behold, it was in the opening of his sack...their hearts sank and they were afraid, saying to one another, "What is this that God has done to us?"[1]

INTRODUCTION

When Yosef's brothers return from buying food in Egypt, they discover, to their alarm, that the money that they had brought with them to purchase food was still in their bags, instead of in the Egyptian coffers where it belonged. With no notion of how this possibly could have occurred, and fearful of the repercussions from the already suspicious

---

1   *Bereishis* 42:27–28.

Egyptian ruler, their eyes turn Heavenwards, trying to fathom what Divine message is intended for them.

This verse, aside from depicting one of many pieces in the story of Yosef and the brothers, also forms the basis for a discussion in the Talmud which could potentially revolutionize the way we look at the three sections that comprise Tanach known as: Torah, *Neviim* (Prophets), and *Kesuvim* (Writings).

R' YOCHANAN'S AXIOM

The Gemara in *Maseches Taanis* relates the following exchange that took place between R' Yochanan and his nephew:[2]

> *R' Yochanan encountered Reish Lakish's son, who was sitting and reciting [the verse], "The foolishness of a man frustrates his way, and [yet] his heart frets against Hashem."*[3]
> *R' Yochanan sat and expressed his astonishment, "Is there anything written in Scripture that is not alluded to in the Torah?"*
> *[The young boy] said to [R' Yochanan], "Is this not alluded to? Behold, the verse states, 'And their hearts sank, they were afraid, saying to one another, "What is this that God has done to us?"""*

First, it is worth noting the novel interpretation R' Yochanan's nephew brings to our verse, for he is saying that rather than the brothers casting their eyes Heavenward and asking why God was doing this to them, they should instead have checked their bags before they left Egypt!

However, of primary interest to our discussion is the axiom implicit in R' Yochanan's words, "Is there anything written in Scripture that is not alluded to in the Torah?" As if to say, anything written later in Tanach must *necessarily* be found in the Torah. As *Rashi* explains, "For

---

2   9a.
3   *Mishlei* 19:3.

the Chumash is the foundation of the *Neviim* and *Kesuvim*, and everything contained therein has an allusion that can be found in the Torah."[4]

FURTHER EXAMPLES: "THE MENTION OF A TZADDIK IS FOR A BLESSING"

This idea finds similar expression elsewhere in the Talmud. The Gemara in *Maseches Yoma* records the following exchange:[5]

> Said Ravina to the rabbi who would recites Aggados before him, "What is the source of that which the Rabbis say, 'The mention of a tzaddik is for a blessing'?"
> He [the rabbi] said to him [Ravina], "For the verse states, 'The mention of a tzaddik is for a blessing.'"[6]
> [Ravina continued]: "From where do we know this in the Torah [i.e., the Chumash]?"
> [The rabbi answered]: "For it is written, 'And Hashem said, "Shall I hide from Avraham that which I am doing?"'[7] And it [then] states, 'And Avraham will be a great and powerful nation.'"[8]

Let us ask, if Ravina does not know *from where* in the Torah the idea that "the mention of a *tzaddik* is for a blessing" is derived, how does he know *that it is* to be derived from there at all? Apparently, it is obvious to Ravina that if something is written later in Tanach, it *must be* contained somewhere within the Torah; all that remains is to find out where in the Torah it is contained.

---

4   *Taanis* loc. cit., s.v. *ve'lo.*
5   38b.
6   *Mishlei* 10:7.
7   *Bereishis* 18:17.
8   Ibid., verse 18. [See glosses of R' Akiva Eiger to *Yoma* loc. cit., who refers to *Rashi's* comments at the beginning of *Parshas Noach* (*Bereishis* 6:9, s.v. *eileh*), where he adduces the principle that "the remembrance of a *tzaddik* is for a blessing" in his explanation of the verse there. With this reference, R' Akiva Eiger is implicitly raising the question as to why the Gemara does not likewise identify this earlier verse as the source of this principle, deriving it rather from the later verses dealing with Avraham.

THE PRINCIPLE: NEVIIM AND KESUVIM
AS EXPLICATING IDEAS OF THE TORAH

The question that now arises is: If, indeed, every idea mentioned in *Neviim* and *Kesuvim* is already to be found in the Torah, what is the purpose of these ideas being "repeated" in *Neviim* and *Kesuvim*?

Clearly, although these ideas are all *contained* within the Torah, they are not necessarily readily *discernible* from reading the Torah itself. To this end, they are stated clearly in the *Neviim* and *Kesuvim*. It is worth noting that R' Yochanan's statement informs us that the relationship between ideas alluded to in the Torah and expressed in *Nach* is *exclusive* in nature; for if there is nothing written in *Nach* that is not alluded to in the Torah, then nothing exists in *Nach* which is not an explication of an idea in the Torah. Moreover, it is for the very purpose of such explication that it is written later on.[9]

To put it differently: The earliest commentary on the Torah is *Neviim* and *Kesuvim*!

"THAT I HAVE WRITTEN"—THESE ARE NEVIIM AND KESUVIM

It is possible to perceive this idea within a statement of Reish Lakish, as recorded in *Maseches Berachos*:[10]

> *What is the meaning of the verse, "And I will give you the tablets of stone and the Torah and the commandment that I have written to instruct them"?[11]*
>
> - *"The tablets of stone"—these are the Ten Commandments.*
> - *"The Torah"—this is Scripture.[12]*
> - *"And the commandment"—this is Mishnah.*
> - *"That I have written"—these are Neviim and Kesuvim.*
> - *"To instruct them"—this is Gemara.*
>
> *This teaches that all of them were given to Moshe at Sinai.*

---

9   With regard to the parameters of deriving halachic teachings from *Neviim* and *Kesuvim* to matters of Torah law, see *Chagigah* 10b, *Bava Kama* 2b, and *Niddah* 23a.

10   5a.

11   *Shemos* 24:12.

12   I.e., the Chumash.

We note that the reference to *Neviim* and *Kesuvim* is contained within the words, "That I have written." Let us suggest that the intention is that although the events described in the *Neviim* and *Kesuvim* had not yet occurred, nor had the verses of those sections of Tanach been written, nonetheless, the ideas which they discuss are all to be found *in the Torah itself*—"which I have [already] written!"

NEVIIM, KESUVIM AND THE SIN OF THE GOLDEN CALF

This idea will help illuminate a statement that is found in *Maseches Nedarim:*[13]

> Said Rav Ada son of Rav Chanina: Had Israel not sinned [with the Golden Calf], they would have been given only the five Chumashim and the Book of Yehoshua, which contains the [allotted] portions of the land of Israel.

On the face of it, this statement is somewhat baffling, for it implies that had we not made the Golden Calf, we would have missed out on all the lessons found within *Neviim* and *Kesuvim*! How can sinning give us access to Torah ideas from which we would otherwise have been deprived?

Rather, the point is that had we not sinned and fallen from the exalted level which we attained at Mount Sinai, we would not have needed *Neviim* and *Kesuvim* to explicate the ideas of the Torah for us. Our vision would have been keen enough to detect these ideas ourselves within the Torah, rendering the formulations of the *Neviim* and *Kesuvim* redundant.[14]

Indeed, in this light, we can understand the statement of the *Talmud Yerushalmi*,[15] as codified by the *Rambam*,[16] that in the future, all the books of *Neviim* and *Kesuvim* will be discontinued, with the exception

---

13 22b.
14 The *Netziv*, Second Introduction *Kidmas Ha'emek* to the *She'iltos* of Rav Achai; R' Yaakov Kamenetsky, Preface *Mevo L'limud Hamikra* to commentary *Emes L'Yaakov* on the Torah.
15 *Megillah* 1:5.
16 *Hilchos Chanukah U'Megillah* 2:8.

of *Megillas Esther*, concerning which it says, "And their remembrance [of the events of Purim] will not depart from their [the Jewish People's] descendants."[17] Needless to say, this statement requires some explanation. Why should works of Torah be discontinued in the future?[18] The commentators[19] explain this assertion based on the above idea: In the future, we will yet return to a level where we will be able to perceive all the concepts contained within the Torah from our study of the Torah itself, and will no longer need the *Neviim* and *Kesuvim* to identify them for us. The only exception will be the book of *Esther*, where there is a specific mitzvah to read it in order to commemorate the miracle described therein.

"JOYOUS AS WHEN THEY WERE GIVEN AT SINAI"

Moreover, this idea will give us further insight into a phrase which is found concerning certain cases in the words of Chazal. The *Talmud Yerushalmi* describes the event of the *bris* of Elisha ben Avuyah.[20] All the notables of Jerusalem were assembled, but the *bris* was late in starting. R' Eliezer and R' Yehoshua, who were also present, decided to use the time to study Torah, which they proceeded to do, whereupon they were enveloped by fire. Avuyah, their host, rushed over to them in alarm and exclaimed, "Have you come to burn down my house?!" The Sages replied:

> Heaven forbid! Rather, we were sitting and reviewing words of Torah, from the Torah to the Neviim and from the Neviim to the Kesuvim, and the words were joyous as when they were given from Sinai. Were the words of Torah not themselves given in fire?

What is the meaning of this distinctive description? What was it about the way these Sages were learning which rendered the words

---

17 *Esther* 9:28.
18 See glosses of *Raavad* to *Rambam* ibid., and Responsa *Radvaz*, vol. 2, sec. 666.
19 See commentary *Manos Halevi* (by R' Shlomo Halevi Alkabetz) and commentary of R' Moshe Alshich to *Esther*, loc. cit.
20 *Chagigah* chap. 2, cited in *Tosafos* ibid., 15a, s.v. *shuvu*.

of Torah "joyous," and why specifically as "when they were given from Sinai"?

Interestingly, this phrase appears elsewhere in the Aggadic literature, and is adduced regarding a similar form of learning Torah. *Midrash Shir Hashirim Rabbah* states:[21]

> Ben Azzai was sitting and expounding and a fire surrounded him. R' Akiva inquired as to what he was involving himself with. Ben Azzai replied, "I was sitting and threading through [chorez] words of Torah, and from the Torah to Neviim and from Neviim to Kesuvim, and the words were as joyous as when they were given at Sinai."

It appears that the unusual distinction of words that were "as joyous as when they were given from Sinai" derives from the particular way in which these scholars were engaged in Torah study. In both cases, they were learning, or "threading through," from Torah to *Neviim* and from *Neviim* to *Kesuvim*. This "threading through" involved identifying the ideas embedded within the Torah as they were subsequently explicated in the *Neviim* and *Kesuvim*.[22] Essentially, they were learning the Chumash with the vision that the Jewish People originally had when the Torah was given to them at Sinai, and, hence, they succeeded as well in reproducing the conditions in which the Torah itself was given and became surrounded by fire.

This fascinating and far-reaching idea of the role of *Neviim* and *Kesuvim* as "the earliest commentary on the Torah" will no doubt serve as a basis for approaching these areas of Tanach with new eyes. Hopefully, it will, in turn, yield further insight into the words of the Chumash itself—rendering its messages "as joyous as when they were given at Sinai!"

---

21 1:10, s.v. *tzavarech*.

22 A simple reading of these words implies that the ideas that Ben Azzai found in the Torah were explicated both in the *Neviim* and the *Kesuvim*. From numerous places in the Gemara, however, it appears that there are only certain noteworthy cases where an idea appears in all three sections of the Tanach; see, e.g., *Megillah* 31a, *Mo'ed Katan* 17b, and *Makkos* 10b.

UNDERSTANDING YOSEF'S ACCUSING THE BROTHERS OF BEING SPIES

וַיֹּאמֶר אֲלֵהֶם מְרַגְּלִים אַתֶּם לִרְאוֹת אֶת עֶרְוַת הָאָרֶץ בָּאתֶם.

He said to them, "You are spies! It is to see the land's weakness that you have come."[1]

INTRODUCTION

Much attention has been devoted by the commentators over the generations to understand Yosef's intention in accusing the brothers of being spies, with all the trauma that this entailed, not only for them, but also for their father, Yaakov. As we will see, this is directly connected to another basic question in these parshiyos: Why did Yosef not make contact with his family at any point during the twenty-two years that he was away? Granted, the early years did not give him much of an opportunity, but once he was effectively ruler of the country, he surely could have found a way.

Classic responses to these questions from the early commentators are either that Yosef's actions were in order to allow for the fulfillment

---

1   *Bereishis* 42:9.

of his dreams or, alternatively, to bring about the rectification of the rupture in family unity that had culminated in the brothers selling him.[2] Other commentators, however, question whether either of these goals lay within Yosef's mandate. This leads them to take a third approach to this matter.[3]

To understand the background to this approach, we need to first appreciate why the brothers originally wanted to kill Yosef, and how that idea then came to be commuted into instead selling him to Egypt.

THE BROTHERS' ORIGINAL VERDICT CONCERNING YOSEF

An idea that is found in numerous commentators is that the brothers saw Yosef as seeking to exclude them from being part of Yaakov's family and spiritual legacy.[4] Already the favored son, Yosef's negative reports to their father about them were seen as an attempt to condemn them as unworthy of being members of the future Jewish People. We should bear in mind that prior to this point, the fact that one was born from one of the Avos did not automatically guarantee a share in their legacy. After all, of Avraham's numerous sons, only Yitzchak remained as a continuation from him. Likewise, of Yitzchak's own two sons, Yaakov alone continued his legacy.

And so, faced with what was thus perceived as an existential spiritual threat, the brothers judged that Yosef himself deserved to be killed. Moreover, we can now understand why, when the avenue presented itself for him to be sold as a slave to Egypt, the brothers modified their plan and availed themselves of that option. Since the primary goal was not to kill Yosef, but merely to remove him as a threat, they judged that anything that would effectively bar him from posing that threat would be an acceptable solution. As a slave in Egypt, Yosef's capacity for communication would be nullified, and hence, there would be no need to actually kill him.

---

2   See, e.g., commentaries of *Ramban, Abarbanel, Akeidas Yitzchak, Kli Yakar,* and *Ohr Hachaim* to *Bereishis* loc. cit.

3   This approach is found in the commentaries *Emes L'Yaakov* of R' Yaakov Kamenetsky and *Ben Melech* of R' Leib Mintzberg.

4   See, e.g., *Roke'ach* and *Malbim,* beginning of *Parshas Vayeishev.*

The implication of this idea is that the only thing which prevented Yosef from being killed by the brothers is the notion that sending him away would remove him from the picture. As such, as long as the brothers' position regarding him remained unchanged, to try and communicate with his father would very simply endanger his life. If the brothers were to see that his being distanced from home did not deter him from his path and that sending him away had not dealt with the problem, they would likely proceed to find him and kill him. Even when Yosef became second in command of Egypt, he did not rely on that position to protect him against the brothers' verdict, for Yosef knew full well not to underestimate what they were capable of doing. In other words, it was eminently clear to Yosef that unless the brothers came to change their view concerning him, he could not communicate with them without endangering his life.

But what could change the brothers' minds? What might bring them to believe that they had, perhaps, misjudged Yosef and wrongly accused him of seeking to expose their flaws for his own gain?

THE OTHER SIDE OF ACCUSATION

This brings us to Yosef's actions toward the brothers when they arrive in Egypt to buy food. Yosef promptly accuses them of being spies. This is the first stage of a process aimed at their reorientation. Here, the brothers experience acutely what it is like to be accused of something that is not true. Hopefully, this will plant within their consciousness the notion that a person can be misjudged.

The next stage in this process is one that can be easily overlooked, but which actually began to effect change within the brothers. Yosef's original offer for the brothers to clear their name was to incarcerate all of them and allow only one to return home and fetch their younger brother. However, after three days, he came to them saying that as a God-fearing person, he was prepared to revise the original plan and let them all go home, keeping only one brother as collateral. Essentially, Yosef was saying, "I may have been overly harsh in my original plan, and I am prepared to reconsider." Here too, the hope was that the brothers may witness a person re-evaluating his initial judgment and apply such a strategy with regard to their own dealings with Yosef. For if the ruler of Egypt can, of his own volition, admit that he may have misjudged someone, then maybe so can they! And, indeed, it is fascinating to note that at this point, the verse relates that the brothers began to voice regret in some form over the sale of Yosef.

This development on the brothers' part, while certainly encouraging, is not enough for Yosef to know that it is safe to reveal his identity, for he will then simply reveal himself as the perpetrator of more trouble for them, thereby undoing any change of heart that he may have engendered up to now. Therefore, although he turns aside and weeps over the sentiments that he is hearing from them, he nevertheless composes himself and prepares for the next stage—bringing Binyamin down to Egypt.

BINYAMIN'S ROLE

The placing of the silver cup in Binyamin's sack enabled the final part of Yosef's plan, for it brought the brothers to again wrongfully suspect one of their number of a crime. It is interesting to consider, in this light, the feast that Yosef has with the brothers when they arrive in Egypt for the second time, eating and drinking with them. Seeing as Yosef had not yet finished presenting them with distressing situations, what was the role of this feast? Perhaps, it was in order to engender a feeling of security vis-à-vis the brothers and himself, so that when the cup was found, they did not suspect him of being behind it, but rather cast their suspicions on Binyamin.

With this element brought to mind, it was finally safe for Yosef to reveal that it was him, for the idea that they had wrongfully suspected him all those years ago was reinforced by the presence of Binyamin, to whom they had done so again right now. Indeed, it is fascinating to consider in this regard that the shock of the brothers upon finding out that this ruler was in fact Yosef, whom they had sold to Egypt so many years ago, must have been exceeded exponentially by Binyamin's shock upon discovering that all this had occurred. As far as we know, this was the first that Binyamin had heard of the sale, and, when that happened, everything changed. We tend to focus on the brothers' feelings of shame and confoundedness regarding Yosef at this moment, but alongside those were similar feelings in terms of Binyamin. At this point, the brothers' accusations toward him abruptly evaporated in light of the revelation of their own guilt. With the foundations of their attitude toward Yosef totally shattered, he was finally able to reveal his identity to the brothers, beginning the process of re-appraising the past, as well as taking stock in terms of the future, for themselves and for their father, Yaakov.

FROM THE COMMENTATORS

TWO ADDITIONAL YEARS

וַיְהִי מִקֵּץ שְׁנָתַיִם יָמִים.

It happened at the end of two years.[1]

Our parsha begins two years after Yosef made his request to the chief butler to remember him to Pharaoh. Indeed, the Midrash states that these two years were a punishment for Yosef's words at that time, for they represented a breach of *bitachon* (trust in Hashem) on Yosef's part.[2] However, we need to understand why this request was looked upon in such a negative light. By that stage, Yosef had been in jail for ten years and the butler's release presented an opportunity for him to secure his own release. Is it not acceptable to engage in *hishtadlus* (effort) alongside *bitachon*? Was he expected to do nothing? Additionally, why did this infraction lead to two extra years?

Bitachon is typically referred to as a "trait." However, a more meaningful understanding of *bitachon* is that it is a mood. After all, when one trusts in someone else and relies on him, one's mood is free from the anxiety that would exist if he had to deal with the situation by himself.

---

1   *Bereishis* 41:1.
2   Cited in *Rashi* to *Bereishis* 40:23, s.v. *vayishkacheihu*.

Indeed, this is the description of *bitachon* as found in the classic work *Chovos Halevavos:*[3]

"Trust" is the peace of mind that one has as he relies on someone else.

In other words, *bitachon* is not defined by what one does or does not do. Those actions are *expressions* of *bitachon*; *bitachon* itself is a mood and a state of being.

In this light, let us consider the following fascinating and profound approach as to where Yosef was found wanting, provided by R' Shlomo Kluger. It may well have been acceptable for Yosef to ask the butler to remember him, as that represents basic *hishtadlus*. However, even if the request itself was legitimate, the question remains—when is the right time to ask? Yosef has just established, through his own interpretation of the dream, that the butler will be released from jail in three days' time. This means that until day three, he is not going anywhere. But Yosef asks him immediately, even though he does not need to mention this to the butler for another two days. Why does he ask now? In terms of the exceedingly high standard of *bitachon* expected of Yosef, making this request two days early was a symptom of unease and anxiety. It was as if he couldn't afford to wait another two days. For the level of reliance expected from Yosef, this was a breach of the mood of *bitachon*, for which he spent another two years in jail. Moreover, we now understand why the extension was for two years specifically, one for each day that he unnecessarily advanced his request.

As always, we are not expected to conduct ourselves in accordance with the level expected of the greats of the Chumash. We are, however, fully expected to learn the relevant lessons from them, to be applied at our own level. Every application of the mood of *bitachon* into our own experience will serve to give more meaning to those two extra years through which the Torah taught it.

---

3   *Shaar Habitachon*, chap. 4.

PHARAOH'S DREAMS—AND THE DAY
YOSEF WAS REMEMBERED

וַיְהִי מִקֵּץ שְׁנָתַיִם יָמִים וּפַרְעֹה חֹלֵם.

It happened at the end of two years, and Pharaoh was dreaming.[4]

The beginning of our parsha relates how, two years after the chief butler was released from prison, Pharaoh had dreams that no one could interpret, at which point the chief butler recalled Yosef who had interpreted his dreams and recommended that he be brought before Pharaoh. Rav Yosef Nechemiah Kornitzer[5] raises two basic questions regarding this episode:

- Verse 8 states that in the morning, Pharaoh was agitated concerning his dreams, whereupon he sent for "all the magicians and wise men in Egypt" to tell them his dreams, yet none could interpret them to Pharaoh's satisfaction. We can only imagine how many hundreds, if not thousands, of wise men existed throughout the land of Egypt; yet the verse says that Pharaoh was able to assemble them all—as well as to hear all their interpretations—within one morning! How was this possible?

- The final verse of the previous parsha informs us that whereas Yosef asked the chief butler to mention him to Pharaoh, the latter forgot about Yosef for two years, remembering him only two years later. The question is: Barring Pharaoh requiring Yosef's services—such as now, when he has had these obscure dreams—what meaningful opportunity would there have been for Yosef to be mentioned? Surely, we do not imagine that the chief butler's relationship with Pharaoh was such that purely apropos of nothing, he could just mention that there was someone in jail whom he recommended should be released. In the

---

4   *Bereishis* 41:1.

5   A great-grandson of the *Chasam Sofer* and the Rav in Krakow in the early part of the twentieth century; *Chiddushei Rav Yosef Nechemiah, Parshas Mikeitz.*

absence of some opportune time to mention Yosef, in what way do we understand that the chief butler "forgot him"?

Rav Kornitzer therefore explains that these two dreams were not experienced by Pharaoh on just one occasion two years after the chief butler had been released. Rather, Pharaoh had these dreams *every night* during these two years. In other words, when the opening verse states *"u'Pharaoh cholem,"* it is not to be translated as, "Pharaoh was dreaming," but "Pharaoh was *still* dreaming"! Accordingly, when the later verse says that in the morning he called all the wise men of Egypt, this describes the scene that would take place *every morning during those two years*, over the course of which Pharaoh had the opportunity to hear from all the wise men in the land, none of whom could successfully interpret the dreams.

We now appreciate the full impact of the idea that the chief butler "did not remember Yosef," for throughout these entire two years when Pharaoh was in dire need of assistance, the idea of Yosef as a worthy candidate eluded him. Indeed, this gives us new insight into his opening words to Pharaoh, "אֶת חֲטָאַי אֲנִי מַזְכִּיר הַיּוֹם"—I recall my sins today."[6] To what is he referring? If it is to the episode that led to him being thrown into jail, that is one sin; why does he mention "sins" in the plural? Rather, says Rav Kornitzer, in mentioning Yosef to Pharaoh only now, he was admitting his sins, i.e., every day over the past two years when he had not brought Yosef to Pharaoh's attention!

That is a *chiddush*!

REMAND, REMORSE, AND REVELATIONS

אִם כֵּנִים אַתֶּם אֲחִיכֶם אֶחָד יֵאָסֵר בְּבֵית מִשְׁמַרְכֶם...וְאֶת אֲחִיכֶם הַקָּטֹן תָּבִיאוּ אֵלַי וְיֵאָמְנוּ דִבְרֵיכֶם...וַיִּקַּח מֵאִתָּם אֶת שִׁמְעוֹן וַיֶּאֱסֹר אֹתוֹ לְעֵינֵיהֶם.

If you are truthful people, let one of your brothers be imprisoned in your place of incarceration...and bring your youngest

---

6 Verse 9.

brother to me, so that your words will be verified…and he took
Shimon from them and imprisoned him before their eyes.[7]

The commentators, starting with *Rashi*, discuss the question as to why, of all the brothers, Shimon was the one chosen by Yosef to stay behind in remand. It is also very interesting to note what appears to be an interruption or digression in this particular exchange. Yosef's words to the brothers are recorded in verses 19–20, while his imprisoning Shimon is described in verse 24. In the intervening verses 21–23, the Torah relates how the brothers began to express remorse over not showing compassion toward Yosef. One of the classic commentators among the Rishonim, Rabbeinu Yosef Bechor Shor, explains that the reason the Torah records the brothers' words at this juncture is because they were responsible for Yosef's choice of Shimon as the brother to stay behind.

The natural choice for who would remain in Egypt was Reuven, who was the oldest of the brothers, and therefore responsible for them. And, indeed, this was Yosef's initial intention. However, he then heard the brothers talking among themselves about their predicament and what had likely caused it. Verse 21 records the brothers saying that it was because they had not heeded Yosef's cries at the time of the sale. Verse 22 then describes how Reuven told them that they should have listened to him when he initially objected to them taking action against Yosef.

Yosef, who, as the verse describes, was listening to their words and understood everything that they were saying, now discovered two things. The first, that they were beginning to regret the sale, was presumably something he was hoping to hear. It is fascinating to consider, however, that the second matter, that Reuven had actually objected to them harming him, was something of which he, heretofore, had *no prior inkling.* After all, his entire experience with the brothers on that fateful day only began from the time that he approached them; he had no knowledge of their discussions before he approached them. Indeed, when verse 24 states that he turned away from them and wept, perhaps

---

7   *Bereishis* 42:19–20, 24.

it was over both of these revelations—those concerning the brothers as well as those concerning Reuven. At any rate, when he returned, he no longer chose Reuven as the one to stay behind on the brothers' behalf, choosing instead Shimon, the next oldest brother, as stated in the end of verse 24.

PARSHAS VAYIGASH

YEHUDAH'S CONFRONTATION WITH YOSEF

"A Word in Your Ear, My Lord"

INTRODUCTION

Our parsha begins with Yehudah's impassioned plea before Yosef on Binyamin's behalf. With the silver goblet having been found in Binyamin's sack, and facing the unbearable prospect of returning home to their father without him, Yehudah steps forward to offer a word "in Yosef's ears," in a desperate attempt to elicit some form of clemency from the Egyptian ruler.

REMEMBRANCE OF THINGS UNSAID

As we survey Yehudah's review of the events that led to this point, it is most interesting—and somewhat baffling—to notice that a number of items in his account do not match up with the events themselves as they occurred. This discrepancy begins with the very first thing that Yehudah says. He recalls:

אֲדֹנִי שָׁאַל אֶת עֲבָדָיו לֵאמֹר הֲיֵשׁ לָכֶם אָב אוֹ אָח.

My master asked his servants, saying, "Do you have a father or brother?"[1]

---

1   *Bereishis* 44:19.

When we look back at the first meeting between Yosef and the brothers, we see that Yosef asked them no such question. All information regarding their family was volunteered by the brothers in order to clear themselves from the charge of being spies.[2] Why, then, does Yehudah open by describing a question that was never asked?

A further famous departure from events as they occurred is where Yehudah states that the brothers had originally said that one of their number was dead.[3] In actual fact, they said that one of the brothers was missing.[4] Why did Yehudah make this change? *Rashi* comments that he was afraid that if he presented the original version, the ruler would tell him to bring the missing brother to him; therefore, he changed it to say that the brother was dead. However, surely to actively deviate from the initial response as given would involve greater and more immediate risk than the potential concern that they might be asked to bring a brother who was, after all, missing! Why was his taking this step of changing "missing" to "dead" considered to be the more preferred option?

ENTRAPMENT AND THE MEANING OF THE WORD "LEIMOR"

According to the *Alshich Hakadosh*, the key word in Yehudah's opening sentence is the word "*leimor*." This word is commonly translated simply as "saying." However, many commentators understand the word "*leimor*" as the infinitive of the verb "*amar*" and translate it as "to say." Within the context of someone asking a question, this word denotes that one is asking for the other person "to say" something back to him.[5] In this light, we understand that Yehudah is not stating that Yosef actually asked them if they had a father or brother; rather, Yosef asked them something with the intent of *them* saying this.

To understand how this is so, let us consider Yosef's opening question, which was: "*Me'ayin basem*—From where are you coming?"[6] Although this inquiry appears simple enough, we note that no sooner had the

---

2   Ibid., 42:9–13.
3   44:20.
4   42:13.
5   See *Rashi, Bamidbar* 12:13.
6   *Bereishis* 42:7.

brothers answered it, saying that they were from Canaan and had come to buy food, than Yosef proceeds to accuse them of being spies! Where in the exchange thus far could we possibly detect the basis for such an accusation? Were these the only people from the entire neighboring land of Canaan who had come to buy grain?

In truth, however, the question "From where are you coming?" is somewhat ambiguous, since it does not simply ask, "Where are you from?"[7] It could be understood as also asking, "and what brings you here?" This open-ended question, together with the harsh tone in which it was asked,[8] led the brothers to feel that they should provide a full response, stating that they are from the land of Canaan and that they have come to buy food. With that response, they have already opened themselves to accusation. For since Yosef did not actually ask them why they had come, to present the reason of buying food could be seen as volunteering *too much information*; for, indeed, wasn't that why everyone was there? Yosef was thus able to claim that their stating the obvious was in order to mask the real reason that they were there—to spy out the land. In this situation, the brothers feel compelled to establish their innocence, including full details of their family back home.[9] In light of Yosef's apparent fixation on their family from that point on, Yehudah, looking back, is able to argue that Yosef's question from the outset was purely "*leimor*," to get them to say that they had a brother.

Indeed, Yehudah further asserts that upon reflection, the accusation of them being spies was clearly a fabrication, seeing as Yosef proceeded to *send them home* to bring down their brother. If he really suspected them of being spies who had gathered information harmful to his country, the last thing he would do would be to allow them to return home, enabling them, thereby, to share their findings with the Canaanites! Clearly, says Yehudah, it was Binyamin who was the focus from the outset.

---

7   Compare Yaakov's question to the shepherds at the well (*Bereishis* 29:4).
8   "And he spoke with them harshly and asked them, 'From where do you come?'" (ibid., 42:7).
9   See *Beis Halevi, Parshas Mikeitz*.

A SHIFT IN VISION

A basic question that arises is: What brought on this sudden change in approach on Yehudah's part, prompting him to reappraise the entire situation and confront the Egyptian viceroy with his findings? This is especially striking when we consider that as recently as the very end of *Parshas Mikeitz*, when the cup was found in Binyamin's sack, Yehudah himself accepted for them all to be slaves to Yosef. What changed now? We might be inclined to respond simply that this was the product of desperation in the face of the prospect of returning home without Binyamin. However, the *Alshich* explains that a more fundamental shift was taking place at this time. As we can see from the verses, already fairly early on in this saga, the brothers related to their predicament as punishment for their actions toward Yosef. As such, they were not inclined to ascribe too much significance *per se* to the individual in front of them or to his unpredictable ways, for they saw him essentially as an instrument of Divine retribution.

All of this came to a sudden crash when the silver cup was found in Binyamin's sack, resulting in the viceroy stating that *Binyamin alone* would stay with him as a slave, while the rest of them were free to return home. This new development completely undermined their interpretation of events; now, the only one who was to endure punishment at the hands of this Egyptian ruler was specifically the only brother who was not involved in the sale! With their prior understanding of their situation lying shattered in pieces before them, they finally began to take a closer look at the viceroy himself, and Yehudah felt it was warranted to shift from a compliant and submissive stance to assuming a more proactive role in confronting him in terms of his behavior.

IN THE SHADOW OF THE BRIS BEIN HABESARIM

There is a further fascinating point to consider in all this, which is mentioned by the *Beis Yisrael* of Gur.[10] Already three generations earlier, Hashem had foretold to Avraham in the episode known as the *Bris Bein*

---

10   Recorded by R' Shiloh Refael and printed in the *Sefer Zikaron* to his memory, p. 599.

Habesarim (Covenant Between the Pieces) that his descendants would be "slaves in a land that was not theirs."[11] Assuming that knowledge of this future event was passed down to the subsequent generations of Avraham's household, we will appreciate that although no one knew how or when this decree would unfold, there was nevertheless an ongoing latent expectation of servitude in a foreign land that would take place at some time. Accordingly, when force of circumstance brought the brothers down to Egypt, with the baffling and bewildering experiences that ensued, there was a sense on some level that those events, which had been foretold to Avraham, were now being initiated. For this reason, the brothers submitted to what they understood as the implementation of a Divine decree, culminating in them *pronouncing themselves Yosef's servants* when the cup was found in Binyamin's sack.

However, this model was also shattered when Yosef announced that they could all return home, with only Binyamin remaining as his servant. With all but one of their number being absolved of any servitude, they were forced to move away from any notion that this was a fulfillment of the decree to Avraham, and to approach the situation in a radically different way.

In fact, it is even possible that upon fundamentally reappraising his understanding of the viceroy's actions toward them, and exploring an alternative explanation for them, Yehudah actually began to consider the unthinkable.

YEHUDAH IN SEARCH OF YOSEF

One of the great Torah Sages of sixteenth-century Tzefas, R' Shlomo Halevi Alkabetz, makes a stunning comment regarding this episode.[12] He states that at this stage, taking stock of everything that had happened, Yehudah actually started to suspect that this viceroy before them was, in fact, Yosef. Although he looked very different from when the brothers last saw him and was speaking a foreign dialect—and even

---

11 *Bereishis* 15:13.
12 Famous as the author of the song *Lechah Dodi*. Rav Alkabetz's words are cited by R' Shmuel Laniado in his commentary *Kli Chemdah* to our parsha.

then, not directly to them—nevertheless, Yehudah could not dismiss the notion that it might be Yosef. The question was, what to do? He could hardly confront him and ask him outright if he was Yosef. This would be too dangerous a move in case he was wrong; in any case, Yosef could simply deny it. Therefore, Yehudah took a different strategy—the first part of which was asking for the interpreter to be removed.

According to the Midrash, when Yehudah asked that he be able to speak a word "in my master's ears," he was requesting to be able to address the ruler and put his case before him directly, a request that he hoped would be granted to him on compassionate grounds.[13] On the face of it, this idea seems like a complete waste of this crucial opportunity, as in using a translator until this point, the ruler has clearly indicated that he does not speak their language! However, based on the approach of Rav Alkabetz, we can understand that this was Yehudah's very intention—to reveal that this ruler really did understand his language, with further revelations, hopefully, following from that. This gives us a completely different picture of this confrontation, for it effectively entailed Yehudah pleading before Yosef *in Hebrew*, laying out their innocence and their father's anguish in full detail, with Yosef, for his part, doing his best to maintain an appearance of not understanding a word Yehudah was saying!

Is there anything Yehudah could say, beyond his impassioned portrayal of their father's grief, that would force Yosef to reveal that he understood what was being said to him? Perhaps, we can now understand Yehudah's motive in modifying the original version, in which they said that Yosef was missing, to saying that he was dead. Since his primary goal was to provoke a reaction from Yosef, who officially did not understand his words, there was no more likely way to do so than to tell him he was dead! On the other hand, if this ruler was not actually Yosef and really did not understand Yehudah's words, then there was no risk anyway, as the change would go unnoticed.

---

13   Cited in *Torah Sheleimah*, sec. 65. See also *Haamek Davar*.

As we know, Yehudah's words found their mark, and by the time he was finished, Yosef could no longer withhold his identity from the brothers. The time for revelation had arrived, as the ensuing verses proceed to describe.

CONCEPT:
TAAMEI HAMIKRA
AS COMMENTARY

וַיִּגַּשׁ אֵלָיו יְהוּדָה וַיֹּאמֶר בִּי אֲדֹנִי...

Yehudah approached him [Yosef] and said, "Please, my master..."[1]

BACKGROUND

One of the features accompanying the words of the Torah are the cantillation notes, known as *taamei hamikra* or *trop*. These notes indicate how the words of the verse should be sung, with each sign having its own distinctive melody. The *taamim* date back to antiquity; according to many opinions, they were given to Moshe together with the Torah at Sinai.[2]

---

1   *44:18.*
2   See, e.g., *Kuzari, maamar* 3, sec. 31; *Rabbeinu Bachya* to *Bereishis* 5:29; Responsa *Radvaz*, vol. 3, sec. 1068; and R' Yaakov Emden, *Migdal Oz, Aliyas Hakesivah.* According to other opinions, the *taamim* were added in the time of Ezra; see, e.g., commentaries of *Tosafos, Rosh* and *Ran* to *Nedarim* 37b and *Abarbanel,* Introduction to *Sefer Yirmiyahu.*

TAAMIM THAT JOIN AND TAAMIM
THAT SEPARATE: SHEM AND YEFES

It is important to realize that in addition to the melodic aspect of the *taamim*, they also contribute to our understanding of the words themselves. The most obvious expression of this idea is the fact that some *taamim* join words together, while others separate them by denoting pauses of varying degrees. Clearly, the way in which we group the words will impact on our understanding of their meaning.

A simple illustration of this idea can be found in the verse[3] which describes Shem as "אֲחִי יֶפֶת הַגָּדוֹל." The word "*hagadol*" means "big" and denotes the eldest brother. The question is: *Who* was the eldest brother? To whom does the word "*hagadol*" refer? Does it qualify the word "Yefes," indicating that he was the eldest, or does it rather qualify the word "*achi*," stating that Shem was the eldest brother? The answer can be derived from the *taamim* of these words. The *taam* under the word "אֲחִי" is known as a *tipcha*. It is—conveniently—shaped like a comma, and indeed, serves as a minor pause. On the other hand, the *taam* under the word "יֶפֶת" is known as a *mercha* and serves to connect it to the word that follows—"*hagadol*." Thus, the *taamim* are informing us that the way to read these words is that Shem was "the brother of (אֲחִי) Yefes the eldest (יֶפֶת הַגָּדוֹל)."[4]

TAAMIM THAT EMPHASIZE: PHARAOH AND YAAKOV

A fascinating example of a more subtle type of meaning to be gleaned from the *taamei hamikra* can be found in our parsha. When Yosef introduces his father, Yaakov, to Pharaoh, we find the following exchange between the two:

וַיֹּאמֶר פַּרְעֹה אֶל־יַעֲקֹב כַּמָּה יְמֵי שְׁנֵי חַיֶּיךָ. וַיֹּאמֶר יַעֲקֹב אֶל־פַּרְעֹה יְמֵי שְׁנֵי מְגוּרַי שְׁלֹשִׁים וּמְאַת שָׁנָה מְעַט וְרָעִים הָיוּ יְמֵי שְׁנֵי חַיַּי.

---

3   *Bereishis* 10:21.
4   See *Sanhedrin* 69b, and *Rashi* to *Bereishis* ibid. For a similar discussion, see *Chagigah* 6b, discussing the understanding of the verse in *Shemos* 24:5.

Pharaoh said to Yaakov, "How many are the days of the years of your life?" Yaakov said to Pharaoh, "The days of the years of my sojourns have been a hundred and thirty years. Few and bad have been the days of the years of my life."

Yaakov's answer to Pharaoh's question is somewhat mystifying. Having been asked by the latter as to how old he was, why did he not content himself by simply replying with his age, continuing instead to comment on the quality of his years?

One of the Rishonim, the *Rashbatz*,[5] explains that Pharaoh's words to Yaakov were not merely asked as a *question*, but were rather said as an *exclamation*. Yaakov looked so worn and weathered that Pharaoh could not help but wonder how old he was! This understanding, he adds, is indicated by the *taamei hamikra*. Had Pharaoh merely been asking, "How old are you?" the *taamim* accompanying his words would have joined them all together as one. However, the *taam* on the word "כַּמֶּה" is known as a *zakef* and denotes a pause for emphasis. In this light, we now understand that Pharaoh was actually exclaiming, "How *old* are you?" which is a somewhat different question, expressing his disbelief that a person could be as old as Yaakov looked. In response to this, Yaakov answered, first by stating his years, and then by proceeding to explain how the difficulties of those years had given him such an aged appearance beyond their actual number.[6]

THE COMMENTARY OF THE TAAMIM: BROKEN LADDERS

Taking this discussion to a completely different level, we now come to an approach to *taamei hamikra* that is found in the writings of the *Vilna Gaon*.[7] According to him, the *taamim* not only tell us how to *read* the words, but can themselves serve as a *commentary* on those words. Let us see one or two examples of this approach before returning to the opening verse of our parsha.

---

5   Rabbeinu Shimon ben Tzemach Duran, *Magen Avos*, vol. 3, p. 56a.

6   See similarly, *Rabbeinu Bachya* to *Bereishis* 39:8, who writes that the *taamei hamikra* reflect the facial expression and gesticulation (body language) that accompany a person's words.

7   In addition to the examples cited below in *Kol Eliyahu*, see also *Aderes Eliyahu, Shemos* 30:15.

The Gemara relates that on one occasion, Rav Papa was ascending a ladder, when one of the rungs of the ladder broke and Rav Papa nearly fell and injured himself. Upon witnessing this, his colleague, Rav Chiya bar Rav, commented, "Perhaps a poor person approached you and you did not respond adequately in giving him tzedakah?" Rav Papa reflected on recent events and realized that this had indeed been the case.[8] The question is, of all the areas which may have been the cause for this near accident, what made Rav Chiya bar Rav think that it might be related to matters of giving tzedakah?

The *Vilna Gaon* explains that the source in the Torah for the mitzvah of giving tzedakah is the words: "כִּי־פָתֹחַ תִּפְתַּח אֶת־יָדְךָ לוֹ"—For you shall surely open your hand."[9] The *taamim* under the words "פָּתֹחַ תִּפְתַּח" are called "*darga*" and "*sevir*." The word *darga* relates to the word *madreigah* and means step, while the word "*sevir*" is Aramaic for "broken." Hence, the Torah is indicating that the consequences for being remiss in the area of giving tzedakah are that a step might be broken. This, says the *Gaon*, was the basis for Rav Chiya bar Rav's suggestion.[10]

LEAVING EGYPT EARLY

There is a well-known question regarding the duration of the Jewish People's stay in Egypt. On the one hand, Hashem foretold to Avraham that his descendants would be strangers in a land which was not theirs for four hundred years,[11] yet in fact, the Jewish People were in Egypt for only two hundred and ten years. How are we to understand this significantly shortened term? Among the many answers that are given is that the intensity of the suffering in Egypt resulted in four hundred years' worth of suffering being compacted into two hundred and ten. Here too, the *Vilna Gaon* explains that this idea is contained within the *taamei hamikra*.[12] The verse which describes how the Egyptians embit-

---

8   *Bava Basra* 10a.
9   *Devarim* 15:8.
10   Cited in *Kol Eliyahu* to *Parshas Re'eh*.
11   *Bereishis* 15:13.
12   *Kol Eliyahu, Parshas Shemos*.

tered the Jewish People's lives states: "וַיְמָרְרוּ אֶת־חַיֵּיהֶם."[13] The *taamim* accompanying these words are known as *"kadma v'azla."* The word *"kadma"* relates to the word *"kodem"* and means "early," while *"azla"* is Aramaic for "to go." As such, the *taamim* on top of the words which described the bitterness and intensity of the exile indicate that this resulted in the Jewish People "going out early," after only being there for two hundred and ten years.

YEHUDAH'S PLEDGE

Returning to the beginning of our parsha, the Torah describes how Yehudah approaches Yosef to plead on behalf of Binyamin: "וַיִּגַּשׁ אֵלָיו יְהוּדָה וַיֹּאמֶר בִּי אֲדֹנִי." We note that Yehudah was not the eldest son; in fact, he was the fourth eldest. Why then, did he step forward to intercede on Binyamin's behalf? The answer is in the previous parsha, where Yehudah undertakes to look after Binyamin, pledging to Yaakov, "If I do not bring him to you and stand him before you, then I will have sinned to you for all days."[14] Commenting on the words "for all days," *Rashi* cites the Midrash which explains that Yehudah was referring to his share in the World to Come, which he was prepared to forfeit if he did not return Binyamin home safely to his father.

The *taamim* accompanying the first six words of our verse are (1) *kadma*, (2) *v'azla*, (3) *revi'i*, (4) *zarka*, (5) *munach*, and (6) *segol*. We have seen that *kadma v'azla* means to go early; *revi'i* means "fourth"; *zarka* means "to throw"; *segol* relates to the word *segulah*, which is "treasure"; and *munach* means "set aside." With this in mind, the *Vilna Gaon* explains that the first three *taamim* are making an observation: "*Kadma v'azla revi'i*—the fourth preceded and went forth." They are noting that Yehudah, the fourth son (*revi'i*), preceded and went (*kadma v'azla*) before his other brothers to plead with Yosef. Why is this so? To this question, the last three *taamim* provide the answer: "*zarka munach segol*—he was throwing away treasure that was set aside."[15] As we mentioned, Yehudah

---

13 *Shemos* 1:14.
14 *Bereishis* 43:9.
15 *Kol Eliyahu, Parshas Vayigash.*

had committed that if he did not return Binyamin to Yaakov, he would thereby be throwing away (*zarka*) the treasure (*segol*) that was set aside (*munach*) for him in the World to Come. Hence, although he was the fourth, he went first to intercede with Yosef.

Truly a remarkable dimension within the aspect of Chumash known as *taamei hamikra*!

SPEAKING LASHON HAKODESH

וְהִנֵּה עֵינֵיכֶם רֹאוֹת...כִּי פִי הַמְדַבֵּר אֲלֵיכֶם.

Behold, your eyes see...that it is my mouth that is speaking to you.[1]

Rashi explains the phrase "that it is my mouth speaking to you" as saying that Yosef was speaking to his brothers in *lashon hakodesh*. This is also the approach of *Onkelos*, who translates: "ארי בלישנכון אנא ממלל עמכון—for I am speaking to you in your language." Through this, Yosef was seeking to verify that it was indeed he who was speaking to them.

WHEREFORE THE PROOF?

It is amazing to consider that even though Yosef had already revealed himself to his brothers, saying, "I am Yosef, your brother, whom you sold to Mitzrayim," he still needed to prove that it was indeed him. The commentators explain that the reason the brothers did not respond when he said that he was Yosef is partly because they were not sure if they could believe him! All they knew about this individual is that he had been confounding and tormenting them since they first met him. Perhaps, he had met Yosef some years back, heard his story of how his brothers had sold him, and decided to further torment them by

---

1   *Bereishis* 45:12.

impersonating their long-lost brother. As such, Yosef needed to provide proof that it was actually him.

THE RAMBAN'S QUESTION: WHAT WAS THE PROOF?

The *Ramban* raises the question of how Yosef speaking in their language constituted any proof as to his identity. After all, it was surely quite common for the ruler of a country to be conversant in the languages of nearby regions!

Interestingly, according to some commentators, the proof came not from the fact that Yosef knew how to speak their language, but from what happened when he did. Having grown up with Yosef, all the brothers really needed was to hear the sound of his voice, for each person speaks in a distinctive way that is recognizable to those who are familiar with him. However, as long as Yosef was speaking Egyptian, a language that the brothers did not understand, they could not recognize that it was him speaking. However, as soon as he reverted to Hebrew, his mother tongue, the brothers were able to recognize that it was him.[2]

HEBREW AND LASHON HAKODESH

Others, however, understand that the proof really did come from the fact that Yosef knew their language. The premise behind the *Ramban's* question, which he states explicitly, is that *lashon hakodesh* was the language spoken by the people of Canaan, i.e., Hebrew. Hence, he asks, the simple fact that he knew Hebrew was no proof as to his identity. Indeed, we may add that the interpreter mentioned in *Parshas Mikeitz* who ferried their words to Yosef clearly spoke their language,[3] yet they did not conclude that he must be related to them! However, one of the classic commentators on *Rashi*, the *Nachalas Yaakov*, points out that sources in Chazal seem to indicate otherwise.

The Gemara relates how, as part of Yosef's meeting with Pharaoh to interpret his dreams, Pharaoh began conversing with Yosef in each

---

2   See commentary of *Radak* and *Tiferes Yehonasan* of R' Yehonasan Eibeschutz to *Bereishis* ibid.
3   See *Bereishis* 42:23.

of the seventy languages known at that time.[4] Yosef, who had been taught these languages by the angel Gavriel the previous night, was able to respond in all these languages. After Pharaoh exhausted all of the languages that he knew, Yosef began speaking to him in *lashon hakodesh*, which Pharaoh did not understand. This resulted in Pharaoh making Yosef take an oath that he would never reveal that *lashon hakodesh* was a language that Pharaoh did not speak. This clearly indicates that *lashon hakodesh* was distinct from the language that was spoken in the neighboring country of Canaan, and was known only to Yaakov and his family. Hence, when Yosef spoke to his brothers in *lashon hakodesh*, it was indeed proof that it was him.

It is most noteworthy in this regard that when *Rashi* describes the role of the translator between Yosef and the brothers,[5] he says that the brothers spoke to him in "*lashon Ivri*—Hebrew," which he then translated for Yosef into Egyptian. It is only when Yosef seeks to verify his identity to his brothers does *Rashi* say that he spoke to them in "*lashon hakodesh*—the Holy Tongue." This further confirms that *Rashi* sees Hebrew and *lashon hakodesh* as two separate languages.

This leaves us with the interesting question as to the relationship between these two languages. Are they simply two completely different languages? If so, then the language we call Hebrew, which is clearly associated with *lashon hakodesh* of the Torah, has no connection to the *lashon Ivri* to which *Rashi* is referring.

WHO CAN SPEAK LASHON HAKODESH?

What makes the situation more mystifying, however, is that the Gemara states that not only did Pharaoh not understand Yosef when he spoke to him in *lashon hakodesh*, but he was also unable to learn it from Yosef, hence, he resorted to swearing Yosef to secrecy. Having mastered the seventy main languages of the world, why would Pharaoh be unable to learn *lashon hakodesh*? Surely, it would be worth the effort rather than to remain beholden to Yosef! To this, the *Chasam Sofer* responds

---

4 *Sotah* 36b.
5 *Bereishis* 42:23, s.v. *ki*.

that in order to speak *lashon hakodesh*, the person himself needs to possess *kedushah*. As such, Pharaoh, who was bereft of *kedushah*, could not learn how to speak it.[6]

This answer is equally mystifying. If *lashon hakodesh* is simply another language—essentially synonymous with what we refer to as Hebrew—why can one not learn it without *kedushah*? Has no one ever learned to speak Hebrew without first attaining a state of sanctity?

Apparently, *lashon hakodesh* is more than a set of words and accompanying grammatical rules. It is the ability to use words in a way that compacts layers of meaning into a minimum of expression, to a degree, the way that the Torah does. That is something one cannot do without *kedushah*; Pharaoh knew enough to realize this. Accordingly, the words themselves which *lashon hakodesh* uses in this special way may well be words from *lashon Ivri*, and using them in a more mundane form may simply be what we call speaking Hebrew.

WHAT WAS YOSEF PROVING?

Looked at in this regard, it is possible that by speaking *lashon hakodesh* to his brothers, Yosef was looking not just to prove his identity, but also that he had not lost the sanctity required to speak in that way. Indeed, in a classic observation, the *Meshech Chochmah* notes that this whole element of Yosef making a point by speaking *lashon hakodesh* seems to appear somewhat late in the proceedings. The verses in the beginning of chapter 45 discussing Yosef's revelation can be divided into three sections:

- Verses 1–4: Yosef revealing his identity, and the brothers' shock upon hearing this.
- Verses 5–8: Yosef comforting and reassuring the brothers that everything that had happened had been guided by Hashem toward a positive outcome.

---

6   *Drashos Chasam Sofer, drashah* for the eighth of Teves.

- Verses 9–13: Yosef discussing sharing the news with Yaakov and bringing him down to live in Mitzrayim, where Yosef would take care of him.

In light of this, we proceed to note that Yosef's words concerning him speaking *lashon hakodesh* appear in verse 12—the third section. If his intent was to verify his identity, this should have taken place someplace within the first four verses, where he dealt with that issue! Rather, says the *Meshech Chochmah*, Yosef speaking *lashon hakodesh* was part of the discussion of bring Yaakov down to Egypt.

For Yaakov to come to Egypt was no simple matter. Aside from his basic reluctance regarding having to leave Eretz Canaan, there was another critical issue. A central component of Yaakov's spiritual level, and of his relationship with Hashem, was his *ruach hakodesh*, which translates as Divine inspiration and is a form of prophecy. Chazal inform us that Yaakov had been without *ruach hakodesh* for the past twenty-two years due to his being in mourning over Yosef, for *ruach hakodesh* only rests upon a person who is in a state of joy. Now, upon hearing that Yosef was alive, he could once again enjoy that exalted level and connection with Hashem[7] and would surely not wish to lose it again. Yaakov would not want to leave Eretz Canaan, a land conducive to this state, and he would certainly not wish to relocate himself to the impure and Godless environment of Mitzrayim, of all places, where he would surely forfeit any significant spiritual level!

It is in the interests of alleviating this concern that Yosef speaks to the brothers in *lashon hakodesh*. He was saying, "When suggesting to our father that he come to live in Mitzrayim, tell him that he will not need to abdicate the *ruach hakodesh* he attained in Canaan by living here. The proof of this is the fact that I have been here for twenty-two years and yet, I am still speaking *lashon hakodesh*—the language of *ruach hakodesh*!"

All of this should serve to give us a deeper appreciation of *lashon hakodesh* and what it means to speak it.

---

7   See verse 27 with *Rashi's* comments.

FROM THE COMMENTATORS

FORGING BONDS OF HISTORY

וְעַתָּה יֵשֶׁב נָא עַבְדְּךָ תַּחַת הַנַּעַר עֶבֶד לַאדֹנִי וְהַנַּעַר יַעַל עִם אֶחָיו.

And now, please let your servant remain instead of the youth as
a servant to my lord, and let the youth go up with his brothers.[1]

Our parsha opens with Yehudah's impassioned plea before Yosef on behalf of Binyamin, offering to remain as a servant in his stead. It is worthwhile reflecting that with this gesture, Yehudah was effectively offering to sacrifice every aspect of his life back home in order for his brother to return. This offer was never realized, as shortly afterwards it was revealed that the Egyptian ruler was in fact none other than Yosef. However, although there was no practical outcome at that time, Yehudah's offer would reverberate in a most profound way many generations later.

At a certain stage in the Jewish monarchy, the tribe of Ephraim seceded and formed its own kingdom in the north of Israel, drawing along with it the majority of the tribes. From this point on, the monarchy from the royal line of David was known as the Kingdom of Yehudah. Notably, the only tribe that remained as part of this

---

1   *Bereishis* 44:33.

southern kingdom was Binyamin.[2] This is most fascinating; after all, Binyamin and Yosef—from whom Ephraim was descended—were brothers from their mother, Rachel. As such, we would naturally have expected Binyamin to be one of the first tribes to join forces with the north! Geographically, Binyamin was no closer to Yehudah than many other tribes who seceded. Yet Binyamin stayed with Yehudah. Some commentators explain that this allegiance was the legacy of the bond that had been forged between these two tribes from the very beginning, when Yehudah offered himself as a servant to Yosef in Binyamin's stead. From that point on, these two tribes were connected. Indeed, it was a connection which ultimately kept the tribe of Binyamin as part of world Jewish history, since the ten tribes of the north were exiled by Sancheriv, and their whereabouts remain unknown until today.[3]

WITH ISRAEL IN EXILE

וַיֹּאמֶר אֱלֹקִים לְיִשְׂרָאֵל...אַל תִּירָא מֵרְדָה מִצְרַיְמָה...אָנֹכִי אֵרֵד עִמְּךָ מִצְרַיְמָה וְאָנֹכִי אַעַלְךָ גַם עָלֹה.

God said to Yisrael..."Do not be afraid of descending to Egypt...I shall descend with you to Egypt and I shall surely bring you up."[4]

The *Beis Halevi* explains that Yaakov's fear when going down to Egypt was that his descendants may not endure the entire term of exile, and may simply either assimilate or dissolve as a people, leaving the entire goal of the exile unrealized. Hashem reassured Yaakov regarding his fears by saying that He would also go down to Egypt with them. The full meaning of this idea is that Hashem pledged to tie His name to that of the Jewish People, whereby humanity's recognition of Him would come about solely through the success of Israel. Thus, when the Jewish People enter a state of exile, so too does Hashem, in the sense that His control of the world is no longer apparent.

---

2   See *Melachim I* 12:21.
3   R' Leib Mintzberg, *Ben Melech, Parshas Vayigash.*
4   *Bereishis* 46:2–4.

The full implication of this idea is that it guarantees that Hashem will not allow the Jewish People to disintegrate in exile, for in so doing, He would negate any possibility of the world's recognition of Him. This would nullify any notion of Godly living and thereby render the entire Creation a worthless process. Thus, Hashem promises Yaakov, "As surely as I will go down with you in your exile, I *will come up together with you* (*aalcha gam aloh*) through the miracles with which I will redeem you."[5]

---

5   Rabbeinu Yonah (commentary to *Rif, Berachos*, chap. 5) explains in this vein the verse in *Yeshayahu* (45:15): "אָכֵן אַתָּה אֵ-ל מִסְתַּתֵּר אֱלֹקֵי יִשְׂרָאֵל מוֹשִׁיעַ"—Indeed, you are a hidden God, the God of Israel saves." The prophet is saying that although for the most part Hashem's presence in the world is concealed, the exception to this concealment is when He acts to save the people of Israel. A basic survey of the experiences of the Jewish People in the land of Israel over the last century will provide more than ample expression to this comment of Rabbeinu Yonah.

PARSHAS VAYECHI

THE BLESSING OF
MENASHEH AND EPHRAIM

BACKGROUND: SYNOPSIS AND SOME QUESTIONS

One of the main episodes in the beginning of our parsha is Yaakov's blessing to Yosef's two sons, Menasheh and Ephraim. A synopsis of this episode would roughly go as follows: Yosef presents his sons to his father with Menasheh, the elder son, at Yaakov's right side and Ephraim, the younger son, at Yaakov's left. Yaakov, however, switches his hands, placing his right hand on Ephraim and his left hand on Menasheh. Yosef objects to this switch and expresses to his father that Menasheh should get the right hand. To this, Yaakov responds that he knows what he is doing and that it is Ephraim who will be the greater of the two.

However, a careful analysis of the verses which the Torah devotes to Yaakov's blessing will reveal a deeper dimension into this entire episode.[1] Let us preface with some questions:[2]

---

1   The present discussion is based on the commentary *Toras Moshe* of R' Moshe Alshich.

2   The *Alshich*'s commentary follows the style of earlier commentators, such as the *Akeidas Yitzchak* and the *Abarbanel*, of prefacing his comments to a particular section with a number of questions, and then proceeding to offer an approach which answers them one by one. In our instance, the *Alshich* opens with twenty-five questions, of which we have presented six, leaving the other questions to be addressed as the presentation of his approach unfolds.

- Verses 8–9: Yaakov sees Yosef's sons and asks, "Who are these?" to which Yosef responds, "They are my sons, whom God gave me in this place." What is behind this question and answer? Are we to assume that until this point Yaakov did not know who his grandchildren were? Additionally, why does Yosef add the detail that they were born to him "in this place"? Having married in Egypt, would we have thought that they would be born to him anywhere else?

- Verse 9: In response to Yosef's answer, Yaakov instructs him, "קָחֶם נָא אֵלַי וַאֲבָרֲכֵם"—Take them to me please, and I will bless them." This phrase sounds self-contradictory. When one "takes" something or someone, he takes it toward himself. Here, however, Yaakov is asking Yosef to move his sons forward closer to him. As such, the verse should have said "haviem na eilai—bring them to me"!

- Verse 12: When Yosef presents his sons to Yaakov, he bows down to the ground. What is the meaning of this act? This is neither the beginning nor the end of the meeting, and nothing seems to have happened at this particular moment which would make such a gesture appropriate!

- Verse 13: The Torah describes how Yosef positioned his sons—"Ephraim at his right side, which was Yaakov's left, and Menasheh at his left side, which was Yaakov's right." Why does the verse inform us of the positioning of the sons in terms of Yosef? While it is true that if one person faces another, then the former's right is the latter's left and vice versa, surely that is irrelevant here, as the only positioning of significance is vis-à-vis Yaakov!

- Verse 14: Yaakov switches his hands, placing his right hand on Ephraim and his left on Menasheh. Given that in Yaakov's estimation, Yosef has positioned his sons wrongly, why does he choose to switch his *hands*? Why not simply ask his *grandchildren* to switch their positions?

- Verses 17–18: When Yosef sees that his father switched his hands, he begins to move them toward the way he feels they should be positioned, saying, "Not so, Father, for this is the firstborn; place your right hand on his head." This action, as well as Yosef's words, seems very forward, to say the least! There is an appropriate way to address one's father if one feels he is mistaken, and Yosef seems to have acted far in excess of any such protocol.

FROM GRANDSONS TO SONS: EVALUATION BEFORE ELEVATION

The *Alshich* explains that the singling out of Menasheh and Ephraim for a special blessing is not merely to bless them with success, but for the purpose of elevating them to the status of tribes of Israel. To this end, when Yaakov is presented with his grandchildren on this momentous occasion, he first assesses them critically to see if they are worthy of attaining such status. This is the meaning of his question, "Who are these?" Yaakov is asking, "What is their essential worth, and are they deserving of being elevated to tribe status?" In fact, as the Sages point out, Yaakov senses that they are not entirely worthy of this elevation and, as such, was expressing his reservations about giving them this blessing.[3]

To this, Yosef responds, "They are *my sons*," expressing his assertion that like him, they are indeed deserving of "tribe" status. In this vein, he adds the words "that God gave me in this place." By emphasizing where they were born, Yosef was arguing that any deficiency Yaakov may have perceived within them was not an expression of an essential lack on their part. Rather, it was the unavoidable consequence of external circumstance—"this place" in which they were born, the land of Egypt which was full of corrupt influence and moral deficiency. The sons themselves, however, says Yosef, are entirely worthy.

Did Yaakov accept Yosef's argument?

In response to Yosef's words, Yaakov says, "Take them to me and I will bless them." We noted that the ideas of "take them" and "to me" contradict each other, for the former connotes Yosef drawing them

---

3   *Midrash Tanchuma,* cited in *Rashi* to this verse.

close to him, while the latter involves moving them forward toward Yaakov. What is the meaning of this phrase? The answer is that Yaakov has assessed that while Menasheh and Ephraim are fundamentally worthy of this blessing, they are not entirely on the level where they can receive it directly. Rather, the blessing will come *through Yosef*. Thus, Yaakov instructs Yosef to take his sons and draw them close to him, since the blessing will be bestowed through him, and thus to present them to Yaakov for blessing.

ENCOURAGING DEVELOPMENTS?

Understandably, this instruction was something of a disappointment for Yosef, who would have liked to have seen his sons blessed directly by Yaakov. That said, however, the events described in the following verses were a source of some encouragement for Yosef, as they gave him reason to conclude that Yaakov had reconsidered.

- Verse 10: Yosef presents his sons to Yaakov, who kisses and hugs them.
- Verse 11: Yaakov says to Yosef, "I never thought that I would see you again, and behold, God has shown me your children as well."

What are the implications of all this? In reality, with these actions and words, Yaakov was endorsing his grandsons' *essential* worthiness to receive the blessing, even though his decision to bless them through Yosef remained unchanged. Yosef, on the other hand, saw the direct contact with his sons and Yaakov's ensuing words as an indication that *he had reconsidered* and was prepared to bless them directly! For this reason, verse 12 states that "Yosef released his sons from between his knees and bowed down to the ground." We asked, what was the meaning of this bowing? The answer, says the *Alshich*, is that one bows down upon hearing good tidings.[4] In Yosef's understanding, he had just heard exceptionally good tidings—that his sons would be blessed directly by Yaakov!

---

4   See *Rashi* to *Bereishis* 24:52.

In reality, however, Yaakov's fundamental position had not changed. The grandsons would receive his blessing, but it would take place through Yosef. The most immediate implications of this question relate to how the sons should be positioned in order to receive the blessing—which brings us to the question of right and left.

THE FIELD OF BLESSING

When it comes to the positioning of Yosef's sons to receive the blessing, two issues need to be considered:

- Which son should receive the right side?
- With reference to whom should the "right" and "left" side be determined?

Regarding the latter question, if the blessing will be given directly from Yaakov, then it will be his right and left side that are significant. However, if the blessing will be delivered through Yosef, then his right and left will be the ones to consider.

In terms of the above, we can appreciate that Yosef's understanding differed from that of Yaakov with regards to both of these questions:

- He felt that Menasheh should receive the right side.
- He thought that the blessing would come directly from Yaakov.

Accordingly, he positioned his sons with Menasheh at Yaakov's right side and Ephraim at Yaakov's left. What is most fascinating is that through acting on these two premises together, he effectively positioned his sons *exactly where they needed to be* in terms of Yaakov's plans:

- Placing Ephraim at *Yaakov's left* side meant that he was placed at *Yosef's right* side.
- Likewise, placing Menasheh at *Yaakov's right* side meant that he was at *Yosef's left* side.

This is why the verse describes the positioning of the sons not only in terms of Yaakov's right and left, but also in terms of Yosef's, for in fact, it was the latter's "coordinates" which would be definitive for the way the blessing was delivered. Additionally, we now understand why Yaakov crossed over his hands to give the right to Ephraim, and did not ask his grandsons to change places. For in reality, they were exactly where they needed to be—with Ephraim at Yosef's right and Menasheh at his left. All Yaakov now needed to do was to align his right and left hands with the corresponding sides of Yosef—which he did by crossing over his hands. With everything in place, verse 15 then introduces Yaakov's blessing to his grandsons by saying, "He blessed Yosef," for, as we have seen, his blessing to them was actually transmitted through Yosef.

UNDERSTANDING YOSEF'S REACTION

We can now understand why Yosef reacted to these events in the way that he did, saying, "Not so, Father, for this is the firstborn," and even trying to physically move Yaakov's right hand to Menasheh. When Yosef saw that Yaakov had crossed his hands, he realized that he had been mistaken in thinking that the blessing was to go to the sons directly from Yaakov. However, he still assumed that Menasheh was meant to receive the right hand. As such, in light of the way he realized the blessing was being transmitted, he thought that he had positioned his sons contrary to Yaakov's wishes! That is why he tried moving Yaakov's hands—not as a protest to what he perceived as *Yaakov's* mistake, but in response to *his own* mistake. He was effectively saying, "I am sure you crossed your right hand over to *my* right side expecting to find Menasheh there, but I mistakenly put him at *your* right side. Here he is!"

However, Yaakov responds by saying, "*Yadati b'ni yadati*—I know, my son, I know." Perhaps the double expression refers to both aspects of the situation: "(1) I know that you thought the blessing would come directly from me, and (2) I also know that you think Menasheh should get the right hand, and that is why you placed Ephraim at my left side. However, the blessing was actually to go through you, and Ephraim—whom you placed at your right side—is the one who will be receiving my right hand, for he will achieve greater eminence than his brother."

Stunning!

CONCLUDING THOUGHTS

The *Alshich* does not specify what the implications are of Yosef's sons receiving the blessing through him and not directly from Yaakov. However, it is interesting to note, as we go through the Chumash, that these two are not always considered separate tribes. There are occasions when they "close ranks" and are treated as one tribe called "Yosef." Perhaps, this "partial" elevation to tribe status is due to the fact that it still involved their father, Yosef.

Another question that remains is that although Yaakov originally stated that the blessing would go through Yosef ("take them to me"), he was aware that his subsequent actions (hugging and kissing them, saying, "Behold, God has shown me your children") led Yosef to conclude that the blessing would be given directly. Since Yaakov had not in fact changed his mind in this regard, why did he allow Yosef to reach this conclusion? Possibly, since Yosef was effectively to be the conduit through which Yaakov's blessing would flow to his grandsons, Yaakov did not want any resistance or interference to that flow on account of Yosef's desire that the blessing not go through him. The optimum way to ensure that the blessing would flow smoothly through Yosef was by arranging for it to flow unconsciously, leaving the explanation for after it had occurred.

YAAKOV'S BLESSINGS
TO HIS SONS

וַיִּקְרָא יַעֲקֹב אֶל בָּנָיו וַיֹּאמֶר הֵאָסְפוּ וְאַגִּידָה לָכֶם אֵת אֲשֶׁר יִקְרָא אֶתְכֶם
בְּאַחֲרִית הַיָּמִים.

Yaakov called his sons and said, "Assemble and I will relate to you what will happen to you in the End of Days."[1]

INTRODUCTION: A WISH DENIED

Commenting on this verse, *Rashi* writes:[2]

ביקש לגלות את הקץ ונסתלקה ממנו שכינה והתחיל אומר דברים אחרים.

[Yaakov] wanted to reveal the end [of the exile], however, the Divine Presence was removed from him, and [thus] he began to say other things.

The basis of *Rashi*'s comment in the text is quite clear, for our verse describes Yaakov's announcement that he will tell his sons about the End of Days, while the ensuing verses contain no such content, comprising, instead, his blessings to his sons. Additionally, verses 1 and 2

---

1   *Bereishis* 49:1.
2   S.v. *v'agidah.*

both begin with Yaakov assembling his sons, implying that the purpose of the assembly in verse 1 was not realized at that time, leading him to convene them again for other matters, i.e., to deliver the blessings.

In a well-known passage, the Talmud in *Maseches Pesachim*, which is the source of *Rashi's* comment, proceeds to describe how Yaakov was afraid that the reason the Divine Presence had departed from him was due to some deficiency in one of his sons.[3] To this, the sons replied in unison: "*Shema Yisrael Hashem Elokeinu Hashem echad*—Hear O Israel,[4] Hashem is our God, Hashem is One," which the Gemara explains to mean, "Just as Hashem is One in your heart, so, too, He is One in all of our hearts." In response to this, Yaakov exclaimed, "*Baruch shem kevod malchuso l'olam va'ed*—Blessed is the name of His glorious kingdom forever and ever." Indeed, as the Gemara concludes, although this latter sentence is not written in the Torah, it is said in an undertone as part of our daily recitation of the *Shema* in recognition of having been expressed by Yaakov on this occasion.

Why does *Rashi* not cite the continuation of the Gemara? Because *Rashi's* job in his commentary is devoted purely to resolving *pshat* issues with the verse. Therefore, he only cites the opening section of that passage, which deals with the shift from foretelling to blessing. For the rest of the discussion, the reader can then consult the Gemara itself—where *Rashi* indeed has prepared another commentary for him; however, in terms of his commentary on the Torah, *Rashi* has cited all that he needs.[5]

---

3   56a.

4   In this context, the reference to "Israel" was to their father. Although one may not call one's parent by their first name, the name Israel, having been given to Yaakov by Hashem, had the status of a title of honor. Therefore, it was not considered disrespectful for the brothers to refer to him by this name.

5   Interestingly, the *Rambam's* discussion of this episode in his *Mishneh Torah* (*Hilchos K'rias Shema* 1:4) specifically begins at the point where *Rashi* left off, i.e., Yaakov's fears concerning his sons' righteousness, their reassurance regarding this matter and his response of "*Baruch Shem.*" Here, too, the reason is based on his purpose of referencing the discussion, which is to explain the background to the way we read the *Shema*. Accordingly, he cites only the second half of the Gemara's discussion that is relevant to this matter.

FROM REDEMPTION TO BLESSING

In light of the above, it is interesting to consider the blessings Yaakov proceeds to dispense, for they would appear to be a kind of "shift in topic" given Yaakov's original intention upon gathering his sons to discuss the redemption.

In truth, however, the shift is not as drastic as it seems. As numerous commentators explain, the blessing for each son pinpointed a unique characteristic of that particular son, which would in turn characterize the members of that tribe. This would identify the strength of that tribe that would enable it to make its unique contribution to the success and destiny of the Jewish People. In other words, in the absence of the ability to *reveal* the End of Days itself—whether this refers to the timing of the final redemption, or the nature of how it will come about and the era that it will usher in—Yaakov instead turned his attention to the more practical matter of *how to bring it about.*

FOLLOWING THROUGH: THEN WHY
WAS THE DIVINE PRESENCE REMOVED?

What is most fascinating to contemplate regarding this entire episode is that it is easy to review it many times, reflecting on Yaakov's fears concerning the brothers and how they allayed those fears, announcing their faithfulness to Yaakov's message, without ever proceeding to ask the question: Why then, was the Divine Presence removed from Yaakov? If the problem with revealing the End of Days did not lay where he suspected it might, where then did it lay?

The answer, very simply, is that it was not appropriate to reveal the date or nature of the final redemption to the Jewish People at the time when they were *embarking on their exile.* Part of the exile itself is not having a clear vision of matters pertaining to the redemption; hence, any detailed discussion of the End of Days was not appropriate at that time. Having said this, we do note that for his part, Yaakov was hoping to reveal this to his sons. How is this to be understood?

To help explain this matter, we recall the fundamental principle concerning the lives of the Avos: "*Maaseh Avos siman l'banim*—the deeds of the Patriarchs are a sign for their descendants." This means that every significant experience of the Jewish People has already been "pre-experienced" by the Avos. With reference to exile, too, Yaakov had already experienced *maaseh Avos* in his sojourn with Lavan, with all the difficulties that it entailed. As such, we ask, at what stage did he experience *maaseh Avos* relating to redemption? The answer, according to the Midrash,[6] is that his final seventeen years, at peace, free of travail and reunited with Yosef, were his redemption years. It is now easy to understand why Yaakov felt it appropriate to discuss the final redemption directly, as this was the stage that he was personally experiencing.

WHEN MAASEH AVOS MET SIMAN L'BANIM

What is fascinating about this idea is that while generally, the "*maaseh Avos*" events of the Patriarchs did not overlap with the "*siman l'banim*" events of their descendants, on this one occasion, they existed simultaneously—and what's more, as opposites! For the very years which marked redemption for Yaakov were the initial years of his children's exile. What are we to make of this unusual situation?

To understand this "dual era," we must realize that *maaseh Avos* do not function merely as a "sign" in the *informational* sense. Rather, the personal experiences of the Avos harnessed the spiritual energy needed for their descendants' unique history, *enabling* it to happen. The full impact of this idea as it relates to our discussion is that the coincidence of Yaakov's redemption experience with the exile experience of his children meant that *they went into exile already possessing the capacity for redemption*! In this regard, the Torah's recording of Yaakov's desire to reveal the End of Days to his sons in verse 1 represented the existence of the potential for redemption which was already in place at that time. In other words, while Yaakov provided the emotional and operational path toward redemption through the blessings that he gave on the last day of his life, the essential capacity for redemption was something he had been providing in the seventeen years leading up to that day through his very existence and experience.

---

6   See *Bereishis Rabbah* 96:1.

The Egyptian exile is looked upon as the root of all our exiles, and likewise, the redemption from Egypt is seen as the root of all future redemptions. It turns out that in providing his children with the potential for redemption from Egypt, Yaakov was ultimately providing the entire Jewish People with the capacity to be redeemed from all future exiles. We look forward to that potential becoming fully actualized in our times, and to encountering the long-awaited epoch that our father Yaakov so sorely wished to reveal all those centuries ago.

CONCEPT: THE WORLDS OF PSHAT AND DRASH

"Yaakov, Our Father, Never Died"

INTRODUCTION: A MYSTIFYING EXCHANGE

The Gemara in *Maseches Taanis* records the following exchange between two Sages of the Talmud, Rav Yitzchak and Rav Nachman:[1]

אמר ליה הכי אמר ר' יוחנן, יעקב אבינו לא מת.

אמר ליה וכי בחנם ספדו ספדנייא וחנטו חנטייא וקברו קברנייא?

אמר ליה מקרא אני דורש, שנאמר: "ועתה אל תירא עבדי יעקב נאום ה' ואל
תחת ישראל כי הנני מושיעך מרחוק ואת זרעך מארץ שבים," מקיש הוא
לזרעו, מה זרעו בחיים אף הוא בחיים.

He [R' Yitzchak] said to him [Rav Nachman]: Thus said Rav Yochanan: "Yaakov, our father, never died."

[Rav Nachman] said to [R' Yitzchak]: "Was it for nothing that the eulogizers eulogized [Yaakov] and the embalmers embalmed him and the buriers buried him?"

[R' Yitzchak] replied: "I am expounding a verse, as it says: 'And you fear not, My servant Yaakov, says Hashem, and do not

---

1 5b.

become broken, Yisrael, for behold, I will deliver you from afar,
and your descendants from the land of their captivity.[2] *[We*
see that] the verse equates him [Yaakov] and his descendants:
Just as his descendants are living, so too, is he living."

The above exchange is most perplexing. With all due respect to
R' Yitzchak's exposition, he appears to have entirely sidestepped Rav
Nachman's objection that the simple meaning of the verses indicates
that Yaakov died!

PSHAT AND DRASH TEACHINGS

Rav Tzadok HaKohen of Lublin[3] explains the matter by taking us
in to the methods of interpretation we call *pshat* and *drash*. These are
not simply two ways of deriving messages from a verse. Rather, they
often represent two different types of messages, reflecting two entirely
different realms:

- In the same way that *pshat* represents that which is openly
  stated and clearly visible to the reader, it likewise reflects the
  situation as would be visibly apparent to the onlooker.
- Conversely, just as *drash* involves looking beneath the surface
  of the Torah's words, so too, the message it communicates
  reflects aspects of that situation which are "hidden" and not
  readily apparent.

Here too, when Rav Nachman challenged the teaching that "Yaakov,
our father, never died" from the fact that he was embalmed, eulogized,
and buried, R' Yitzchak responded by saying, "*Mikra ani doresh*—I am
expounding a verse." With this he was indicating that the realm to which
his teaching refers was not the one apparent to the onlookers, reflected
by the *pshat* reading of the verse, but to a more hidden realm, whereby
Yaakov, although physically dead, lives on in his descendants.

---

2   *Yirmiyahu* 30:10.
3   *Takanas Hashavin, maamar* 6.

DEAD MAIDENS WALKING

This fundamental idea is already discussed in earlier sources. In the course of the Torah's description of Pharaoh's daughter going to wash in the Nile, where she would meet the baby Moshe who had been set afloat there by his mother, the verse relates: "וְנַעֲרֹתֶיהָ הֹלְכֹת עַל יַד הַיְאֹר—and her maidens were walking on the side of the Nile."[4] Commenting on these words, Rashi cites the following Midrash:

ורבותינו דרשו "הולכות" לשון מיתה...הולכות למות לפי שמיחו בה.

Our Sages expounded the word "going" [here] as an expression of death...they were "going" to die because they protested her [taking the child].[5]

The *Maharal* explains that here too, the Midrash does not mean to say that these maidens dropped dead at the side of the Nile when they protested. Rather, it means that they found themselves somehow unable to prevent Pharaoh's daughter from taking the child. This lack of ability was the result of their strength being withheld from them from On High, and it is to this that the Midrash refers when it says that they "died," since their connection with life in the higher realms was diminished.[6]

The *Maharal's* words confirm Rav Tzadok's principle that a message derived through the medium of *drash* reflects an inner or higher reality, beyond that which is readily visible to the onlooker.

IN CONVERSATION

The above idea regarding *pshat* and *drash* also relates to the Midrash's expositions on people's words in the Torah. In the beginning of *Parshas Vayigash*, when Yehudah approaches Yosef to plead for Binyamin's freedom, he prefaces by saying, "*Ki chamocha k'Pharaoh*—for you are

---

4   *Shemos* 2:5.
5   The simple understanding of the basis of this exposition is the fact that the word "*holchos*" is written "deficiently," i.e., without either letter *vav*, indicating a deficiency in the state of the maidens themselves; see *Pachad Yitzchak, Pesach, maamar* 52.
6   *Gevuros Hashem*, chap. 17.

like Pharaoh."[7] *Rashi*, commenting on these words, cites no fewer than four interpretations, starting with the *pshat* and from there proceeding to *drash*:

חשוב אתה בעיני כמלך, זהו פשוטו.

ומדרשו: סופך ללקות עליו בצרעת כמו שלקה פרעה על ידי זקנתי שרה.

דבר אחר: מה פרעה גוזר ואינו מקיים, מבטיח ואינו עושה, אף אתה כן.

דבר אחר: אם תקניטני אהרוג אותך ואת אדוניך.

You are as important in my eyes as a king; this is the pshat meaning.

The midrashic meaning is: Your end will be to be afflicted with leprosy just as [the earlier] Pharaoh was afflicted on account of my ancestress, Sarah.

An alternative explanation: Just as Pharaoh decrees and does not fulfill, promises and does not act, so too do you.

An alternative explanation: If you antagonize me, I will kill you and your master.

In this instance, the midrashic explanations seem to not only differ from the *pshat* meaning, but also contradict it! If the *pshat* says that Yehudah's words meant to convey his respect for Yosef, how can the *drash* then say that in fact, they meant to indicate criticism and even threats of a most extreme nature?

R' Yaakov Kamenetsky explains that here, too, the *pshat* and *drash* interpretations reflect the overt meaning and implicit messages within Yehudah's words.[8] The outermost layer was undoubtedly one that expressed respect, and that is the *pshat*. However, people often accompany a straightforward message with additional undertones, insinuations, and implications. Together, these form a composite or blended message. It is these added messages that the *drash* draws out from a deeper analysis of Yehudah's words. After all, for a person in his position, standing accused both of spying and of theft, to state that the

---

7 *Bereishis* 44:18.

8 *Emes L'Yaakov, Bereishis* ibid.

second-in-command is like the king himself is at best redundant, and at worst, potentially dangerous. Additionally, the words *"Ki chamocha k'Pharaoh"* literally translate as: "for like you, like Pharaoh," indicating further layers of comparison between the two personalities. R' Yaakov concludes that this is a major idea when learning Midrashim such as these, whereby the interpretations of *pshat* and *drash* in the verse reflect the *"pshat"* and *"drash"* within the person.

A LEVEL DEEPER: HIDDEN ELEMENTS WITHIN REVEALED EVENTS

Taking this discussion one stage further, there are times when the hidden or inner element identified by the *drash* refers not to the event itself, but to its role within the episode being described in the Torah. An example of this is in the episode of the Golden Calf, where the verse states, "וַיַּרְא אַהֲרֹן וַיִּבֶן מִזְבֵּחַ לְפָנָיו"—Aharon saw, and built an altar before him."[9] The verse does not explain exactly what Aharon saw that led him to build the altar for the people. *Rashi* cites the explanation of the Midrash that Aharon saw that Chur, who protested the making of the calf, was killed by the people. Aharon reasoned that if he, too, were to protest, the people would kill him as well, rendering their sin so grievous as to be beyond any hope of rectification. Therefore, he made the altar.

In this instance, this discussion takes place in the realm of *drash*, not because Chur was murdered in a hidden or "inner" way, but because that murder constituted the inner reason for why Aharon acquiesced to the people's demand to make the altar.[10]

This example demonstrates the latitude we sometimes need to take with this idea, when we come to consider which aspect of the element identified by the *drash* was hidden from open view at that time.

IN HALACHAH

In light of the above, let us conclude by considering the relative roles of *pshat* and *drash* in halachah, where seemingly, their relationship with

---

9   *Shemos* 32:5.
10   Heard from R' Beryl Gershenfeld, *shlita*.

visible reality appears to be reversed, i.e., it is reflected specifically in the interpretation of *drash* and not of *pshat*.

A classic example of this is the famous verse in Parshas Mishpatim: "עַיִן תַּחַת עַיִן—An eye for an eye."[11] The simple meaning of this verse is that a person who takes someone's eye out is punished by having his own eye taken out. As we know, based on the midrashic exposition of the verse, the halachah does not require this, but rather obligates the aggressor to pay monetary compensation equal in value to the victim's eye.[12] In this case, we see that the visible reality is as indicated by the *drash* and not by the *pshat*! How is this to be understood in light of their relative roles, as discussed above?

Here too, the "apparentness" expressed by the *pshat* is that the literal penalty of an eye for an eye is what we would expect to be the verdict. The actual punishment of financial restitution is the product of deeper considerations, as expressed by the Talmud in its discussions of this matter, and hence is reflected in the *drash*.

All of this is certainly food for thought and should give us much to contemplate as we seek to further develop our understanding of the worlds of *pshat* and *drash*.

---

11   *Shemos* 21:14.
12   See *Bava Kama* 83b–84a.

FROM THE COMMENTATORS

GIVING STRENGTH

וַיְהִי אַחֲרֵי הַדְּבָרִים הָאֵלֶּה וַיֹּאמֶר לְיוֹסֵף הִנֵּה אָבִיךָ חֹלֶה...וַיַּגֵּד לְיַעֲקֹב וַיֹּאמֶר הִנֵּה בִּנְךָ יוֹסֵף בָּא אֵלֶיךָ וַיִּתְחַזֵּק יִשְׂרָאֵל וַיֵּשֶׁב עַל הַמִּטָּה.

It came to pass after these things that someone said to Yosef, "Behold, your father is ill"...It was told to Yaakov, "Behold, your son Yosef has come to you," and Yisrael strengthened himself and sat up on the bed.[1]

The Gemara informs us that when one visits a sick person, if there is commonalty between the visitor and the patient, such that the latter is buoyed by the visit,[2] a sixtieth of the illness is removed.[3] On its most basic level, the Gemara is noting that the mood and spirits of the patient can have a direct impact on their physiological state.

A precedent for this idea can be seen in our verses. When the ailing Yaakov was (just) informed that his son, Yosef, was coming to visit him, he strengthened himself and sat upright. That strength came from Yosef's visit. However, the matter is alluded to on a more detailed level still. When Yosef is informed in verse 1 of his father's condition,

---

1   *Bereishis* 48:1–2.
2   Commentary of *Meiri* to *Nedarim* ibid.
3   *Nedarim* 39b.

it says that he was told, "הִנֵּה—behold, your father is sick." The *gematria* (numerical value) of the letters that make up the word "הנה" is sixty. However, in the next verse, when Yosef visits Yaakov, the latter is strengthened so that he is able to sit up "עַל הַמִּטָּה—on the bed." The *gematria* of the word "המטה" is fifty-nine, reflecting the sixtieth of his illness that had been removed, enabling him to sit up![4]

ASSEMBLING YAAKOV'S SONS

וַיִּקְרָא יַעֲקֹב אֶל בָּנָיו וַיֹּאמֶר הֵאָסְפוּ וגו'.

Yaakov called his sons and said, "Assemble…"[5]

The Midrash states that at the time Yaakov called his sons, they were scattered, citing two opinions as to how they were gathered together. The first opinion states that it was through an angel, while the second states it was through *ruach hakodesh*—Divine inspiration.[6]

There are two ways the Jewish People can achieve unity and overcome any differences or divisions that keep them apart from one another. The first is borne of the holiness that resides within each and every Jew, which spontaneously senses the commonality that exists with all other Jews and seeks to be one with them. This is called *ruach hakodesh*—a Divine spirit or inspiration. However, if that spirit is not awakened within the Jewish People, then a second means of uniting them exists, known as an "angel" or messenger. In this form, Hashem brings about a human agent to oppress them in a way which forces them to resolve their differences and unite in the face of an adversary who seeks their misfortune or worse.[7]

These two paths toward unity have been expressed from our very earliest days. *Ruach hakodesh* as a form of prophecy has not been with us for centuries now. However, as a basis for Jewish unity, it has never

---

4   *Alshich Hakadosh.*
5   *Bereishis* 49:1.
6   *Bereishis Rabbah* 98:3.
7   Based on the commentary of R' Yehoshua Leib Diskin.

left us, and is beckoning to be accessed in full, ushering us into the era of ultimate blessing.

A MESSAGE FOR YOSEF

אָבִיךָ צִוָּה לִפְנֵי מוֹתוֹ לֵאמֹר. כֹּה תֹאמְרוּ לְיוֹסֵף אָנָּא שָׂא נָא פֶּשַׁע אַחֶיךָ וְחַטָּאתָם כִּי רָעָה גְמָלוּךָ וְעַתָּה שָׂא נָא לְפֶשַׁע עַבְדֵי אֱלֹקֵי אָבִיךָ וַיֵּבְךְּ יוֹסֵף בְּדַבְּרָם אֵלָיו.

"Your father commanded before his death, saying, 'Thus shall you say to Yosef, "Please forgive the crime of your brothers and their sin, for they did you evil."' And now, please forgive the crime of the servants of your father's God." And Yosef wept when they spoke to him.[8]

The Torah does not relate that Yaakov instructed his sons to communicate this message to Yosef. Indeed, the Gemara states that Yaakov did not do so; rather, the brothers fabricated the message out of fear that Yosef would take revenge against them now that their father was dead.[9]

We note that the brothers' words to Yosef comprise two parts: first, the message they "quote" in Yaakov's name and, second, their own plea for forgiveness. On the face of it, their words are purely a reiteration of those of Yaakov. However, when we look closer, we will see that the two are not identical. Specifically, the message that they relay in Yaakov's name refers to their actions as both a *"pesha*—crime" and a *"cheit*—sin," while their own plea mentions only the term *"pesha."* What is behind this shift?

Rav Chanoch HaKohen Ehrentrau,[10] in his sefer *Kometz Haminchah*, explains as follows. In their message from Yaakov, the brothers sought not only to ask for *forgiveness* for their actions, but also to provide an *explanation* of them. The term *"pesha"* refers to a willful crime, while the term *"cheit"* denotes more of an unintentional sin. Thus, the message is

---

8   *Bereishis* 50:16–17.
9   *Yevamos* 65b.
10   Rav of Munich, grandfather of *yblcht"a* Dayan Chanoch Ehrentrau of London.

that the sale of Yosef was not just a pure *pesha*, but had an element of *cheit* as well. Yet how can this be so?

The answer, says Rav Ehrentrau, lies in the word "*gemalucha*," which is commonly translated as "done to you." However, the word "*gomel*" means "to repay," so that in the realm of action, it denotes *a response to someone else's deed*. With this word, the brothers were saying in Yaakov's name that Yosef should not only forgive them for what they did, but should also understand why they did it. Their actions against him were a reaction to his deeds: bringing negative reports about them to their father in a way which they perceived threatened to exclude them from being part of the future of the Jewish People.[11] Appreciating the background to their deeds would serve to mitigate them drastically in Yosef's appraisal, turning what would seem to be an unpardonable crime (*pesha*) into an understandable mistake (*cheit*). Having expressed this idea on their father's behalf, the brothers themselves made no mention of anything other than the crime itself (*pesha*) as they pleaded with Yosef for forgiveness.

Additionally, when repeating Yaakov's words, they refer to themselves vis-à-vis Yosef as "your brothers," appealing to him to have compassion on brotherly grounds. Understandably, the brothers themselves do not refer to themselves in this way, since their own actions were anything but brotherly. Rather, they use the term "the servants of the God of your father," Whom you might emulate in showing compassion on them.[12]

The verse concludes by saying: "And Yosef wept when they spoke with him." The Torah does not specify why Yosef cried at this point. Maybe we cannot know, or alternatively, the answer might be straightforward and obvious. He may have been simply overwhelmed with compassion at their pitiful plight, or perhaps he was anguished at the thought that they feared reprisal on his part. However, in light of Rav Ehrentrau's

---

11   See commentaries of *Roke'ach* and *Malbim*, beginning of *Parshas Vayeishev*.
12   R' Avraham Korman (*Haavos V'hashevatim* p. 211) suggests that even with this term, the brothers were making a veiled reference to their motivation in their actions against Yosef, for they saw him as threatening their status as being part of the continuation of the community who served the God of Yaakov.

explanation of the brothers' words, perhaps we may suggest that Yosef's weeping was because, for the first time, he considered his part in the events that led to him being sold to Egypt, something of which he was completely unaware at the time and indeed, in the decades that ensued, until this moment.

CHUMASH
SHEMOS

PARSHAS SHEMOS

CONCEPT: COMPOSITE WORDS IN TORAH REFLECTING COMPLEX SITUATIONS

INTRODUCTION

Lashon hakodesh consists of clearly defined categories, both in terms of its nouns (e.g., masculine and feminine), as well as its various grammatical forms (e.g., active, passive, causative, etc.). However, once in a while, something unusual happens. There are times when the Torah appears to depart from these rules, using words in a way which either seems incongruous with the context in which they are stated, or alternatively, which do not reflect any recognized category at all! This phenomenon leads certain commentators to develop a fascinating idea regarding the Torah's use of language: At times, the formal boundaries between the categories are relaxed, *grafting together different elements into one word*, in order to reflect an additional or complex element within the situation to which the word relates. Let us consider some classic examples of this idea as found in our parsha.

BLENDED NOUNS: YISRO'S DAUGHTERS

Chapter 2 describes how, when Moshe runs away from Egypt, he arrives at the well in Midyan, where the daughters of Yisro also presently arrive to draw water. Verse 17 then states:

וַיָּבֹאוּ הָרֹעִים וַיְגָרְשׁוּם וַיָּקָם מֹשֶׁה וַיּוֹשִׁעָן.

The shepherds [then] came and drove them away, and Moshe rose up and saved them.[1]

If we look at this verse, we will notice something unusual. The final *mem* of the word "וַיְגָרְשׁוּם" denotes the pronoun "them," in this case, Yisro's daughters. However, a final *mem* is always used when describing a plural *masculine* noun; for a plural *feminine* noun, a final *nun* is used.[2] As such, the appropriate spelling of this word should have been "וַיְגָרְשׁוּן"!

R' Yaakov Tzvi Mecklenberg explains that through this unusual spelling, the Torah is indicating an additional element within the situation.[3] The harassment of Yisro's daughters was not an arbitrary occurrence. The Midrash informs us that Yisro was originally the priest of Midyan.[4] However, at a certain point, he saw through the falsehood of paganism and abdicated that position. As a result of this, Yisro became a persona non grata in town, and his family became subject to hostility on the part of its inhabitants, including the trouble his daughters encountered when they went to draw water at the well. In order to indicate the background to the daughters' distress, i.e., the moral stand of their *father*, the Torah uses a final *mem* in the word that describes them being driven away, thereby incorporating a masculine element within that word![5]

BLENDED VERBS: MIRIAM'S VIGIL

In the beginning of chapter 2, the Torah describes how Yocheved, who was no longer able to hide Moshe, placed him in a basket near the banks of the Nile. Verse 4 then states:

---

1   *Shemos* 2:17.

2   As indeed we find in the following phrase—"וַיּוֹשִׁעָן."

3   *Hakesav V'hakabbalah, Parshas Shemos.*

4   Cited in *Rashi* to our verse.

5   In a similar vein, R' Mecklenberg explains that the use of the final *mem* in the concluding phrase "וַיַּשְׁקְ אֶת צֹאנָם"—and he watered their flock" serves as a reference to the idea stated in the Midrash that Moshe proceeded to water the flock of all those present, hence, the more generic masculine pronoun is used. For further examples of this idea in his commentary, see *Hakesav V'hakabbalah* to *Bereishis* 29:32 and 41:8, *Bamidbar* 22:33, and *Devarim* 21:8.

וַתֵּתַצַּב אֲחֹתוֹ מֵרָחֹק לְדֵעָה מַה יֵּעָשֶׂה לוֹ.

His sister [Miriam] stood at a distance to know what would be done with him.

The word "וַתֵּתַצַּב" is most interesting. On the one hand, the presence of two letter *tav*'s indicates that it is a reflexive verb, the translation of which would be, "she stood herself." However, the correct spelling for the reflexive form is actually "וַתִּתְיַצֵּב," whereas the *tzeirei* under the first *tav* in this word as the Torah presents it is more indicative of the passive form—"she was made to stand." In other words, this word does not entirely fit into either of the above categories, appearing instead to have elements of both!

What are we to make of all this? What does it tell us about Miriam's decision to stay behind and see what would happen?

The *Maharal* explains that the background to Miriam's actions, as discussed in the Gemara,[6] was the prophecy that she received which stated that Moshe would be the future savior of the Jewish People.[7] With Moshe now being set on the Nile, Miriam felt compelled to stay and see what would happen in light of her prophecy. As such, says the *Maharal*, her staying behind was comprised of two elements:

- On the one hand, she *chose* to stay, for no one told her to do so.
- On the other hand, given the prophecy that she had received regarding Moshe, force of destiny dictated that she *had* to stay behind and see what would happen to him.

This blended situation, says the *Maharal*, is reflected in the word "וַתֵּתַצַּב" which, as we noted, combines both reflexive and passive elements. This combination gives us the composite picture of someone who both chooses (reflexive) *and* is compelled (passive) to stay!

---

6   *Sotah* 13a.
7   *Gevuros Hashem*, chap. 17.

NOUNS AND VERBS BLENDED TOGETHER:
THE MEANING OF "SAREI MISIM"

The opening chapter of our parsha describes Pharaoh's persecution of the Jewish People. Verse 11 relates that he placed "sarei misim" over them. What are "sarei misim"?

- *Rashi* associates this term with the word "mas," which means "tax," explaining that they were tax-officers.
- In contrast, *Onkelos* translates "shiltonin mav'ishin," which means "officers who did evil."

The *Netziv* explains that in fact, *both of these connotations combined* emanate from the word "misim."[8] On the one hand, if it only referred to tax, then it should have said "masim" with a *patach*—the plural of "mas"! Rather, the reason the word is spelled with a *chirik* is because it also derives from the word "memasim," which means "melting,"[9] i.e., subjugating and disheartening the Jewish People through persecution. This is the basis of *Onkelos'* translation—"officers who did evil." Having said that, the word "misim" cannot just mean "doing evil," for it is clearly a plural noun denoting *things*, not a verb denoting *actions*. Hence, through a combined use of the letters for the word "taxes" with the vowelization of the word "persecuting" in describing these officers, the Torah presents a composite description of their role![10]

FROM WORDS TO VOWELS: AVRAHAM'S GUESTS

Moving beyond our parsha and taking this discussion one stage further, we will discover that the idea of combining different elements to

---

8   *Haamek Davar* to *Shemos* ibid.
9   See, e.g., *Yeshayah* 10:18.
10   See also the *Netziv's* Introduction *Kidmas Ha'emek* to *Haamek Davar*, sec. 7, and *Harchev Davar* to *Bereishis* 2:25. For an example of a composite word in the realm of halachah, see *Malbim* to *Vayikra* 4:23, who explains that the word which denotes a person's awareness of a sin which obligates him to bring a sin-offering—"אוֹ הוֹדַע אֵלָיו חַטָאתוֹ"—combines both passive and causative elements. This indicates that a person can be liable for such an offering through being informed of it by someone else (causative), provided that he accepts and believes their testimony, whereby the sin is known (passive) to him.

express a composite message can express itself not only within a single word—but even within a single vowel. The beginning of *Parshas Vayeira* describes how Hashem appears to Avraham, who presently notices three wayfarers standing nearby.[11] Verse 3 then reads:

וַיֹּאמַר אֲדֹנָי אִם נָא מָצָאתִי חֵן בְּעֵינֶיךָ אַל נָא תַעֲבֹר מֵעַל עַבְדֶּךָ.

He [Avraham] said, "Adonoy, if I have found favor in your eyes, do not pass on from your servant."

Who is Avraham addressing with these words? The Midrash offers two possible explanations:[12]

- Avraham was addressing the guests, beseeching them to stop and enjoy his hospitality. According to this explanation, the word *"adonoy"* is the plural of the word *"adoni"* and means "my masters."
- Avraham was addressing Hashem, asking Him not to depart while he tended to his guests. According to this explanation, the word *"Ado-noy"* denotes Hashem's name.

The commentators, however, point out a basic problem:

- The word *"אֲדֹנָי"* in the verse is spelled with a *kamatz* under the *nun* (Ado-noy). This is indeed the vowelization for this word when used as Hashem's name.
- In contrast, the word *"אֲדֹנַי,"* when spelled in the plural denoting "my masters," is *"אֲדֹנַי"* (adonay) with a *patach*.[13]

As such, the presence of the *kamatz* in this word in our verse clearly indicates that Avraham was addressing Hashem! How is it even possible to suggest an alternative explanation, i.e., that he was addressing his guests?

---

11   *Bereishis* 18:1–2.
12   *Bereishis Rabbah* 48:10, cited in *Rashi* to that verse.
13   As used, e.g., by Lot when addressing the angels later in that parsha (19:2): "וַיֹּאמֶר הִנֶּה נָּא אֲדֹנַי."

The *Shelah Hakadosh* explains that *Rashi* himself notes that the rest of the verse is phrased in the singular ("*b'einecha...avdecha*"), while only the following verse uses the plural ("*Yukach na me'at mayim v'rachatzu ragleichem*—Take please some water and wash your feet")! How can this be reconciled with the approach whereby Avraham was addressing his guests already in the first verse? *Rashi* explains that while Avraham was indeed addressing them as a group, he nonetheless intuited that one of them was the senior member, by whose decision the other two would abide; hence, he specifically addressed his initial plea to that individual. This, says the *Shelah*, is why the word "*adonoy*" in the verse has a *kamatz*, even if it is not the name of Hashem! As we have noted, when addressing one person as one's master, the word is spelled with a *chirik* under the *nun*—"*adoni*," while, when addressing a number of people, it is spelled with a *patach*—"*adonay*." Yet, what happens when one is simultaneously addressing *both* a group of people in general *and* one individual in particular? What vowel should be used then? The answer is: A vowel which combines both a *chirik* and a *patach* under the *nun*, which results in a *kamatz*—"*adonoy*"![14]

It is simply incredible to behold how the nuance of the simultaneous duality within Avraham's comments to his guests, as described by *Rashi*, is communicated by the Torah with a single vowel!

---

14   *Parshas Vayeira.*

THE REQUEST FOR THREE DAYS

נֵלְכָה נָּא דֶּרֶךְ שְׁלֹשֶׁת יָמִים בַּמִּדְבָּר וְנִזְבְּחָה לַה' אֱלֹקֵינוּ.

Let us please go on a three-day journey in the wilderness and we shall bring offerings to Hashem, our God.[1]

INTRODUCTION: WAS THIS A REAL REQUEST?

When Hashem appears to Moshe at the burning bush, He instructs him to go to Pharaoh and request a three-day leave for the Jewish People. Many commentators raise the question of how to understand this request. It quite clearly states just one verse earlier that Hashem was planning to take the Jewish People out of Egypt permanently and bring them to the land of Israel! Why then, send Moshe to ask for something which was less than what He really wanted?

An approach adopted by numerous commentators is that on the eve of receiving punishment that would be both dramatic and decisive, it was crucial to expose the full extent of Pharaoh's wickedness, leaving no doubt in anyone's mind as to how deserving he was of receiving it. Not only was he not prepared to release the Jewish People permanently—a position which, although still wrong, would at least be understandable—he refused to allow them out for even three days! In light of

---

1   *Shemos* 3:18.

this, there could be no doubt that his punishment was justly deserved, allowing people to fully engage in and connect with the lessons learned therefrom. This was the role of the request for three days.[2]

TWO MESSAGES FOR PHARAOH

A spectacular analysis of the messages Hashem wished to convey to Pharaoh is found in the writings of one of the great Torah luminaries of pre-war Lithuania, R' Aharon Walkin.[3] He explains that alongside the request for three days, whose role we have discussed, it is equally important that Pharaoh should also hear from the outset the full extent of Hashem's demands—a complete emancipation of the Jewish People. Pharaoh should not be able to claim that this bigger demand was not part of the original message from Hashem.

And indeed, in addition to the message that was told to Moshe at the burning bush, cited in chapter 3 of our parsha,[4] chapter 4 records that when Moshe is apparently already on the way back to Egypt, Hashem tells him the following:[5]

וְאָמַרְתָּ אֶל פַּרְעֹה כֹּה אָמַר ה' בְּנִי בְכֹרִי יִשְׂרָאֵל. וָאֹמַר אֵלֶיךָ שַׁלַּח אֶת בְּנִי וְיַעַבְדֵנִי.

You shall say to Pharaoh, "So said Hashem: My son, My firstborn is Israel. And [so], I say to you, send out My son that he may serve Me."

Having already been told at the burning bush what to say to Pharaoh, what need was there to repeat the message at this stage? And yet, when we look carefully at the verses, we will see that this is not a repetition of the original message, but rather, an *entirely different message.*

---

2   See also, concerning this request, *Ohr Hachaim Hakadosh Shemos* 3:18; *Beis Halevi, Parshas Shemos,* s.v. *b'Yalkut;* and *Emes L'Yaakov* ibid., 3:18.

3   *Drashos Metzach Aharon,* vol. 1, *drush* 1.

4   Verse 18.

5   Verses 22-23.

Let us consider:

This second message makes no reference whatsoever to a duration of three days. On the contrary, the Hebrew word "*shalach*" typically denotes sending someone away with no expectation of seeing him again, in which case the word "*v'yaavdeini*" means the Jewish People will enter Hashem's service *fully*, never again to return to Egypt. In other words, accompanying the first request for three days, there is also a request demanding the total release of the Jewish People.

However, this leads us to a different question: How can Moshe request two different things without simply sounding as if he is contradicting himself? The answer, says R' Walkin, is that these two messages did not come from the same person...

TWO DELEGATIONS TO PHARAOH

If we look again at the verses in these two chapters, we will notice something most interesting:

- The verse in chapter 3 indicates that the first message, asking for three days, is to be said by Moshe *together with the elders of Israel*.
- In contrast to this, the second message, demanding full emancipation, has no participation from the elders; it is to come from Moshe alone in Hashem's name.

As Pharaoh's subjects, the elders of Israel cannot meaningfully ask for more than a temporary reprieve. Moshe, on the other hand, who is not subject to Pharaoh's rule, can communicate a demand for the people's full release. In this way, Pharaoh gets to hear both messages—each one for its own goal and purpose, as outlined above—without them coming from the same source and thereby sounding contradictory to each other.

In fact, there are a couple of additional, nuanced differences between the two messages which can be explained with this approach:

- The second message to Pharaoh is an explicit demand from Hashem: "Send out My son." A literal reading of the first message contains no such demand, and actually implies that it is *the peo-ple's own idea*: "And now [i.e., given that the God of the Hebrews has appeared to us], please let us go on a three-day journey..." This further separates the two messages from each other, in order to minimize a sense of contradiction between them.

- At the burning bush, Moshe is told to go together with the elders to "the king of Egypt." In the second message, he is told to come to "Pharaoh." Given that these two terms undoubtedly refer to the same person, what is behind the shift in reference? Here too, the answer lies in who is talking. The first message comes from the elders of Israel, who are under Pharaoh's dominion; therefore, they need to address him as their king. The second message, coming from Moshe who is not subject to Pharaoh, can address him with his official title, but no more.

Having thus arrived at an understanding of the two different mes-sages to Pharaoh coming from two different sources, all we need now is to understand how the actual message that is subsequently recorded as being said to Pharaoh is...*neither of the above two messages!*

WHEN THE MANY BECAME THE FEW

When Moshe and Aharon finally come to Pharaoh, the verse records their demand as follows:

כֹּה אָמַר ה' אֱלֹקֵי יִשְׂרָאֵל שַׁלַּח אֶת עַמִּי וְיָחֹגּוּ לִי בַּמִּדְבָּר.

So said Hashem, the God of Israel, "Send out My people that they may celebrate for Me in the wilderness."[6]

Which of the two messages is this?

- On the one hand, Moshe uses the term "*shalach*," which implies a demand for complete emancipation, as per the message of chapter 4.

---

6   5:1.

- On the other hand, he concludes, "that they may celebrate for Me in the wilderness," implying that the request is only for the duration of that festival, as per the message of chapter 3!

Why is Moshe grafting together parts of the two messages to create a message that is neither of them?

The answer is in a comment of *Rashi's* to the beginning of the verse, which states: "וְאַחַר בָּאוּ מֹשֶׁה וְאַהֲרֹן וַיֹּאמְרוּ אֶל פַּרְעֹה"—Afterwards, Moshe and Aharon came and said to Pharaoh." We notice that part of the delegation to Pharaoh is missing—namely, the elders! Where did they go? *Rashi* explains:

> But the elders slipped away, one by one, until all of them had disappeared before they arrived at [Pharaoh's palace] because they were afraid to go.

The elders could not bring themselves to come before Pharaoh and request anything. This left only Moshe and Aharon. However, we can appreciate that Moshe now faced a problem: The two groups were required in order to communicate two different messages. Now that there was only one group left, how were both of those messages to come across?

It is for this reason that Moshe "blends" the two messages into one in his first communication to Pharaoh—using the word "*shalach*" on the one hand, while mentioning "celebration" in a general sense on the other. With the message containing both elements, it was now a question of which one Pharaoh heard as primary, which would then allow Moshe to follow up with the other request.

And which element did Pharaoh "hear" more? Verse 2 records his reply:

וַיֹּאמֶר פַּרְעֹה מִי ה' אֲשֶׁר אֶשְׁמַע בְּקֹלוֹ לְשַׁלַּח אֶת יִשְׂרָאֵל לֹא יָדַעְתִּי אֶת ה' וְגַם אֶת יִשְׂרָאֵל לֹא אֲשַׁלֵּחַ.

Pharaoh said, "Who is Hashem that I should heed His voice to send out Israel? I do not know Hashem, nor will I send out Israel!"

We see that Pharaoh understood Moshe's words as demanding a full release of the Jewish People, to which he stated his categorical refusal. At this stage, with the demand for full release having been stated, Moshe himself shifts to the other message, which was originally meant to have been made by the elders:

וַיֹּאמְרוּ אֱלֹקֵי הָעִבְרִים נִקְרָא עָלֵינוּ נֵלְכָה נָּא דֶּרֶךְ שְׁלֹשֶׁת יָמִים בַּמִּדְבָּר וְנִזְבְּחָה לַה' אֱלֹקֵינוּ.

They said, "The God of the Hebrews happened upon us. Let us please go for a three-day journey in the wilderness, and we shall offer sacrifices to Hashem, our God."

However, as the next verse records, Pharaoh refused this request as well:

וַיֹּאמֶר אֲלֵהֶם מֶלֶךְ מִצְרַיִם לָמָּה מֹשֶׁה וְאַהֲרֹן תַּפְרִיעוּ אֶת הָעָם מִמַּעֲשָׂיו.

The king of Egypt said to them, "Moshe and Aharon, why would you disturb the nation from its work?"

In these verses, too, we see that when refusing to release the people entirely, the verse refers to him as "Pharaoh," while when refusing to let them go for even three days, he is called "the king of Egypt."

Thus, with both requests having been put to Pharaoh, albeit in a different form than originally intended, and with him having, nonetheless, categorically refused both of them, the stage was now set for initiating the Ten Plagues and the Exodus from Egypt, as described in the parshiyos to come.

SIGNS FOR THE
NON-BELIEVERS

וַיַּעַן מֹשֶׁה וַיֹּאמֶר וְהֵן לֹא יַאֲמִינוּ לִי וְלֹא יִשְׁמְעוּ בְּקֹלִי כִּי יֹאמְרוּ לֹא נִרְאָה אֵלֶיךָ ה'.

Moshe responded and said, "But they will not believe me and they will not listen to my voice, for they will say, 'Hashem did not appear to you.'"[1]

INTRODUCTION: "BUT THEY WILL NOT BELIEVE ME"

The middle section of our parsha discusses the episode of the burning bush, where Hashem appears to Moshe and charges him with taking the Jewish People out of Egypt. As our verse relates, Moshe was concerned that the people would not believe him. In response to this, Hashem provided him with three signs to perform in order to verify his status as Hashem's emissary.

SHOULD MOSHE HAVE HAD CAUSE FOR CONCERN?

If we reflect on the situation of the Jewish People at that time, we will better understand where Moshe's concerns were coming from:

---

1   *Shemos* 4:1.

- Timing: First, it was well known to the people that the exile had been foretold to Avraham, who had been informed that it would last for four hundred years. The Jewish People had currently been in Egypt for a little over two hundred years. Even if they harbored hope for the future redemption, that was not something they were expecting to see in their lifetimes.

- Identity of the Redeemer: Additionally, even if the Jewish People accepted the idea that they could be redeemed now, no one was expecting that the redeemer would be Moshe, whom they had not seen for decades. If anyone, it would be Aharon, who had been together with them and prophesying for them in Egypt during this time.

It would appear, then, that Moshe was correct in suspecting that his message would be met with reservations on the part of the people. Moreover, the very fact that Hashem responded by providing Moshe with signs to verify his words, as opposed to simply saying, "Don't worry, they will believe you," indicates that Moshe was right in suspecting that such measures might be needed.

And, yet, at the same time, this entire matter is completely astounding. For when we look just a few verses earlier,[2] we see that Hashem has already addressed this matter, *explicitly assuring Moshe, "V'sham'u l'kolecha*—They will listen to you"! How then, could Moshe say—in direct contradiction of these words—that the people would *not* listen to him?[3]

TWO TYPES OF LISTENING

To answer the above question, let us consider that the idea of "listening to someone" can have more than one meaning:

- It is possible to "listen to someone" in the sense of giving the person a hearing and considering what he has to say, without necessarily then going along with it.

---

2   3:18.

3   See commentaries of the *Ibn Ezra* and *Ramban* to our verse, and *Moreh Nevuchim*, sec. 1 chap. 63.

- Another type of "listening to someone" denotes heeding the person's words and following what he says.

How can we know to which of these types of listening the Torah is referring? The key is in noting whether the "listening" is followed by the letter *lamed*—"lishmoa *l'kol*"—or the letter *beis*—"lishmoa *b'kol*":

- The letter *lamed*, which means "to," denotes distance from A to B. Hence, listening "*l'kol*" indicates that the listener is distinct from the speaker and it is he who will determine whether or not he follows the speaker's wishes.
- The letter *beis*, which means "with" or "in," denotes the proximity of A to B. Accordingly, listening "*b'kol*" entails B heeding A's words and following them.

For example, in *Parshas Lech Lecha* we are told of how Sarah (then Sarai), upon seeing that she had not borne children, advises Avraham (then Avram) to take Hagar as a wife.[4] The verse describes Avraham's response:

וַיִּשְׁמַע אַבְרָם לְקוֹל שָׂרָי.

Avram listened to Sarai's voice.

In that instance, Avraham heard Sarah's idea, considered it, and concurred with it. Hence the term "*l'kol*" is used.

In contrast to this, after the birth of Yitzchak, when Sarah sees that Yishmael is a danger to him, she demands of Avraham to banish Hagar and Yishmael from the house. We are told by the Torah that Avraham did not concur with this idea, rather, "the matter was very bad in his eyes"![5] Nevertheless, Hashem told Avraham to heed Sarah's voice in spite of his objections, and hence, the term used is "*b'kol*":

כֹּל אֲשֶׁר תֹּאמַר אֵלֶיךָ שָׂרָה שְׁמַע בְּקֹלָהּ.

Everything that Sarah tells you, heed her voice.[6]

---

4   *Bereishis* 16:2.
5   Ibid., 21:11.
6   Ibid., verse 12.

Applying this idea to our verses, we can see that here too, Hashem's original assurance to Moshe was *"v'sham'u l'kolecha."* With these words, Hashem was telling Moshe that the people would give him a hearing. This, however, did not guarantee him a following, or that they would necessarily even believe him. This is especially understood when we consider why they would listen to him in the first place. *Rashi* explains that their attention was guaranteed on account of Moshe using the words *"pakod pakadeti*—I have indeed taken account,"[7] which were known to be the words with which the redeemer would introduce himself. However, the very fact that this was known meant that a person using these words did not necessarily mean he was the redeemer. It did ensure, however, that people would hear what he had to say, as denoted by the words *"v'sham'u l'kolecha."* In light of this, Moshe proceeds to raise the concern that even after having heard his voice, *"v'lo yishme'u b'koli*—they will not heed my voice." This concern was indeed validated by Hashem, Who then gave Moshe the signs to perform before the people.[8]

A truly stunning example of how attention to detail, down to the letter, opens up the words and messages of the verses.

THE FIRST TWO SIGNS: WAS THE SECOND SIGN BETTER THAN THE FIRST?

In response to Moshe's concerns, Hashem provided him with three signs in order to verify his status as the emissary for the redemption. Let us focus for now on the first two signs:

- Upon being thrown onto the ground, Moshe's staff turned into a snake, and returned to being a staff when he picked it up.
- When he placed his hand in his tunic, it became leprous, becoming healed again when he replaced it there.

---

7   *Shemos* 3:16.
8   Based on the *Gur Aryeh* and *Malbim* to our verse. See also *Shemos* 18:19 and 24.

After presenting the second sign, Hashem informs Moshe:

וְהָיָה אִם לֹא יַאֲמִינוּ לָךְ וְלֹא יִשְׁמְעוּ לְקֹל הָאֹת הָרִאשׁוֹן וְהֶאֱמִינוּ לְקֹל הָאֹת הָאַחֲרוֹן.

It shall be that if they do not believe you and do not listen to the voice of the first sign, they will believe the voice of the latter sign.[9]

The basic question is: Why would they believe the second sign more than the first? Given that both signs were miraculous, why would one miracle be more convincing than another?

Rashi presents a most astonishing answer to this question:

Once you tell them, "I was stricken on your account because I spoke lashon hara [slander] about you," they will believe you; for they have already learned regarding such matters that those who attack them in order to harm them are stricken with tzaraas, as were Pharaoh and Avimelech on account of Sarah.

The background to *Rashi's* explanation is the idea that the second sign, which involved Moshe's hand becoming leprous, came as a punishment for him speaking negatively about the Jewish People. Once he communicated this aspect of the sign to the people, they would be more convinced that he was indeed Hashem's emissary.[10]

What emerges from this explanation of *Rashi* is that there was nothing about the second sign *per se* that made it more convincing than the first; rather, it was specifically the accompanying commentary that it came as a punishment that would hopefully bring the people around.[11]

---

9   *Shemos* 4:8.
10   It is amazing to consider that the Jewish People, who had by now been subjected to decades of systematic, nationwide oppression, with their tormentors apparently free of any repercussions, were convinced by the fact that Moshe, who had merely spoken negatively about them, was punished for doing so. This means that although sorely tried, their expectation of Divine justice had not been extinguished.
11   *Rashi* actually explains that the first sign also contained elements of censure for Moshe over his negative comments concerning the people: Hashem informed him that he deserved to be struck by the staff in his hand for speaking ill of them, and the staff then turned into

Needless to say, this explanation is categorized as *drash*, as it draws on an aspect of the sign which is not contained in the words of the verses themselves. This, then, leaves us wondering: Is there a *pshat* answer to why the second sign would be more convincing?

One of the great commentators on *Rashi*, the *Be'er Yitzchak*, explains that in fact, there is no *pshat* answer to this question because, on a *pshat* level, the question doesn't begin.

PSHAT AND DRASH: LITERAL AND NON-LITERAL?

When coming to formulate the difference between *pshat* and *drash*, we might be inclined to phrase it as being that *pshat* represents the literal meaning of the words, while *drash* is the non-literal meaning. However, that formulation is not only imprecise, but sometimes, the exact opposite is true.

Pshat represents the straightforward reading of the verse. Sometimes, in order to arrive at the straightforward meaning, one is required to exercise a certain degree of latitude with the words, not necessarily taking them literally as stated. In our instance, there are commentators who explain that when Hashem says, "If they do not listen to the first sign, they will listen to the second," it means, "the second sign *together with the first*." According to this approach, the contribution of the second sign was not *qualitative*, but *corroborative*. In other words, there was not necessarily anything inherently more convincing about the second sign; rather, now there will be two signs, and two signs are more convincing than one.

Thus far on a *pshat* level. However, says the *Be'er Yitzchak*, one of the classic methods of *drash* is specifically to engage in the words *as they were literally stated*. In this instance, the words literally imply that the second sign by itself would be more convincing than the first, and hence,

---

a snake, the archetypical symbol of *lashon hara*. It is interesting, therefore, that the response in the event that the people did not believe the first sign was to provide a second sign, the compelling factor of which would be the accompanying commentary of punishment for *lashon hara*, and not simply to provide the same commentary for the already existing first sign.

the *drash* proceeds to explain why this is so, referencing the fact that it was a punishment for Moshe speaking negatively about the people.[12]

This is a truly fascinating idea in the world of the concepts of *pshat* and *drash*, as the *Be'er Yitzchak* himself describes it: "*Klal gadol b'derech hadrashos*—a major principle regarding *drash* expositions!"[13]

CONCLUDING THOUGHTS: WHAT DID MOSHE SAY WRONG?

The question that remains is: Why is Moshe considered to have spoken *lashon hara* about the Jewish People? As we have seen, his concerns that the people would not automatically believe him were perfectly legitimate and indeed, corroborated by Hashem giving him signs to verify his status!

It appears that the answer lies in Moshe's opening word: "*V'hein.*" This word simply appears to mean, "And they [will not believe me]." However, if so, why does Moshe use the feminine form instead of the masculine form, "*v'heim*"?

In truth, the word "*hein*" has another meaning—it means "behold" or "indeed," and denotes emphasis and certainty. When Moshe said, "*V'hein lo yaaminu li*," he was saying, "It is certain that they will not believe me." In this regard, Moshe was considered to have slandered the Jewish People, for even if he was entitled—and, perhaps, even required—to address the *possibility* that the people might not believe

---

12   For this reason, when it comes to the third sign of turning water into blood, *Rashi* does not discuss why that sign would be more convincing than the first two. Since Hashem did not say regarding the third sign, "If they don't believe the first two, they will believe this third one," it is understood that the contribution of this sign was purely corroborative, i.e., there being three signs instead of two (*Be'er Yitzchak* ibid.).

13   Another classic illustration of this idea comes from *Rashi's* comments on various verses that mention peoples' hands, e.g., Yaakov sending gifts to Eisav "from that which came to his hand" (*Bereishis* 32:14), or a lesson regarding Korach that came "from Moshe's hand" (*Bamidbar* 17:5). *Rashi* first presents the *pshat* explanation, which in the former case means "from his domain," and in the latter case is "through his agency." However, he then adds the *drash* explanation, which translates the word "hand" literally—in the first case referring to jewels that Yaakov gave Eisav, and in the second case referring to Moshe's actual hand which turned leprous when he spoke negatively about the Jewish people at the burning bush. Regarding this matter, it is fair to say that the *drash* has the ability to translate these words literally, since it has the option of then explaining them in a way that does not rely on *pshat* context.

him, he was not, however, entitled to assert that they would *definitely* not believe him.

This understanding is corroborated by a passage in the Midrash regarding Moshe's final days, during which Hashem informed him, "הֵן קָרְבוּ יָמֶיךָ לָמוּת—Behold, your days are drawing near to die."[14] The Midrash states:[15]

> כָּךְ אָמַר מֹשֶׁה, רִבּוֹנוֹ שֶׁל עוֹלָם, בִּ'הֵן' קִלַּסְתִּיךָ שֶׁכֵּן כְּתִיב "הֵן לַה' אֱלֹקֶיךָ הַשָּׁמַיִם וּשְׁמֵי הַשָּׁמָיִם," וּבִ'הֵן' אַתָּה גּוֹזֵר עָלַי מִיתָה? אָמַר לוֹ הַקָּדוֹשׁ בָּרוּךְ הוּא...אִי אַתָּה זוֹכֵר בְּשָׁעָה שֶׁשְּׁלַחְתִּיךָ לִגְאוֹל אוֹתָם מִמִּצְרַיִם וְאָמַרְתָּ לִי "וְהֵן לֹא יַאֲמִינוּ לִי"?

> *So said Moshe, "Master of the universe, I praised You with the word "hein," as it says, 'Behold [hein], to Hashem, your God, are the Heavens and the highest Heavens,' and with the word "hein" You are decreeing death upon me? Said the Holy One, Blessed be He, [to Moshe], "Do you not remember at the time that I sent you to redeem them from Egypt that you said, 'Behold [hein] they will not believe me?'"*

With these words, Hashem was telling Moshe, "You may have been entitled to consider the possibility that they may not believe in you, but you were not entitled to not believe in them."

We may not be on Moshe's level, where a single misplaced word can have such dire consequences, but we can, and should, certainly extrapolate from this episode to our own lives in our dealings and interactions with our fellow Jews. As we regard others whose standards or sensitivities may be lacking in some respects, we can never consign them to such conduct or discount the possibility that they might change. They too, are children of our Patriarchs and Matriarchs, and one never knows when their Jewish soul will shine through.

---

14 *Devarim* 31:14.
15 *Devarim Rabbah* 9:6.

FROM THE COMMENTATORS

LOST WITHOUT TRANSLATION

וְאֵלֶּה שְׁמוֹת בְּנֵי יִשְׂרָאֵל הַבָּאִים מִצְרָיְמָה.

And these are the names of the B'nei Yisrael who were coming to Mitzrayim.[1]

The Gemara states that a person is obligated to review the weekly parsha, reading the verses twice and then translating them—"*sh'nayim mikra v'echad targum.*"[2] Various commentators point out that this mitzvah is alluded to in the opening words of our parsha: "וְאֵלֶּה שְׁמוֹת" serves as an acronym for, "וחייב אדם לעבור הפרשה שנים מקרא ואחד תרגום"— A person is obligated to review the parsha, twice with Scripture and once with *targum*." It is most interesting to ponder this choice of verses through which to allude to this mitzvah. How is it connected to the Jewish People coming to Mitzrayim?

The onset of the persecution of the Jewish People is recorded in verses 6–8:

וַיָּמָת יוֹסֵף וְכָל אֶחָיו וְכֹל הַדּוֹר הַהוּא. וּבְנֵי יִשְׂרָאֵל פָּרוּ וַיִּשְׁרְצוּ...וַתִּמָּלֵא הָאָרֶץ אֹתָם. וַיָּקָם מֶלֶךְ חָדָשׁ עַל מִצְרָיִם אֲשֶׁר לֹא יָדַע אֶת יוֹסֵף.

Yosef died, and all his brothers, and that entire generation.

---

1   *Shemos* 1:1.
2   *Berachos* 8a.

And the B'nei Yisrael multiplied profusely...and the land was filled with them. And a new king arose over Mitzrayim who did not know of Yosef.

The *Chasam Sofer* explains that the relationship between these verses is not just *sequential*, it is *causational*. After all, we note that the Jewish People had been in Mitzrayim for a number of decades without experiencing any oppression. What brought on such a drastic change? The Sages comment that the phrase "and the land was filled with them" is stated in a negative light. With the death of Yosef and his generation, the people lost their connection with the distinct outlook and values embodied by their forebears and began to try and integrate into Egyptian culture. The result was that "the land was filled with them," including places which were not appropriate for them or in keeping with the values they were meant to uphold. The result of this tragically misguided move is recorded in the third verse: "And a new king arose over Mitzrayim who did not know of Yosef," enacting oppressive edicts for them, and, ultimately, engineering their enslavement and persecution.

What led to the people's abandonment of the ways of their fathers? The answer is that although they were well aware of how the earlier generation lived and, no doubt, appreciated its value, they could not see how this could be applied to their new surroundings. It may have been appropriate for "the *heim*" of Canaan, but not for modern Egypt. Confronted with the perceived conflict between an ancient way of life and the need to adapt to a new society, they chose the latter.

What is the solution to their quandary? *Sh'nayim mikra v'echad targum*. Wherever a person is, he needs to read the Torah—and then he needs to read it again. Success begins by fully absorbing the Torah's message and values. Once that has been accomplished, the next stage is *"targum"*—to know how to translate the Torah's timeless values into one's current situation in a way that will be both faithful to the former and yet, compatible with the latter. This is the message of *sh'nayim mikra v'echad targum*; it is, quite literally, a message for all times.[3]

---

3   R' Ze'ev Freund, *Shabbos U'Moadim*.

PHARAOH'S FEARS

הָבָה נִתְחַכְּמָה לוֹ פֶּן יִרְבֶּה וְהָיָה כִּי תִקְרֶאנָה מִלְחָמָה וְנוֹסַף גַּם הוּא עַל שֹׂנְאֵינוּ
וְנִלְחַם בָּנוּ.

*Come, let us deal wisely with them, lest they increase, and it
may be that there will be a war, then they, too, will join our
enemies and wage war against us.*[4]

It is worthwhile considering whether Pharaoh truly believed that
the Jewish People would ally themselves with his enemies in the event
of war and turn against him, and, if so, on what basis did he believe that
they would act in such a treasonous way?

Interestingly, our verse has the distinction of having commentary
provided for it from another verse later in the Torah. In the beginning
of *Parshas Ki Savo*, the Torah describes the procedure for the mitzvah
of bringing *bikkurim* (first fruits), which involves reciting a number of
verses that encapsulate our experiences in Egypt. This section forms
the core of the mitzvah of telling the story of the Exodus on the Seder
night, as we take each phrase and elaborate with a proof-text from the
relevant sections in *Chumash Shemos*. The second verse of that section
begins: "וַיָּרֵעוּ אֹתָנוּ הַמִּצְרִים—the Egyptians were evil to us," and the proof
text cited is our verse: "Let us deal wisely with them, lest they increase,
etc." Of all the expositions in that section of the Haggadah, this one is
most puzzling, for the proof-text seems to be describing Pharaoh's fear
as to the evil that *we* might do to *them*! How then, does it serve as an
elaboration on the evil that *they* did to *us*?

However, upon closer inspection of that verse, we can appreciate the
Haggadah's teaching. Although the words "*vayarei'u osanu*" are commonly
translated as "they did evil to us," the more straightforward way to say
that in Hebrew is "*vayarei'u lanu*"![5] A more accurate translation of the
words "*vayarei'u osanu*" is "they *made us* evil." Is this true, and if so, how?

The *Beis Halevi* explains. As Pharaoh considered his plans for the

---

4   *Shemos* 1:10
5   Indeed, this is the phrase that the Torah uses elsewhere in describing the Egyptians' treatment of the Jewish People; see, e.g., *Bamidbar* 20:15.

Jewish People, he knew that in order to achieve his goal, he would need both the support of his nation and the understanding of nations in the region. To spontaneously single out a group of people for persecution may have led to feelings of unrest among his citizens and neighbors. How could Pharaoh create an atmosphere which would be conducive to complicity among his people in implementing his policies of persecution against an innocent people in their midst?

The solution to this problem is: *Vayarei'u osanu*—they made us evil, i.e., they portrayed us as an evil people who were only looking to exploit the weaknesses of their gracious host country in order to take over when the time was right. Looked at in this way, any preemptive measures taken against this dangerous and subversive people would be no more than those of a faithful monarch defending the interests of his people. This was all the idealistic justification necessary to pave the way for national sympathy and complicity in his plans for the Jewish People.

Therefore, the Haggadah cites our verse, which describes the meeting where Pharaoh voiced his concerns that the Jews were set to take over his country, thereby "making them evil."

According to R' Shlomo Kluger, Pharaoh and his court really did believe that this people in their midst would try to overthrow and expel them. We asked, what basis might they have had for such grave suspicions? The answer is—none. But Pharaoh still believed that they would try and take over the country for one simple reason. They were so successful and powerful that it was simply inconceivable to Pharaoh that they would *not* be plotting a takeover, because that was what *he* would be doing if he would have been in their situation. Hence, it was clear to Pharaoh that this is what they would do, if only given the chance.

This brings us back to the words "*vayarei'u osanu.*" Rav Kluger explains that the root of the word *vayarei'u* in this verse is from the word *rei'a*, one's fellow or peer. In other words, "*vayarei'u osanu*" means they *equated us with them* in terms of our perceived national goals, and projected onto our situation all the things that they would do if they were us. Accordingly, the Haggadah proceeds to cite our verse, which gives full and graphic expression to these suspicions.

Our exile in Egypt is described as the prototype exile experience. In

this regard, too, our parsha presents us with themes that were originally formulated in Egypt and would be echoed many times after that.

DISCOVERING MOSHE

The Torah tells of how, in the course of surveying the tribulations
of his brethren, Moshe came upon an Egyptian taskmaster beating
a Hebrew slave. The verse states:

וַיִּפֶן כֹּה וָכֹה וַיַּרְא כִּי אֵין אִישׁ וַיַּךְ אֶת הַמִּצְרִי וַיִּטְמְנֵהוּ בַּחוֹל.

*He looked this way and that way and saw that there was no one,
and he slew the Egyptian and buried him in the sand.*[6]

The simple meaning of the verse is that Moshe first checked that
there was no one around who might report him to Pharaoh, and then
proceeded to take action against the Egyptian.

One of the great Chassidic masters interpreted the verse as follows:
Moshe was of Hebrew descent, and yet grew up in an Egyptian palace.
He was inclined to see himself as being a composite person with an
integrated identity, i.e., a "Hebrew-Egyptian." However, this way of
defining himself became untenable on that day, when he saw the two
sides of himself in irreconcilable conflict: an Egyptian beating a Hebrew.

What was Moshe to do? It was impossible to look upon this scene and
respond appropriately as a Hebrew-Egyptian, for there was no course of
action which would not pit one side of himself against the other.

In this defining moment, Moshe had to decide who he really was. Thus,
the verse says: "He looked this way and that way," i.e., Moshe looked at
one side of himself and saw a Hebrew, and the other side of himself and
saw an Egyptian, "and he saw that there was no one"—Moshe saw that
the person who he thought he was didn't really exist, for now he realized that he could not be both. He would have to choose. "And he slew
the Egyptian and buried him in the dust." Moshe killed the Egyptian
inside of himself, for he realized that although he had been brought up
in Egypt, that was not who he was. He was a Hebrew.[7]

---

6   *Shemos* 2:12.
7   Heard from my father, Rabbi Isaac Bernstein, *zt"l*.

PARSHAS VA'EIRA

FOUR REDEMPTIONS INSIDE ONE EXODUS

לָכֵן אֱמֹר לִבְנֵי יִשְׂרָאֵל אֲנִי ה' וְהוֹצֵאתִי אֶתְכֶם מִתַּחַת סִבְלֹת מִצְרַיִם וְהִצַּלְתִּי אֶתְכֶם מֵעֲבֹדָתָם וְגָאַלְתִּי אֶתְכֶם בִּזְרוֹעַ נְטוּיָה וּבִשְׁפָטִים גְּדֹלִים. וְלָקַחְתִּי אֶתְכֶם לִי לְעָם וְהָיִיתִי לָכֶם לֵאלֹקִים וִידַעְתֶּם כִּי אֲנִי ה' אֱלֹקֵיכֶם הַמּוֹצִיא אֶתְכֶם מִתַּחַת סִבְלוֹת מִצְרָיִם.

Therefore, say to the B'nei Yisrael, "I am Hashem, and I shall take you out from under the burdens of Mitzrayim, and I shall rescue you from their service, and I shall redeem you with an outstretched arm and with great judgments. And I shall take you to Me as a people, and I shall be a God to you; and you shall know that I am Hashem your God, Who takes you out from under the burdens of Mitzrayim."[1]

These two verses, stated by Hashem to Moshe at the beginning of our parsha, contain what are known as "the four expressions of redemption." However, as many commentators point out, this depiction does not do full justice to these terms, as "four expressions" of something sounds like four ways of saying the same thing. In reality, these four terms represent four distinct stages in the redemption from

---

1   *Shemos* 6:6–7.

Mitzrayim; and indeed, the *Talmud Yerushalmi* thus refers to them as "four redemptions."

RAV HIRSCH: A SYSTEMATIC REVERSAL OF THE EGYPTIAN EXILE

There have been many different interpretations of these four stages offered by the commentators over the generations, both in the Rishonim and the Acharonim.[2] A classic approach to this matter is found in the commentary of Rav Hirsch, who explains that if we wish to understand the specific connotation of each of these "redemption terms," we must remind ourselves of the way the Torah itself originally described this exile.

In *Parshas Lech Lecha*, Avraham is foretold of the exile that his descendants will experience:

וַיֹּאמֶר לְאַבְרָם יָדֹעַ תֵּדַע כִּי גֵר יִהְיֶה זַרְעֲךָ בְּאֶרֶץ לֹא לָהֶם וַעֲבָדוּם וְעִנּוּ אֹתָם אַרְבַּע מֵאוֹת שָׁנָה.

[Hashem] said to Avram, "You shall surely know that your descendants will be strangers in a land that is not theirs, and they will serve them, and they will oppress them, for four hundred years."

We see that the exile is described as comprising three increasing levels: (1) being strangers in a foreign land, (2) serving the Egyptians, and (3) being oppressed by them. As such, the redemption from that exile will likewise take the form of undoing those levels, beginning, of course, with the most difficult:

- "*V'hotzeisi*—I will take you out from the burdens of Mitzrayim," refers to releasing them from the burden of oppression.
- "*V'hitzalti*—I will save you from their service," refers to freeing them from having to serve the Egyptians.
- "*V'gaalti*—I will redeem you," refers to the indignity of being aliens in a foreign land, with no status, standing or recognition.

---

2   See, e.g., commentaries of *Rabbeinu Bachya*, the *Abarbanel, Malbim,* and *Netziv,* among others.

It is most interesting to note that in contrast with the first two expressions, which specify *from what* the people will be redeemed ("the burdens...their service"), this third expression instead focuses on *how*: "with an outstretched arm and with great judgments." This addresses one of the most basic questions regarding the entire Exodus from Egypt. Arguably, the whole process could have taken place on a much lower key, with Pharaoh being afflicted with some debilitating condition until the people were released and a safe distance away. Instead, it was a year-long production, full of miracles and wonders, as well as devastating and humiliating judgments for the Egyptians. A crucial goal served by this method is that it *restored the prestige of the Jewish People*. After having been regarded as people of no worth, more or less from the time that they entered the land, Hashem demonstrated that in His eyes, they were of *immense* value, deserving of great miracles through which their oppressors would be punished. This was the final point of their redemption, leading to the fourth stage:

- "*V'lakachti*—I will take you to Me as a people," expresses the purpose of the entire Egyptian experience—to enable the Jewish People to receive the Torah.

BETWEEN סבלת AND סבלות—OPPRESSION AND RECOGNITION

Having discussed the four stages of redemption in a general sense, let us consider for a moment a fascinating detail within these verses. The word "*sivlos*—burdens" appears twice: first in the beginning of verse 6, and then again at the end of verse 7. However, there is a difference between these two appearances. The first time that it is written, it is missing the letter *vav* at the end—"סִבְלֹת," while the second time, it is written "in full," with the *vav*—"סִבְלוֹת." What is behind this shift?

R' Yosef Salant offers a most profound explanation.[3] It is clear from the Midrash and classic commentators that the damage sustained by the Jewish People in Egypt was twofold in nature; alongside the physical and material oppression of the slavery itself, there was also a spiritual

---

3   *Be'er Yosef, Parshas Va'eira.*

decline. This is summed up in the statement of the *Zohar* that by the time they left, the people were on the forty-ninth level of impurity.[4] Whether this damage was inflicted knowingly and intentionally by the Egyptians or was simply a by-product of the general Egypt experience is a matter of some discussion among the commentators,[5] but the damage was done. The corollary of this idea is that redemption from Egypt, in the fullest sense of the word, incorporated spiritual rehabilitation as well as physical deliverance.

It is normal that if a person has a problem of a physical nature, be it medical, economic, or otherwise, that person will be aware of the fact. By contrast, if a person has a spiritual problem, he might not be aware of it at all. Indeed, it is practically a trademark of spiritual problems that a person becomes desensitized to spiritual matters, including his own spiritual situation. Ironically, sometimes it is only after a person manages to recover to a certain degree that he is then able to look back and realize that he initially had a problem.

The commentators explain that when a plural word is spelled without a *vav* at the end, it is in order to denote an element of singularity as well. This brings us to the spelling of the word "*sivlos*." As we noted, the first time it appears, when Hashem says, "I will take you out from under the burdens of Egypt," the word is written without a *vav*—"סִבְלֹת." The reason is because, at the time that they were being rescued, the people were only aware of being under one type of burden: the physical oppression. However, the next verse describes Hashem taking the people to Him as His people, culminating in the giving of the Torah, at which point they will then be able to look back from their spiritually recovered state and realize that Hashem had taken them out from two types of oppression, both physical and spiritual—hence, the word "סִבְלוֹת" is written with a *vav*, indicating multiple burdens!

---

4   One of the major questions regarding this matter is understanding how the subjugation in Egypt can, on the one hand, have inflicted such massive spiritual damage on the Jewish People, while on the other hand, the entire experience was preparing them to be able to receive the Torah! It would appear that one needs to differentiate between the reconstruction that was taking place on a *core* level and the negative fallout that accrued on a *behavioral* level.

5   See, e.g., *Beis Halevi, Parshas Shemos.*

It is both fascinating and moving to see how the Torah communicates such a profound idea by simply removing one letter from one of its words.

FROM FOUR STAGES TO FOUR REDEMPTIONS

Taking this discussion one stage further, the *Shem MiShmuel* adds an entirely new dimension to our understanding of the "four redemptions" in our verses. As we know, beyond the exile in Egypt, the Jewish People have undergone four exiles in their history: (1) Babylon, (2) Persia and Media, (3) Greece, and (4) Edom or Rome, with the latter continuing until the coming of the Mashiach. Moreover, the exile in Egypt is seen as the root-exile experience, of which the subsequent four exiles are all considered branches. This idea is contained in the verse which describes the Jewish People's arrival in Egypt: "וְאֵלֶּה שְׁמוֹת בְּנֵי יִשְׂרָאֵל הַבָּאִים מִצְרָיְמָה—And these are the names of the Children of Israel, who were coming to Egypt." We note that the form used is not *"asher ba'u*—who came," but rather, *"haba'im."* The letters of the word באים correspond to the four subsequent "branch" exiles:

- ב—*Bavel* (Babylon)
- א—*Edom* (Rome)
- י—*Yavan* (Greece)
- מ—*Madai* (Persia)

In this regard, not only did the exile in Egypt constitute the root of the four exiles, but the Exodus from there, likewise, represents the root redemption experience, of which all subsequent redemptions are branches. With this in mind, let us return to the "four redemptions" in our parsha and we will see that they correspond to the redemption from the four later exiles:

- The first exile involved the Jewish People being physically exiled from their land to Babylon. As such, the redemption from that exile was removing them from that land back to the Land of Israel. Hence, the key term regarding that redemption is *"v'hotzeisi*—I will take them out."

- The second exile was that of Persia, where the Jewish People faced the threat of extinction at the hands of Haman. Hence, the redemption from that exile was being saved from that decree, so that the key term for that redemption is *"v'hitzalti*—I will save them."
- The third exile was that of Greece, which took place in the land of Israel. The goal of the Greeks was not to exterminate the Jewish People, but to shift their allegiance from Hashem to the Greek outlook. The redemption from that exile took the form of reaffirming the Jewish People's relationship with Hashem. The concept of *geulah* in Torah denotes restoring something to its rightful owner. Hence, the term which reflects that redemption is *"v'gaalti*—I will redeem."
- The fourth and final exile, that of Rome, will complete the tribulations the Jewish People need to experience in their history in order to fully realize their destiny and connect with Hashem as His people. Hence, the fourth term of redemption is *"v'lakachti*—"I will take you to Me as a people."

It is most interesting to note in this regard that the four redemption terms are not divided equally as two in each verse; rather, the first verse contains three, while the second verse contains the fourth. This parallels the statement of the Midrash regarding the four exiles that states that when Daniel had his visions of the four exiles,[6] he dreamt about the first three on one night and the fourth on the next night; to teach you, says the Midrash, that the fourth exile is equal to all the first three.[7]

POSTSCRIPT: FOUR THAT ARE FIVE

Throughout the discussion of the "four terms of redemption," it is important not to lose sight of the fifth, which describes where the previous four stages will lead us to: "וְהֵבֵאתִי אֶתְכֶם אֶל הָאָרֶץ אֲשֶׁר נָשָׂאתִי אֶת

---

6   Described in *Daniel*, chap. 7.
7   *Vayikra Rabbah, Parshas Shemini.*

יָדִי לָתֵת אֹתָהּ לְאַבְרָהָם לְיִצְחָק וּלְיַעֲקֹב וְנָתַתִּי אֹתָהּ לָכֶם מוֹרָשָׁה אֲנִי ה׳—And I shall bring you to the land about which I raised My hand [in an oath] to give it to Avraham, to Yitzchak, and to Yaakov, and I shall give it to you as a heritage, I am Hashem."[8]

May we merit to see the fulfillment of all of these stages and elements of redemption, speedily in our days!

---

8   Verse 8.

UNDERSTANDING
THE HARDENING
OF PHARAOH'S HEART

וַאֲנִי אַקְשֶׁה אֶת לֵב פַּרְעֹה...וְלֹא יִשְׁמַע אֲלֵכֶם פַּרְעֹה וְנָתַתִּי אֶת יָדִי בְּמִצְרָיִם
וְהוֹצֵאתִי אֶת צִבְאֹתַי אֶת עַמִּי בְנֵי יִשְׂרָאֵל מֵאֶרֶץ מִצְרָיִם בִּשְׁפָטִים גְּדֹלִים.

I shall harden Pharaoh's heart...Pharaoh will not listen to you,
and I shall put My hand upon Egypt, and I shall take out My
legions—My people, the B'nei Yisrael—from the land of Egypt,
with great judgments.[1]

INTRODUCTION: PUNISHMENT WHEN
"YES" WAS NOT AN OPTION

One of the major questions pertaining to our redemption and the
Exodus from Egypt relates to the hardening of Pharaoh's heart. As our
verses state, Hashem removed Pharaoh's capacity to agree to let the
Jewish People go, in response to which he was visited with Hashem's
retribution in the form of ten plagues. This presents us with a basic
problem: If Pharaoh was rendered unable to say "yes," how could he
then be punished for saying "no"?

---

1   *Shemos* 7:3–4.

Various classic answers have been provided for this question by the early commentators:

- The *Rambam* states that in subjugating and persecuting the Jewish People as he did, Pharaoh had sinned to such a heinous extent that his punishment itself entailed having his free will removed from him and then being punished for saying no.[2]
- The *Ramban*, based on the Midrash, explains that Pharaoh hardened his own heart during the first five plagues, in response to which Hashem hardened his heart regarding the second five.[3]

THE MAASEH HASHEM: A NATURAL PROCESS

A fascinating and illuminating approach to the entire concept of Hashem hardening Pharaoh's heart is found in the writings of the *Maaseh Hashem*.[4] Rather than understanding that Hashem reached into Pharaoh's decision-making apparatus and turned off the switch, leaving him fundamentally incapable of deciding to let the Jewish People go, the *Maaseh Hashem* explains this idea in a much more natural way.

Often, people are in situations where they may say that they "have no choice" but to pursue a certain course of action, when in reality, what they mean is that the personality traits that govern them leave them no choice. For example, someone who has been insulted may feel that he is "forced" to leave the room. Of course, he *can* choose to stay if he wants, but his pride will not allow him to do so. Similarly, someone who subscribes to the notion that he is all-knowing or all-powerful may feel "compelled" to cover up a mistake or a weakness. In truth, he is fully capable of admitting his error, but the way in which he wishes to see—or project—himself effectively bars this option from him.

The *Maaseh Hashem* explains that it was in this sense that Hashem hardened Pharaoh's heart.

---

2   *Hilchos Teshuvah* 6:3.
3   See commentary to *Shemos* 7:3; see also commentary of *Seforno* to *Shemos* ibid.
4   *Shemos*, chap. 11

FIRST ENCOUNTER: STEPPING BACK TOWARD REDEMPTION

It is quite striking to note that the first meeting between Moshe and Pharaoh did not go very well at all. In fact, as a result of that meeting, things only got worse for the Jewish People, and Pharaoh actually increased their workload. Indeed, following that first episode, Moshe returns to Hashem and complains on the Jewish People's behalf: Not only had the redemption not begun moving forward, things had actually moved backwards!

To this, Hashem responds:

עַתָּה תִרְאֶה אֲשֶׁר אֶעֱשֶׂה לְפַרְעֹה כִּי בְיָד חֲזָקָה יְשַׁלְּחֵם.

Now you will see what I will do to Pharaoh, for with a strong hand he will send them out.[5]

Let us ask: How has Hashem's response addressed Moshe's complaint? Moshe asks why things went badly *so far*, and Hashem responds that *from this point on* things will go well! Seemingly, the question persists: why did the first meeting have to go badly?

Hashem is telling Moshe that now that things have gone badly in the first meeting, *that* is what has set the scene for Pharaoh to send the Jewish People out "with a strong hand." According to numerous commentators, the term "strong hand" refers to the idea of the hardening of Pharaoh's heart. Why is Hashem mentioning this idea to Moshe at this stage? Because it is this effect that was achieved through the first meeting going badly for Moshe and well for Pharaoh! This initial victory allowed Pharaoh to conclude that he was indeed stronger than whatever force Moshe represented—a conclusion which he was egotistically only too happy to embrace. Once Pharaoh had adopted this view, it was then possible to smite him with any number of plagues with confidence that he would not relent, for to do so would be for him to admit that his initial assessment of the situation had been mistaken. Pharaoh's ego would never allow him to make such an admission; as such, his heart was hardened.

---

5   Ibid., 6:1

VIEWING COMPASSION AS WEAKNESS

This idea will also explain to us something else that happened during that first encounter: Moshe's threat in Hashem's name that He will smite Pharaoh's firstborn.[6] As we know, the smiting of the firstborn was the last of the ten plagues. That being the case, we may wonder why Moshe is warning Pharaoh about it before the first plague has even begun!

This too was part of the hardening of Pharaoh's heart. Being the tenth plague, the smiting of the firstborn was clearly the most severe blow to Pharaoh and to Egypt, and indeed, Hashem brought nine relatively lesser plagues first. The reason why Pharaoh was warned about the tenth plague first was that being the most severe, it was also the plague whose foretelling was most likely to cause Pharaoh to consider letting the Jewish People go. Indeed, had Pharaoh responded to this warning, he could have thereby avoided all of the plagues.

In Pharaoh's mindset, however, the exact opposite was true. For if *he* was capable of inflicting such a harsh blow to his enemy, he would not settle for a milder one. In his lexicon, there was only one possible reason why one would not inflict the harsher blow—because he was unable to do so! The alternative suggestion, that Hashem was fully capable of killing his firstborn, but was refraining from doing so as an act of compassion, sadly did not register with Pharaoh. And, thus, he weathered the first nine plagues clinging on to his conviction that Moshe's Deity was not as powerful as He seemed to be; after all, had He not threatened to kill Pharaoh's firstborn, and yet had not done so?[7]

Here too, the hardening of Pharaoh's heart took the form of presenting him with a statement which the corrupt forces that governed him were then able to develop into a narrative that effectively guaranteed that he would not relent.

---

6 *Shemos* 4:23
7 R' Yaakov Ettlinger, *Minchas Ani, Parshas Tazria*, quoting his father.

SECOND ENCOUNTER: AN INDECISIVE VICTORY

In a similar vein, the second meeting between Moshe and Pharaoh sees Pharaoh demanding a sign to demonstrate the veracity of Moshe's claim. In response to this, Moshe tells Aharon to throw his staff on the ground, where it turns into a snake. Pharaoh then tells his magicians to do likewise, and their staffs also turn into snakes, at which point Aharon's staff devours those of all the magicians.[8] This encounter too, requires some reflection. For while it ultimately ended in victory for Moshe and Aharon and defeat for the Egyptians, nonetheless, there was a stage early on where they seemed quite capable of matching Aharon's sign. As such, the victory somehow does not seem to have been quite as decisive as we might have hoped. To phrase it in more contemporary terms, Moshe and Aharon would appear to have won this encounter on points, while we might have rather been expecting a knockout.

Here we see a progression in the process of hardening Pharaoh's heart by allowing him to form the initial impression that his magicians' powers were equal to those of Aharon. After all, didn't they, too, all turn their staffs into snakes? In manipulating his ego-driven tendency to reach conclusions instantly and then stick with them even as they unraveled before his eyes, Hashem was furthering the hardening of his heart, allowing him to conclude that he was winning even as he was losing! And so, while Pharaoh's wise men all left that meeting in a hurry to go and acquire new magic staffs, Pharaoh went home to celebrate another round of victory.

Indeed, the commentators point out that this process continued in each of the ten plagues. Even as his country was being systematically devastated in front of him, there existed some form of anomaly in each plague, whereby the way in which the plague arrived or was removed did not match up entirely with the way that was predicted. Although these discrepancies did nothing to mitigate against the essential impact of the plague even slightly, nonetheless, they allowed Pharaoh to cling to his assessment that Moshe's God was not as powerful as He claimed

---

8   *Shemos* 7:8–13.

to be. Each plague contained, as it were, a "loophole for delusion," such that Pharaoh's heart was effectively hardened on an ongoing basis during the plagues by the plagues themselves!

FROM EGYPT TO THE RED SEA

In truth, it is possible to see the *Maaseh Hashem*'s more "natural" approach to our topic in the verses that describe the final chapter of the Exodus—the splitting of the Red Sea. In the prelude to that episode, Hashem instructs Moshe regarding drawing Pharaoh out from Egypt to the sea:

דַּבֵּר אֶל בְּנֵי יִשְׂרָאֵל וְיָשֻׁבוּ וְיַחֲנוּ לִפְנֵי פִּי הַחִירֹת...וְאָמַר פַּרְעֹה לִבְנֵי יִשְׂרָאֵל נְבֻכִים הֵם בָּאָרֶץ סָגַר עֲלֵיהֶם הַמִּדְבָּר. וְחִזַּקְתִּי אֶת לֵב פַּרְעֹה וְרָדַף אַחֲרֵיהֶם וְאִכָּבְדָה בְּפַרְעֹה וּבְכָל חֵילוֹ.

Speak to the B'nei Yisrael and let them turn back and encamp before Pi Hachiros...And Pharaoh will say of the B'nei Yisrael, "They are confused in the land, the wilderness has locked them in." I will strengthen the heart of Pharaoh and he will pursue them, and I will be glorified through Pharaoh and his entire army.[9]

Let us ask: Through what means, practically, was Pharaoh drawn out? The first verse implies that it was done through the Jewish People acting as if they were lost, thereby emboldening Pharaoh to chase after them. However, the second verse states that Hashem would "strengthen" Pharaoh's heart so that he would pursue them. If so, then why was the ruse necessary?

Here, we see quite clearly that these two ideas are not distinct from each other; rather, they work together. The "strengthening" and "hardening" of Pharaoh's heart took the form of his acting in accordance with his interpretation of events, as presented to him by Hashem.

---

9   *Shemos* 14:2–4.

LATER EXAMPLES: SICHON

It is most interesting to note a similar discussion of the concept of "hardening someone's heart," as relates to a lesser-known case of this phenomenon later on in the Chumash.

When the Jewish People were approaching the land of Israel at the end of their forty-year sojourn in the wilderness, Sichon, the king of the Emorites, went out to wage war against them.[10] The Midrash points out that this was an act of great folly on his part, for his cities were heavily fortified, and, by leaving that protected setting, he exposed himself to enormous harm. Why did he leave his cities? In referring to this event later on in the Torah, the verse states:

כִּי הִקְשָׁה ה' אֱלֹקֶיךָ אֶת רוּחוֹ וְאִמֵּץ אֶת לְבָבוֹ לְמַעַן תִּתּוֹ בְיָדֶךָ.

For Hashem hardened his spirit and fortified his heart, in order to deliver him into your hands.[11]

Once again, we encounter the idea of Hashem hardening someone's heart and forcing him to make a decision which he would otherwise not have made. How was this done? The *Sefer HaIkarim* explains that the background to this event is described earlier on, when the Jewish People sent a delegation to the king of Edom and asked for safe passage through his territory into the land of Israel. The king of Edom refused this request, and then threatened the Jewish People with military action should they try and pass through his land. In response to this threat, the Jewish People backed away, moving toward the territory of Sichon with the same request.[12] Sichon viewed the evasive action of the Jews as a sure sign of weakness, for he reasoned that if they were capable of conquering the army of Edom, surely they would have done so! Having thus concluded that the Jews were not as strong as Edom, Sichon, who was stronger than Edom, was convinced that he would be

---

10 See *Bamidbar* 21:21–24.
11 *Devarim* 2:30.
12 See *Bamidbar* 20:17–21

able to go out and destroy them. Thus, he left his fortified cities and rushed headlong to his defeat.[13]

Here too, we see the idea of Hashem "hardening someone's heart" through a presentation of events which is then interpreted by his corrupt perception, leading him to make decisions which are ultimately his undoing.

CONCLUSION: ACTING ON EGO AND PLEADING EGOMANIA

In light of this approach, let us now return to the question with which we opened this discussion. We will appreciate that understanding the idea of the hardening of Pharaoh's heart in this way will have major implications when we come to consider whether he was ultimately responsible and culpable for his decisions. At every point in the proceedings, he was *essentially* capable of choosing the right path, but his corrupt character traits prevented him from doing so. A person cannot claim immunity from the consequences of his wrongful actions simply because those actions are a product of ego and stubbornness. With the fundamental capacity to say "yes" left intact, Pharaoh was thus accountable and culpable for each of the times he said "no."

---

13   *Sefer HaIkarim*, sec. 4, chap. 25.

WHAT HAPPENED IN THE PLAGUE OF BLOOD?

This parsha presents seven of the ten plagues that Hashem brought against Egypt, the first of which involved turning all the water in Egypt into blood for seven days.

THE NILE AND THE OTHER WATERS: TWO OBSERVATIONS

As we know, the plague of blood affected not only the River Nile, which was the main source of water for Egypt, but also included every body of water in the land—even water that was inside vessels of wood or stone.[1] Having said that, if we look closely at the relevant verses, we will discover that the Torah's presentation of the plague as it affected the Nile versus all the other waters differs in two noteworthy respects.

- The way the plague is described:
  - Verse 17 states concerning the water in the Nile: "וְנֶהֶפְכוּ לְדָם—it will *turn into* blood." Likewise, verse 20, which describes the plague as it happened, states: "וַיֵּהָפְכוּ כָּל הַמַּיִם אֲשֶׁר בַּיְאֹר לְדָם—All the water in the Nile *turned into* blood."

---

1   *Shemos* 7:19.

- In contrast, the term used in verse 19 with respect to all the other waters in Egypt is: "וְיִהְיוּ דָם"—and they will *become* blood." Likewise, verse 21 states: "וְיְהִי הַדָּם בְּכָל אֶרֶץ מִצְרַיִם—There was blood in all the land of Egypt."

Now, seemingly, these two verbs—"turning into" and "becoming"—represent two ways of describing exactly the same thing; by definition, any water that *turns into* blood *becomes* blood! Why, then, does the Torah use one term for the Nile and a different term for the other water in Egypt?

- The act which brought about the plague:

  - Verses 17 and 20 relate that the water in the Nile was turned into blood by being struck with a staff.
  - In contrast, the other waters in Egypt became blood by having a staff extended in their direction, as described in verse 19.

Here too, we ask: Why would the very same plague be brought about through two different acts?

All of this leads us to consider that although the plague of blood affected both the Nile and all the water in Egypt, nevertheless, it did not affect them in the same way. In other words, the plague of blood actually contained *two different plagues!*

THE BECHOR SHOR'S CHIDDUSH

The basis of our suggestion is a fascinating comment on our parsha made by one of the Rishonim, Rabbeinu Yosef Bechor Shor.[2] He writes as follows:

> It appears to me that the Nile only became blood for a short while—during which the water became blood and all the fish died—and then it became water [again]. My proof that this is so is the fact that [the verse] does not give the reason [the Egyptians] could not drink from the Nile as the fact that it

---

2   One of the *Baalei HaTosafos*, a student of Rabbeinu Tam.

was blood, rather, as since the fish had died and putrefied [the water].[3]

Furthermore, it states that the [Egyptian] magicians did likewise, turning water into blood.[4] *Yet, how could they do so, seeing as everywhere there was only blood, even in the vessels? Rather, it is clear that there was blood for [only] a short while throughout Egypt, which then turned back to water, at which point the magicians turned some of it back into blood. Indeed, for this reason Pharaoh did not instruct them simply to turn the blood back into water.*

ON THE COATTAILS OF THE RISHONIM

Now, a simple reading of the *Bechor Shor*'s words indicates that his explanation of the plague is that it affected all the water in Egypt. However, if this is so, we should note two things:

- The *Bechor Shor* adduces proof for his thesis from the fact that the reason given for the Egyptians' inability to drink the water was not that it was blood, but rather that it had become putrefied from the rotting fish. The verse in question (verse 18) reads, "The fish in the Nile will die and the Nile will putrefy, and Egypt will tire from trying to drink water from the Nile." We note that this verse explicitly mentions the Nile three times.

- Likewise, verse 21 reads, "The fish in the Nile died and the Nile putrefied, and Egypt could not drink water from the Nile." Why the repeated emphasis on the Nile?

- Since the plague affected every collection of water, including that which was inside vessels, where there were no fish, what would be the result of the water momentarily becoming blood and then turning back into water? With nothing to kill and putrefy, it would simply revert to being drinkable water, exactly as it was before the plague happened!

---

3   Verses 18 and 21.
4   Verse 22.

In light of these questions, let us suggest that it was *in this respect* that the other waters differed from the Nile, namely, that the water in the Nile was turned into blood only temporarily, whereas the other waters remained blood for seven days.[5]

If this is so, we can now answer the two questions that we raised at the beginning of this discussion. First, this will explain why there are two different verbs used to describe the plague, for they are essentially describing two different effects:

- With regard to the Nile, the term used is "*nehepach*—turning into," which emphasizes the *transition* from water to blood, if only for a moment.
- With regard to the other waters, however, the term used is "*yihiyeh*—will be," which implies that they will not only turn into blood, but will *remain so.*

We now also understand why the different waters were affected by different actions, each one appropriate to the way in which that water would be affected:

- The Nile turned into blood after being struck by Aharon's staff, an act which was abrupt in nature, representing a *momentary* transition.
- The other waters became blood after Aharon extended his staff toward them, representing the fact that their newly acquired state would also exist for an *extended* period of time.

LOOPHOLES FOR DELUSION:
EXPLAINING THE DUALITY WITHIN THE PLAGUE

Having discovered that the plague of blood actually took on two distinct forms, the question now is: What is behind all of this? Why would the one plague affect different waters in different ways?

---

5   As we will appreciate, the second proof of the *Bechor Shor*, that there was also water available for the magicians to turn into blood, likewise does not necessitate an understanding that all the water which had turned into blood turned back into water after a moment. It would be sufficient for some of the blood to revert to water in order that some would then be available; specifically, the water of the Nile, around which they were all congregated.

To answer this question, we need to remind ourselves that in addition to being the largest source of water for Egypt, the Nile was also an object of worship.[6] An idea mentioned by numerous commentators is that the concept of "hardening Pharaoh's heart" was essentially the process of manipulating his natural stubbornness and egotism.[7] This process continued throughout the year of the plagues, with each plague containing a loophole of sorts for Pharaoh to latch onto, insisting that he was right and that Moshe was a charlatan. Here too, by allowing the Nile to revert to being water after just a moment, Hashem gave Pharaoh the option of perceiving his deity as having "defended itself," and recovered expediently. It is true that this thesis is not particularly cogent, for the waters of the Nile hardly emerged fresh from the plague. Nonetheless, the opening was there for Pharaoh to reach the conclusions which suited him. He did not allow the unbearable stench of rotting fish rising from his deity to dissuade him. For Pharaoh, that was nothing other than the smell of victory. This was a pattern that was to repeat itself with each of the ensuing plagues, so that while the people of Israel were progressively becoming free of Pharaoh's rule, Pharaoh himself was becoming ever increasingly enslaved by his obstinacy and egocentricity.

FURTHER OBSERVATIONS:
MOSHE AND THE PLAGUE OF BLOOD

This explanation might also help us answer another question regarding the plague of blood. *Rashi* famously comments that the reason Moshe was instructed to tell Aharon to initiate this plague is because he was saved by the Nile when he was set afloat upon it as a baby, thereby making it inappropriate for him to strike it.[8] However, it is most interesting to note that the words on which *Rashi* comments, "say to Aharon," were not stated with reference to the Nile, but rather in the verse which refers to him extending his staff toward the *other waters*

---

6   See *Rashi* to Verse 17.
7   See, e.g., *Maaseh Hashem* to our parsha.
8   Verse 19, s.v. *emor*.

of Egypt! Clearly, *Rashi* understands that Aharon's substitution for Moshe, likewise took effect with regards to hitting the Nile, effectively having him initiate both parts of the plague. However, let us ask a simple question: Given that the "default" situation is for Moshe to initiate the plagues, and given also that his gratitude pertained to the Nile specifically, why were the two aspects of the plague not *divided between them*—with Aharon striking the Nile and Moshe extending his staff toward the other waters? If anything, this division would underscore Moshe's particular gratitude toward the Nile!

Perhaps we may suggest based on our discussion, that such a division would not be acceptable. Since the temporary nature of the plague as it affected the Nile in contrast to the other waters was designed in order for Pharaoh to conclude that he was right, that discrepancy could not be ascribed to any external factor, such as the fact that the Nile was afflicted through Aharon, while the other water was afflicted through Moshe. Hence, once Aharon took over the one aspect of afflicting the Nile, he resultantly also had to take over the other aspect of afflicting all the water in Egypt.

FROM THE COMMENTATORS

MOSHE AND AHARON

וַיֹּאמֶר ה' אֶל מֹשֶׁה רְאֵה נְתַתִּיךָ אֱלֹהִים לְפַרְעֹה וְאַהֲרֹן אָחִיךָ יִהְיֶה נְבִיאֶךָ.

Hashem said to Moshe, "See, I have made you as elohim for Pharaoh, and Aharon, your brother, shall be your navi."[1]

This verse, in which Hashem assigns the respective roles of Moshe and Aharon in dealing with Pharaoh, certainly requires explanation. Specifically, the two terms "*elohim*" and "your *navi*," which we have deliberately left untranslated, are both very challenging. In what way is Moshe as "*elohim*" to Pharaoh? Why is Aharon considered to be "Moshe's *navi*"? A *navi* is someone who receives prophecy, which can only come from Hashem!

Clearly, it is in response to these questions that *Rashi* offers his explanation of these two terms:

- "I have made you as *elohim* for Pharaoh": The word "*elohim*" in the Torah does not only refer to Hashem, for the term itself means "powerful being." Of course, Hashem is the Ultimate Powerful Being, but this term also refers to a judge.[2] Here too,

---

1   *Shemos* 7:1.
2   See, e.g., *Shemos* 22:3. When this word is referring to Hashem, out of respect, it is commonly

says *Rashi*, Moshe is appointed as a judge to mete out punishment to Pharaoh.[3]

- "And Aharon your brother shall be your *navi*": *Rashi* explains that the term "*navi*" essentially derives from the term "*niv sefasayim*—speech."[4] Here too, when Aharon is referred to as "Moshe's *navi*," it means not that he is Moshe's prophet, but his spokesperson.

There is a fascinating explanation of this verse which is found in the commentary of Rabbeinu Avraham, son of the *Rambam*, who cites it in the name of his grandfather, Rabbeinu Maimon. The basis of this explanation is the idea that even when a prophet receives prophecy from Hashem, it is not transmitted to him directly, but rather through an angel who serves as a conduit between Hashem and the prophet.[5] This is true for all prophets, with the exception of Moshe Rabbeinu, whose prophecy, as we know, was unique in many ways. In this respect too, Moshe had the unique capacity to receive prophecy directly from Hashem.

As we know, in terms of communicating Hashem's word to Pharaoh, it was Aharon who spoke with him. Moreover, Rabbeinu Maimon explains that Aharon, who was himself a prophet, received his messages for Pharaoh through the medium of prophecy. What then, was the role of Moshe in this process?

Since Aharon was like other prophets, he needed to receive his prophecy via an angel. And this is where Moshe came in. Just as Moshe was able to receive prophecy directly from Hashem, he was likewise able to function as the conduit for Hashem's word to another prophet. In

---

pronounced "Elokim." When it is used to refer to someone like a judge, it is extremely important *not* to pronounce it "Elokim," but rather "*elohim*."

3   Even the idea of explaining Moshe being "*elohim*" as a judge still contains a *chiddush*. The term "*elohim*" as a judge that we find in the Torah refers to the judge who *renders a verdict*, while others carry it out. Here, it was Hashem Who judged Pharaoh as being guilty, while Moshe's role was to carry out the punishment.

4   See *Yeshayahu* 57:19.

5   See *Mishneh Torah, Hilchos Yesodei HaTorah* 7:6.

other words, Moshe was the "angel" in the transmission of Aharon's prophecy![6]

The other usage of the word "*elohim*," when not referring to Hashem, is to refer to an angel, again, as a powerful being.[7] Thus, coming back to our verse, Rabbeinu Maimon explains that Moshe was an "*elohim*" for Pharaoh, i.e., the conduit through which the prophetic messages intended for Pharaoh flowed, while Aharon was "his prophet" who received the prophecy from Hashem that flowed through him.

WHO WAS AFFECTED BY THE FIRST THREE PLAGUES?

וְהִפְלֵיתִי בַיּוֹם הַהוּא אֶת אֶרֶץ גֹּשֶׁן אֲשֶׁר עַמִּי עֹמֵד עָלֶיהָ לְבִלְתִּי הֱיוֹת שָׁם עָרֹב...וְשַׂמְתִּי פְדֻת בֵּין עַמִּי וּבֵין עַמֶּךָ.

And I shall set aside on that day the land of Goshen upon which My people stands, that there will be no wild beasts there...I shall make a distinction between My people and your people.[8]

These verses, which describe the differentiation between the Egyptians and the Jewish People, are written concerning *arov* (wild beasts), the fourth of the ten plagues. What are we meant to conclude regarding the first three plagues? Did a similar distinction pertain, and if so, why is it only being mentioned now?

---

6   The *Sifri* at the beginning of *Parshas Matos* (*Bamidbar* 30:2, cited in *Rashi* ibid., s.v. *zeh*) states that while all other prophets introduce their prophecy with the words "*Koh amar Hashem*—Thus says Hashem," Moshe has the unique level of introducing prophecy with the words "*Zeh hadavar*—This is the word [that Hashem commanded]." Throughout our parshiyos, Hashem's messages to Pharaoh are all introduced with "*Koh amar Hashem*," which prompts many commentators to ask why Moshe wouldn't use his unique signature introduction of "*Zeh hadavar*" (see, e.g., commentaries of the *Mizrachi* and *Gur Aryeh* to *Rashi*, *Bamidbar* loc. cit. The *Sifri* itself states that Moshe prophesied using "*Koh amar Hashem*," but doesn't specify when). According to Rabbeinu Maimon, the reason why "*Koh amar Hashem*" is used in our parshiyos is because it is not Moshe who is prophesying, but Aharon; hence, he introduces his messages in the way that all other prophets do.

7   See, e.g., *Bereishis* 33:10.

8   *Shemos* 8:18–19.

Indeed, the *Ibn Ezra* infers from our verses that the first three plagues also affected the Jewish People to some degree. This approach receives stark criticism from one of the later medieval authorities, the *Radvaz*.[9] First, he notes that the Mishnah in *Pirkei Avos* clearly indicates that the Jewish People did not experience any of the plagues, for it states that our forefathers in Egypt experienced ten miracles there, referring to them being spared from each of the plagues.[10] Additionally, the verses that describe the earlier plagues themselves emphasize that they affected the Egyptians only:

- Regarding the plague of blood, it states that *the Egyptians* were unable to find drinking water.[11]
- Likewise, when Moshe warns Pharaoh concerning the plague of frogs, he states that they will come upon "the houses of *your servants and your people.*"[12]

However, if this is so, then the question returns: Why is the matter of distinguishing between the two peoples mentioned only now, in the plague of *arov*?

R' Shimon Schwab explains that the distinction referred to here is not between *peoples*, but between *locations*.[13] For the first three plagues, the Egyptians were affected wherever they were, and the Jewish People were spared wherever they were. With the fourth plague, a new development was introduced, whereby the land of Goshen, where the Jewish People lived, would be plague-free *for whoever was there*—including an Egyptian! This further underscored Hashem's love for His people, whereby anyone who was even in their environs was also spared the plague. It also brought with it an added indignity for Pharaoh, as it became known among the Egyptians that whoever would make his way to Goshen at this time would be spared. Outside of Goshen, the

---

9   Responsa, sec. 813.
10   5:5; see commentary of the *Rambam* ibid.
11   7:21 and 24.
12   Ibid., verse 28. For an explanation of the *Ibn Ezra's* position, see *Likutei Sichos*, vol. 11, pp. 31–32.
13   *Maayan Beis Hashoeivah, Shemos* 8:18–19. See also *Haamek Davar* ibid.

general distinction between Jew and Egyptian continued to pertain, as described in verse 19.

R' Schwab adds that with this in mind, we can gain deeper insight into Pharaoh's response to the plague, where he calls Moshe and says, "Go and serve Hashem in the land." On a simple level, this appears to be a partial concession on Pharaoh's part. However, R' Schwab explains that Pharaoh was claiming that in light of the special providence that had been exhibited toward the land of Goshen during this plague, the people no longer needed to leave Egypt in order to find a holy place in which to worship Hashem—they were living in one!

PARSHAS BO

THE KORBAN PESACH
AND ITS ROLE IN THE EXODUS

INTRODUCTION: ONE THREAD TOO MANY?

Our opening discussion of *Parshas Bo* begins by taking a look at a mitzvah that will not actually appear until the middle of *Chumash Bamidbar*. Although not formally one of the mitzvos that commemorate the Exodus—and there are many of those—the mitzvah of tzitzis, nonetheless, has a significant connection with that event. Indeed, the parsha of tzitzis, which we read daily as the third paragraph of the *Shema*, concludes with the Exodus from Egypt:

אֲנִי ה' אֱלֹקֵיכֶם אֲשֶׁר הוֹצֵאתִי אֶתְכֶם מֵאֶרֶץ מִצְרַיִם לִהְיוֹת לָכֶם לֵאלֹקִים.

I am Hashem, your God, Who took you out of the land of Egypt, to be a God unto you.[1]

Developing this theme further, *Rashi* quotes his teacher, R' Moshe HaDarshan, who explains numerous details within this mitzvah as reflecting aspects of the Exodus:[2]

---

1   *Bamidbar* 15:41.
2   Commentary to *Bamidbar* ibid., s.v. *ani*.

- The place on the garment where the tzitzis are attached, the "*kanaf*" (corner), corresponds to the verse which states that Hashem took us out from Egypt "*al kanfei nesharim*—on eagles' wings."[3]
- The tzitzis are attached specifically to a garment that has four corners, corresponding to the four expressions of deliverance from Egypt mentioned in the beginning of *Parshas Va'eira*.[4]
- The eight strings of the tzitzis correspond to the eight days from when the Jewish People left Egypt until they sang at the banks of the Red Sea.

This last comment of *Rashi's* has been the focus of much discussion over the generations for a very simple reason: There were not *eight* days between us leaving Egypt until crossing through the Red Sea, there were *seven*—including both the day of leaving and that of the crossing! Indeed, *Rashi* himself states this explicitly in his commentary to *Parshas Beshalach*.[5] How then, can he say elsewhere that the crossing took place eight days after leaving?

THE EXODUS: PROCESS AND PURPOSE

Coming back to the verse at the end of the parsha of tzitzis, we note that it not only mentions the event of the Exodus, but also emphasizes its purpose: "לִהְיוֹת לָכֶם לֵאלֹקִים—to be a God unto you." Indeed, to lack awareness of this goal is to see the Exodus purely in a negative light, that is to say, to define it solely in terms of what we are *not*—i.e., no longer slaves to Pharaoh. However, it doesn't define what we *are*—Hashem's people—so that the sum total of our freedom would be simply defined as the absence of slavery. It is our singular connection to and relationship with Hashem that was formed through the Exodus that gives a positive definition to that process. Moreover, the verse later on in *Chumash Devarim* refers to Egypt as a "*kur habarzel*—smelting furnace,"[6]

---

3   *Shemos* 19:4.
4   Ibid., 6:6–7.
5   *Shemos* 14:5, s.v. *vayugad*.
6   4:20.

informing us that everything that we experienced there was in order to refine us of core impurities and enable us to become Hashem's nation. In light of this defining statement, to lose sight of that goal would be to render the entire Egypt experience—both the subjugation therein and the deliverance therefrom—not only incomplete, but effectively meaningless.

"A FESTIVAL FOR HASHEM"—FOR ALL GENERATIONS

This fundamental idea will not only give us a fuller and more meaningful understanding of the Exodus from Egypt, it will also explain both its scope and its permanence. The Jewish People have not always enjoyed the political freedom that they attained on that first Pesach. There have been many times in our history when we have found ourselves in conditions that were not too dissimilar to those in Egypt—if not worse. And yet, the attainment of our status as Hashem's People has never left us. It is with reference to that aspect of the Exodus to which we refer in the *Maariv* prayer when we say:

ויוצא את עמו ישראל מתוכם לחירות עולם.

And He took His nation Israel out from [the Egyptians'] midst to everlasting freedom.

Political freedom has not always been with us, but the freedom of becoming Hashem's nation is eternal and ongoing. According to the *Meshech Chochmah*, this profound idea is expressed in a simple reading of one of the verses in our parsha concerning the Pesach festival:

וְחַגֹּתֶם אֹתוֹ חַג לַה' לְדֹרֹתֵיכֶם חֻקַּת עוֹלָם תְּחָגֻּהוּ.

And you shall celebrate it as a festival for Hashem, for your generations, as an eternal law shall you celebrate it.[7]

As if to say: If you celebrate Pesach primarily as a festival over your temporal freedom, there may be generations where such celebration is not warranted nor appropriate. However, when you celebrate it as

---

7   *Shemos* 12:14.

a festival *for Hashem*, over the relationship with Him as His people that you attained upon leaving Egypt, then it will be a festival worthy of celebration every year—in all generations and for all time.

INITIATING THE RELATIONSHIP

All of this should give us a new appreciation of the significance of the *Korban Pesach* that we brought on the day preceding the Exodus. For it turns out that although the *full realization* of the purpose of the Exodus, namely, becoming Hashem's people, took place at Har Sinai seven weeks after we had left Egypt, the *first step* of that process was actually initiated *before we left*—with the offering of the *Korban Pesach*! Our relationship with Hashem is expressed by us being His servants. As such, the actualization of our status as *avdei Hashem* (servants of Hashem) occurred through the *avodah*—Divine service—of the *Korban Pesach*.[8] Indeed, this idea was especially accentuated with the first *Korban Pesach*, which incorporated a public repudiation (and renunciation) of idolatry: taking a lamb, which was worshipped by the Egyptians as a deity, and leaving it tied to a bedpost for four days before offering it as a *korban* to Hashem.

Understanding the *Korban Pesach* as the initiation of our relationship with Hashem will explain why neglecting to bring this *korban* carries the unusually severe punishment of *kares* (Divine excision). Failure to fulfill a positive mitzvah almost never results in any punishment, certainly not one as severe as *kares*. In fact, there is only one other example of this, and that is for one who fails to perform *milah*. And indeed, we now understand that the reason for both of these is the same. They are not "only" mitzvos; rather, they both represent our entry into a covenantal relationship with Hashem. Hence, their neglect carries such severe consequences.

Moreover, in this light, we can further understand that the *Korban Pesach* that is to be brought each year in subsequent generations is not

---

8   *Maharal, Gevuros Hashem*, chap. 35 and 60.

merely commemorative in nature, but rather represents a *renewal* of the relationship that began with the original *Korban Pesach* in Egypt.[9]

PESACH AS THE NAME OF THE OFFERING

Developing this idea further, we know that the *Korban Pesach* is intimately bound up with the plague of the firstborn, with its very name deriving from the fact that Hashem "passed over" (*pasach*) the houses of the Jewish People during that plague, whose doorposts and lintels were smeared with the blood of the Pesach offering. Here too, the full significance of this act was not just that the blood on the doorposts acted as a sign that there were Jews inside so that Hashem would "know" to pass over the house. Rather, it was a sign that the occupants of the house had involved themselves in the service of Hashem, thereby connecting themselves to Him and elevating themselves beyond reach of the plague.

Indeed, the placing of the blood on the doorposts also had a basic function within the mitzvah of bringing the *korban*. Every *korban* requires the application of some of its blood on a *mizbeiach* (altar). The Gemara states that on the original Pesach, the doorposts and lintels of the Jewish houses assumed this role, and the blood that was smeared on them fulfilled the requirement of applying the blood of a *korban* on the altar![10] Although this appears to be a distinct idea from the blood as a "sign" for Hashem to pass over the house, upon deeper reflection, they are the same. The fact that the doorposts attained the status of a *mizbeiach* was the product of the Divine Presence having entered the homes of the Jewish People to initiate the relationship, thereby elevating those homes to the status of the *Mishkan*. Hence, the blood on the doorposts, as the sign of that elevation, indicated that the occupants of the house were likewise elevated beyond the harmful effects of the plague.

---

9   R' Leib Mintzberg, *Ben Melech, Parshas Bo.*
10   *Pesachim* 96a.

FEASTING AT GOD'S TABLE

Appreciating the role of the *Korban Pesach* as establishing our unique connection with Hashem as His people will give us a deeper insight into one of the central features of the offering—partaking of its meat. Although there are numerous offerings which contain a mitzvah to partake of their meat, this element is highlighted in the *Korban Pesach* to a degree not found in any other offering. Thus, for example:

- If an animal is brought as a *Korban Pesach* but none of its participants are capable of partaking of its meat, the offering is disqualified.[11]
- A *Korban Pesach* that is brought when the people are in a state of *tum'ah* (impurity) can also be consumed by them, even though they are *tamei*. This is in contrast to other communal offerings, which, although they can be brought in a state of *tum'ah*, cannot be consumed in that state.[12]

The central importance of partaking of the *Korban Pesach* is also reflected in the *Rambam*'s codification of the mitzvos. Whereas with other *korbanos* that are eaten, the *Rambam* categorizes the eating of the *korban* as a detail within the mitzvah of that *korban*, when it comes to the *Korban Pesach*, he codifies the eating of the *korban* as a separate mitzvah from actually bringing the *korban*.

Why does the eating of the *Korban Pesach* enjoy such central status within the *korban*? In truth, the very idea of eating from an animal that has been brought as an offering to Hashem is itself most unusual. Surely, having been sanctified and offered to Hashem as part of Divine service, the notion of people then partaking of it seems inappropriate in the extreme! Rather, the aspect of the Kohanim—or the owners of the *korban*—partaking of a *korban* is an indication of the fact that they, *too, are sanctified*, to the extent that they have an affinity with food even of such consecrated status. Indeed, the Talmud phrases this idea

---

11 Ibid., 61a.
12 Ibid., 76b.

most profoundly and beautifully by saying: "They receive [this food] from the table of On High."

The sanctification of the Jewish People to the degree that they could partake of *korbanos* took place at the time of the original Pesach offering, for it is an expression of the relationship that was initiated with Hashem as His people. Hence, this element of eating the offering receives such special emphasis within the *Korban Pesach*.[13]

THE CLOCKS OF REDEMPTION

Let us now return to the strings of the tzitzis, which *Rashi* informed us correspond to the days from when we left Egypt until we sang at the Red Sea. The connection of the mitzvah of tzitzis to the Exodus is that tzitzis serve as a reminder to fulfill all of Hashem's mitzvos, which is itself the very purpose of Hashem taking us out of Egypt. Hence, a garment must have four corners to be obligated in tzitzis, corresponding to the four expressions of redemption. The first three of those expressions refer to Hashem saving us from the Egyptians, while the fourth expresses the goal of that salvation, "And I shall take you to Me as a people and I will be a God unto you."[14]

As we have seen, this relationship began with the bringing of the *Korban Pesach* the day before we exited Egypt—the fourteenth of Nisan. We can now appreciate why, in terms of the association of tzitzis with the Exodus, it is *that day* that will be considered the first day of our freedom, with the day on which we sang *Az Yashir* then being the eighth—represented by the eight threads of the tzitzis![15]

---

13 *Ben Melech* ibid.

14 *Shemos* 6:7.

15 See *Maharal, Gur Aryeh* to *Shemos* 14:5. (The *Maharal* points out that while the mitzvah of eating matzoh does not begin until the fifteenth of Nisan, the prohibition against eating chametz already starts from midday on the fourteenth, expressing, thereby, that in some sense, the festival has already begun at that time. Indeed, the *Taz* [*Orach Chaim*, sec. 432] points out that in commanding us to destroy chametz, the Torah [*Shemos* 12:15] refers to the fourteenth as "*yom harishon*," which generally means "the first day." Although *Rashi* explains, based on *Pesachim* 5a, that the word "*rishon*" can also mean "prior," nonetheless, the simple reading also indicates that while this is not the first of the seven days of the "Festival of Matzos," it is still in some way the first day of the festival celebrating our freedom.)

EXAMINING THE RELATIONSHIP BETWEEN THE SALE OF YOSEF AND THE EXILE IN EGYPT

INTRODUCTION: DRAWING FORTH REDEMPTION

A central feature within the Exodus from Egypt—and one which commemorates it in every subsequent year—is the *Pesach* offering. Moshe's instructions to the Jewish People regarding this offering open with the words:

> *Draw forth and take for yourselves [one of the] flock for your families and slaughter the Pesach offering.*[1]

The commentators ponder the meaning of the first instruction: "Draw forth." What does it add to the subsequent command of "take for yourselves"? *Rashi*, for example, explains:

- "Draw forth"—One who has a flock shall draw from among his own.
- "Take for yourselves"—One who does not have shall take, i.e., acquire from the market.

---

1   *Shemos* 12: 21.

A most fascinating explanation of this matter is found in the commentary of Rabbeinu Bachya. He writes:

> Since our forefathers' initial descent to Egypt was through "drawing forth," as it says, "They drew Yosef forth and raised him out of the pit."[2]

The verse cited describes the lifting of Yosef out of the pit into which the brothers had cast him and selling him to Egypt. According to Rabbeinu Bachya, the first step in the *Pesach* offering, "drawing it forth" from among the flock, is a response to that initial "drawing out" and the subsequent sale!

The implications of this statement are profound in the extreme, for it identifies an entirely new dimension within the *Pesach* offering—and by extension, the entire Egyptian exile. For, if the *Pesach* offering, heralding the redemption from the Egyptian exile, represents a recovery from the sale of Yosef, the exile from which we are redeemed itself is thereby identified as a consequence of that sale. In other words, we are being informed that the relationship between the sale of Yosef and the ensuing Egyptian exile is not merely *sequential*, it is *causational*.

FROM THE SAGES

Indeed, the notion that the exile in Egypt was on account of the sale of Yosef appears to be stated clearly in the Gemara. In *Maseches Shabbos*, we find the following:[3]

> Rava bar Machsia said…in the name of Rav: One should never favor one child over other children, for on account of two shekels' weight of fine wool [the special coat which Yaakov made for Yosef], the brothers became jealous, and the matter resulted in our ancestors descending to Egypt.

The Gemara here seems to be clearly implicating the tensions between Yosef and the brothers, which resulted in his sale to Egypt, as

---

2   *Bereishis* 37:28.
3   10b.

the matter which *caused* our eventual descent there. Likewise, *Midrash Tehillim* states, "Said the Holy One, Blessed is He, to the tribes: You saw to it that Yosef was sold as a slave, by your lives, *you will say about yourselves* every year [on Pesach] that 'we were slaves.'"[4]

CAUSING AN EVENT THAT HAD ALREADY BEEN CAUSED?

However, there is a basic question here. The exile had already been foretold to Avraham many years prior, seemingly on account of the doubt he expressed regarding whether he would receive the land of Israel.[5] In the episode known as the *Bris Bein Habesarim* (Covenant Between the Pieces), Hashem informs Avraham:[6]

> *You shall surely know that your descendants will be strangers in a land which is not theirs, and they will enslave and oppress them for four hundred years.*

Naturally, we are moved to ask: If the exile was already foretold to Avraham many years before Yosef and his brothers were born, how can the Gemara identify the sale of Yosef as the cause of that exile?

This question is raised by *Tosafos* in the above-mentioned Gemara.[7] They answer that even though the exile had already been decreed (and thus would have happened regardless of the sale of Yosef), nonetheless, perhaps the persecution would not have been as difficult as it eventually was. We know, for example, that the four hundred years of exile actually began with the birth of Yitzchak. This means that the first one hundred and ninety years of the decree took the form of Avraham's descendants being regarded as "strangers" *in the land of Israel*! While this was, undoubtedly, an unpleasant situation, it did not entail any exile, enslavement, or persecution. This tells us that there was no fixed time for those additional elements of slavery and torture to begin, nor was there a fixed level of persecution that had to accompany those four

---

4   Chap. 10, s.v. *b'gaavas.*
5   *Bereishis* 15:8.
6   Ibid., verse 13.
7   S.v. *nisgalgel.*

hundred years. Thus, the sale of Yosef contributed to exacerbating the conditions set down in the original decree of exile.

In other words, although the sale of Yosef was clearly not the *initial* cause of the exile itself, it was, however, a *contributive* cause for how it was eventually experienced.

In a similar vein, another of the Rishonim, the *Ritva*, points out that Hashem did not originally specify to Avraham in which "land that is not theirs" the exile would take place.[8] It could have happened in some other country, which may not have been so oppressive for the Jewish People. The eventual location of Egypt as the setting for the exile, says the *Ritva*, with the particular harshness experienced there, was the product of the sale of Yosef, as observed by the Gemara.[9]

Indeed, identifying the sale of Yosef as one of two causes for the exile finds expression in the words of the Sages as well. *Midrash Hachefetz* to *Bereishis* 15:13 comments on the double expression *"Yado'a teida*—You shall surely know," with which Hashem told Avraham about the exile, explaining that the two words refer to the two causes of the exile: (1) the doubt originally expressed by Avraham over receiving the land, and (2) the sale of Yosef.[10]

CEMENTING JEWISH UNITY

Having arrived at an understanding of the sale of Yosef as a contributory cause for the Egyptian exile, we now proceed to ask: How was the exile deemed a fitting consequence of that act, and did it, in any way, serve to fix it?

---

8   Commentary to *Shabbos* ibid. This explanation is also advanced by later commentators, see, e.g., *Iyun Yaakov* to *Ein Yaakov, Shabbos* ibid., and *Torah Temimah* to *Bereishis* 37:3.

9   The *Vilna Gaon* (commentary to *Shabbos* ibid.) has a different approach to this Gemara. According to his view, the Gemara does not mean to say that the exile in Egypt happened *as a result* of the sale of Yosef, for it was destined to happen anyway. Nevertheless, the very fact that the event which inaugurated this difficult time was the favoring of Yosef, and his ensuing sale into slavery, should be enough to tell us that favoring one child is an incorrect practice. In other words, for this event to serve as the trigger for such a terrible exile can't help but reflect negatively on the triggering event itself.

10   Cited in *Torah Sheleimah*, loc. cit.

The answer is that the sale of Yosef represented a level of fragmentation that had developed between the brothers, which the exile in Egypt was aimed at treating. The experience of being subjugated and persecuted as a people by an external oppressor served to diminish the internal differences which divided the Children of Israel, fostering a sense of unity among them and bringing them closer together. In this regard, the "smelting furnace" of the Egyptian exile[11] served not only to refine us as *people*, but also bind us as *a* people.

This will help us resolve a simple question that arises from this understanding of the Exile, namely, why did Yosef's descendants also need to undergo it? They were descendants of *the victim!* By the same token, Binyamin, who was not involved in the sale at all, should likewise not have needed his descendants to go into exile. And yet, as we know, the exile in Egypt was experienced by the *entire* Jewish People. For the point was not the incident of selling Yosef *per se* which was responsible for the exile, but rather, the lack of unity among the brothers it represented that came to the fore in the sale. This was something which constituted a problem for *all* of the brothers. The divisiveness which was present in the formative years of what would later become the Jewish People could have had disastrous consequences as the nation developed. This breach in unity had to be repaired, and the exile experience in Egypt was part of what would repair it, at least on a fundamental level.[12]

A UNIQUE OFFERING

This brings us back to the *Pesach* offering. As we have seen through the words of Rabbeinu Bachya, aside from having the Jewish People express their rejection of the idolatrous ways of the Egyptians, this offering had the additional element of addressing the sale of Yosef. When we consider the *Pesach* offering in light of the issue of Jewish unity, we will

---

11   See *Devarim* 4:20.

12   For further discussion regarding the connection between the sale of Yosef and the exile in Egypt, see *Rabbeinu Bachya, Bereishis* 44:17, *Abarbanel, Bereishis* 15:12, and *Devarim* 26:5, and *Maharal, Gevuros Hashem*, chap. 9.

uncover an entirely new dimension within it, which can be discerned by noting a number of unique laws that apply to this offering:

- The Pesach offering in Egypt had the requirement of taking a bundle of hyssop and dipping it in the blood of the *Pesach*.[13] This is reminiscent of an earlier act of dipping into blood, where the brothers took Yosef's coat, dipped it in goat's blood, and brought it back to their father.

- The verse specifies that the *Pesach* offering be taken "for your families."[14] The *Pesach* is to be offered and eaten as a family. This event is meant to strengthen the family unit, which was ruptured all those years ago with the sale of Yosef. This is especially significant when we consider that as soon as the brothers completed the sale, the verse relates that "they sat down to eat bread"![15] The *Pesach* meal as a *unifying* experience for the family serves to counteract the original meal that took place following the event which left the family fragmented.[16]

- The *Pesach* offering can only be eaten *in one place*. It cannot be divided.[17]

- Unlike all other offerings, which may be cooked in any fashion, the *Pesach* offering must specifically be roasted.[18] Whereas all other forms of cooking serve to "loosen" the meat and weaken its consistency, roasting has the effect of contracting the particles and bringing them closer together.[19]

Thus, the theme of unity pervades the laws of the *Pesach* offering which we ate on the eve of the Exodus, for achieving this state was one of the core goals of the Egyptian exile, and a matter of utmost priority in order for us to merit our deliverance from there.

---

13 *Shemos* 12:22
14 Ibid., 12:21
15 *Bereishis* 37:25
16 R' Leib Heyman, *Chikrei Lev*, Shemos, sec. 9.
17 Ibid., 12:46
18 Ibid., 12:9
19 *Maharal, Gevuros Hashem*, chap. 60.

RESONANCE AND RE-SENDING

When seeking to study the Chumash carefully, we wish to pay attention not only to the meaning of each and every word, but also to their atmosphere. When a distinctive phrase appears only twice in the entire Torah, our ears should be attuned to hear a resonance between those two places. When Yaakov calls Yosef to send him to see how his brothers are faring, he says, "לְכָה וְאֶשְׁלָחֲךָ אֲלֵיהֶם—Go and I will send you to them."[20] How fascinating it is to see that when Hashem appears to Moshe at the burning bush, the words with which He charges Moshe with the mission of redeeming the Jewish People are: "וְעַתָּה לְכָה וְאֶשְׁלָחֲךָ אֶל פַּרְעֹה—And now, go and I will send you to Pharaoh."[21] The very phrase that had originally led to Yosef being sold to Egypt, with his brothers eventually following him there, was now being used to deliver the Jewish People from there and bring the entire process to its conclusion.[22]

Redeeming Considerations

This idea will explain to us an additional feature of the redemption from Egypt. The Torah relates that when Hashem tells Moshe to go and serve as the agent for the deliverance from Egypt, Moshe does not wish to go.[23] The reason for this is that he is sensitive to the fact that his older brother, Aharon, may feel slighted at his younger brother assuming the role of redeemer. Indeed, it is only after Moshe is assured by Hashem that Aharon will, in fact, be truly happy for him that he finally agrees to go.

In light of our discussion, these sentiments of Moshe take on an entirely new significance. Given that one of the primary goals of the exile in Egypt was to strengthen feelings of unity and goodwill between

---

20 *Bereishis* 37:13.
21 *Shemos* 3:10.
22 An additional point of correspondence can be seen when Moshe was set afloat on the Nile and his sister, Miriam, stood from afar to watch over him (2:4). The last time someone was watched "from afar" was when Yosef approached his brothers in Dosan (*Bereishis* 37:18), on which occasion they plotted to kill him, eventually settling on selling him. This time, a brother was watched from afar in order to protect him. (R' Moshe Chesir).
23 See *Shemos* 4:13–14

Jews, it would have been *categorically antithetical* to their redemption for Moshe to appear as the redeemer if the result would be for his brother, Aharon, to feel slighted. To do so would merely be giving entry to the type of ill feeling which was responsible for the exile in the first place![24]

CONCLUSION: SYNERGY AND SANCTITY

It is important to note that although the goal of unifying the Jewish People appears to be distinct from the primary focus of the Exodus—i.e., leaving Egypt in order to become Hashem's people—in reality, the two are very much connected. It is only when the Jewish People themselves are united as one that they are able to fully realize their connection with Hashem.[25] As we say in the *Minchah* prayer on Shabbos afternoon:

אתה אחד ושמך אחד ימי כעמך ישראל גוי אחד בארץ.

You are One, Your Name is One; and who is like Your people Israel, one nation on earth.

In other words, the Jewish nation fully actualize their unique relationship with the One God as His people when they, like Him, are one people!

---

24   *Chikrei Lev* ibid.
25   *Gevuros Hashem* ibid., *Ramchal, Maamar Hachochmah.*

FROM THE COMMENTATORS

NISH'AR AND NOSAR

וְאָכַל אֶת יֶתֶר הַפְּלֵטָה **הַנִּשְׁאֶרֶת** לָכֶם מִן הַבָּרָד.

[The locusts] shall consume the remnant that was left over for you from the hail.[1]

Our verse uses the word "*nish'eres*" to describe the produce that re-mained from the plague of hail. By contrast, verse 15, which describes the plague, states: "וַיֹּאכַל אֶת כָּל עֵשֶׂב הָאָרֶץ וְאֵת כָּל פְּרִי הָעֵץ אֲשֶׁר **הוֹתִיר הַבָּרָד**"—it consumed all the grass of the land and all the fruit of the tree that the hail left over." We see that the second verse uses the word "*hosir*" to denote the leftover produce. What is behind this shift?

The *Malbim* explains that the two terms "*nish'ar*" and "*nosar*" reflect two ways that something can be left over:

- *Nosar*—refers to something which simply remains on account of the fact that whatever happened did not affect everything. For example, if one is eating something, but simply does not finish it, what is left is called "*nosar*."

---

1   *Shemos* 10:5.

- *Nish'ar*—refers to something that was specifically set aside. In the above example, if one *set aside from the outset* a portion that was not to be consumed, that would be called "*nish'ar.*"

In our instance, the first verse refers to the produce of the field that was left over from the hail. As the Torah informs us at the end of *Parshas Va'eira*, the wheat and spelt were specifically spared from that plague, hence they are referred to with the term "*nish'ar.*" The latter verse, however, refers to the fruit of the trees that was left over from the hail. There, the trees were not excluded from the plague of hail, rather, it simply did not destroy every single piece of fruit. Hence, the term used for whatever fruit was left is "*nosar.*"

Perhaps, we can use this distinction to illuminate another matter. In *Parshas Beshalach*, we are told that the waters of the Yam Suf covered over Pharaoh's army to the extent that "*Lo nish'ar bahem ad echad*—There did not remain of them even until one." The *Mechilta* records a dispute as to whether the word "*ad*" is meant to be taken as meaning "up to and including" (i.e., not even one remained), or "up to and excluding" (i.e., one did remain—Pharaoh). However, later commentators question how there could be a dispute about this, seeing as the verse in *Tehillim* explicitly states regarding the Egyptians at the Yam Suf: "וַיְכַסּוּ מַיִם צָרֵיהֶם אֶחָד מֵהֶם לֹא נוֹתָר—And the water covered their oppressors, not one of them remained!"[2]

Based on the *Malbim*, we may suggest that this verse presents no difficulty. We note that these two verses also contain the two different terms for "remaining." The view that Pharaoh remained understands that he was specifically excluded from drowning in the sea in order to witness those events and recognize Hashem's glory. In this respect, the verse says: "*Lo nish'ar bahem ad echad,*" namely, no one was intentionally left over (*nish'ar*), with the one exception of Pharaoh. What is certainly true, however, is that not one of the Egyptians survived that episode simply because the waters of the sea did not reach them (*nosar*); and it is concerning this that the verse in *Tehillim* states: "*Echad me'hem*

---

2   106:11.

*lo **nosar**.*" Hence, it is possible that while no one was "*nosar*," one per-son—Pharaoh—was indeed "*nish'ar*"!

WHAT'S THE STORY ON SEDER NIGHT?

וְהִגַּדְתָּ לְבִנְךָ בַּיּוֹם הַהוּא לֵאמֹר בַּעֲבוּר זֶה עָשָׂה ה' לִי בְּצֵאתִי מִמִּצְרָיִם.

You shall tell your son on that day, saying, "For this Hashem did for me when I left Egypt."[3]

This verse is the source of the mitzvah of telling the story of the Exodus on Seder Night. The Mishnah in *Maseches Pesachim*[4] in-forms us that the way to tell the story is, "*Maschil b'g'nus u'mesayem b'sh'vach*—One should begin with the negative and end with the posi-tive."[5] The Mishnah does not specify exactly what the "negative" and "positive" are. In this matter we find a dispute among the rabbis of the Talmud:

- Rav holds that the negative is the fact that "*Mitechilah ovdei avodah zarah hayu avoseinu*—Initially, our forefathers were idol worshippers," and the positive is, "*v'achshav keirvanu haMakom laavodaso*—and now, the Omnipresent has drawn us near to His service."
- Shmuel holds that the negative is "*Avadim hayinu*—we were slaves," and the positive is "*vayotzi'enu*—Hashem took us out of slavery."

Of these two opinions, Shmuel's clearly seems to be the more intu-itive. Surely, the focus on Pesach should be on the events which took place on Pesach! Why, then, does Rav insist that the story on this night

---

3   *Shemos* 13:8.

4   116a.

5   According to the *Ohr Hachaim Hakadosh* (*Shemos*, loc. cit.), this progression is also alluded to in our verse, which begins with the word "*v'higadeta*" and ends with "*leimor*." *Rashi* (*Shemos* 19:3) informs us that the term "*hagadah*" has a somewhat harsh connotation, while "*amirah*" has a much warmer connotation. Hence, our verse is an instruction to begin with the harsher aspects of the story ("*v'higadeta*") and to move on from there to the more positive aspect ("*leimor*").

is much broader, beginning generations prior to our descent to Egypt and concluding after we had left?

Perhaps, the answer can be found by taking a closer look at our verse which, as we noted, is the source for the mitzvah of telling the story. Although we would loosely translate the verse as commanding us to tell the story of the Exodus, we note two elements within its phraseology:

- The verse commands us to tell the son "*Baavur zeh*—**For** this," i.e., the focus of the story is not the Exodus per se, but why it occurred.

- The focal events in the verse are not those of the Exodus itself, but rather that which "Hashem did for me **when** I left Egypt," i.e., the events which accompanied the Exodus.

With these observations in mind, we can better understand Rav's position. The verse is telling us to relate to our sons not just the story of the Exodus, but the reason why it occurred, which was in order for us to enter into Hashem's service. Moreover, to this end, we are to relate that which happened when we left, referring to the miracles that accompanied the Exodus. The goal of those miracles was to establish our connection with Hashem as the Sole Ruler of the world. The reason we required those miracles was to remove any latent impediment to that connection, due to the fact that "initially our forefathers were idol worshippers." That careful reading of the verse, then, is the basis of Rav's formulation of the story.

PARSHAS BESHALACH

WHAT HAPPENED
AT THE RED SEA?

SOME PRELIMINARY QUESTIONS

The opening section of the parsha is devoted to Egypt's pursuit of the Jewish People, culminating in the miraculous splitting of the Red Sea, through which the Jewish People traversed and in which the Egyptian army was drowned. The Torah describes these events at length, with many questions to be raised concerning the relevant verses. Let us consider three sets of questions at this stage, leaving others to be mentioned as the discussion unfolds:

QUESTIONS PART I

In *Az Yashir* (The Song of the Sea) we read:

מַרְכְּבֹת פַּרְעֹה וְחֵילוֹ יָרָה בַיָּם וּמִבְחַר שָׁלִשָׁיו טֻבְּעוּ בְיַם סוּף.

*Pharaoh's chariots and army, He [Hashem] threw into the sea,
and the choice of his officers were drowned in the Red Sea.*[1]

- This verse is effectively doubled over, with Pharaoh's officers receiving separate mention in the second half. Why? Are they

---

1   *Shemos* 15:2.

not also part of his army mentioned in the first half of the verse?

- The first half of the verse simply mentions "the sea," referring obviously to the Red Sea. Why then, does the second half specifically mention "the Red Sea"? If the identity of the sea did not need to be specified in the first half of the verse, why would it become necessary in the second?

QUESTIONS PART II

Verse 22 of chapter 14 reads:

וַיָּבֹאוּ בְנֵי יִשְׂרָאֵל בְּתוֹךְ הַיָּם בַּיַּבָּשָׁה וְהַמַּיִם לָהֶם חוֹמָה מִימִינָם וּמִשְּׂמֹאלָם.

The B'nei Yisrael entered in the middle of the sea on dry land, and the water was a wall for them on their right and on their left.

A few verses later, we find:[2]

וּבְנֵי יִשְׂרָאֵל הָלְכוּ בַיַּבָּשָׁה בְּתוֹךְ הַיָּם וְהַמַּיִם לָהֶם חֹמָה מִימִינָם וּמִשְּׂמֹאלָם.

The B'nei Yisrael went on dry land in the middle of the sea, and the water was a wall for them, on their right and on their left.

- Why is the same idea mentioned twice in two verses so close to each other?
- There is a subtle difference between the two verses: The first verse refers to them traveling "in the middle of the sea on dry land," while the second verse reverses the terms, describing them as going "on dry land in the middle of the sea." What is behind this reversal, seeing as, by definition, both aspects were true in both verses?

---

2   Verse 29.

The verse which describes the splitting of the sea reads as follows:

וַיֵּט מֹשֶׁה אֶת יָדוֹ עַל הַיָּם וַיּוֹלֶךְ ה' אֶת הַיָּם בְּרוּחַ קָדִים עַזָּה כָּל הַלַּיְלָה וַיָּשֶׂם
אֶת הַיָּם לֶחָרָבָה וַיִּבָּקְעוּ הַמָּיִם.

*Moshe stretched out his hand over the sea, and Hashem moved
the sea with a strong easterly wind all the night, and He turned
the sea to dry land, and the water split.*

- The verse describes the split as having been effected by Hashem
  blowing an easterly wind. How are we to understand this?
  Presumably, an easterly wind blowing on the sea would have the
  effect of *moving it westwards*, but not of causing it to *split in half!*
- The word in the verse which describes the sea's movement is
  "*vayolech*," which literally means "to transport." To where was
  the sea transported?
- The word which describes the turning of the sea to dry land is
  "*vayasem*," yet this word literally means "to place." How does
  one "place" a sea into dry land? Surely the word should have
  been "*vayehafech*—He turned"!
- The end of the verse mentions the seabed becoming dry land
  before mentioning that the waters split. Isn't this backwards?
  Surely, the water first split and *then* the exposed seabed became dry land!

PHARAOH AND EGYPT: A TALE OF TWO ARMIES

A classic understanding of the entire episode of the splitting of the
Red Sea is found in the commentary *Maaseh Hashem*.[3] The key to his approach lies in noting that throughout the parsha, the Torah refers sometimes to "Pharaoh's army" and sometimes to "Egypt." It is important to

---

3   Various elements of the *Maaseh Hashem's* approach are adopted and developed by numer-
    ous later commentators, including R' David Tevel of Minsk (*Drashos Beis David, drush* 10),
    R' Yehudah Aidel of Slonim (*Drashos Afikei Yehudah, drush* 33), as well as in the commentar-
    ies of the *Malbim* and the *Netziv* on the Torah.

realize that these are not two ways of referring to the same army, rather, they are *two separate armies.* "Egypt" refers to the general Egyptian army, comprised of its citizenry, which numbered many, many thousands of soldiers. In contrast, "Pharaoh's army" refers to his personal guard, which consisted of a few hundred soldiers. Moreover, Hashem's plans for these two armies diverge:

- **Pharaoh's guards** are, without exception, evil to the core. They are intensely loyal to Pharaoh and have been intimately involved in his persecution of the Jewish People. As such, they are all liable and deserving of meeting their end at the bottom of the Red Sea.
- **The Egyptian army** is more diverse: some of them, indeed, also deserve to be killed, but most of them do not. Therefore, while the wicked among them are to be drowned, the goal for most of them is to witness directly the salvation of the Jewish People and the retribution meted out to Pharaoh and his guard.

This is the meaning of verse 4 of chapter 14, which states:

- "And I will be glorified through **Pharaoh and his entire army**"—through meting out Divine retribution by bringing the sea over them.
- "And **Egypt** will know that I am Hashem"—the greater Egyptian army will be there to witness it.

In light of this, the process of drawing the Egyptians out of Egypt is twofold in nature:

- Both armies need to be drawn out toward the Red Sea.
- Given the differing plans for each of these two armies, they *cannot be brought out together,* but rather need to be kept separate from each other.

DRAWING OUT PHARAOH'S GUARD

The first stage is thus to bring out Pharaoh's guard by themselves. This will be accomplished by making him feel that there is no need to mobilize the entire nation's army. This will happen by making Pharaoh think that not only are the Jewish People *lost* and can be easily pursued, but also that they are *scared* and can be easily retrieved without mobilizing the general army.

- The notion that they are lost is accomplished by having them backtrack toward Egypt, as mentioned in verses 2 and 3.
- Interestingly, the second notion, that they are scared, has been cultivated over the course of the preceding six days. Verse 21 of chapter 13 informs us that the people were "traveling day and night." This seemingly minor detail is most striking. A nation that is confident does not travel nonstop without rest! One who observes people who cannot afford to stop moving is looking at a people who is scared.

It was this combination of factors which convinced Pharaoh that he only needed to pursue them with his personal guard in order to bring them back. Thus, verse 5 states that "Pharaoh was informed that the people had run away." Why is this relevant? Was not the point for him to be informed that they were *lost*? Rather, the fact that they had been "running away" from Egypt meant that they were scared as well as lost. All this led to Pharaoh's decision, as recorded in verses 6–8:

> He took his people with him. He took six hundred chariots, and all the chariots of Egypt, with officers on them all...and he pursued the Children of Israel.

The phrase "his people" refers to his personal army, for whose purposes he enlisted the country's chariots. In Pharaoh's estimation, the mere sight of his elite guard with chariots would cow the people into submission. The general Egyptian army was left behind, with its mobilization and presence deemed unnecessary.

And thus were a king and his country's army parted.

Pharaoh's optimism, however, was short-lived. Upon getting close enough to observe the Jewish People firsthand, he received something of a surprise, described in the end of verse 8: "The Children of Israel were going out *with an upraised arm*." The phrase "upraised arm" depicts a people who are confident and in high spirits. At this stage, Pharaoh was hit with a startling realization: Somehow, he had been misled, for the Jewish People were not actually scared at all!

CALLING UP THE EGYPTIAN ARMY

In light of this discovery, Pharaoh does not feel confident advancing accompanied by just his private guard to confront an exultant people who outnumber him a thousand to one. He therefore does what he would have done originally, had he known the triumphant mood of the Jewish People—he calls for the Egyptian army! The arrival of this second army is described in verse 9: "Egypt pursued after *them*," i.e., after Pharaoh's army whose own pursuit was mentioned earlier in verse 7, "and they caught up with them encamped by the sea."[4]

With his nation's army behind him, Pharaoh once again feels emboldened to advance with his guard to retrieve the Jewish People. Thus, verse 10 reads:

> *Pharaoh advanced, and the Children of Israel raised their eyes and, behold, Egypt was traveling after them and they were very afraid and they cried out to Hashem.*

Let us ask: Did no one inform the Jewish People that the goal of their backtracking was to draw out the Egyptian army? If not, why not? Moreover, why would the people consent to traveling back toward Egypt for no reason? But if they were told, then why were they so surprised to see the Egyptians coming after them? Was that not the plan? Rather, the people understood that Pharaoh would come out with just his guard, numbering a few hundred soldiers, a confrontation for which they felt confident. They were not prepared to see *all of Egypt* "traveling after them," i.e., after Pharaoh's personal army! Moshe, however, allays

---

4   In other words, the "horses and chariots of Pharaoh" are the *objects* of the verse, i.e., those with whom Egypt caught up. This is why the verse describes them as being encamped "*Al Pi Hachiros*—by Pi Hachiros," a short distance from the Jewish People who were instructed to encamp "*Lifnei Pi Hachiros*—before Pi Hachiros" (verse 2).

their fears and assures them that Hashem will do battle on their behalf against the army of Egypt (verses 13–14).

CHASING TO THE CUT

We are now ready to head toward the Red Sea, with a different goal in mind for each of the three groups:

- **The Jewish People** need to enter the sea, traverse it, and emerge on the other side.
- **Pharaoh's army** needs to enter the sea and *not* emerge on the other side, but to be drowned within.
- **The Egyptian army** *cannot be allowed to enter the sea!* For the most part, they are not meant to be drowned. Rather, they are to reach the banks of the sea, from which point they will witness the demise of Pharaoh's army, as stated in verses 17–18.

In order for all this to happen, it is imperative to keep all these groups separate from each other. How is this achieved? Verses 19 and 20 describe how the pillar of cloud, which normally went before the Jewish People, now went behind them, plunging the entire Egyptian camp into darkness. This allowed for two results.

First, it meant that Pharaoh's camp would continue to move forward, even entering the Red Sea after it had split, completely oblivious to the fact that this had occurred. Had they known, it is highly unlikely that they would have followed the Jewish People in, as they would have to know by that stage that it was not being miraculously parted for them.

Second, the two armies of Pharaoh and Egypt would not be able to successfully regroup and reconnect. This is described in the final words of verse 20: "Neither one drew near the other the whole night." Who is the verse talking about? If it is the Jewish People and the Egyptians, we have a basic problem, for these words imply a *mutual interest* on the part of these groups to draw near to each other. In our case, that interest was decidedly one-sided, for while the Egyptians would have wanted to draw near the Jewish People, the opposite is hardly true! Rather, it refers to Pharaoh's army and the Egyptian army, who were unable to unite, in spite of their desire to do so.

In this way, the three groups continue moving forward until the first of the groups, the Jewish People, arrive at the Red Sea.

CUTTING AND PLACING: THE DAY THE SEA WAS SUMMONED

As we noted in our introductory comments, the verse which describes the splitting of the Red Sea begs a number of questions:

- It states that the split was caused by an easterly wind, which should seemingly have had the effect of moving the sea westwards, not dividing it in half.
- It uses the word "*vayolech*," which means "to transport." To where was the sea transported?
- It uses the word "*vayasem*," which means "to place." Where was the sea placed?
- It appears to mention the water splitting *after* the sea becoming dry land.

All of this brings us to a completely new understanding of how the miracle occurred. In order for the Jewish People to make their way through the sea, a path had to be cleared for them, with the water occupying that path displaced. Where did that water go? The answer is that Hashem caused an easterly wind to blow, which transported (*vayolech*) *that water westwards* out of the sea! To where? Onto the seashore, as the verse then states: "וַיָּשֶׂם אֶת הַיָּם לֶחָרָבָה—He placed the sea onto dry land"! However, given that the Jewish People were *directly in the path* of this water coming out to meet them, how did they not get deluged by it? The answer is in the final phrase of the verse: Upon that portion of the sea being moved out toward the shore, the waters split!

Indeed, says the *Maaseh Hashem*, it is to this aspect of the miracle at the Red Sea that the prophet refers when he says, "He [Hashem] is the One…Who summons the waters of the sea and pours them on the face of the Earth."[5]

---

5   *Amos* 5:8. This understanding of the miracle may give us a new insight into the verse in *Tehillim* (136:13): "לְגֹזֵר יַם סוּף לִגְזָרִים"—Who tears the Red Sea into strips." If the miracle consisted purely of creating a divide within the sea, the two halves of the sea would not be called

On Dry Land in the Sea—and in the Sea on Dry Land

It turns out that the Jewish People were surrounded by water on both sides even before they had entered the sea. This is the meaning of verse 22, which states that "the B'nei Yisrael entered the sea on dry land, and the water was a wall for them, on their right and on their left." In other words, the verse is emphasizing that they were entering the sea *while still on dry land*. This is in contrast to verse 29, which, as we noted, sounds almost identical, except it reverses those two terms, saying, "The B'nei Yisrael went on dry land in the middle of the sea, etc." That verse refers to the later stage when the people had already entered the sea, at which point the miracle was reversed: For while initially they were "in the sea while on dry land," they were subsequently "on dry land while in the middle of the sea"![6]

Thus, with a path having been cleared for them, the Jewish People enter the sea—pursued by the Egyptian army as well as Pharaoh's own army, both of whom are still engulfed in darkness. This continues until Pharaoh's army is entirely within the Red Sea (verse 23), while the Egyptian army is still at its banks. At this stage, Hashem illuminates the area, allowing the Egyptians to see that although they have not actually entered the sea, they too are surrounded by water on both sides. The Egyptians try to head back, but Hashem disables their chariots and immobilizes them (verses 24–25).

With everyone where they need to be, it is time for the waters to return.

SHAKING OUT EGYPT AND COVERING UP PHARAOH

The returning of the water is mentioned twice in two consecutive verses:

---

strips. (Indeed, the Midrash learns from these words that each tribe had its own individual path within the sea.) According to the *Maaseh Hashem's* understanding, however, a strip of water was indeed cut out of the sea and then itself divided in two strips.

6   *Afikei Yehudah.*

- **Verse 27** states that the sea returned to its original form.
- **Verse 28** states that the waters returned and covered over Pharaoh's chariots.

In light of our discussion, we appreciate that these two verses refer to two separate stages of the water's return.

As we have seen, the water that was displaced to create a path through the sea was moved out of the sea onto dry land. Why was this so? Why did it not simply pile up on either side in the sea itself? The answer lies in the fact that although most of the Egyptians were meant only to witness the drowning of Pharaoh's army in the sea—for which reason they were brought only to its banks and no further—a number of them were deserving of that fate as well. How were they to end up there? The answer is in verse 27. The water which was on either side of the Egyptians while on dry land closed on them from behind as it was returned to the sea,[7] taking with it all of those who deserved to be drowned. This process is described with the words, "וַיְנַעֵר ה' אֶת מִצְרַיִם בְּתוֹךְ הַיָּם"—Hashem shook Egypt into the sea," i.e., He shook out the Egyptian camp of those deserving to be drowned, washing them into the sea.

When the water returned to the sea, it then covered over Pharaoh's army, as described in verse 28, concerning whom the verse concludes: "לֹא נִשְׁאַר בָּהֶם עַד אֶחָד"—Not even one remained from them."

From the Chumash to the Siddur

Understanding that the retribution at the sea was meted out to two separate groups will illuminate the way in which we refer to that event in our prayers. In the blessing which follows the evening *Shema*, it states: "את רודפיהם ואת שונאיהם בתהומות טבע"—Those who pursued them and those who hated them He [Hashem] drowned in the depths." Let us ask: What is the meaning of this double reference? Are "their pursuers"

---

7 This is the meaning of the words "*U'Mitzrayim nasim likraso*—Egypt was fleeing toward [the water]." If the Egyptians were trying to head backwards, how would that make them fleeing toward the water on either side? Rather, since the water had closed in behind them, in trying to head back, they were effectively fleeing toward it (*Beis David*).

and "their enemies" not one and the same? In light of our discussion, we now understand that they are, in fact, two distinct entities:

- "Those who pursued them" refers to Pharaoh's army, who were directly in pursuit of the Jewish People.
- "Those who hated them" refers to those among the broader Egyptian army who displayed particular hatred and cruelty toward them and thus, also deserved to be drowned.[8]

Likewise, in the blessing after the morning *Shema*, we say: "וזדים טבעת...ויכסו מים צריהם אחד מהם לא נותר—You drowned the wanton sinners...and the waters covered their oppressors, not one of them remained." Here too, the double reference can be explained as per the above:

- "You drowned the wanton sinners" refers to those among the Egyptians who were especially evil in their enslavement of the Jewish People, and who thus deserved to be drowned in the sea.
- "And the waters covered their oppressors" refers to Pharaoh's army, who as a group oppressed them, and who were thus entirely covered over with the water, as it proceeds to state: "not one of them remained."

BETWEEN "THE SEA" AND "THE REED SEA"

The dual nature of the splitting of the sea is expressed in the two phrases of the verse from *Az Yashir* which we quoted in the opening to our discussion:

- "Pharaoh's chariots and army, He [Hashem] threw into the sea"—This refers to the drowning of Pharaoh's army.
- "And the choice of his officers were drowned in the Red Sea"—This refers to those among the Egyptian army who likewise deserved to be drowned. The word "*mivchar*" comes from

---

8   *Haamek Davar.*

the word "*livchor*—to select," and literally means "those who were selected from among his officers."[9]

Additionally, this will allow us to understand why the Yam Suf is mentioned in the second half of the verse, but not the first. As is well known, the term Yam Suf, commonly translated as the "Red Sea," is more accurately translated as the "Reed Sea," on account of the reeds (*suf*) which grow near its banks. When Pharaoh's army was drowned, they had by that time entered deep inside the sea. In contrast, the Egyptians who had been shaken out into the sea from dry land, were much closer to its banks. Therefore:

- The first phrase, which describes Pharaoh's army, simply refers to "the sea," as the middle portion of the sea in which they were drowned was largely similar to any other sea.
- In contrast, the second phrase, which refers to the Egyptian army, refers more specifically to "the Reed Sea," as the portion of the sea where they drowned was near its banks where the reeds are found, after which the sea received its distinct name![10]

And so, through a careful analysis of the verses, guided and inspired by the masterful commentary of the *Maaseh Hashem*, a fascinating vision of the monumental events leading up to the splitting of the Reed Sea unfolds before us.

---

9   *Beis David.*
10   *Malbim.*

THE REVELATIONS
OF K'RIAS YAM SUF

PART I: TRUE TO FORM

INTRODUCTION: A DEFINING EXPERIENCE

The splitting of the Yam Suf is well known to us as both the final chapter in our salvation from Egypt and the retribution meted out to the Egyptians. It is worthwhile pondering, however, whether this event introduced any new element in our formation and development as a nation. This is especially so in light of a comment in the Midrash regarding one of the primary names by which the Jewish People are known—*Ivrim*. The Midrash explains that the word *Ivrim* is a contracted form of the two words "*avar yam*—they passed through the sea." This is notwithstanding the fact that we were known as *Ivrim* prior to this event; nevertheless, the title received full import and meaning at the time of *k'rias Yam Suf*. This comment appraises us of the fact that passing through the Yam Suf is not merely something that *happened* to us, but rather it is something that *defines* us as a people. This idea certainly requires further investigation.

TRIBUTARIES: YOSEF AND THE YAM SUF

There is a fascinating comment elsewhere in the Midrash regarding the words we say in *Hallel* when describing *k'rias Yam Suf*: "הַיָּם רָאָה וַיָּנֹס—The sea saw and it fled."[1] The verse does not specify exactly what it was that the sea saw which caused it to flee. Concerning this, the Midrash explains that it saw the coffin of Yosef, which Moshe had brought out from Egypt.[2] The connection between these two is that Yosef, too, had fled when he was tempted by Potiphar's wife, as described in *Parshas Vayeishev*.[3] Therefore, upon witnessing the coffin of the one who had fled, the sea did likewise.

Here too, it is worthwhile reflecting on the relationship between these two events. Needless to say, Yosef displayed extreme righteousness at that time, and every righteous deed deserves to be rewarded; nonetheless, we need to understand how the particular event of the sea splitting was considered a fitting reward for Yosef's good deed.

WHEN WATERS BECAME WISE

One of the verses in *Az Yashir* (the Song of the Sea) describes the parting of the waters by saying:

וּבְרוּחַ אַפֶּיךָ נֶעֶרְמוּ מַיִם.

And with the wind from Your nostrils water became piled up [on either side].[4]

The translation of the word "*ne'ermu*" as "piled up" relates it to the word "*areimah*—pile." Interestingly, however, *Onkelos* translates these words as "*chakimu maya*—the waters became wise," relating the word "*ne'ermu*" to the word "*armah*," which is a term for wisdom. More fascinating still is a comment of the *Vilna Gaon*, who draws our attention to the opening words of the verse, which state that this effect was caused by "the wind from Hashem's nostrils." In other words, the wind which

---

1   *Tehillim* 114:3.
2   *Midrash Shocher Tov* to *Tehillim* ibid.
3   See *Bereishis* 39:12.
4   *Shemos* 15:8.

caused the sea to split was not merely effected by Hashem, but rather came, so to speak, from within Hashem Himself![5] What is the significance of this idea?

We cannot help but be mindful of the only other place in the Chumash where the verse describes Hashem blowing into something, namely, the original creation of man, where Hashem "blew the soul of life into man."[6] Here too, by blowing into the sea "from within Himself," Hashem endowed it with a Godly quality, one which *Onkelos* defines as "wisdom."

Yet still, the matter requires our understanding. Ultimately, all agree that the waters split and piled up on either side. What are we meant to learn further from the fact that this effect was brought about through the water "attaining wisdom"?

MOSHE AND THE MEANING OF WATER

To better understand this matter, let us ponder certain ideas that are associated with water. As we know, the background to the name "Moshe," as stated in the Torah, lies in the fact that he was "drawn up from the water."[7] On the face of it, this name does not seem to do full justice to Moshe. After all, a person's name is meant to represent his essence. Considering everything that Moshe achieved—leading the Jewish People out of Egypt through the Red Sea to Mount Sinai, transmitting the Torah to them, being the one in whose merit the manna fell for forty years, and achieving a level of prophecy unparalleled in history either before his time or afterward—is the only thing that we can say about him that he was drawn up from the water?

According to the *Maharal*, Moshe being "drawn up from the water" actually encompasses *all the above achievements*.[8] How so?

Water represents formlessness. It has no form of its own and, moreover, can wear away the form of other things with which it comes into

---

5   Cited in *Kol Eliyahu, Parshas Beshalach.*
6   *Bereishis* 2:7.
7   *Shemos* 2:10.
8   *Gevuros Hashem* ibid.

contact. The most dramatic expression of this formless quality of water can be seen in the flood at the time of Noach. The Hebrew word for flood is "*mabul*," which *Rashi* explains as relating to the word "*mevaleh*—to wear away,"[9] and indeed, the waters of the flood wore away the form of everything that was in the world at that time. We know that Hashem's punishments are *middah k'neged middah*—measure for measure. The appalling moral decline into which that generation had sunk could be summed up by saying that they had lost their **form** and **distinction**—their Divinely-oriented qualities and characteristics known as *tzelem Elokim* (the Divine image). Therefore, they were punished by a flood of water which erased the form of the face of the entire world.

In light of this, we can now appreciate the significance of Moshe's name referring to him as being "drawn up from the water." What does this tell us about the essence of Moshe Rabbeinu? In fact, explains the *Maharal*, it says everything! Everything that Moshe achieved was a product of the fact that he removed himself to the greatest degree humanly possible from the formlessness represented by water, attaining instead the ultimate level of *tzelem Elokim*—the Divine image—in all that he did.

A MIRACLE—AND A MESSAGE

In light of the above, the events of the Yam Suf will take on an entirely new dimension; they not only represented the final stage in our departure from Egypt, but also contained a foundational message for where we were headed. Before our eyes and at Hashem's command, water—the epitome of formlessness—attained form and definition. This is a profound expression of what our task was to be upon receiving the Torah: to impose form and higher meaning on an otherwise formless physical world. This is the deeper meaning of the water solidifying as a result of "receiving wisdom" from Hashem, indicating that we, too, can impart form on ourselves and the world around us by developing and empowering the higher, Godly aspects within ourselves.

---

9   *Bereishis* 6:17.

REFLECTED IN THE WATER

In this regard, one event which embodies the idea of imposing *tzurah* on *chomer*, form onto formless material, was that of Yosef and his experiences with Potiphar's wife. Through identifying fully with his higher faculties and bringing them to bear on the situation, Yosef was able to withstand that trial and avoid giving in to temptation. Hence, the Midrash says that the waters of the sea fled when they saw Yosef's coffin; in response to him giving precedence to *tzurah* over *chomer*, the sea did likewise.

Indeed, the Jewish People themselves had already begun to take steps in this direction. Taking the lamb for the *Pesach* offering in full view of the Egyptians, with the potential risk that this entailed, as well as following Moshe out into the desert without any provisions, were both gestures that represented being guided by ideals and idealism and not by mundane concerns of material comfort and security. This too, was instrumental in causing the waters themselves to attain form and allow the Jewish People to pass through.

In contrast, the Egyptians epitomized a life of excess with no physical restraint.[10] As such, the waters, which attained *tzurah* for the Jewish People, lost it again when the Egyptians entered the sea. In this regard, we could say that each group found itself in the water's response to its presence.

EMULATING THE DIVINE

It turns out that through the splitting of the Yam Suf, Hashem demonstrated the concept of giving *tzurah* to *chomer*—a concept which then became a motif for the mission of the Jewish People themselves. It is most interesting to note that the concept of imitating Hashem, i.e., following in His ways, which is discussed in numerous verses in *Chumash Devarim*, receives its first expression in *Az Yashir*. The Gemara cites the opinion of Abba Shaul, who explains the words: "זֶה קֵלִי וְאַנְוֵהוּ"—This is my

---

10   See *Vayikra* 18:2, where the Jewish People are specifically warned not to conduct their physical relationships in the immoral manner that they had witnessed in Egypt.

God and I will glorify Him," to mean, "and I will emulate Him."[11] *Rashi* expounds that the word "*v'anvehu*" is to be understood as a contracted form of the words "*ani v'hu*—I and Him," expressing the desire that we should be as similar as we can be to Hashem by emulating His ways. The relevance of this concept to the Song of the Sea is that it received profound demonstration in the splitting of the sea itself, as Hashem was saying, "Just as I gave *tzurah* to the formless, so too, shall you!"

Finding Man

Indeed, this concept forms part of the very definition of man. The Hebrew word for man is *adam*, which has two meanings. The lower meaning is related to the word *adamah* (earth), denoting the place from which man's physical being was formed. However, the higher definition is related to the word *adameh* (I shall emulate),[12] reflecting man's capacity to emulate the Divine. Thus, we may say that in experiencing the splitting of the sea, the Jewish People discovered a higher definition of man. It is most interesting to note how this idea is alluded to in the words themselves. The word for water—*mayim*—has the numerical value of 90. Accordingly, the splitting of *mayim* gives a result of 45, which is the numerical value of the word *adam*. For indeed, with the splitting of the sea, a true picture of man emerged.[13]

In light of all this, we can well understand the comment of the Midrash cited above, that the experience of "*avar yam*—passing through the sea," became part of the definition of the Jewish People as "*Ivrim*." This historic event exposed us to both our capacity and our mission as Hashem's people.

---

11   *Shabbos* 133b.
12   See *Yeshayahu* 14:14.
13   Rav Uri Yungreis, *Ori V'Yishi, Parshas Beshalach.*

PART II: CREATION AND HISTORY

A MAIDSERVANT'S VISION

Another aspect of revelation at the Yam Suf is referred to in a comment of the Midrash on the words in *Az Yashir*: "זֶה אֵ-לִי וְאַנְוֵהוּ—This is my God and I will glorify Him." The *Mechilta* states:

ראתה שפחה על הים מה שלא ראה יחזקאל בן בוזי.

[Even] a maidservant saw at the sea what [the prophet] Yechezkel ben Buzi did not see.[14]

The basis of this comment is that the Hebrew word "*zeh*" always denotes something that is present or visible. Understandably, this Midrash is somewhat enigmatic:

- What did the maidservant "see" at the Yam Suf that she had not already seen during the year of the plagues?
- Why is her experience contrasted specifically with that of the prophet Yechezkel?

OF HORSES AND RIDERS

Before answering these questions, let us note another aspect of the events at the Yam Suf which receives particular emphasis in the beginning of *Az Yashir*:

סוּס וְרֹכְבוֹ רָמָה בַיָּם.

The horse and its rider [Hashem] threw into the sea.

Rashi explains that this phrase is highlighting the fact that the Egyptians were thrown into the sea while they were yet atop their horses, as opposed to first being knocked off their horses and then being thrown into the sea. Evidence of the significance of this idea is

---

14   *Mechilta D'Shirah*, sec. 3

found in Miriam's condensed version of the song,[15] which contains just this one line:

שִׁירוּ לַה' כִּי גָאֹה גָאָה סוּס וְרֹכְבוֹ רָמָה בַיָּם.

Sing unto Hashem, for He is exalted above the arrogant; the horse and its rider He threw into the sea.

Why is this detail so significant? What difference does it make whether or not the Egyptians were on their horses when they were thrown into the sea?

MAASEH BEREISHIS AND MAASEH MERKAVAH

A highly esoteric area of Torah with which Yechezkel is closely associated is the vision of the *Merkavah* (Chariot), which he describes at length in the first chapter of his *sefer*. Rav Tzadok HaKohen of Lublin provides a glimpse into this area, allowing us to at least attain a working formulation.[16] He does so by contrasting it with another mystical area of Torah known as *Maaseh Bereishis*:

- *Maaseh Bereishis*—discusses the concept of Hashem's creation and guidance of the physical world.
- *Maaseh Merkavah*—discusses the concept of Hashem's guidance of world history. In the same way that a chariot comprises many different parts, yet all of them are steered by the rider in the direction to which he wishes the chariot to go, so too, the manifold and diverse courses of nations and their leaders are ultimately steered by Hashem in the direction toward which He wishes to guide the world.

In this regard, we could say that the year of the plagues gave the Jewish People insight into *Maaseh Bereishis*—as they witnessed Hashem's control of the forces of Creation, which were miraculously enlisted in the punishment of the Egyptians. *K'rias Yam Suf*, on the

---

15 Verse 21.

16 *Sefer Zichronos* 29b, cited in *Mi'maamakim, Parshas Beshalach, maamar* 17.

other hand, provided an encounter with *Maaseh Merkavah*, as it enlisted the plans of Pharaoh and the Egyptians against the Jewish People to lead them exactly where Hashem wanted them to end up. This is what lies behind the emphasis on them being drowned while the riders were yet atop their horses. The Egyptians were never more fearsome or impressive as they were at that moment, mounted on their horses and chariots and galloping in full pursuit of their defenseless quarry. It was with this very power that they played their role in Hashem's Divine orchestration of that slice of history.

It is in respect to this idea that the Sages say that a maidservant beheld more than the prophet Yechezkel. The manipulation of historic human forces, known as the *Merkavah*, that he saw in a prophetic vision, the entire people experienced in epic form as a tangible reality.

ONE BEHIND SEVEN

According to the *Maharal*, this fundamental concept is contained within the opening word of the Song of the Sea. The word "*az*" consists of the letter *zayin* with an *aleph* behind it. In the Torah, the number seven is used to denote something that is happening in all directions.[17] Accordingly, the word "*az*" expresses the idea that behind the multifarious forces in play in the world, there is the *Aleph*, the One God Who is guiding and directing them toward their ultimate purpose.

K'RIAS YAM SUF AND KINGSHIP

This will also explain the introduction of another concept within the events of *k'rias Yam Suf*, namely, that of *malchus*—kingship. The song of *Az Yashir* itself culminates with the words: "ה' ימלך לעולם ועד—Hashem shall reign forever." Likewise, in the blessing after the *Shema* in the morning, we introduce this verse by saying: "יחד כולם הודו והמליכו—together they all gave thanks and acknowledged [Your] kingship," and in the evening we say: "ומלכותו ברצון קיבלו עליהם...מלכותך ראו בניך—His kingship they accepted willingly upon themselves...Your children

---

17   See, e.g., *Devarim* 28:7.

beheld Your kingship." Why is this concept associated with the Yam Suf specifically, and not with the earlier plagues in Egypt?

The concept of Hashem's kingship is this very idea: that Hashem steers the events of the world and the designs of its leaders toward His ultimate purpose. As we have seen, this central idea was impressed upon the Jewish People in most dramatic fashion at the Yam Suf. Indeed, the Midrash explains that the words in *Tehillim*: "נכון כסאך מאז—Your throne was established from antiquity,"[18] refer to the moment of *Az Yashir* (אז)! The experience at the Yam Suf served to establish and embed the concept of kingship within the consciousness of the Jewish People—in a way that would fortify them for their tumultuous history, during which they would witness the raging and diverse forces of the world firsthand. The ability to endure and maintain their faithfulness to the Divine mission was provided for them in this formative experience at the sea.

IN CONCLUSION

What emerges from all the above is that although the concept of Revelation is one we normally do not associate with the Exodus until we reached Har Sinai, nonetheless, it was present in a most profound manner during the splitting of the Yam Suf. Through the events that happened there, Hashem revealed to us ideas of most major import, both regarding the way in which He runs the world, as well as our role and capacity in expressing His will and introducing His message to the world. In this regard, *K'rias Yam Suf* was not merely historical in nature—it was historic in that it enlightened and empowered us to move toward our unique history. As such, we look back at those events from our point in history in order to look forward to the full realization of the vision that we attained there, when Hashem's kingship will be recognized by all.

---

18   93:2.

SYMPHONY IN SEA MAJOR

The Content and Vision of Az Yashir

FIRST MOVEMENT (VERSES 1-12):
CELEBRATING REDEMPTION AND DIVINE JUSTICE

The climactic event in our Exodus from Egypt, the splitting of the Red Sea, was followed by the exultant song of *Az Yashir*, well known to us from our prayers. Indeed, as the *Yerushalmi* points out, the Exodus itself seven days earlier was not accompanied by a song, for *shirah* (song) over redemption is only appropriate when that redemption has been concluded.[1] Having said that, we note that the song does not go back to mention the earlier stages of the Exodus, but focuses solely on the splitting of the sea—both for the salvation it brought for the Jewish People as well as the final justice meted out against their Egyptian oppressors.

SECOND MOVEMENT (VERSES 13-16):
TOWARD THE LAND OF ISRAEL

Having noted that the song does not go back earlier than the events at the Red Sea, we do see that at a certain point, it extends a good deal into events that were to follow. For while the first twelve verses discuss the splitting of the sea and the drowning of the Egyptian pursuers,

---

1   *Pesachim* 10:6.

verse 13 until the end—roughly a third of the song—looks forward toward the land of Israel. This is actually rather puzzling. For all the importance of the land of Israel, what is it doing in the Song of the Sea?

In truth, entering the land of Israel ultimately represents Exodus from Egypt in its fullest sense, for if the Exodus is about us becoming Hashem's people, it reaches full realization when we are in His land, the land He has chosen for us. Indeed, this formulation of the Exodus was expressed by Hashem to Moshe at their very first encounter at the burning bush:

וָאֵרֵד לְהַצִּילוֹ מִיַּד מִצְרַיִם וּלְהַעֲלֹתוֹ מִן הָאָרֶץ הַהִוא אֶל אֶרֶץ טוֹבָה וּרְחָבָה אֶל אֶרֶץ זָבַת חָלָב וּדְבָשׁ.

I shall descend to rescue them from the hand of Egypt and to bring them up from that land to a good and spacious land, to a land flowing with milk and honey.[2]

Likewise, in the beginning of *Parshas Vaeira*, Moshe is sent to the people with five expressions of redemption, four of which would take place around the time of the Exodus itself, with the fifth being:

וְהֵבֵאתִי אֶתְכֶם אֶל הָאָרֶץ אֲשֶׁר נָשָׂאתִי אֶת יָדִי לָתֵת אֹתָהּ לְאַבְרָהָם לְיִצְחָק וּלְיַעֲקֹב וְנָתַתִּי אֹתָהּ לָכֶם מוֹרָשָׁה אֲנִי ה'.

And I shall bring you to the land, about which I raised My hand [in oath] to give it to Avraham, Yitzchak, and Yaakov, and I shall give it to you as a heritage, I am Hashem.[3]

Beyond that point, however, we do not hear of the land of Israel as the end goal of the Exodus. The background to this is the people's reaction to Moshe's words, as recorded in the next verse:

וְלֹא שָׁמְעוּ אֶל מֹשֶׁה מִקֹּצֶר רוּחַ וּמֵעֲבֹדָה קָשָׁה.

They did not listen to Moshe, on account of shortness of spirit and hard work.

---

2 *Shemos* 3:8.
3 Ibid., 6:8.

This reaction seems difficult to understand. Surely, if they are suffering on account of the hard work they should welcome the idea of it ending! The *Meshech Chochmah* explains that the people did, indeed, welcome the message of being released from slavery. However, their repressed spirit, along with the grinding labor, meant that they could not hear of any tidings that went beyond the cessation of their present troubles. In this constricted state, their vision could not encompass what would happen beyond that point. It was of little help to point to the land of Israel on the horizon at a time when they did not have any horizons. Hence, the ensuing verse states that Moshe's mission was limited at that stage to the immediate task of freeing them from oppression. Any talk of the land of Israel was temporarily put on hold.

However, having crossed through the Red Sea, and with their salvation from Egypt now complete, the people were able to expand their consciousness to embrace the future. In other words, part of the emotional liberation that took place at the Red Sea was that it enabled the land of Israel to be put back on the map of their national spiritual aspirations! Hence, the anticipation of journeying toward that land constitutes a significant part of their song of liberation.

WAVES AND REVERBERATIONS

Indeed, not only did the events at the sea allow the Jewish People to again begin to *think about* entering the land of Israel, they actually played an active role in *enabling it to happen*. Verses 14–16 inform us that when the nations inhabiting the land of Israel heard about what happened at the sea, they were seized with fear and trembling. Astonishingly, this situation remained even forty years later, as Rachav described to the two spies who had been sent by Yehoshua to assess the strength and capabilities of the inhabiting nations:

יָדַעְתִּי כִּי נָתַן ה' לָכֶם אֶת הָאָרֶץ וְכִי נָפְלָה אֵימַתְכֶם עָלֵינוּ...כִּי שָׁמַעְנוּ אֶת אֲשֶׁר הוֹבִישׁ ה' אֶת מֵי יַם סוּף מִפְּנֵיכֶם בְּצֵאתְכֶם מִמִּצְרָיִם...וַנִּשְׁמַע וַיִּמַּס לְבָבֵנוּ.

I know that Hashem has given you the land, and that fear of you has fallen upon us...For we have heard how Hashem dried up the waters of the Yam Suf when you went forth from Egypt...We heard and our hearts melted.[4]

In this regard, it is fair to say that crossing through the Red Sea constituted the first step in conquering the land of Israel. Indeed, this will explain to us an unusual feature of the way in which we went through the sea. The Midrash[5] informs us that the sea split not into one pathway, but into twelve, with each tribe crossing via a separate path. Why did the people cross the sea as tribes? The division into tribes is generally for purposes that relate to entering and apportioning the land of Israel! How is that relevant here? However, once we appreciate that crossing the sea was itself an act that made the conquest of the land easier when the time came, it is entirely appropriate for the people to cross accordingly—as twelve tribes.[6] Moreover, we can further appreciate the experiential resonance within the fact that our actual entry into the land also took the form of passing through waters that had parted for us—just like the initial steps through the sea forty years prior.[7]

THIRD MOVEMENT (VERSES 17–18): BEIS HAMIKDASH AND HASHEM'S KINGSHIP

Having directed our focus forward to the land of Israel, the song culminates by referring to the location at the epicenter of that land from which its ultimate message and meaning shine forth—the Beis Hamikdash. Thus, verse 17 states:

תְּבִאֵמוֹ וְתִטָּעֵמוֹ בְּהַר נַחֲלָתְךָ מָכוֹן לְשִׁבְתְּךָ פָּעַלְתָּ ה' מִקְּדָשׁ אֲדֹנָ-י כּוֹנְנוּ יָדֶיךָ.

You will bring them and implant them on the mount of Your heritage, the foundation of Your dwelling-place that You, Hashem, have made, the Sanctuary, Hashem, that Your hands established.

---

4   *Yehoshua* 2:9–11.
5   *Tanchuma, Parshas Beshalach,* sec. 10.
6   Harav Shlomo Fisher, *Beis Yishai, drush* 23.
7   R' Leib Mintzberg, *Ben Melech,* Haggadah Shel Pesach.

The song then concludes with our declaration that "הֹ יִמְלֹךְ לְעֹלָם וָעֶד—Hashem shall reign for all eternity." This represents the sum of our national aspirations, that Hashem should come to be recognized as King over Israel—and the entire world. In this regard, the Song of the Sea is ultimately not just about the event that took place there, but the vision that was established there. As such, the song is of relevance to us on a daily basis and hence, forms the culmination of the *Pesukei D'Zimrah* section of our morning prayers, as well as its final verse, proclaiming Hashem's kingship, ushering us into the *Shemoneh Esreh* prayer in the morning and the evening.

Indeed, commenting on the fact that the word *"yashir"* is in the future tense, our Sages state that this song will again be sung by Moshe and the people of Israel in the future when the vision of the song is ultimately realized.[8] May we merit to participate in that rendition of *Az Yashir* speedily in our days!

_____

8   *Sanhedrin* 91b.

FROM THE COMMENTATORS

TWO TYPES OF WALL

וַיָּבֹאוּ בְנֵי יִשְׂרָאֵל בְּתוֹךְ הַיָּם בַּיַּבָּשָׁה וְהַמַּיִם לָהֶם חוֹמָה מִימִינָם וּמִשְּׂמֹאלָם.

The Children of Israel came within the sea on dry land, and the water was a wall for them on their right and on their left.[1]

This idea of the water forming walls on either side of the Jewish People is reiterated a few verses later, in verse 29, but, in the second verse, the word *"chomah"* is written without a *vav*—"חֹמָה." What is behind this change?[2]

Perhaps we can explain the matter based on a comment of the *Ibn Ezra*,[3] who writes that Hashem did not wait for the Jewish People to exit the sea before closing the water in on the Egyptians. Rather, as soon as all the Egyptians had entered the sea, the walls closed in on them, even while those same walls remained open for Jewish People in front of them who were still passing through the sea.[4]

---

1   *Shemos* 14:22.
2   See *Kol Eliyahu*.
3   *Shemos* 15:19.
4   Indeed, according to the *Ibn Ezra*, this phenomenon is expressed in what he considers to the be the final verse of *Az Yashir*, verse 19 of chap. 15: "כִּי בָא סוּס פַּרְעֹה בְּרִכְבּוֹ וּבְפָרָשָׁיו בַּיָּם וַיָּשֶׁב ה' עֲלֵהֶם אֶת מֵי הַיָּם וּבְנֵי יִשְׂרָאֵל הָלְכוּ בַיַּבָּשָׁה בְּתוֹךְ הַיָּם—When Pharaoh came with his chariots and horsemen into the sea, Hashem returned the waters of the sea upon them, [while] the Children of

As such, the earlier verse which describes the Jewish People as they were entering the sea has the word "*chomah*" written in full, denoting the fact that the walls of the sea were themselves full at that time, i.e., open along the entirety of the passage through the sea. The second verse, by contrast, describes the people passing through after the Egyptians had already entered the sea and the water at the rear section had already returned to cover them over.[5] At that stage, the walls of the sea were not complete, and hence the word "*chomah*" in that verse is likewise written incomplete.

MILESTONES AND MIRACLES: FROM NATION TO FAMILY

It is interesting to note a significant distinction between the miracles in Egypt and those at the Red Sea.

In Egypt, the focus of Hashem's miraculous power were the Egyptians who were punished by the plagues. For the Jewish people, the miracle took the form of them not being affected by the plagues.

At the Red Sea, it was the Jewish people who were the direct recipients of the miracle, as Hashem split the sea before them. In this case, it was the Egyptians who were the secondary "recipients," as the miracle simply ceased when they entered the sea.

What is behind this shift?

The Beis Halevi[6] explains that while they were in Egypt, the people did not have sufficient merits to warrant them being the direct recipients of a miracle. The Egyptians, on the other hand, were fully deserving of being punished. Therefore, the miracles affected the Egyptians, with the Jewish people benefiting vicariously. All of this changed, however, in the days after they left Egypt, during which they demonstrated their

---

Israel walked on dry land amid the sea." This is in contrast to the view of the *Ramban*, who sees verse 18, "ה' יִמְלֹךְ לְעֹלָם וָעֶד—Hashem shall reign for all eternity," as the final verse of the Song, with verse 19 describing when the Song took place, i.e., while the people were still crossing through the sea. See *Magen Avraham, Orach Chaim*, sec. 51, for a discussion of the practical ramifications of this dispute for the way in which we recite *Az Yashir* in *Pesukei D'Zimrah*.

5   As described in verses 27–28.

6   Parshas Beshalach s.v. *vayir'u*.

faith in Hashem, following Him out into the wilderness, "in a land where nothing was sown."[7] This merit enabled them to qualify to become the direct recipients of a miracle—the splitting of the Red Sea.

It is fascinating to see the above-mentioned shift expressed in our daily prayers. In the blessing after the evening Shema, we say:

ויוצא את עמו ישראל מתוכם לחירות עולם. המעביר בניו בין גזרי ים סוף.

He took out His people from their [the Egyptians'] midst toward everlasting freedom. Who causes His children to pass through the parts of the Red Sea.

We note that the first sentence refers to the Jewish people as "His nation," while the second sentence calls them "His children." The Chasam Sofer explains that being called Hashem's nation refers to our fundamental connection with Him, even if we are not on a particularly high spiritual level. By contrast, being called his children reflects us being attuned and responsive to His will.[8] Accordingly, these words, which chart our departure from Egypt until we passed through the Red Sea, likewise reflect the transition we underwent at that time from being Hashem's nation to being His children.[9]

---

7   *Yirmiyahu* 2:2.
8   See *Kiddushin* 36a.
9   *Derashos Chasam Sofer*, p. 676.

PARSHAS YISRO

CONCEPT: THE WAY THE TORAH QUOTES PEOPLE'S WORDS

When Did Yisro Discover His Name Was Yisro?

וַיֹּאמֶר אֶל מֹשֶׁה אֲנִי חֹתֶנְךָ יִתְרוֹ בָּא אֵלֶיךָ.

He said to Moshe, "I, your father-in-law, Yisro, am coming to you."[1]

INTRODUCTION: WHO?

Our discussion opens by referring to a statement of the Midrash,[2] cited by *Rashi* at the very beginning of the parsha.[3] The Midrash notes that Yisro actually had no fewer than seven names and provides the background to each one. Among these, the Midrash says that he was called Yeser on account of the fact that he caused a section to be added to the Torah, namely, his recommendation to Moshe to appoint

---

1   *Shemos* 18:6.
2   *Mechilta, Parshas Yisro*, sec. 1.
3   Verse 1, s.v. *Yisro.*

a network of judges so that he should not have to judge the people alone.[4] Subsequently, when he converted to become part of the Jewish People, another letter was added to his name—becoming Yisro.

With this in mind, let us ask a very simple question: How could Yisro say, "I, Yisro, am coming to join you"? After all, the events which led him to be given this name had not yet occurred—he had not yet added a section to the Torah, nor had he converted! And thus we ask, how did Yisro know at that stage that his name was Yisro?

Now, it is true that the Torah calls him Yisro already from the beginning of the parsha;[5] however, that is a different matter. For the Torah will often refer to something by the way in which it would be called in the future, even if it was not known as such at the time. Thus, for example, in *Parshas Lech Lecha*, the Torah describes how the four kings waged war against the five "in the field of Amalek,"[6] even though Amalek, after whom those fields were named, had not yet been born.[7] It is one thing for the Torah to use a term that would only come into use later in history than the events it is describing, because (1) Hashem knows the future and (2) at the time the Torah is written, these terms were already known and could be applied in retrospect.[8] Yisro, by contrast, is speaking in "real time." How then, could he call himself by a name that did not yet exist?

---

4   See verses 21–23.
5   Indeed, he is already referred to by this name in the opening verse of chapter three of *Shemos*.
6   *Bereishis* 14:7.
7   *Bereishis Rabbah* 42:7, cited in *Rashi* to *Bereishis* ibid. Another very interesting example is that of Yehoshua whose name was changed by Moshe from Hoshea prior to being sent to spy out the land of Canaan, as related by the verse in the beginning of *Parshas Shelach* (*Bamidbar* 13:16). And yet, in the end of the previous parsha, when the people are attacked by Amalek, the verse says, "Moshe said *to Yehoshua*, choose men for us" (*Shemos* 17:9). Here, too, the Torah refers to him by a name that did not exist at the time, but that he would go by in the future (*Maharsha, Sotah* 34b, c.f. commentary of *Rashbam* to *Bamidbar*, loc. cit.)
8   See *Tosafos, Kesubos* 10b, s.v. *al shem*, who explain that the idea of the Torah referring to a term that would only exist in the future (*al shem he'asid*) can take one of two forms: (1) A term that did not exist at the time that the Torah is discussing (e.g., an episode dealing with Avraham), but did exist by the time the Torah was written. (2) A term that did not exist even when the Torah was written, and would only come into existence afterwards.

The key to answering this question lies in raising a more basic question still. Throughout the Torah, we read of things that various people said; some of them righteous personalities such as the Avos (Patriarchs) and Moshe Rabbeinu, others decidedly unrighteous, such as Eisav, Lavan, and Pharaoh. In these instances, we ask: Whose words are we reading, the Torah's or those people's?

On the one hand, the Torah has deemed it correct to include these words, such that if even one letter from any of these quotations would be missing from a Torah scroll, the entire thing would be disqualified. In this respect, they are an indispensable part of the text and are included in the sanctity of the Torah. On the other hand, it is clear that not all of these words reflect the Torah's message and viewpoint. Indeed, in some cases, we know that they do not, as the Torah's own presentation specifically contrasts with the one being quoted.

To illustrate with a simple example, when Pharaoh recounts his dream to Yosef, he states:

בַּחֲלֹמִי הִנְנִי עֹמֵד עַל שְׂפַת הַיְאֹר.

*In my dream, behold, I was standing on **the bank of** the Nile.*[9]

Now, we happen to know that this is not exactly where Pharaoh dreamt he was standing, for the Torah itself mentioned that Pharaoh dreamt he was standing "עַל הַיְאֹר—**over** the Nile!" Leaving aside the question of what lay behind Pharaoh's adjustment of this detail within his dream, we see that his words do not match up with the Torah's, and yet they are part of Torah! In other words, in this instance, the full measure of what the Torah wanted us to know about Pharaoh's dream included both what he actually dreamt, as well as what he said that he dreamt.

Needless to say, a willful departure from the truth is hardly surprising from someone like Pharaoh, who has no loyalty to the truth, while the righteous individuals whom the Torah quotes will clearly be

---

9   *Bereishis* 41:17.

infinitely more aligned with its values and message. However, to the extent that it illustrates the point that the Torah quotes people's words as their words, this principle is true for everyone who is quoted—it is their words being quoted, not the Torah's.[10]

...AS QUOTED BY THE TORAH

However, the full understanding of the matter is somewhat more nuanced. For while it is true that the Torah presents people's words, at the same time, it is the Torah presenting them. Every word in the Torah is written on a level which allows it to be expounded through the prisms of *pshat* (plain meaning), *drash* (hermeneutical exposition), *remez* (allusion), and *sod* (mystical meaning). It is unlikely that the Jewish People, when complaining to Moshe about the manna, instructing Aharon to make for them a Golden Calf, or wailing in response to the spies' report about the land of Israel, crafted their words to be worthy of all these levels of interpretation—nor would they be capable of doing so even if they tried! Rather, as much as the Torah cites the essential content of their words when quoting them, the way in which it does so is in keeping with how the Torah "itself" expresses ideas. In this regard, the words that the Torah chooses to present what someone said will be governed by the definitions of those words as they would reflect the Torah's own ideas.[11]

---

10 See, regarding this, *Gur Aryeh* to *Bereishis* 42:2 and ibid., 43:20 and *Torah Temimah* ibid., 27:16. The topic of the Torah's quotation of people's words is discussed at length by R' Yehudah Copperman, *zt"l*, in his sefer *Pshuto Shel Mikra*, sec. 2, ch. 4.

11 The implications of this idea are that it should be possible to adduce proof regarding the definition of a certain word in the Torah from a verse where someone is quoted in the Torah, as indeed we find in numerous cases (see, e.g., *Berachos* 34a based on *Bereishis* 37:10 regarding the definition of "*hishtachavaah*"; *Bava Kama* 65b based on *Bereishis* 31:38 regarding the word "*ayil*"; ibid., 2b based on *Melachim I* 22:11 regarding the term "*yigach*"; and *Makkos* 11a based on *Bereishis* 42:30 regarding the term "*dibbur*"). The converse side of this idea is that when we say regarding *nedarim* (vows) that we follow the parameters of how people define the relevant terms—for which reason we do not generally adduce definitions for those terms from verses in the Torah—it would be equally inappropriate to cite verses in which it quotes people based on the notion that these verses reflect how people speak. See concerning this, *Tzafnas Paaneach*, *Hilchos Nedarim* 2:8.

AVRAHAM AND THE ANGELS

A classic illustration of this idea can be seen in a comment of *Rashi*'s in the beginning of *Parshas Vayeira*. In verse 5 of *Bereishis* 18, Avraham tells the three wayfarers:

וְאֶקְחָה פַת לֶחֶם וְסַעֲדוּ לִבְּכֶם.

I will fetch a morsel of bread, that you may satiate your hearts.

Commenting on the words "*v'saadu lib'chem*," *Rashi*, citing the Midrash, writes:[12]

"לבבכם" אין כתיב כאן אלא "לבכם," מגיד שאין יצר הרע שולט במלאכים.

It is not written here "levav'chem,"[13] but rather "lib'chem";[14] this teaches us that angels do not have an evil inclination.

Now, it seems quite clear that Avraham himself did not intend to phrase his words as specifically appropriate for angels, for *Rashi* has already informed us in the previous verse that Avraham thought these three men were idol-worshipping nomads! Rather, we see that at the same time that the Torah is quoting what Avraham said, it is doing so in a way which also serves to impart lessons that the Torah itself wishes to teach. (Indeed, we see that the Midrash is particular to express itself regarding that which is "*kasuv kan*—written here." In other words, the Sages' observation does not relate to *what Avraham said*, but rather to *what is written in the verse*.)

CHANAH'S PRAYER

A further illustration of this point can be found in a stunning comment of R' Yosef Chaim of Baghdad, the *Ben Ish Chai*. When Chanah prays to Hashem for a child, she says, "אִם רָאֹה תִרְאֶה בָּעֳנִי אֲמָתֶךָ—If You will see the suffering of Your maidservant."[15] The Talmud records a dispute between the Sages as to whether or not to expound the double

---

12 *Bereishis Rabbah* 48:11.
13 לבבכם—with two *beises*.
14 לבכם—with one *beis*.
15 *Shmuel I* 1:11.

expression "*ra'oh tireh*" as denoting two separate ideas.[16] The Gemara explains that the opinion which does not expound anything extra from this double expression subscribes to the viewpoint that "*dibrah Torah ki'leshon b'nei adam*—The Torah speaks in the way of people." In other words, in the same way that people will typically double over their words for emphasis, not to denote another idea, so too the Torah speaks in this way and hence, the second word is not to be viewed as redundant, requiring or warranting exposition.

The *Ben Ish Chai* asks a fascinating question.[17] While there may be a dispute among the Sages regarding whether *the Torah* speaks in the way of people, all agree that *people* speak in the way of people; in this instance, it is a person talking! As such, why should *any* of the Sages expound her words?

It is clear from here, says the *Ben Ish Chai*, that even when the Torah presents someone's words, it presents them in its own format and with its own parameters. For this reason, according to the view that the Torah does not double up its words "as people do," the verse would not have included a double expression within Chanah's words—even if she herself had spoken that way—unless it intended for it to be expounded. Hence, only the opinion that holds that "the Torah speaks as people do" maintains that the double expression is no cause for comment or exposition.

Coming back to our opening question, we can now understand how Yisro is quoted in the Torah as referring to himself as Yisro, even though he did not yet know at that time that this would become his name. As surely as the Torah chooses to refer to him from this point with the name Yisro—"as per the future"—likewise, it presents his message to Moshe as calling himself by this name.[18]

---

16   *Berachos* 31b.
17   Commentary *Ben Yehoyada* to *Berachos* ibid.
18   See further regarding the way the Torah quotes people in *Ramban* to *Bereishis* 2:9, and *Pardes Yosef, Parshas Bereishis*, sec. 29.

THE TENTH COMMANDMENT

At the center of our parsha is the Revelation at Sinai and the *Aseres Hadibros*—the Ten Commandments—presented to us by Hashem on that occasion. The tenth of the commandments is: "*Lo sachmod*—do not covet" your fellow's house, wife, etc.[1]

OF VILLAGERS AND PRINCESSES: VISION AND THOUGHT

Probably the most famous question regarding this commandment is raised by the *Ibn Ezra*: How can the Torah tell me not to desire something? If my neighbor has a nice house or wife, etc., it is only natural for me to desire them! Granted, in terms of acting on this thought, the Torah can instruct me not to take these items from him, but the thought itself is surely in a realm that is beyond a person's control, no?

Actually, says the *Ibn Ezra*, no.

Many of the things that we think or feel are shaped by the way we see things. Let us use as a parable a common villager who sees a beautiful princess; he may admire her beauty, but the notion of, "I would like her for myself" does not even cross his mind. Why not? Because it is clear to him that it could never happen. We see that one's perspective on things can, indeed, prevent even a thought from entering his mind. Likewise,

---

1   *Shemos* 20:14.

says the *Ibn Ezra*, if it is fundamentally clear to a person that what his fellow has is what has been ordained for them by Heaven, which means Hashem has decided that it is for them and not for him, then the notion of even desiring it will be as far removed from his consciousness as the princess is from the villager.

In addition to answering his basic question, this idea of the *Ibn Ezra* gives us profound insight regarding the entire commandment of *Lo Sachmod*. As we know, mitzvos are divided into two categories: *bein adam laMakom* and *bein adam l'chaveiro*—between man and God and between man and his fellow man. Now, the prohibition against coveting one's fellow's property would surely appear to fit squarely within the second category, and to a certain degree it definitely does. Yet, at the same time, *the perspective which enables its fulfillment* derives specifically from an idea that lies in the realm between man and God!

Additionally, although *Lo Sachmod* is stated in the negative ("Do not covet"), which generally identifies the prohibited entity as the focus of the command, in this case, the way to fulfill the command is actually positive. For ultimately, the commandment is not, "Do not think or feel that," but rather, "Develop a perspective whereby such a thought will not enter your mind."[2]

LO SACHMOD: IN THOUGHT OR DEED?

The above discussion of the *Ibn Ezra* touches on a most basic question regarding the prohibition of *Lo Sachmod*: What exactly is it prohibiting? It is clear from his question that the *Ibn Ezra* identifies the prohibition as pertaining to the realm of thoughts and feelings regarding someone else's things. However, when we consult the words of the *Rambam* on this matter, we see that he does not share this view of the mitzvah. He writes:

---

2   It is important to note that although coveting is closely associated with jealousy, it specifically relates to desiring an object that belongs to someone else. Often, a feeling of jealousy regarding someone else's possessions will motivate a person to obtain a similar item for himself. This is commonly known as "Keeping up with the Joneses," and while it can often be very costly and fretful, it does not entail a violation of *Lo Sachmod*. *Lo Sachmod* is about seeking to obtain Mr. Jones's house and wife, etc., for oneself.

Anyone who covets…anything belonging to his fellow that he could acquire from him and pressures him until he actually acquires it, even if he pays the person a large sum of money, he has violated a negative commandment, as it says, "Do not covet"…and one does not violate this prohibition until he has acquired the item that he coveted.[3]

Evidently, for the *Rambam*, the prohibition of *Lo Sachmod* pertains to the *realm of action*, not of thought. Indeed, this is the position adopted by the *Shulchan Aruch.[4]* We will appreciate that according to this approach, the *Ibn Ezra's* question concerning the Torah prohibiting a thought does not even appear to begin, for it turns out that the Torah does not actually forbid the initial thought!

However, if we just give it a little time and patience, it is possible that the *Ibn Ezra's* question will find expression even within the *Rambam's* approach. In *Parshas Va'eschanan*, we have a second presentation of the Ten Commandments (paralleling the second set of *Luchos*). In the tenth commandment there, it states: "לֹא תַחְמֹד...וְלֹא תִתְאַוֶּה—Do not covet…and do not desire [your fellow's house, etc.]."[5] We see that in addition to prohibiting coveting one's fellow's possessions, the Torah also prohibits desiring them.[6] Now, while "coveting" can be explained as pertaining to the realm of action, "desire" clearly relates to thought! This means that ultimately, the question of the *Ibn Ezra* will need to be addressed by all opinions—if not in relation to *Lo Sachmod* as found in our parsha, then in relation to *Lo Sisaveh* later on in *Parshas Va'eschanan.[7]*

---

3   *Hilchos Gezeilah* 1:9.

4   *Choshen Mishpat* 359:10.

5   *Devarim* 5:18.

6   Indeed, the *Rambam* in his *Sefer Hamitzvos* codifies these as two separate prohibitions in his list of the 613 mitzvos (negative mitzvos 265 and 266).

7   A close reading of the *Rambam*, however, might reveal that even the prohibition of *Lo Sisaveh* does not relate to the actual desire for that object. He writes (*Hilchos Gezeilah* 1:10): "Anyone who desires his fellow's house, wife, etc.…*As soon as he has thought in his heart* how he might acquire this object and he is taken in by the idea, he has violated a negative commandment, as it says, '*Lo Sisaveh*.'" It appears that even *Lo Sisaveh* is not violated by the initial thought, but by developing it into a plan to acquire the object. Perhaps, the basis for this formulation is the fact that the prohibition is phrased in the reflexive form "*v'lo sisaveh*," rather than

A beautiful perspective on the basis for the commandment of *Lo Sachmod* is found in the words of the Sages themselves. The Midrash in *Parshas Kedoshim* explains that the opening verses of that parsha parallel the Ten Commandments.[8] Some of these parallels are immediately apparent: both parshiyos contain references to keeping Shabbos, respecting parents, belief in Hashem, and avoiding idol worship. But what about *Lo Sachmod*? Which verse in *Kedoshim* parallels that commandment? The answer, says the Midrash, is the verse which states: "וְאָהַבְתָּ לְרֵעֲךָ כָּמוֹךָ—Love your neighbor as yourself"![9]

This is a most profound and elevating statement. The Midrash is informing us that ultimately, the background to the Torah commanding us not to covet someone else's possessions is not just to be content ourselves with what we have, but *to be happy for them* regarding what they have! The goal of the mitzvah is not for a person to remove his fellow's possessions from his thoughts; it is to bring his fellow, together with his possessions, into his heart and to rejoice in his success.

The Mishnah in *Pirkei Avos*[10] states: "איזהו עשיר? השמח בחלקו—Who is rich? One who is happy with his portion." The simple reading of this Mishnah is that it refers to someone who is content and happy with what he owns; wealth is not a function of the amount of money that one has amassed, but of one's perspective regarding that wealth. However, the Kotzker Rebbe would explain the Mishnah as saying: "Who is rich? A person who can regard *his fellow* and be *sameach b'chelko*—happy with *his*, i.e., his fellow's, portion!" One who can see someone else's prosperity and be happy on that person's behalf is truly rich.

---

simply *"v'lo s'aveh"* (compare *Devarim* 12:20). This form denotes not merely *having* the thought, but *developing* it into a strategy.

8   *Vayikra Rabbah* 24:5.

9   *Vayikra* 19:18.

10   4:1.

POSTSCRIPT TO THE
ASERES HADIBROS

The Final Section of Parshas Yisro

וַיֹּאמֶר ה' אֶל מֹשֶׁה כֹּה תֹאמַר אֶל בְּנֵי יִשְׂרָאֵל אַתֶּם רְאִיתֶם כִּי מִן הַשָּׁמַיִם
דִּבַּרְתִּי עִמָּכֶם.

*Hashem said to Moshe, "So shall you say to the Children of
Israel, 'You have seen that I have spoken to you from Heaven.'"*[1]

INTRODUCTION: WHAT DOES ONE SAY
AFTER THE REVELATION AT SINAI?

Our parsha ends with Hashem commanding Moshe to address the
people after the *Aseres Hadibros*, during which he is to present to them
a number of mitzvos:

- Not to make images of celestial beings, nor any graven images
  of silver and gold.[2]

---

1   *Shemos* 20:19.
2   Verse 20.

- Not to use a sword while fashioning the stones for the *Mizbeiach*.[3]
- Not to have steps leading up to the *Mizbeiach*, but instead to have a ramp.[4]

This section is somewhat enigmatic. Why are these mitzvos specifically chosen to be communicated immediately following the Revelation at Har Sinai? In what way do they form a fitting "postscript" to the epic event of hearing the *Aseres Hadibros*?

The commentators explain that with these mitzvos, Hashem was indicating to the people the quality of what it means to receive the Torah. Let us consider: Three of the *Aseres Hadibros* are the three prohibitions against idolatry, murder, and adultery. These areas are not only elemental, they are actually already incumbent upon all human beings as three of the seven Noachide mitzvos! Why does Hashem address His chosen people at Sinai with mitzvos that apply to everyone?

This is the background to the follow-up communication, where Moshe informs the people that part of being Jewish means that even these basic laws assume an infinitely higher level of observance and sensitivity. Not only are those sins themselves forbidden, they cannot exist *even in trace form*. When we consider the mitzvos Moshe presents here, we see that they pertain to the domains of the three cardinal prohibitions:

- Not only is serving idols itself prohibited, even making images of celestial beings or other forms is also forbidden.
- Not only is murder prohibited, but even an implement associated with bloodshed is not allowed to be used in fashioning the *Mizbeiach*.
- Not only is physical immorality prohibited, it is forbidden to ascend to the *Mizbeiach* in a way which even appears to be immodest, such as would happen if stairs were used, as explained by *Rashi*.

---

3   Verse 22.
4   Verse 23.

Through this, Hashem is informing the people that having received the Torah, everything—even basic things—takes on an entirely new level of observance and fulfillment!

A LISTENING EAR FOR MITZVOS

Regarding the final prohibition of having stairs lead up to the *Mizbeiach*, which is considered immodest and degrading even though the Kohanim are wearing *michnasayim* (trousers), *Rashi* adds the following fascinating comment:

והרי דברים קל וחומר, ומה אבנים האלה שאין בהן דעת להקפיד על בזיונן אמרה תורה הואיל ויש בהן צורך לא תנהג בהן מנהג בזיון, חבירך שהוא בדמות יוצרך ומקפיד על בזיונו על אחת כמה וכמה.

Behold, the matter is a kal vachomer:[5] If with regard to these stones, which do not have knowledge to be upset over their degradation, [still] the Torah says, since there is use for them, do not act toward them in a degrading way—your fellow, who is in the image of your Creator and who cares about his disgrace, how much more so [should you not act in a degrading way toward him]!

What is so interesting about this comment of *Rashi*'s is that it appears to have nothing to do with *Rashi*'s stated goal in his commentary, which is: "*pshuto shel mikra*—to explain the straightforward meaning of the verse." Here, *Rashi* has already explained to us the *pshat*, namely, that using stairs appears immodest. Beyond this point, any further comment—however worthy and important—would appear to be extraneous!

It appears that *Rashi* felt he could not take leave of the parsha of *Kabbalas HaTorah* (receiving the Torah) without expressing what that concept means in its fullest sense. Beyond the essential requirement to fulfill the mitzvos of the Torah, they also contain concepts and lessons to be absorbed and applied to broader areas of life beyond which they

---

5   An *a fortiori* argument.

were stated. In this regard, the Torah encourages us not just to perform the mitzvos, but to "listen" to them.[6] If a person takes great care to accord respect to the stones of the Beis Hamikdash but then tramples all over his peers, degrading and besmirching them, he may have *fulfilled* the mitzvah, but he has not *listened* to it—and hence, he has not "received" it in the full sense of the word.

A classic and thought-provoking illustration of this idea of "listening to mitzvos" can be gleaned from an episode involving a Torah luminary closer to our times. It is told that a student in the Slabodka Yeshiva was in the habit of walking around with a dour countenance. After a while, Rav Nosson Tzvi Finkel, the Alter[7] of Slabodka, called him over and said, "It is forbidden for you to be in the *beis midrash* wearing an expression like that." The student, who was punctilious in the fulfillment of mitzvos and halachah, inquired, "Where, may I ask, does the Torah prohibit such a thing?" The Alter replied, "The Torah forbids a person to dig a pit in the public thoroughfare, because a passersby can fall in and be injured. The *beis midrash* is a public thoroughfare, and your face is a pit, since people who look at you scowling instantly feel worse. What difference does it make if you damage someone's arm or leg or you damage his mood?"

And so, *Rashi* concludes *Parshas Yisro* with a departure from his general sphere of comment, reminding us that the messages of Torah are communicated not only by the words it uses, but also by the mitzvos it commands.

---

6   See *Shemos* 15:26: "אִם שָׁמוֹעַ תִּשְׁמַע לְקוֹל ה' אֱלֹקֶיךָ...וְהַאֲזַנְתָּ לְמִצְוֹתָיו—If you shall surely heed Hashem's voice...and listen to His mitzvos."
7   Lit., "the Elder," the spiritual dean of the yeshiva.

FROM THE COMMENTATORS

THE BEGINNING OF PARSHAS YISRO: CLASH OF THE TITLES

וַיִּשְׁמַע יִתְרוֹ כֹהֵן מִדְיָן חֹתֵן מֹשֶׁה אֵת כָּל אֲשֶׁר עָשָׂה אֱלֹקִים לְמֹשֶׁה וּלְיִשְׂרָאֵל עַמּוֹ כִּי הוֹצִיא ה' אֶת יִשְׂרָאֵל מִמִּצְרָיִם.

Yisro, the priest of Midyan, the father-in-law of Moshe, heard everything that God did for Moshe and for Israel, His people—that Hashem took Israel out of Egypt.[1]

Let us begin our discussion by raising some simple questions on this well-known opening verse:

- It is interesting to note how the verse presents Yisro with all of his titles. Apparently, as we have not heard from him for a while, it is appropriate for him to be placed in context as we meet him here again.
- Of particular note is his title "priest of Midyan." *Rashi* has informed us that while Yisro was, at one time, the head priest of Midyan, he abdicated that post when he saw through the falsehood of idolatry. Indeed, this was the reason behind the harassment of his daughters at the well, as described in the end of the second chapter of *Shemos*. Given that his position of priest

---

1   *Shemos* 18:1.

was a thing of the past, it is interesting that the verse should still refer to him as such.

- The opening verse refers to him with two titles: "priest of Midyan" and "father-in-law." Curiously, in the verses that follow, the first title is dropped, but not the second: Verses 2, 5, and 6 refer to him as "Yisro, father-in-law of Moshe," while verses 7 and 8 do not even refer to him by name, calling him simply, "Moshe's father-in-law." It is only in verse 9 that we finally hear him simply being called by his name—Yisro. What is behind these shifting references?

FROM "EVERYTHING" TO ONE THING— UNDERSTANDING THE FLOW OF THE VERSE

Let us approach the above points by first raising a more basic question regarding our opening verse: It begins by mentioning that Yisro heard "everything Hashem did for Moshe and Israel," and then concludes by saying, "that Hashem took Israel out of Egypt." What is the meaning of this second clause? Presumably, the first phrase includes everything Hashem did when He took the Jewish People out of Egypt. As such—and having literally mentioned everything—what is added by saying, "that Hashem took Israel out of Egypt"? If anything, paring things down in this way would seem to diminish the scope of the earlier phrase!

The *Chasam Sofer* offers a fascinating explanation. Indeed, as the first part of the verse relates, Yisro heard about everything that Hashem had done for the people of Israel. However, Yisro was not inclined to believe everything that he heard. After all, he spent much of his life following different faiths, each one with claims more fantastical than the next, yet he had come to see through all of them. As such, the only thing Yisro was prepared to accept as fact—reflected in the second part of the verse—was the idea itself that the people had somehow left Egypt, and even then it wasn't clear whether this was a permanent release or a temporary reprieve. Everything beyond that was met by Yisro with suspicion of being fanciful exaggeration. It was only once Yisro traveled to the Jewish People and saw their situation firsthand that he came to realize that all the reports he had heard were actually true. Thus, whereas originally, Yisro was only prepared to believe that Hashem had "*taken Israel out* of Egypt"—perhaps only temporarily—he subsequently exclaimed,[2] "Blessed is Hashem Who *saved you* from under the hand of Egypt," i.e., permanently.

THE PRIEST OF MIDYAN VS. THE FATHER-IN-LAW OF MOSHE

Perhaps, bearing the above in mind, we can return to the question of Yisro's titles and see them as conflicting elements within him.

- On the one hand, he is the "priest of Midyan," which, as we mentioned, reflects the fact that he has seen everything and has learned not to believe everything he hears.
- On the other hand, he is "the father-in-law of Moshe," and he knows that if there is anyone concerning whom such a report might possibly be true, it is Moshe.

These two elements generated conflicting responses within Yisro. The priest of Midyan might not be inclined to pursue the matter further, while the father-in-law of Moshe would want to go and see if all the reports were really true. It was this second element that prevailed; hence, from verse 2 and onwards Yisro is referred to only as Moshe's father-in-law, reflecting his high regard for and appreciation of Moshe. The "priest of Midyan" was, in a sense, left behind in Midyan. This situation persisted until he visited the people and heard from Moshe firsthand everything that had happened. After this, his appraisal of the situation was no longer one of conjecture, but rather, was verified by his own direct experience. Thus, at this stage, we finally hear a reaction from Yisro "himself," i.e., with no titles, in verse 9: "Yisro rejoiced over all the good that Hashem had done for Israel."

---

2   Verse 10.

THE OPENING WORDS OF THE ASERES HADIBROS

אָנֹכִי ה' אֱלֹקֶיךָ אֲשֶׁר הוֹצֵאתִיךָ מֵאֶרֶץ מִצְרַיִם מִבֵּית עֲבָדִים.

*I am Hashem, your God, Who took you out of the land of Egypt,
from the house of slavery.[3]*

With these words, Hashem "introduces Himself" to the Jewish People
at Har Sinai. The commentators wonder: Why did Hashem present
Himself in terms of the specific event of the Exodus from Egypt, and not
more all-encompassingly as the Creator of the heavens and the earth?[4]

One of the most crucial ideas regarding Torah is that it does not merely
represent Hashem's instructions for how we are to lead our lives in this
world, but it is the basis of our relationship with Him. Through performing mitzvos, we elevate ourselves—and, ultimately, the world—to
a state of Godliness and attach ourselves to Him. Indeed, the commentators point out that the root of the word "מצוה"—"צו," in addition to
meaning "commandment," also means "connection," for it is through
the mitzvos that we achieve a meaningful connection with Hashem.

Accordingly, by introducing Himself as the One Who took us out
of Egypt, Hashem was emphasizing that the mitzvos He was about to
command us represent an extension of the special relationship that He
initiated with us when He delivered us from slavery. Indeed, Hashem's
opening words were, "I am Hashem, your God," as if to say, "Not only am
I 'Hashem, Creator of all,' but I am furthermore 'Your God,' interested
in having a special relationship with you." This introduction served to
provide us with an orientation for all the mitzvos that were to follow,
beginning with the *Aseres Hadibros* and continuing throughout the
entire program of mitzvos.

DRAWING STRENGTH FROM SINAI

Following the presentation of the *Aseres Hadibros*, the verses relate
how the people were traumatized when they experienced the awesome

---

3   *Shemos* 20:2.

4   See, e.g., the *Ibn Ezra* and *Ramban* to *Shemos* ibid.

sights and sounds of Sinai. They approached Moshe, asking that he be the one to speak to them and not Hashem, lest they die. To this request, Moshe responded:

אַל־תִּירָאוּ כִּי לְבַעֲבוּר נַסּוֹת אֶתְכֶם בָּא הָאֱלֹקִים.

Do not fear, for it is in order to test you that God has come.

These words require some explanation. Notwithstanding the traumatic nature of the people hearing Hashem Himself speaking, in what way did that experience constitute a "test"? Indeed, *Rashi* relates "נַסּוֹת" not to the word "נִסָּיוֹן"—a test, but to the word "נֵס"—a banner that is raised aloft. The experience of being addressed directly by Hashem was in order to endow the Jewish People with the elevated status of the only nation among humankind to have enjoyed such direct communication.

The *Rambam*, however, does explain the word "*nasos*" as denoting a test. The background to his explanation is that although many religions have laid claim to being the true faith and carrying the authentic word of God, without exception these claims all begin with an individual saying that God appeared to him and revealed to him the true path. After a while, if enough people believe that individual and promote his claims, the new movement will gain momentum. Judaism alone states that the original revelation took place in front of everyone. This is a claim that would have no credibility if it weren't true—which is the very reason why no one else claims it. One cannot reasonably tell an entire people what they saw, and instruct them concerning every aspect of their lives based on it, if they did not actually see what they were told they saw! Thus, the implications of Hashem revealing Himself directly to the people extended beyond the generation that witnessed the revelation; it allowed for the authentication of our belief in Torah for all times.

In his famous epistle to the community of Yemen, known as *Igeres Teiman*,[5] the *Rambam* writes:

---

5   In the *Rambam's* time, the Jewish community in Yemen was beset with troubles, not least of which was ongoing pressure from their Muslim neighbors to accept the tenets of Islam. In their distress, they sent a letter to the *Rambam* asking him to guide them through all their difficulties. *Igeres Teiman* is the *Rambam's* response to that call.

It is fitting for you, our brothers, to promote and extol that great event [of the Revelation at Sinai]...for it is the pillar upon which our faith stands and the proof which allows one to arrive at the truth...as indeed, the Holy One, Blessed be He, extolled it, as it says, "For inquire now regarding the early days that preceded you, from the day that Hashem created man on earth, and from one end of the heaven to the other end of the heaven: Has there ever been anything like this great thing or has anything like it been heard? Has a people ever heard the voice of God speaking from the midst of the fire as you have heard, and lived?"[6]

There was never an event like it nor will there ever be again, namely, that an entire nation will hear the word of God and witness His glory directly. And the reason for this experience was in order to strengthen our faith to the degree that no force could ever change it. This truth was made known to us directly in order that our stance be firm and that we would not falter in trying times such as these, when there is unrest or oppression against the Jews, Heaven forbid.

And thus did Moshe inform the people of the purpose of hearing Hashem directly: "For it was in order to test you," as if to say, Hashem appeared to you in this manner so that you would be able to withstand any subsequent tests to your faith that may befall you in the End of Days, that your hearts will not swerve and you will not err.[7]

FROM THE HAFTARAH: TWO KINDS OF PROPHECY

וָאֶשְׁמַע אֶת קוֹל אֲ-דֹנָי אֹמֵר אֶת מִי אֶשְׁלַח וּמִי יֵלֶךְ לָנוּ וָאֹמַר הִנְנִי שְׁלָחֵנִי.

I heard the voice of Hashem saying, "Whom shall I send, and who shall go for us?" And I said, "Here I am, send me."[8]

---

6   *Devarim* 4:32–33.

7   See the *Ramban* on our verse for a different understanding of how the Revelation was a "test" for the Jewish People.

8   *Yeshayahu* 6:8.

Our haftarah describes the Navi Yeshayahu's first prophetic experience, as well as his initiation as Hashem's emissary to the Jewish People. As we consider the verse in which this is described, three questions arise:

- Hashem's question appears doubly phrased: "Whom shall I send, and who shall go for us?"
- The first phrase is in the singular, "Whom shall I send," while the second is in the plural, "who shall go for us."
- When Yeshayahu responds, he says only, "Send me," addressing the first part of Hashem's question, but does not respond to the second, saying, "And I will go for you."

R' Azaryah Fego, in his classic *Drashos Binah La'itim*, explains as follows.[9] There are, in reality, two kinds of prophecy: positive ones, which foretell redemption and bright times in the future, and negative ones, which entail chastising the people and foretelling the destruction which could ensue if they persist in their evil ways. These two kinds of prophecy differ in a number of ways:

- Our Sages state that "The Holy One, Blessed is He, does not associate His name with evil." This means that although negative events and experiences are sometimes necessary, they are never the essential purpose, but are rather for purposes of rectifying faults or expiating evil deeds in order to allow for a positive outcome.
- Hashem's judgment always begins by consulting His Heavenly tribunal. However, that tribunal often judges in accordance with the strict letter of law. When this happens, Hashem will often break away and judge by Himself, allowing for a more benevolent verdict.

We should also note that the concept of "*shelichus*" entails the emissary not just transmitting a message from the sender, but also representing him. With all this in mind, we return to our verse and see

---

9   *Drush* 62.

that the question Hashem was sending out regarding a prophet and spokesman was addressing these two types of prophecies:

- "Whom shall I send"—refers to positive prophecies, hence the term "*eshlach*" is used, denoting a complete identification with the prophet. Additionally, the singular is used, as the prophet represents the verdict of Hashem alone.
- "And who shall go for us"—refers to negative prophecies. These are not "*shelichus,*" for Hashem issues them only in a detached way. Additionally, regarding these prophecies, the plural form is used, as the prophet relays the verdict of Hashem together with the Heavenly tribunal.

In light of this, we can now understand Yeshayahu's selective response, "Here I am; send me." Yeshayahu does not wish to foretell doom and destruction to his people, nor to reprimand them for their wrongdoings. He seeks only to speak good of them and to them. Hence, he asks that he be sent by Hashem as His emissary, but not that he should go for the Heavenly tribunal. However, on this occasion, Hashem informs him that the message is not one of comfort, but he is charged with delivering it anyway; for it is only when the people take stock of their actions and rectify that which is corrupt that they can look forward to all the good things that Yeshayahu in time will prophesy for them.

PARSHAS MISHPATIM

THE OPENING RASHI

וְאֵלֶּה הַמִּשְׁפָּטִים אֲשֶׁר תָּשִׂים לִפְנֵיהֶם.

And these are the laws that you shall place before them.[1]

Commenting on these words, *Rashi* writes:

כל מקום שנאמר "אלה" פסל את הראשונים, "ואלה" מוסיף על הראשונים, מה הראשונים מסיני אף אלו מסיני. ולמה נסמכה פרשת דינים לפרשת מזבח? לומר לך שתשים סנהדרין אצל המזבח.

Whenever it says "eileh—these," it denotes detachment from that which was stated previously; "v'eileh—and these" adds to that which was stated previously. [In our instance, the word "v'eileh" teaches]: Just as the earlier section [i.e., the Aseres Hadibros] are from Sinai, so, too, these [commandments of Parshas Mishpatim] are from Sinai.

And why was the section dealing with judgments juxtaposed with the section dealing with the Mizbeiach (Altar)? To tell you that you should place the Sanhedrin near the Mizbeiach.

---

1   *Shemos* 21:1.

SOME QUESTIONS

Rabbeinu Eliyahu Mizrachi, among the foremost commentators of *Rashi*, raises a number of questions here which are fascinating, not only for the light they shed on this particular comment of *Rashi*'s, but on his methodology and approach in general:

- As a rule, when *Rashi* comments on the matter of *semichus haparshiyos*—the juxtaposition of two sections in the Torah—it is his first comment in that parsha.[2] Indeed, this makes perfect sense, as this is a general comment which should, thus, be made before proceeding to deal with more particular matters in the verse. Here, *Rashi* begins by discussing the significance of the letter *vav* in the opening word and only then goes on to discuss *semichus haparshiyos*. Why does he reverse the order in which he normally addresses these things?

- *Rashi*'s goal in his commentary is not to provide information, but to resolve *pshat* issues in the verse. As such, he only ever discusses why one section is juxtaposed with another if there is reason to expect that these two *should not have been* juxtaposed, e.g., if we know that the sections were transmitted or the de-scribed events occurred in a different order to the one in which they are written. If so, in our case, why does *Rashi* feel the need to explain why the parsha of judgments was written next to the parsha of the *Mizbeiach*? What reason do we have for thinking that this was not simply the order in which they were given, whereby one should naturally be written after the other?

- Regarding the first part of *Rashi*'s comment, why do we need a special message—in this case, the letter *vav*—to inform us that *Parshas Mishpatim* is also from Sinai? *Rashi* famously in-forms us in the beginning of *Parshas Behar* that all the mitzvos of the Torah were given at Sinai—both their general principles and their particular details.[3]

---

2   See, e.g., *Rashi* to *Bamidbar* 13:2.
3   *Vayikra* 25:1.

- Given that our parsha immediately follows the Har Sinai experience described in *Parshas Yisro*, with no indication whatsoever of the people having moved away from there, we should naturally assume that its contents are from Sinai, even without the letter *vav*!

All of these questions beckon us to take a closer look at this opening *Rashi*.

"SO TOO, THESE ARE FROM SINAI"

The *Mizrachi* explains that when *Rashi* states that the *mishpatim* are "from Sinai," he does not mean only to indicate that they were transmitted from Sinai. This, as we have noted, is something that is true for all the mitzvos of the Torah. Rather, the meaning is that like the *Aseres Hadibros*, the *mishpatim* were transmitted at the time of *Maamad Har Sinai*—the Revelation at Sinai! This is in contrast to the other mitzvos, which were transmitted to Moshe during the forty days he spent on Har Sinai after the revelation.

However, in light of this idea, we now need to consider the final section of *Parshas Yisro*, which begins with Hashem's message to the people, "You have seen that I have spoken to you from Heaven." These words clearly indicate that this section was said to the people after the revelation. As such, we will now realize that it has been written *out of chronological order*—for it divides between two parshiyos that were both said on the same occasion by presenting something that was said after that occasion! Naturally, we are moved to ask: Why is this so?

Actually, says the *Mizrachi*, someone has already asked this for us, for this is, in fact, *Rashi's* second question. When *Rashi* asks, "And why was the section dealing with laws juxtaposed with the section dealing with the *Mizbeiach?*" it is because we would not expect these two sections to be together—and now we know why. Since the *Aseres Hadibros* and the content of *Parshas Mishpatim* were said during the same event, we would not expect the later section—which concludes with the laws of building a *Mizbeiach*—to be written in between them. Hence, this question of *Rashi*, as with all his questions in matters of juxtaposition, is motivated by *pshat* concerns.

However, at the same time, we understand why this question regarding juxtaposition could not be *Rashi's* opening comment. Prior to addressing the message of the opening letter *vav*, we have no notion that any of these sections are written out of order, and hence, no meaningful reason to involve ourselves in why one was written after the other. It is only after we have learned from the *vav* that *Parshas Mishpatim* was said together with the *Aseres Hadibros*, prior to the section with the laws of the *Mizbeiach*, that we can now ask why that section was juxtaposed with the beginning of our parsha!

SETTING THE TONE
FOR MISHPATIM

וְאֵלֶּה הַמִּשְׁפָּטִים אֲשֶׁר תָּשִׂים לִפְנֵיהֶם.

These are the laws that you shall place before them.[1]

BEGINNINGS: LETTERS AND LAWS

The discussion in this week's parsha does not take long to get started—it begins with the very first letter, the letter *vav* of the word *"v'eileh."* Seemingly, it would be appropriate for a new parsha to open afresh with the word *"eileh,"* while the word *"v'eileh"* appears to link this to the previous parsha, making it a continuum of sorts. Indeed, *Rashi* comments on the link, citing the words of the *Mechilta*:

מה ראשונים מסיני אף אלו מסיני.

Just as the above [commandments, i.e., the Aseres Hadibros] were from Sinai, so too, are these [laws] from Sinai.

What exactly is this Midrash informing us? Why does it need to emphasize that the contents of our parsha are from Sinai? Are not all the mitzvos of the Torah from Sinai?

---

1   *Shemos* 22:1

Let us preface our answers to this question by raising another one: Why does *Parshas Mishpatim* open with the laws of *eved Ivri*—the Hebrew servant?

Although we may answer practically that the parsha has to start somewhere, the question nevertheless persists, for the law of *eved Ivri* is actually based on another law that is stated *later on* in our parsha,[2] namely, that if one steals and does not have the wherewithal to pay off his debt, he is sold into servitude in order to do so. As such, our parsha seems to begin *in the middle of a situation*! That demands an explanation.

Apparently, there is something about *eved Ivri* which sets the tone for the body of Torah law known as *mishpatim*.

THE MITZVOS OF MISHPATIM

It is interesting to note that although the other nations of the world are also enjoined by the Torah to set up courts and adjudicate criminal cases—indeed, to do so is one of the seven Noachide Laws—there is no insistence whatsoever that they base their criminal justice systems on the *mishpatim* of the Torah.[3] We may ask, why not? After all, we assume that the Torah's system is the best one!

The answer to this question will lead us to a fundamental idea regarding *mishpatim*. Although these laws fall in the domain of what we might call "civil law," nevertheless, they are ultimately part of Torah and, as such, are infused with the spiritual quality and makeup that pertains to every mitzvah. Indeed, as an integral part of the Divine system of mitzvos, they are *interconnected* with the rest of the mitzvos—to the extent that there are elements of other mitzvos that can be found in the *mishpatim* as well. This idea finds very clear expression in the laws of *eved Ivri*.

---

2   *Shemos* 22:2.
3   Cited in Responsa of the *Rama*, Responsa sec. 10.

The Torah states that a Hebrew servant works for six years and then goes free in the seventh.[4] What is behind this timing? The Midrash explains that there is a parallel between the six days of the working week, which come to a halt on Shabbos, and the six years of servitude, which are terminated in the seventh year. In both cases, it is to remind those involved that Hashem, Creator of the world, continues to run it.[5] We note that we are barely one verse into the *mishpat* of the Hebrew servant and we have already encountered an aspect of it that relates to the mitzvah of Shabbos!

Additionally, the Torah states that if the *eved* wishes to stay on past the sixth year, he may do so only until the *Yovel* (Jubilee) year. The basis for this is stated explicitly later on in the Torah, namely, that the Jewish People are all, ultimately, Hashem's servants,[6] and hence, there is a point beyond which no Jew can exert ownership or mastery of any kind over another Jew. When did we all become Hashem's servants? When He took us out of Egypt. Now, the *eved Ivri* comprises not only elements of Shabbos, but of Pesach as well!

Perhaps, we can now understand why gentiles are not required by the Torah to employ the *mishpatim* of the Torah. If gentiles do not have the mitzvah of Shabbos itself, there is certainly no reason for them to adopt *mishpatim* that have aspects of Shabbos in them. Likewise, if they have no mitzvah of Pesach on Pesach itself, it will hardly be of relevance to them in the *Yovel* year![7]

And so, *eved Ivri* is most illustrative of the nature of the Torah's *mishpatim* and how they are intertwined with mitzvos from other areas of Torah. As such, this mitzvah opens the parsha of the Torah dedicated to the category of mitzvos called *mishpatim*.[8]

---

4   *Shemos* 21:2.
5   *Shemos Rabbah* 30:15.
6   *Shemos* 25:42.
7   Rav Yaakov Kamenetsky, *Emes L'Yaakov, Shemos* loc. cit.
8   See *Drashos HaRan*, beginning of *drush* 11.

Chukim and Mishpatim

This interconnectedness of *mishpatim* with other types of mitzvos is referred to by David HaMelech in *Tehillim*, when he states:

מַגִּיד דְּבָרָיו לְיַעֲקֹב חֻקָּיו וּמִשְׁפָּטָיו לְיִשְׂרָאֵל. לֹא עָשָׂה כֵן לְכָל גּוֹי וּמִשְׁפָּטִים בַּל יְדָעוּם.

He makes known His word to Yaakov, His statute (chok) and law [mishpat] to Yisrael. He did not do so for all the other nations, and they do not know mishpatim.[9]

The first verse expresses the idea that even mitzvos as diverse from each other as *chukim* and *mishpatim* are, in fact, intertwined. The second verse proceeds to state that as a result of this, Hashem did not transmit even the area of *mishpatim* to the gentiles, for it is intimately bound up with the other areas of Torah, which belong to Yisrael alone.

In this regard, we can understand why our parsha opened with the letter *vav*, linking it, as the Midrash explained, with Sinai. This was not in order to apprise us of the origins of these mitzvos, but to alert us regarding their *nature*—as an integral part of the Divine program of mitzvos given by Hashem to the Jewish People at Sinai.

THE VISION OF MISHPATIM

A second approach to this question begins by referring to an observation of the Midrash. Our parsha is not the first occasion where the Torah presents us with *mishpatim*, for we also received a number of such laws while at Marah, even before arriving at Har Sinai. The Midrash comments:[10]

This may be compared to a noblewoman, who travels with a guard both before and after her. So too, the Torah has monetary laws both before and after it, while it is in the middle.

---

9 *Tehillim* 147:19.
10 *Shemos Rabbah*, beginning of *Parshas Mishpatim*.

What is the meaning of this parable? In what way do the *mishpatim* function as "guards" for the Torah given at Sinai?

The *Be'er Yosef* explains. A striking feature of many of the *mishpatim* is the generosity of spirit that they demand in their implementation. For example:

- Money lent to a fellow Jew cannot have interest charged on it.
- If a borrower defaults on a loan, the lender cannot enter his house to take collateral; rather, he must wait outside for the borrower to bring it to him. As the Gemara notes, it is unlikely that the borrower will choose his most valuable possessions to give as collateral.[11] Additionally, if the item is something the borrower needs at certain times, the lender must return it to him at those times.[12]

What is behind these *mishpatim* that while they ultimately ensure that the lender gets his money back, certainly do not seem to bring the full weight of the law to bear on the one who has to pay? Where does this measure of compassion within the *mishpatim* come from?

The answer is: from Sinai.

The events of Sinai were not just about *revelation*, they were about *elevation*. If we were to ask anyone among the B'nei Yisrael standing at Har Sinai what his goal in life was, we can be sure that no one would respond: "To make as much money as possible and ensure that anyone who owes me money pays it back—come what may!" The entire atmosphere was one which brought the people to an entirely higher plane, with the accompanying higher vision of how to use their assets—for the betterment of society, while ultimately being protected against loss.

This noble vision of Sinai, says the *Be'er Yosef*, is preserved in the *mishpatim* of the Torah. That is why they are looked at as the "guards" which protect the Torah that was given there.

Nowhere is this vision more manifest than in the laws relating to *eved Ivri*. Someone stole money and does not have the wherewithal to

---

11 *Bava Kama* 8a.
12 *Shemos* 22:25–26.

pay it back, resulting in his being sold into servitude in order to do so. We would have imagined that the only priority in this situation is the person working off his debt, yet we find a host of laws regarding how to treat this servant. He cannot be given work that is demeaning.[13] His basic needs are to be provided for in a manner no less than his master,[14] to the extent that the *Yerushalmi*[15] famously says that if there is only one pillow available, the master must give it to his servant, while he himself must sleep without one! The entire situation is summed up by the Gemara that states: "Whoever acquires a servant has thereby acquired a master for himself."

What is behind these laws? The vision of Sinai, whereby the goal with regards to this thief is not just one of *remuneration*, but of *rehabilitation*! Perhaps, we can now understand why *eved Ivri* opens *Parshas Mishpatim*, for it so strikingly portrays the Torah's Higher Program of monetary law.

This will give us new insight into the *Mechilta* cited in the beginning of our discussion which comments on the opening letter *vav*, linking the *mishpatim* to Sinai: Just as the earlier commandments are infused with the ethos and atmosphere of Sinai, so too are the *mishpatim*, beginning with—and stunningly represented by—*eved Ivri*!

---

13 See *Rashi* to *Vayikra* 25:39.
14 *Kiddushin* 20a.
15 Cited in *Tosafos* ibid.

FOLLOWING THE MAJORITY

Finding the Halachah

אַחֲרֵי רַבִּים לְהַטֹּת.

Incline the matter after the majority.[1]

BACKGROUND

Parshas Mishpatim introduces us to the world of the Torah's laws that are relevant *bein adam l'chaveiro*—between man and his fellow man." At the center of this world is the *beis din*, whose job it is to determine which party is guilty in any given altercation and to oversee the appropriate administration of justice. One of the bedrock principles for deciding Torah law is expressed in our verse. In the event that the judges of the *beis din* are not all in agreement as to what the ruling should be regarding a particular question, the Torah states that they should rule in accordance with the majority opinion among the judges.

UNDERSTANDING THE CONCEPT

It is worthwhile raising the simple question of why this is so. On the one hand, one has to do something, and it is not practical to hold off

---

1   *Shemos* 23:2.

from ruling on any case unless and until all judges are in agreement. On the other hand, there is still room to ponder as to the meaning behind this principle and its implications regarding the minority opinion which was outvoted. After all, it is not impossible that the correct answer lies with them. Indeed, answering this question will lead us to consider the very meaning of the concept that we call halachah—Torah law.

In fact, there are two possible ways to respond to the above question:

- It is possible that the Torah is simply endorsing the notion that the majority is *more likely* to arrive at the correct conclusion than the minority, and therefore, it is to be followed. According to this approach, there does exist the possibility that the actually correct conclusion was arrived at by the minority; nevertheless, as a rule, the truth will more likely rest with the majority and hence, their opinion is to be followed in all cases.
- However, it is possible that in telling us to follow the majority, the Torah is defining for us what halachah is. Halachah—Torah law—is *by definition* the conclusion of the majority of qualified judges on a *beis din*. "Halachah" literally translates as "going." The way that Hashem wants us to go in life is in accordance with the decision of the majority of the *beis din*.

"NOT IN HEAVEN": CONTESTED OVENS AND HEATED DEBATES

This second approach would appear to be corroborated by the fact that we follow the majority even in a case where we are appraised of the correct decision as arrived at in Heaven. Indeed, such a situation is famously described in the dispute between R' Eliezer and the Sages regarding whether a certain oven was susceptible to receiving *tum'ah* (ritual contamination) or not. Initially, R' Eliezer advances a number of arguments for his position, but these were not accepted by the Sages. At that stage, R' Eliezer called for all sorts of miracles to demonstrate that his opinion was correct, all of which were ignored by the Sages. Finally, the Gemara relates:

> He then said to them, "If the halachah is like me, let them prove it from Heaven." A Heavenly voice [bas kol] issued forth

and said, "Why do you take issue with R' Eliezer, whom the
halachah follows in all places?"
R'Yehoshua stood up on his feet and said, "Lo baShamayim
hi—It [the Torah] is not in Heaven!"[2]
What is the meaning of, "It is not in Heaven?" R'Yirmiyah said,
"For the Torah has already been given from Sinai. We do not pay
any attention to a bas kol, for You [God] have already written
in the Torah at Mount Sinai, 'The matter shall be inclined
toward the majority.'"[3]

With these three words, *"lo baShamayim hi,"* R' Yehoshua encapsulated halachah's attitude toward Heavenly intervention in matters of halachah. The arena of halachic discussion is solely in the *beis din,* and the tools for deciding halachah are those that were handed down to the judges along with the Torah at Sinai; and when they are in disagreement—we follow the majority.

The *Rambam,* in his introduction to his Commentary on the Mishnah, phrases the matter thus:

And know that prophecy influences neither the explanations of
the Torah nor the deriving of the details of its commandments
through the principles of exegetical derivation. Rather, the
way Yehoshua and Pinchas conducted their investigation and
reasoning is the same way Ravina and Rav Ashi performed
theirs...God has not allowed us to learn from prophets, rather,
only from chachamim, men of reasoning and knowledge. The
Torah does not say, "You shall come to the prophet who will be
in those days," rather, "You shall come to the Kohen and to the
judge."[4]

Yet we ask: *Why* is this so? To put it in the simplest terms, do we not assume that a *bas kol*—a voice emanating from Heaven—represents

---

2   *Devarim* 30:12.
3   *Shemos* 23:2.
4   See also *Hilchos Yesodei HaTorah* 9:1.

the ultimate truth, making it the "right" answer? If that is the case, then how can we ignore it? In the case cited by the Gemara, did the *bas kol* siding with R' Eliezer not indicate that in this case, the majority of Sages were in error?

In light of our discussion, we can understand why a Heavenly voice is inadmissible in the *beis din*, for even if it represents the theoretical "true answer," it does not define the halachah as Hashem wishes us to follow it. This is why the Sages ignored the *bas kol* which supported R' Eliezer's view.[5]

DEFINING THE LAW AND PROTECTING THE LAW

The above explanation of why we ignore a *bas kol* fits in very well with the second answer offered above as to why we follow the majority, namely, that it defines the halachah. However, according to the first answer, whereby the majority is simply more likely to find the correct answer, why did the Sages ignore it when it was presented to them in the form of a Heavenly voice?

The *Chasam Sofer* explains that according to this approach, the principle of "*lo baShamayim hi*" exists as a means to protect the halachah.[6] If a Heavenly voice were admissible as a basis for a halachic ruling, it could lead to a breakdown of effective halachic adjudication, for any person could simply say that his ruling is based on a Heavenly voice, thereby placing it beyond any potential investigation or refutation. Therefore, the Torah demands that halachic rulings must be based solely on evidence and arguments that can be demonstrated and authenticated.

A very interesting potential difference between these two approaches would arise in a situation where the *beis din* is unable to reach a decision with regard to a certain case. Under those circumstances, would they be allowed to follow the ruling of a *bas kol*? According to the *Chasam Sofer's* approach, which we could call "Protecting the Halachah," the medium of

---

5   *Drashos HaRan*, drush 7. See also Author's Introduction to *Ketzos Hachoshen*, and Rav Elchanan Wasserman, *Kuntres Divrei Sofrim*, part 1, § 5. See also commentaries *Be'er Yosef* and *Emes L'Yaakov* to our verse.

6   Responsa, *Orach Chaim* § 208.

a *bas kol* is categorically inadmissible in a halachic discussion, and hence, would be unacceptable even if there were no other means of determining the halachah. By contrast, according to the second approach, which we could refer to as "Defining Halachah," lacking the wherewithal to arrive at the halachah on their own, the *beis din* might then be entitled to follow a *bas kol*.[7]

Another instance which might result in a difference between the two approaches is a case where the halachah was initially known and then subsequently forgotten. Would it be possible to rely on a *bas kol* to reinstate it? Here too, according to the approach of "Protecting the Halachah," the *bas kol* would be inadmissible, since in order to preserve the halachic system, no entry can ever be given to Heavenly input, even for a halachah that was once known. However, according to the approach of "Defining the Halachah," in this instance, the halachah was originally formulated by the *beis din*! All the *bas kol* is doing is informing people of what the *beis din* had once decided, and hence it would be permissible.[8]

---

7   See *Chida, Devash L'fi, os nun,* § 12. It is apparent from numerous sources that the exclusion of Heavenly input from a halachic ruling refers specifically to the ruling itself; however, the evidence upon which the ruling is based can be attained through Heavenly means. See, e.g., *Tosafos, Chullin* 4b, s.v. *al pi; Kuntres Divrei Sofrim* sec. 5; and at length in *Maharatz Chiyus, Toras Neviim,* chap. 2. It is interesting to consider this distinction in terms of the two approaches we have presented to the principle of "*lo baShamayim hi.*" According to the second approach ("Defining Halachah"), although gathering correct information is crucial as the basis for the correct ruling, it is only the ruling itself that is actually "Torah," about which we say that it is no longer in Heaven. In terms of the first approach ("Protecting the Halachah"), seemingly one could argue that the proceedings in the *beis din* could break down as much through claims of Heavenly voices regarding evidence as with regard to the rulings themselves, so that both should be inadmissible! However, apparently the worry over a breakdown applies specifically to the ruling, perhaps because that would have implications for all such cases, as opposed to the question of evidence, which relates only to that particular case.

8   See *Temurah* 16a regarding three thousand halachos that were forgotten during the mourning period for Moshe. The people asked Yehoshua to reclaim them using prophecy, to which he replied, "It is not in Heaven." The Gemara concludes that ultimately, Osniel ben Kenaz restored them by means of *pilpul* (halachic analysis). This Gemara seems to indicate clearly that Heavenly input is not allowed even with regards to halachos that were once formulated and subsequently forgotten. Elsewhere (see *Megillah* 3a), the Gemara states that the final letters were instituted by the prophets. When challenged that a prophet cannot innovate

THE GIVING OF THE TORAH:
TOWARD CROWNING ACHIEVEMENTS

According to numerous commentators, the shift of authority from Heaven to Earth in deciding the halachah represents the full meaning of the term "*Matan Torah*"—the Giving of the Torah. In other words, not only were the mitzvos of the Torah *transmitted* to us to fulfill, but the ability to determine the halachah in any given situation was *transferred* to us.[9]

In his introduction to the first volume of his responsa *Igros Moshe*, Rav Moshe Feinstein discusses this concept of the Torah being "not in Heaven" as it applies throughout the generations. By definition, this means that there must exist a criterion whereby the Torah scholars of each generation are qualified to make halachic rulings. Thus, he writes, after having mastered the relevant sources, and accompanied by fear of Heaven, the scholar should engage himself in the question posed to him and issue the ruling that he feels is correct. And while it is possible that his ruling is in error, the Torah is "not in Heaven," and he has acted properly in delivering the answer which he believes to be correct.

With this in mind, Rav Moshe refers to the Gemara in *Maseches Menachos* that describes when Moshe ascended on high to receive the Torah, he found Hashem attaching "crowns" to the letters, referring to

---

a halachah, the Gemara explains that these letters were originally known, but then forgotten, so that all the prophets did was to reinstate them. Based on the above Gemara in *Temurah*, the commentators conclude that the prophets could not have used prophecy to reinstate the letters, for, as we have seen, this is unacceptable even for things that were merely forgotten. Rather, they did so through means of *pilpul*, as Osniel did in his time (see *P'nei Yehoshua* to *Megillah* ibid. In *Maseches Sukkah* 44a, the Gemara says that the circling of the *Mizbeiach* with the *aravah* on Sukkos is a Torah law that was forgotten and then reinstated by the prophets. *Rashi* there comments that they did so via prophecy. The commentators raise a difficulty on this comment from the abovementioned Gemara in *Temurah*, which seems to disqualify prophecy even in such cases. The *Pardes Yosef* (*Vayikra* 27:34) explains *Rashi's* position that where there is the possibility of restoring the halachos via *pilpul*, then prophecy is not accepted. However, a "standalone" mitzvah such as *aravah* in the Beis Hamikdash could not feasibly be deduced via halachic analysis. In such an instance, a forgotten mitzvah can be reclaimed via prophecy).

9   Commentary of *Vilna Gaon* to *Shir Hashirim* 3:11; R' Yaakov of Lisa, Introduction to commentary *Nachalas Yaakov* on the Torah; R' Yisrael Salanter, *Ohr Yisrael*, footnote to sec. 30 part 3; *Beis Halevi, Parshas Shemos*, s.v. *l'havin*.

the vertical lines attached to the top of certain letters. When Moshe inquired as to the purpose of these crowns, Hashem responded that in the future, R' Akiva would expound halachos from them.[10]

Why are the lines above the letters called "crowns"?

Rav Moshe explains that part of the process of Hashem giving the Torah to the Jewish People is that He also grants them the authority to derive halachic rulings based on their understanding of the words written therein. As such, the "crown," which represents that authority, has passed to the words and letters themselves, for it is the Sages' understanding of those words and letters which will henceforth determine the halachah!

10   29b.

FROM THE COMMENTATORS

THE TREIFAH AND BEING HOLY

וְאַנְשֵׁי קֹדֶשׁ תִּהְיוּן לִי וּבָשָׂר בַּשָּׂדֶה טְרֵפָה לֹא תֹאכֵלוּ לַכֶּלֶב תַּשְׁלִכוּן אֹתוֹ.

You shall be holy people to me; you shall not eat the flesh of an animal that was torn in the field, [rather] you shall throw it to the dogs.[1]

Although the topic of permitted and forbidden foods will be presented at length in *Chumash Vayikra*,[2] our parsha already mentions an example of food that is prohibited for consumption. Indeed, the latter half of our parsha contains numerous brief references to various mitzvos, such as Shabbos, *shemittah*, *terumah* and *maaser*, the three *Regalim* festivals, etc. The *Ramban* explains this phenomenon based on his understanding that *Parshas Mishpatim* is the "*Sefer Habris*—the Book of the Covenant" mentioned at the end of the parsha which Moshe read to the people at the time of the giving of the Torah.[3] Hence, it contains these brief presentations of many different types of mitzvos of the Torah.

---

1   *Shemos* 22:30.
2   Chap. 11.
3   24:7.

The *Ramban* further explains the reason the Torah introduces this prohibition with the words, "You shall be holy people to me" is in order to emphasize that the prohibition of the various foods and species is not based on *physical* health concerns. Rather, these are foods which the Torah informs us are *spiritually* damaging to a person and hence, by way of preface, it states that we must be holy and avoid any food that will be detrimental to that state of holiness. Indeed, the *Netziv* adds that this is why the Torah gives the specific example of an animal that has been "torn in the field." Although conversationally we use the term "*treif*" to include all non-kosher food, the concept of *treifah* refers specifically to a rupture to one of various organs in the animal, resulting in a life expectancy of less than twelve months. While some kinds of internal *treifah* ruptures might be seen as rendering the animal unhealthy for consumption, an animal that was torn apart in the field was one hundred percent healthy prior to that incident! By highlighting this kind of *treifah* in the prohibition, the Torah is emphasizing that the commandment is not related to physical health concerns, but to spiritual ones.[4]

The verse concludes that an animal that has become forbidden for consumption due to being a *treifah* should be thrown to the dogs. *Rashi* provides the background to this unusual mitzvah. At the time of the plague of the firstborn in Egypt, in order to further emphasize the miraculous nature of that event, Moshe informed Pharaoh that no dog would whet its tongue against the Jewish People or their animals. Although it is natural for dogs to become agitated and incited when surrounded by death and confusion, in this instance, they would not act in a violent manner. Since Hashem does not withhold reward for any man or beast, He mandated that henceforth, *treifah* animals should be given to the dogs as their reward.

R' Shmuel Birnbaum offers a most beautiful insight here. It emerges that the verse contains two mitzvos:

- The negative mitzvah of not eating a *treifah*.
- The positive mitzvah of throwing it to the dogs.

---

4   *Haamek Davar* to our verse.

As we noted, the verse opens by exhorting us to be holy people. Those words, says R' Birnbaum, introduce *both mitzvos* of the verse. Let us ask, what exactly did the dogs do that made them deserving of reward? The fact that they did not act in a violent manner was not due to a decision on their part, but because they were rendered unable to do so! Rather, the dogs' inability to act on their instincts on that occasion was a cause of distress for them. It is in recognition of that distress that the Torah says that they should receive their reward, and this too is a fulfillment of the command to be holy. Ultimately, the verse is teaching us that holiness is expressed not only in the things that we do or do not eat, but also in the sensitivity that we have to the feelings of every living being, both human and animal.

Beautiful!

WISDOM AND PERCEPTIVENESS

וְשֹׁחַד לֹא תִקָּח כִּי הַשֹּׁחַד יְעַוֵּר פִּקְחִים וִיסַלֵּף דִּבְרֵי צַדִּיקִם.

And do not accept a bribe, for a bribe will blind the eyes of those who have sight and falsify the words of the just.[5]

This verse spells out clearly the consequences of a judge taking a bribe. Even if he is wise, nevertheless, once he has become partial to one of the parties, he will be blinded to aspects of the case that would be to that party's detriment. The prohibition against taking a bribe is reiterated later in the Torah, in *Parshas Shoftim*, in an almost identical manner. There, however, the verse concludes: "כִּי הַשֹּׁחַד יְעַוֵּר עֵינֵי חֲכָמִים—for a bribe will blind the eyes of the wise."[6] What is the difference in connotation between these two verses?

The *Vilna Gaon* explains that in order for a judge to rule correctly on any given case, he needs two qualifications: wisdom and perceptiveness.[7]

---

5   *Shemos* 23:8.
6   *Devarim* 16:29.
7   *Aderes Eliyahu.*

- The quality of wisdom refers to expertise in Torah law, knowing exactly which verdict is appropriate for each case as presented by the witnesses in their testimony.
- The quality of perceptiveness relates to knowing how to relate to the testimony itself, being able to assess whether it sounds as if the witnesses are being truthful or not. This involves a knowledge of people, being able to pick up on things such as their body language, suspicious discrepancies between the accounts of each of the witnesses—and even suspicious similarities! In such cases, the judge will know to investigate the matter further until he is satisfied that their testimony is genuine.

We will appreciate that without the second faculty, the judge is liable to render a decision that is fully accurate in terms of what he has heard, while at the same time completely inappropriate to that case. It is specifically through both faculties that the true and correct verdict will emerge. Indeed, we find that the Sages praise a judge who is *dan din emes l'amito*—renders true judgment in its truth."[8] The double phraseology in this praise is as per the above; the judge who is worthy of praise is one whose judgments are not only "true" in terms of being the correct ruling based on the witnesses' testimony, but also "in its truth" in terms of establishing whether that testimony is genuine.

Having identified the two criteria for a successful judgment, our verses inform us that both of these faculties can be critically compromised by receiving a bribe, leaving the judge blind not only to what the correct verdict should be, but also to whether he can rely on those testifying before him. Moreover, as both verses conclude, a bribe can also "falsify the words of the just." The *Vilna Gaon* explains that in addition to corrupting the judge's vision in that particular case, a bribe can also lead to later cases being falsified, even if there is no bribe given then. Once he has rendered the flawed verdict here, later cases will likewise be influenced so that they don't clash with the precedent set in the initial case.

---

8   See *Shabbos* 10b.

וּמַרְאֵה כְּבוֹד ה' כְּאֵשׁ אֹכֶלֶת בְּרֹאשׁ הָהָר.

And the vision of Hashem's glory was like a consuming fire at the top of the mountain.[9]

The concluding chapter in our parsha describes the *Bris Torah* (Covenant of Torah) that the Jewish People entered into when they received the Torah at Har Sinai.[10]

Regarding our verse, a couple of basic question arise. First, what are we to learn from this description? Hashem's glory is not a physical entity to be perceived visually, so why then does the verse liken it to a consuming fire? Additionally, what is the meaning of the phrase "a consuming fire"? Does not all fire consume?

We may be inclined to understand that when the Israelites were assembled around Mount Sinai to receive the Torah, they all received it to the same uniform degree. However, upon further reflection, this is neither likely nor reasonable. The Jewish People had seven weeks to prepare themselves to receive the Torah, with the experience at Mount Sinai being the product of that preparation. In the same way that not every single person prepared to exactly the same degree, so too not every person experienced *Matan Torah* in exactly the same way. Those who prepared themselves more received more, and those who prepared less received less. It is fascinating to consider that there may have been two people who were literally standing side by side at Mount Sinai, seeing and hearing the same thing, but receiving the Torah to a significantly different degree.

A helpful analogy to illustrate this varying effect is the consuming effect of fire. The same fire applied to different materials will not affect them all in the same way. Certain materials are highly combustible and will burst into flames almost instantly, while others may take a while

---

9   *Shemos* 24:17.

10   Regarding the question of whether this covenant was enacted prior to the people receiving the Torah or afterwards, see commentaries of *Rashi* and the *Ramban* to the opening verse of chapter 24. See also *Chiddushei Maran Riz Halevi al HaTorah*, end of *Parshas Mishpatim*.

longer; yet other materials, such as stone, will not catch fire at all. This is the intent of the Torah in likening Hashem's glory to "a consuming fire." It is not a *description* of what the glory looked like, but an *assessment* of the way it affected the Jewish People; it was like the way fire consumes. Those who had prepared more were more "combustible" and "caught fire" to a greater degree, while others who prepared less were affected to a lesser degree.[11]

---

11   Based on *Hakesav V'hakabbalah* to *Shemos*, loc. cit.

PARSHAS TERUMAH

THE PRINCIPLE OF EIN MUKDAM U'MEUCHAR BATORAH

BACKGROUND: THE MISHKAN AND THE CHEIT HAEIGEL

The final five parshiyos of *Chumash Shemos* are devoted, in the main, to matters relating to the *Mishkan* and the *bigdei kehunah* (priestly garments), with the notable exception of the *Cheit HaEigel* (Sin of the Golden Calf), which features in the middle. The basic breakdown is as follows:

- *Parshas Terumah*—Hashem's command regarding the *Mishkan* and its vessels
- *Parshas Tetzaveh*—Hashem's command regarding the *bigdei kehunah*
- *Parshas Ki Sisa*—The *Cheit HaEigel*
- *Parshas Vayakhel*—The Torah's description of the construction of the *Mishkan*
- *Parshas Pekudei*—The Torah's description of the manufacture of the *bigdei kehunah*

Rashi states that although the *Cheit HaEigel* is written in the Torah *after* the commands regarding the *Mishkan*, etc., it actually occurred beforehand.[1] In stating this, *Rashi* is invoking the principle of "*Ein*

---

1   *Shemos* 31:18.

mukdam u'meuchar baTorah—There is no "earlier" or "later" in the Torah." In other words, the order in which events are *written* in the Torah does not necessarily reflect the order in which they *occurred historically*.

Where does this idea come from?

THE SOURCE: COUNTING ISRAEL, THE KORBAN PESACH— AND CHUMASH BAMIDBAR

The idea that an event which happened earlier in history can be written later in the Torah is discussed in the Gemara,[2] based on a case where the Torah itself explicitly states that this was the case:

- The *opening* chapter of *Chumash Bamidbar* deals with the counting of B'nei Yisrael, which the verse describes as having happened in the *second month* of the second year.[3]
- Chapter 9 of *Bamidbar* discusses the *Korban Pesach* that was offered in the wilderness, specifying that this instruction was given in the *first month* of the second year![4]

The Gemara cites these two verses and concludes with the formulation: We see from here that there is no "earlier" and "later" in the Torah.

This principle is applied by *Rashi* several times throughout his commentary on the Torah,[5] with our situation being a classic example: Although the *Cheit HaEigel* is discussed in the "middle" parsha of *Ki*

---

2 *Pesachim* 6b.
3 *Bamidbar* 1:1.
4 Ibid. 9:1.
5 Actually, in one respect, *Rashi* applies the principle even beyond the parameters set forth by the Gemara. The Gemara (*Pesachim* ibid.) states that the principle of *ein mukdam u'meuchar* can only be invoked with respect to two sections of the Torah, but not within one section. *Rashi*, however, does apply this principle even within one section (see, e.g., *Bereishis* 18:3, s.v. *vayomar* and *Shemos* 4:20, s.v. *vayashav*). In this, *Rashi* seems to be more basing himself on the *Yerushalmi* (*Shekalim* 6:1), which invokes the principle of *ein mukdam u'meuchar* with regards to the verse in our parsha (25:21) that describes the placing of the *Kapores* (covering) on the lid of the *Aron* before mentioning the placing of the *Luchos* inside, even though the latter would happen beforehand. See also *Tosafos Chullin* 95b, s.v. *k'Eliezer*.

Sisa, it occurred *before* the events discussed in the prior parshiyos of *Terumah* and *Tetzaveh*.[6]

UNDERSTANDING RASHI

Having seen the basis of the principle, we now proceed to ask: Why did *Rashi* invoke it *here*? In other words, *Rashi* must have had reason to conclude that the parshiyos of the *Mishkan* and the *Cheit HaEigel* are not in chronological order. What would that reason be?[7]

R' Leib Heyman offers a fascinating suggestion.[8] *Rashi* notes that prior to the *Cheit HaEigel*, the *avodah* of *korbanos* was performed by the *bechorim* (firstborns), while the introduction of Kohanim from the tribe of Levi specifically to perform the *avodah* was a result of the *Cheit HaEigel*.[9] Having said this, we note that the following parsha, *Tetzaveh*, already records the command to initiate Aharon and his sons, i.e., the Kohanim, into the *avodah*—an event which did not occur until after the *eigel*! This, says R' Heyman, is what led *Rashi* to conclude that these parshiyos were not written in chronological order.

A thought-provoking point, indeed!

---

6 This is in contrast to the *Ramban*, who understands that the order in which these events are written reflects the order in which they actually occurred:

1. Hashem initially commanded Moshe regarding the *Mishkan* and *bigdei kehunah* during the forty days he was on Mount Sinai (*Terumah* and *Tetzaveh*).
2. While Moshe was on the mountain, the people made the *eigel*, at which point the project of constructing the *Mishkan* was "shelved" until the people recovered from that sin (*Ki Sisa*).
3. Once B'nei Yisrael received atonement for the *eigel* (on Yom Kippur), Moshe was then able to tell them about the *Mishkan*, which they proceeded to build (*Vayakhel* and *Pekudei*).

This position reflects the *Ramban's* general approach regarding the principle of *ein mukdam u'meuchar*, which he sets forth elsewhere in his commentary (*Vayikra* 8:2 and *Bamidbar* 16:1), which is very restricted. According to the *Ramban*, this principle can only be invoked if *the Torah itself specifies*—either through date or location—that the event written later actually happened earlier. In this regard, *Rashi* is more liberal in his understanding of the parameters which allow for the application of this principle. Interestingly, the most frequent application of *ein mukdam u'meuchar* is found in the commentary of the *Ibn Ezra*; see, e.g., *Bereishis* 12:1 and *Bamidbar* 16:1.

7 See commentaries of *Mizrachi* and *Gur Aryeh* to *Rashi*, loc. cit., who discuss this question.

8 *Chikrei Lev, Parshas Terumah*.

9 See *Rashi* to *Shemos* 24:5 and *Bamidbar* 3:39.

UNDERSTANDING THE PRINCIPLE: GENERAL AND SPECIFIC APPROACHES

Having discussed the circumstances which might lead us to invoke the principle of *ein mukdam u'meuchar*, we come now to consider the principle itself: *Why*, if we may ask, does the Torah not always preserve the chronological sequence in its presentation of events? What is behind this idea?

It is possible to identify two different approaches to this question:

General Approach—The *Sefer Hachinuch*, in his introduction to *Chumash Devarim*, writes that in addition to teaching us how to perform mitzvos, the Torah includes and alludes to all forms of wisdom, which can be gleaned from it in many different ways. Moreover, says the *Sefer Hachinuch*, the inclusion of these other aspects of wisdom can sometimes result in the order of the parshiyos not paralleling the order in which the events occurred, since including those additional forms of wisdom contained within the Torah may take precedence over presenting the chronological order.

This is a profound and stunning idea.[10] Moreover, we will appreciate that it is one that potentially explains all cases where we see *ein mukdam u'meuchar* in action, whereby, in all of those cases, we could say that the Torah set aside the chronological order for purposes of teaching some additional point of wisdom which required a different order.

Specific Approach—From *Rashi*, however, we can see that the answer to why a topic may have been presented out of chronological order will rest in a concern *relating to that topic itself*. Thus, for example, while discussing the cases in *Chumash Bamidbar* which are presented out of order (counting the people before *Korban Pesach*), *Rashi* raises the question as to why, in fact, the *Korban Pesach* was not discussed first. He answers that it is because it reflects negatively on the B'nei Yisrael, since throughout all the forty years they were in the wilderness, they only offered this one *Korban Pesach*.[11]

---

10   See similarly Responsa *Radvaz* sec. 1,086 and *Shelah Hakadosh*, Shavuos, *Torah Ohr*, sec. 90.

11   *Rashi* to *Bamidbar* 9:1.

As such, with regards to our situation, we ask: What is it *about the Mishkan and the Cheit HaEigel* which would lead to them not being discussed in the order in which they occurred?

Now, we could answer simply that it is similar to the Pesach case: We prefer to mention something positive, like the *Mishkan*, before something negative, like the *Cheit HaEigel*. However, it appears that there is a deeper point here.

FORGET ME NOT

The Gemara recounts a most unusual exchange between Hashem and the people of Israel:[12]

> *Israel says: Seeing as there is no forgetting before You, perhaps You will not forget the episode with the eigel?*
> *Hashem responds: I will [nevertheless] forget the eigel.*
> *Israel says: Seeing as You are prepared to forget the eigel, perhaps You will also forget the events of Sinai?*
> *Hashem responds: I will not forget Sinai.*

What is the meaning of this exchange?

- How are the ideas of Hashem being prepared to forget the *eigel* and potentially forgetting Sinai linked to each other?
- More specifically, what is the meaning of Hashem "forgetting" either of those events, seeing as Hashem is All-Knowing and does not forget anything?

The *Maharal* explains that the Jewish People were concerned that the fact that they could have erred with the *eigel* so soon after having received the Torah was indicative of an essential disconnect between them and Hashem.[13] If so, then Hashem would never forget the *eigel*, for it would always represent something about their essential makeup. To this, Hashem responded that He *would* "forget" the *eigel*, that is to say, He would not associate it with them in an essential manner, for

---

12   *Berachos* 32b.
13   *Ner Mitzvah.*

it did not express their true nature. For, in truth, the making the *eigel* was not the product of any such disconnect. Rather, it was a result of the vestiges of Egyptian culture to which they had been exposed for so many years, and from which they had only recently been removed.

At this stage, having been reassured by Hashem, the concern of the Jewish People now becomes reversed. If their actions with the *eigel* during this formative period were not necessarily an expression of their essential nature, then perhaps their experiences at Sinai did not reflect their true essence either—and were thus likewise, prone to being "forgotten" by Hashem! To this, Hashem responds that he would not forget Sinai, as the level attained by Israel at that time really was an expression of their true nature.

BETWEEN HISTORY AND DESTINY

With the above in mind, we will appreciate that the order of events as presented by the Torah in these parshiyos can express one of two truths:

- The truth about the order of events
- The truth about the Jewish People

Now we can understand why the Torah reversed the order of events regarding the *Mishkan* and the *eigel*. Had it presented them in the order that they occurred, this may have been accurate regarding the events themselves, but would have belied the truth about what each event says about the Jewish People. To this end, the *Mishkan* is presented first, expressing thereby the *fundamental truth* that the Jewish People have an essential connection with the Divine Presence represented by the *Mishkan*, while they have no such connection with the prior episode of the *eigel*. And while it may be true that those who don't learn from history are destined to repeat it, those who *mis*-learn what history says about them risk compromising their destiny itself.

This is the lesson from the Torah's use of *ein mukdam u'meuchar* in our parsha.

AN ARK IN THE SANCTUARY

The Relationship of the Aron with the Vessels of the Mishkan

וְאֶל הָאָרֹן תִּתֵּן אֶת הָעֵדֻת אֲשֶׁר אֶתֵּן אֵלֶיךָ.

And into the Aron you shall put the Testimony that I shall give you.[1]

INTRODUCTION: A QUESTION FROM RASHI

Rashi, in his comment to this verse, raises a simple question. This selfsame instruction has already been stated just a few verses earlier:

וְנָתַתָּ אֶל הָאָרֹן אֵת הָעֵדֻת אֲשֶׁר אֶתֵּן אֵלֶיךָ.

You shall put into the Aron the Testimony that I shall give you.

Thus, *Rashi* asks, why would the Torah see fit to repeat an instruction it had just given?

Rashi himself proceeds to offer an answer to this question; however, once he has opened the matter for discussion, we will not be surprised to hear that other answers are forthcoming from later commentators.

---

1   *Shemos* 25:21.

THE MAHARAL: WHAT REPETITION REVEALS

Let us consider a fascinating response to this question by the *Maharal* in the *Gur Aryeh*. First, he identifies the Testimony to which these verses refer as the two *Luchos* (tablets of stone) with the *Aseres Hadibros* engraved on them. Although the earlier verse has already stated that Moshe is to place the *Luchos* inside the *Aron*, there may yet have been room to understand that while this is a mitzvah that pertains to the *Aron*, it is not critical. If so, then even if there were to be no *Luchos* to place inside, there would still be a requirement to make the *Aron*. To this end, the Torah repeats the instruction of placing the *Luchos* in the *Aron*. Through this, it indicates that this is something that is indispensable to the *Aron*; indeed, it expresses the idea of what the very definition of the *Aron* is: "A repository for the *Luchos*"!

RESONANCE IN THE VERSES

This fundamental idea regarding the purpose of the *Aron* is expressed in various ways in other verses as well. In the beginning of *Parshas Ki Sisa*, the Torah lists the component parts of the *Mishkan*.[2] Within that list, the *Aron* is referred to as: "אֶת הָאָרֹן לָעֵדֻת—The *Aron* **for** the Testimony." With these words, the Torah clearly indicates that the *Aron* is not simply "a place in which the *Luchos* reside," but rather that it exists specifically *in order* for them to reside inside.[3]

The matter receives striking emphasis from a verse in the beginning of *Sefer Shmuel*, which describes the defeat the Jewish People suffered in battle against the Philistines, during which the *Aron*—which they had taken with them out to the battle—was captured. The verse describes this tragic event with the words: "וַאֲרוֹן הָאֱלֹקִים נִלְקָחָה—and the Ark of God was taken."[4] Now, the Hebrew word *"aron"* is a masculine noun, and treated as such throughout the Chumash and Prophets. If

---

2   *Shemos*, chap. 31.
3   Comments of *Rashash* to *Yoma* 53b.
4   *Shmuel I* 4:17. See, likewise, *Divrei Hayamim II*, "אֲשֶׁר בָּאָה אֲלֵיהֶם אֲרוֹן ה'"—For the Ark of Hashem had come to them."

so, the verse should not have used the feminine form "*nilkachah*" when describing it, but rather the masculine form—"*nilkach*"!

What is behind this anomaly?

R' Yaakov Kamenetsky presents a stunning answer to this question, beginning by referring to a classic idea regarding *lashon hakodesh*.[5] There are occasions where the Torah introduces and combines an element within a word that is not warranted by the laws of grammar in order to reflect an additional aspect of what that word represents. As we have seen, the *Aron* exists in order to house the *eidus* (Testimony) in the form of the *Luchos*. So intimately is the *Aron* bound up with this purpose that the verse actually ends up referring to it in the feminine form, as appropriate for the feminine word "*eidus*"!

Indeed, according to Rabbeinu Bachya, the very name "*Aron*," which we translate as "Ark" and assume denotes a container, actually derives from the word "*ohr*" (light), reflecting the fact that it houses the *Luchos*, which are a source of spiritual illumination.

PRACTICAL IMPLICATIONS—THE SECOND BEIS HAMIKDASH

Once we understand how crucial the presence of the *Luchos* are for the *Aron* to fulfill its function—and even its very definition—we will appreciate that if there were to be no *Luchos* to place inside, there would be no point in making an *Aron*. And indeed, this was the situation during the time of the second Beis Hamikdash. All of the vessels required were remade—with the exception of the *Aron*. Since the *Luchos* resided in the original *Aron*, wherever that was located at that time, there was no purpose in making a new *Aron* without *Luchos* to place inside it.

Moreover, it is noteworthy that when the *Rambam* discusses the prohibition of an individual replicating the vessels of the Beis Hamikdash, he mentions all the vessels with the exception of the *Aron*. If we say that the *Aron* is defined by the presence of the *Luchos* inside, then in order to violate the prohibition of replicating the *Aron*, one would likewise have to place the *Luchos* inside—for without them, it is not an *Aron*. Since there is only one set of *Luchos* and it is in the original *Aron*, it is actually

---

5   Commentary *Emes L'Yaakov, Parshas Terumah.*

impossible to replicate it, and hence, the *Rambam* does not include it in the prohibition![6]

THE ARON: A VESSEL "OF THE MIKDASH"
OR "IN THE MIKDASH"?

Bearing the above in mind, let us approach the words of the *Rambam* regarding the mitzvah of building the Beis Hamikdash,[7] the source for which he identifies as verse 8 in the beginning of our parsha: "וְעָשׂוּ לִי מִקְדָּשׁ—They shall make for Me a Sanctuary." The *Rambam* further states that this mitzvah includes not only the making of the building of the *Mishkan*/Beis Hamikdash itself, but also its vessels:

> We have already explained[8] that this general command also includes particular items, and that the Menorah, Shulchan, and Mizbeiach and their like are all considered part of the "Mikdash."

Noticeably absent from this list of items included in "the Mikdash" is the *Aron*! Likewise, in the *Mishneh Torah*,[9] the *Rambam* lists seven items within the Mikdash:

1. The *Mizbeiach* for *korbanos*
2. Its ramp
3. The *Kiyor* for washing the Kohanim's hands and feet
4. Its base
5. The *Mizbeiach* for *Ketores*
6. The *Shulchan*
7. The *Menorah*

Here too, the *Aron*, which we might have expected to be at the top of the list, is not on the list at all!

---

6   Rabbi Isaac Bernstein, *shiur* on *Parshas Terumah*.
7   *Sefer Hamitzvos*, positive mitzvah 20.
8   In *shoresh* 12 of *Sefer Hamitzvos*.
9   *Hilchos Beis Habechirah* 1:6.

Rav Moshe Soloveitchik explains that the reason for this is as per the above.[10] All of the above-mentioned vessels play a role in the *avodah* of the Mikdash and are thus considered as part of it. By contrast, the *Aron* is not involved in any *avodah*; it exists solely to house the *Luchos*. Therefore, while it understandably resides in the innermost point within the Mikdash, it is not itself a "vessel of the Mikdash"! In this regard, we could say that while the other vessels serve the Mikdash *around* them, the *Aron* serves the *Luchos within* it.[11]

FOLLOWING THE COMMANDMENTS IN PARSHAS TERUMAH

Let us conclude this discussion by returning to our parsha and seeing how the above idea is reflected in the phraseology of the various commands therein. We note that while the initial command to make the *Mishkan* is phrased in the third person plural, "*v'asu*—they shall make," all the subsequent commands are in the second person singular, "*v'asisa*—you shall make."

R' Yitzchak Ze'ev Soloveitchik, the Rav of Brisk, explains that the initial command, "*v'asu*," represents the mitzvah of building the Mikdash which, as we have seen, incorporates its vessels as well.[12] Since the mitzvah of building the Mikdash is one that falls upon the community, the command is phrased in the plural—"they shall make." Beyond this point, the additional commands are not new mitzvos, but are rather specifications and details regarding how to make the various component parts. Hence, these commands are phrased in the singular, as they are addressed to Moshe or whomever he will delegate to perform those particular tasks.

---

10   Cited in *Imrei Chen*, vol. 2 sec. 11.

11   It is extremely interesting to note the resonance of this idea in the Gemara's famous account (*Berachos* 55a) of the dialogue between Moshe and Betzalel, regarding the order of building the *Mishkan* vis-à-vis the vessels. The Gemara relates that Moshe told Betzalel the order of: "the *Aron*, the vessels and then the *Mishkan*," while Betzalel intuited Hashem's instruction to Moshe to first make "the *Mishkan* and then the *Aron* and vessels." Leaving aside the question of what lay behind these two viewpoints, we see that in both orders, the *Aron* receives distinct mention apart from "the vessels." This corroborates the understanding that the *Aron* does not fully fall into the category of those vessels as "*keilim* of the Mikdash."

12   Cited in *Imrei Chen* ibid.

Having established this, we proceed to note that the exception to the above rule is the *Aron*, the construction of which is also commanded in the plural "*v'asu*"! We can now understand why this is so. Since, as we have seen, the *Aron* is not one of the vessels of the Mikdash, its manufacture is not covered by the initial mitzvah of "*V'asu Li Mikdash.*" As such, the making of the *Aron* is an independent mitzvah that likewise falls upon the community, and hence, the command to make it is phrased in the plural form.[13]

---

13 Throughout our parsha, the *Mishkan* is referred to with the term "*Mishkan*," with the exception of the initial command, which uses the word "Mikdash." One the one hand, we can understand the use of this term as *broadening the scope* of the mitzvah to include the contents of the *Mishkan*, as well as extending to future Batei Mikdash. However, it is also possible to see that the verse is *qualifying* the mitzvah as pertaining specifically to items which are part of the *avodah* in the Mikdash. The *Aron*, by contrast, has no part in the *avodah*, but is there to house the *Luchos*, and hence is not included in the mitzvah of making a Mikdash. See further regarding the mitzvah to make an *Aron* in the *Kli Chemdah* to *Parshas Terumah*, sec. 3, *Chasam Sofer* ibid. 25:21, and in Responsa *Chasam Sofer*, *Yoreh Deah* sec. 236.

BETWEEN THE HOLY AND THE HOLY OF HOLIES

Understanding the Role of the Paroches

וְעָשִׂיתָ פָרֹכֶת...וְהֵבֵאתָ שָׁמָּה מִבֵּית לַפָּרֹכֶת אֶת אֲרוֹן הָעֵדוּת וְהִבְדִּילָה
הַפָּרֹכֶת לָכֶם בֵּין הַקֹּדֶשׁ וּבֵין קֹדֶשׁ הַקֳּדָשִׁים.

You shall make a Paroches partition...and you shall bring there, inside the Paroches, the Ark of the Testimony, and the Paroches shall separate for you between the Holy and the Holy of Holies.[1]

ROLE I: "AND THE PAROCHES SHALL SEPARATE FOR YOU"

The *Paroches* (dividing curtain) in the *Mishkan* is well known to us. Indeed, within our synagogues, which are known as "*mikdashei me'at*—small sanctuaries," the curtain which sections off the Ark that contains the Torah scrolls is modeled on the *Paroches* of the *Mishkan*.[2]

If we were to be asked what the role and purpose of the *Paroches* in the *Mishkan* was, we would likely respond that the answer is explicitly stated in our verse: to serve as a division between the two domains

---

1   *Shemos* 26:31–33.
2   See R' Moshe Feinstein, *Igros Moshe, Orach Chaim* 4:40.

of the *Kodesh* (Main Sanctuary) and the *Kodesh Hakodashim* (Holy of Holies). Indeed, *Rashi* states that the word "*Paroches*" is an expression of "*mechitzah*—partition." *Hakesav V'hakabbalah* elaborates that the root letters of the word are כ-ר-פ, which means to break, as the *Paroches* provided a break or division between the two domains of the *Mishkan*. Moreover, the "dividing" function of the *Paroches* was not always provided by a curtain made of material—in the first Beis Hamikdash, it was a wall of stone that divided between the Main Sanctuary and the *Kodesh Hakodashim*.

ROLE II: "AND YOU SHALL BRING THERE... THE ARK OF THE TESTIMONY"

However, while the above response is undoubtedly correct, a closer look at our verse will reveal that the *Paroches* served not one function, but two. The earlier part of the verse states: "And you shall bring there, inside the *Paroches*, the Ark of the Testimony." As the *Ramban* points out, these words are not describing the way the *Mishkan* is to be set up, for that is something that is not dealt with until the end of *Parshas Pekudei*.[3] Rather, the verse here is describing a second role of the *Paroches*, namely, that it serves to "cover" the holy *Aron* and shield it from view. This second purpose is reiterated in the Torah's instructions for setting up the *Mishkan*, where it states: "וְשַׂמְתָּ שָׁם אֵת אֲרוֹן הָעֵדוּת וְסַכֹּתָ עַל הָאָרֹן אֶת הַפָּרֹכֶת—You shall place there [in the *Mishkan*] the Ark of the Testimony, and you shall shield the Ark with the *Paroches*."[4]

DIVIDING BETWEEN THE ROLES

Having identified the two purposes of the *Paroches*—dividing between the two domains in the *Mishkan* and covering the *Aron* from view—it is most interesting to note that there were times when the *Paroches* fulfilled only the first purpose, and other times when it fulfilled only the second.

---

3   *Shemos*, chap. 40.

4   Loc. cit., verse 3.

- During the second Beis Hamikdash, there was no *Aron* in the *Kodesh Hakodashim*, so there was no requirement for a *Paroches* to shield it from view. At that time, the *Paroches* served only the function of dividing between the two domains of the Sanctuary and the *Kodesh Hakodashim*.

- In chapter 4 of *Parshas Bamidbar*, the Torah describes how the *Mishkan* and its vessels were to be transported as the people journeyed through the wilderness. Verse 5 reads: "וּבָא אַהֲרֹן וּבָנָיו בִּנְסֹעַ הַמַּחֲנֶה וְהוֹרִדוּ אֵת פָּרֹכֶת הַמָּסָךְ וְכִסּוּ בָהּ אֵת אֲרֹן הָעֵדֻת—Aharon and his sons shall come when the camp is to journey, and they shall take down the *Paroches* and cover the Ark of the Testimony with it." With the people in transit, there were no domains for the *Paroches* to divide between; yet, even then, it continued to fulfill the function of shielding the *Aron* from view by covering it.[5]

Moreover, when we return to the situation in the first Beis Hamikdash—where both roles of the *Paroches* were fulfilled—we will see that each role was taken care of by a different component: At that time, the *Paroches* consisted of a wall, with an entrance in the center that was covered by a curtain.

- On the one hand, the division between the Main Sanctuary and the *Kodesh Hakodashim* was provided by the wall. Even had the entrance in the center not been covered with a curtain, that would in no way have negated the wall's status as a partition.

- On the other hand, the curtain which covered the entrance served the function of shielding the *Aron* from view.[6]

ROLE III: CREATING SPACE

Looking yet more carefully at the verse, we will discover a third element within the *Paroches*. The verse concludes:

---

5   R' Aharon Dovid Goldberg, *shlita*, *Shiras Dovid*, *Parshas Terumah*.
6   R' Menachem Kasher, *Torah Sheleimah*, endnotes to *Parshas Terumah*, sec. 18.

וְהִבְדִּילָה הַפָּרֹכֶת לָכֶם בֵּין הַקֹּדֶשׁ וּבֵין קֹדֶשׁ הַקֳּדָשִׁים.

And the Paroches shall divide for you between the Holy and the Holy of Holies.

The *Netziv* asks: What is the meaning of the seemingly redundant word "*lachem*"—for you? This word does not appear with regard to any other aspect of the building of the *Mishkan* or the manufacturing of its vessels. In what way was the *Paroches*'s division between the two domains any more "for the Jewish People" than anything else mentioned in our parsha?

TWO TYPES OF DIVISION

The *Netziv* further draws our attention to the verse's phrasing the division as "בֵּין הַקֹּדֶשׁ וּבֵין קֹדֶשׁ הַקֳּדָשִׁים," in light of a most interesting principle of *parshanut*. In *lashon hakodesh*, there are two ways to describe something that divides between two things:

- With the letter "*lamed*" in between the two things being divided. For example: "וַיְהִי מַבְדִּיל בֵּין מַיִם לָמָיִם."[7]
- With the word "*u'vein*" in between the two things. For example: "וַיַּבְדֵּל אֱלֹקִים בֵּין הָאוֹר וּבֵין הַחֹשֶׁךְ."[8]

What is the difference between these two forms? The *Netziv* explains:

- If the division is described with a "*lamed*," then the divider serves only to divide between the two things, but does not partake of any quality of either of them.
- If the word "*u'vein*" is used, it means that the item that is in between the two things is also a "middle ground" that has qualities of the two things it is dividing between.

Applying that principle to our verse, we conclude that the *Paroches* served to effect a division that enjoyed a status somewhere between

---

7   *Bereishis* 1:6.

8   Ibid., verse 4.

the Holy and the Holy of Holies. The question is: Where did this take place and to what end?

ENTERING THE IMPOSSIBLE

The meaning behind this lies in a Midrash that states that although Aharon could not enter the *Kodesh Hakodashim* at any time apart from Yom Kippur, Moshe was able to enter whenever he wanted. Indeed, he did so regularly in order to commune with the Divine Presence and receive Torah from there.[9] The problem is, at the end of *Chumash Shemos* we are told that Moshe was unable to enter the *Mishkan* on the day of its inauguration, on account of Hashem's cloud that hovered over it.[10] However, Hashem's cloud was constantly over the *Kodesh Hakodashim*! If so, how could Moshe ever enter there?

The solution is found in our verse: create a zone between the Holy and the Holy of Holies where Moshe could stand. Yet how could such a zone be created? Surely, one is either in the one domain or the other! To this end, Hashem informs Moshe that the *Paroches* shall divide "for you" between the two domains. This means that specifically for Moshe, the dividing line was whether he was in front of or behind the *Paroches*, whereas for Hashem, the division was between the innermost ten cubits and that which lay beyond. Although these two dividing points generally coincided, they could be caused to diverge—and indeed, they were. It is well known that the poles of the *Aron* protruded eastward into the main sanctuary somewhat, moving the *Paroches* one *amah* back.[11] The purpose of this protrusion? To create a space that on the one hand, was behind the *Paroches*, while at the same time, not within the final ten *amos*! This was the middle ground where Moshe was able to stand and receive Torah from Hashem.

Truly a new dimension in our understanding of these domains!

---

9   *Toras Kohanim* to *Vayikra* 16:2.
10   40:35.
11   See *Yoma* 54a.

FOLLOW-UP: FROM MOSHE TO AHARON

In light of this idea, it is further fascinating to consider the way in which Aharon's own entry into the *Kodesh Hakodashim* on Yom Kippur is phrased by the Torah. In the beginning of *Parshas Acharei Mos*, in words well known to us from the *leining* on Yom Kippur morning, Hashem instructs Moshe:

דַּבֵּר אֶל אַהֲרֹן אָחִיךָ וְאַל יָבֹא בְכָל עֵת אֶל הַקֹּדֶשׁ מִבֵּית לַפָּרֹכֶת.

Speak to your brother, Aharon, and he shall not come at all times into the Sanctuary that is behind the Paroches.[12]

Here too, the Torah refers to the place where Aharon can enter only on Yom Kippur not as the "*Kodesh Hakodashim*," but as "the *Kodesh* (Sanctuary) that is behind the *Paroches*." For indeed, entry into the *Kodesh Hakodashim* itself was off-limits for Aharon even on Yom Kippur—as it was for Moshe during the forty years in the wilderness. What the special *avodah* of Yom Kippur did allow Aharon to do was for him to enter "the *Kodesh* that was behind the *Paroches*," the middle ground that was "between the Holy and the Holy of Holies."[13]

---

12   *Vayikra* 16:2.
13   *Haamek Davar* ibid.

FROM THE COMMENTATORS

TREES, ROOTS, AND REDEMPTION

One of the materials involved in the construction of the *Mishkan* was cedar wood, from which the beams were formed. *Rashi*, citing the Midrash, informs us regarding where this wood came from:[1]

יעקב אבינו צפה ברוח הקודש שעתידין ישראל לבנות משכן במדבר, והביא ארזים למצרים ונטעם, וצוה לבניו ליטלם עמהם כשיצאו ממצרים.

Our forefather, Yaakov, saw through Divine inspiration that his descendants would in the future, build a Mishkan in the wilderness, and so he brought cedar trees to Egypt and planted them, and he instructed his sons to take them with them when they would leave Egypt.[2]

What is the meaning behind Yaakov making provisions for his descendants to be able to make the *Mishkan*? Presumably, Hashem, Who will command them to do this, will also see to it that the necessary materials are available at the time!

R' Yaakov Kamenetsky explains that Yaakov's intent in planting these trees was twofold.[3] As the exile in Egypt was about to commence,

---

1 *Shemos* 25:5, s.v. *vaatzei* and 26:15, s.v. *v'asisa*.
2 *Tanchuma, Parshas Terumah*, sec. 9.
3 *Emes L'Yaakov, Bereishis* 46:1 and *Shemos* 26:15.

Yaakov was apprehensive that as time went on and the exile continued and possibly even intensified, his descendants may lose hope in the idea of redemption and lose sight of their unique identity and destiny. And while it is true that he had informed them that they would, in time, be redeemed and told them to pass this idea on to their children, there were grounds for concern that words alone might not be enough to keep the Jewish people going. Therefore, he planted cedar trees, in order that they would have a tangible entity to point to and say, "When the time comes, Hashem will redeem us and take us out from here, and we will build a *Mishkan* for Him—with these trees!" With something concrete with which to associate their redemption, the people would be more strengthened and encouraged.

Additionally, the Midrash informs us that the trees Yaakov planted were taken from Be'er Sheva. Here too, Yaakov wished to forestall the possibility that the people would, over the course of their exile, lose sight of the fact or simply forget that Egypt was not where they were meant to remain and that they had a homeland elsewhere. To this end, he brought and planted "trees from home" so that in this regard too, they would have a constant and tangible reminder of their true homeland to where they would keep alive the dream of someday returning.

THE GOLDEN BLEND: LESSONS FROM THE KERUVIM

וְהָיוּ הַכְּרֻבִים פֹּרְשֵׂי כְנָפַיִם לְמַעְלָה...וּפְנֵיהֶם אִישׁ אֶל אָחִיו.

The Keruvim shall be with wings spread upward...and their faces, one toward his fellow.[4]

The mitzvos of the Torah are divided broadly into the two realms of *bein adam laMakom* (between man and God) and *bein adam l'chaveiro* (between man and man). The *Kli Yakar* explains that these two realms are depicted by the positioning of the *Keruvim* atop the Holy Ark:[5]

---

4   *Shemos* 25:20.
5   *Vayikra* 19:18.

- On the one hand, their wings are spread upwards, representing their aspirations in terms of their connection with Hashem.
- At the same time, they are facing one toward his fellow, representing them keeping their fellow in sight and fulfilling their obligations between man and man.

The fundamental and beautiful message emanating from the *Keruvim* is to remind us that these two categories of mitzvos, together, form the Divine program of mitzvos. Not only should one not detract from the other, they are meant to be harmonized together to develop the complete Torah Jew.

THE CROWN OF WEALTH

וְעָשִׂיתָ שֻׁלְחָן עֲצֵי שִׁטִּים...וְעָשִׂיתָ לוֹ מִסְגֶּרֶת טֹפַח סָבִיב וְעָשִׂיתָ זֵר זָהָב לְמִסְגַּרְתּוֹ סָבִיב.

You shall make a Table of cedar wood...you shall make for it a boundary of one handbreadth all around, and you shall make a gold crown on the boundary all around.[6]

The Table in the *Mishkan* symbolizes material prosperity, with its crown representing the crown of wealth. Our Sages inform us in *Pirkei Avos*[7]: "איזהו עשיר השמח בחלקו—Who is wealthy? He who is happy with his portion." A person who is blessed with wealth but is not happy with what he has, focusing only on what he is lacking, is the poorest of men. For this reason, the Torah stipulates that the crown of the *Shulchan* be placed around its *misgeres* (boundary), for a person who not only enjoys material prosperity, but also knows how to set boundaries for his needs has truly attained the crown of wealth.[8]

---

6   *Shemos* 25:23–25.
7   4:1.
8   R' Reuven Grozovsky, cited in *Peninim Mishulchan Gavoah*.

THE ADORNMENTS OF THE MENORAH

וְעָשִׂיתָ מְנֹרַת זָהָב טָהוֹר...גְּבִיעֶיהָ כַּפְתֹּרֶיהָ וּפְרָחֶיהָ מִמֶּנָּה יִהְיוּ.

You shall make a Menorah of pure gold...its cups, globes, and flowers shall be [hammered] from it.[9]

The Talmud indicates that the *Menorah* symbolizes Torah.[10] Rabbeinu Bachya elaborates on this and notes that in fact, there are two vessels in the *Mishkan* symbolizing Torah—the *Aron* and the *Menorah*. These correspond to the two areas of Torah—*Torah She'bichsav* (the Written Torah) and *Torah She'baal Peh* (the Oral Torah)—respectively.[11]

Torah She'baal Peh itself can be divided into three categories:

- Laws received through oral transmission from Moshe at Sinai (*Halachah l'Moshe miSinai*), such as the details of tefillin.
- Protective measures to safeguard against infraction of Torah laws (*gezeiros*), such as *muktzeh*.
- Laws propounded through the tools of *midrash halachah* (halachic exposition), as well as additional Rabbinic enactments, such as Purim and Chanukah.

It is possible to discern these three areas of *Torah She'baal Peh* as reflected in the three adornments of the *Menorah*:

- Cups—represent the laws that were received from Sinai, in the same way that a cup receives that which is poured into it.
- Globes—represent the protective measures, ensuring that Torah laws remain whole and intact with no breach or crack.
- Flowers—represent the laws that grow out from the Torah, both in terms of *drashos* and Rabbinic enactments.

---

9   *Shemos* 25:31.
10   See, e.g., *Berachos* 57a and *Bava Basra* 25a.
11   *Kad Hakemach,* "Ner Chanukah."

PARSHAS TETZAVEH

STONES, LIGHT, AND PERFECTION

The Avnei Miluim and the Urim V'Tumim

וְעָשִׂיתָ חֹשֶׁן מִשְׁפָּט...וּמִלֵּאתָ בוֹ...אַרְבָּעָה טוּרִים אָבֶן.

You shall make a Breastplate of Judgment...You shall fill it with...four rows of stones.[1]

INTRODUCTION: TWELVE PRECIOUS STONES

One of the fascinating elements among the Priestly Garments discussed in this parsha are the twelve *Miluim* stones that were attached to the *Choshen* (Breastplate), worn by the Kohen Gadol (High Priest). Each stone bore the name of one of the twelve tribes, so that the Kohen Gadol bore their remembrance with him wherever he went during his service in the Beis Hamikdash.

R' Levi Yitzchak of Berditchev explains the special significance of this idea in terms of understanding the true role of the Kohanim in general, and the Kohen Gadol in particular.[2] Although the Kohanim had been separated from the other tribes in order to perform the *avodah*,

---

1   *Shemos* 28:15–17.
2   *Kedushas Levi.*

this was not in the interests of *detaching* themselves from the Jewish People, but of *representing* them. The *avodah* is something that only Kohanim can do, but it is done on behalf of the entire people and with their ultimate blessing in mind. In order to keep this crucial idea in mind, the most distinct and distinguished among the Kohanim—the Kohen Gadol—could not be allowed to perform his *avodah* without having the names of all twelve tribes constantly before him.

HOW WERE THE NAMES ENGRAVED ON THE STONES?

Verse 21 states that each of the twelve *Miluim* stones had the name of one of the tribes engraved on it:

וְהָאֲבָנִים תִּהְיֶיןָ עַל שְׁמֹת בְּנֵי יִשְׂרָאֵל שְׁתֵּים עֶשְׂרֵה עַל שְׁמֹתָם עַל שְׁמֹתָם פִּתּוּחֵי חוֹתָם אִישׁ עַל שְׁמוֹ.

The stones shall be according to the names of the sons of Yisrael, twelve according to their names, engraved like a signet ring, each according to [that tribe's] name.

Some commentators have observed that the analogy to a signet ring does not appear to be accurate in every respect. For while it is true that a name on a signet ring is engraved, it is actually engraved *backwards*, so that when the ring is applied to make a seal, the letters in the seal read forwards. Presumably, this was not the case with the engraving on the *Miluim* stones.

However, R' Yehoshua Leib Diskin says that in reality, the verse's analogy is a complete one. To explain how, he draws our attention to the beginning of our verse: "וְהָאֲבָנִים תִּהְיֶיןָ עַל שְׁמֹת בְּנֵי יִשְׂרָאֵל." The literal translation of these words is that "the stones shall be *on* the names of B'nei Yisrael." Naturally, this does not sound right—for it was not the stones that were on the names, but rather the names that were on the stones! For this reason, the translation given for the word "*al*" is "according," so that the stones were not "on the names," but "according to the names."

Rav Diskin, however, says that the word "*al*" *should* be translated as "on," for the stones were in fact "on the names of B'nei Yisrael"! How so? The names of the tribes were not engraved on the side of the stones that faced outwards. Rather, they were engraved on the part of the stone that was attached to the *Choshen*; seeing as the stones were translucent, the names could be read through the stones by anyone who looked at the *Choshen*. Thus, the verse says that the stones were indeed "on the names of B'nei Yisrael," for the stones actually lay on the names!

There is just one problem, though. If the side of the stones with the names engraved was attached to the *Choshen*, with the name being read through the stone, it would then be read backwards! This, says Rav Diskin, is why the verse instructed the original engraving to be "like that of a signet ring," i.e., backwards. In other words, the names were engraved backwards onto the stones, so that they would subsequently be read forward when seen through the stones.

A *chiddush* in *peshuto shel mikra*!

THE CHOSHEN AND THE TZITZ: READING UP ON THE JEWISH PEOPLE

An additional insight into the names engraved on the *Choshen* comes when considering it in conjunction with another of the Kohen Gadol's garments—the golden *Tzitz* worn across his forehead. Verse 36 informs us that the *Tzitz* had the two words "קֹדֶשׁ לַה׳"—Holy for Hashem engraved on it. The Gemara (*Sukkah* 5a) cites the opinion of the Sages that "*Kodesh la*" was engraved below, and Hashem's name was engraved above it. The commentators wonder why these words would be written in this way, rather than in a straight line as words are normally written.

There is an additional question to be considered here: What exactly is being referred to with the words "Holy to Hashem"? The Torah has already informed us that *all* the priestly garments are holy! Why, then, would one of them need to be marked especially as such?

The *Rashash* explains that the words "Holy to Hashem" are not to be read by themselves, and they do not refer to the *Tzitz*.[3] Rather, they are referring to the twelve tribes whose names are engraved below on the *Choshen*! It is the Jewish People who are holy to Hashem, with the *Choshen* and the *Tzitz* combining to communicate that message.

---

3   Comments to *Maseches Sukkah* ibid.

Therefore, says the *Rashash*, since the flow of reading goes upwards from the *Choshen* to the *Tzitz*, the descriptive phrase on the *Tzitz* itself likewise goes from down to up, with "*Kodesh la*" below and Hashem's name above.

In is worthwhile noting, in this regard, that the names of the tribes of Israel are engraved on two sets of stones worn by the Kohen Gadol; in addition to the twelve *Miluim* stones, there are also two *Shoham* stones on the shoulders of the *Ephod* which have the names of six tribes engraved on each stone.[4] These two engravings represent the two capacities in which the twelve tribes of Israel exist:

- On the one hand, they are all part of the nation of Israel. In this regard, their names are all listed together on the two identical *Shoham* stones.
- At the same time, each tribe has its individual character and mission within the Jewish People. This is reflected by the twelve *Miluim* stones, all of different colors, which are then embedded within the framework of the *Choshen*.

THE URIM V'TUMIM

An additional element within the *Choshen* is mentioned in verse 30:

וְנָתַתָּ אֶל חֹשֶׁן הַמִּשְׁפָּט אֶת הָאוּרִים וְאֶת הַתֻּמִּים.

And you shall place in the Breastplate of Judgment the Urim and the Tumim.

The *Urim V'Tumim* allowed for messages to be received from Heaven in answer to questions that were of national or communal concern. The Gemara explains the background to this name:[5]

- "*Urim*—their words illuminated,"[6] signifying the illumination they brought to the questions that were posed through them.

---

4   See verses 9–10.
5   *Yoma* 73b.
6   From the word *ohr*—light.

- *"Tumim*—their words completed,"[7] reflecting the idea that an answer received through them was final and irrevocable.

As the Gemara proceeds to describe, when a question was addressed via the *Urim V'Tumim*, the answer would be transmitted by the relevant letters on the *Miluim* stones either protruding or illuminating.[8] What emerges is that in addition to the institution of prophecy, which existed primarily as a means through which Hashem communicated His will to the Jewish People via a prophet, the *Urim V'Tumim* existed as a vehicle through which the people could ask certain vital questions of Hashem and receive His answer. In this regard, the Gemara lists the *Urim V'Tumim* as one of the five things that were absent during the period of the Second Beis Hamikdash, within which the Divine Presence resided to a lesser degree than it did in the First Beis Hamikdash.[9]

What Were the Urim V'Tumim?

The Torah does not specify exactly what the *Urim V'Tumim* were. Indeed, more intriguing still, it does not even mention a command to make them! The only instruction concerning them is the one mentioned in our verse: to place them in the *Choshen*. Of further interest is that the Torah refers to them as *"the Urim* and *the Tumim,"* apparently denoting a prior known entity, even though this is the first time they are being mentioned.

Rashi states that the *Urim V'Tumim* was a small scroll of parchment with Hashem's Ineffable Name (*Shem Hameforash*) written on it. This approach is endorsed and elaborated upon by the *Ramban*.[10]

---

7   From the word *tamim*—complete.
8   How did the Kohen know in which order to arrange the letters that formed the answer? Some commentators explain that the letters lit up in the order the words were to be spelled (Rav Saadya Gaon). The *Ramban* explains that the *Urim* and *Tumim* were two separate names of Hashem (see below), with the first enabling the letters to light up (*"Urim*—illumination"), and the second allowing the Kohen to understand how they were to be arranged (*"Tumim*—completion").
9   *Yoma* 21b.
10   The basis for this approach can be found in *Targum Yonasan ben Uziel* to our verse, and in *Zohar* 2:234.

The *Rambam* does not specify what the *Urim V'Tumim* were. However, in *Hilchos Beis Habechirah*, he writes that they were still worn during the time of the Second Beis Hamikdash.[11] He explains that even though the Gemara lists them among the items that were absent during that era, this means that they did not perform their prophetic function but, nonetheless, they still needed to be worn; otherwise, the Kohen Gadol would be lacking the required number of special garments required in order to perform the *avodah*.

There are certain commentators who understand that the *Rambam* concurs that the *Urim V'Tumim* were Hashem's names written on parchment, and, moreover, maintains that their presence within the folds of the *Choshen* was critical to its status as one of the priestly garments. Hence, the *Rambam* says that even when they no longer functioned as the *Urim V'Tumim*, they still needed to be in the *Choshen*.[12] However, other commentators explain that the *Urim V'Tumim* were, in fact, the *Miluim* stones themselves, not an additional item that was added to the *Choshen*. The name *Urim V'Tumim*, according to this approach, does not indicate a separate entity, but rather an additional quality of the stones—of transmitting prophetic messages.[13]

A GOOD HEART

It is fascinating to consider this prophetic aspect of the *Choshen*—one that is certainly very different from the general function of the priestly garments, which are focused on the *avodah* in the *Mishkan*. Indeed,

---

11 4:1.

12 *Maharash Algazi, Ratzuf Ahavah.* See also commentary of *Radvaz* to *Hilchos Klei Hamikdash* 9:6. This would also appear to be the *Raavad's* understanding of the *Rambam* (*Hasagos* to *Hilchos Beis Habechirah*, loc. cit.), who questions why the absence of the *Urim V'Tumim* would render the number of garments incomplete.

13 Rabbeinu Avraham, the son of the *Rambam*, cites this approach as "the words of our Sages." This is also the opinion of Rav Sherira Gaon and Rav Hai Gaon, as found in a responsa cited by Rav Menachem Kasher in his endnotes to *Parshas Tetzaveh*, sec. 11. *Tosafos* in *Yoma* 21b (s.v. *Urim*) likewise concur with this approach; see notes of *Rashash* ibid. Later commentators point out that *Rashi's* approach would seem to be borne out by the simple reading of our verse (see also *Vayikra* 8:8), which implies that the *Urim V'Tumim* were something that was added to the *Choshen after* the stones had been attached; see *Hakesav V'hakabbalah* for a discussion of this question.

according to one of the Rishonim, the *Ran*, this point is addressed by our Sages in the Talmud.[14] When Moshe is first told to go and act as the redeemer for B'nei Yisrael, Hashem informs him that on his return to Egypt, he will be met by Aharon, who will be glad in his heart to see him.[15] Commenting on these words, the Gemara says:

בשכר "וראך ושמח בלבו" זכה אהרן ל"ונשא אהרן את משפט בני ישראל על לבו."

In reward for fulfilling "he will see you and be glad in his heart," he [Aharon] merited, "And Aharon shall carry the judgment of the B'nei Yisrael on his heart."[16]

The *Ran* asks: What does the Gemara mean to say? If it is that Aharon merited to be the Kohen Gadol in reward for being glad on Moshe's behalf, why is the *Choshen* mentioned specifically as his reward? Rather, he explains, Aharon's heartfelt joy for Moshe reflected an extremely lofty quality. After all, Moshe was coming to Egypt as Hashem's prophet to redeem the people from their exile there. Aharon had already been a prophet for the people there for many years. In effect, he was stepping aside for Moshe to assume the role that had been his until this point!

The graciousness and magnanimity of this gesture, as well as what Hashem Himself testified to as heartfelt joy for Moshe, is truly worthy of our profound contemplation and appreciation. In fact, it could be said to be one of the most beautiful elements within the entire Exodus story. And it did not go unrewarded.

Aharon's role as Kohen Gadol only needed to be focused on matters of *avodah*. However, Hashem rewarded him with the *Urim V'Tumim*, a vehicle for prophecy that he carried on his heart, in recognition of the role of prophet that he allowed Moshe to assume during the Exodus.

---

14   *Drashos HaRan, drush* 3.
15   *Shemos* 4:14.
16   *Shabbos* 139b.

MAKING A MATERIAL DIFFERENCE

Lessons from the Bigdei Kehunah

The first half of our parsha is devoted to the making of the *bigdei kehunah* (priestly garments). Seemingly, this section is of no practical relevance to most of the Jewish People: Four of the eight garments are worn only by Kohanim, while the other four are worn by the Kohen Gadol specifically, with none of them currently being worn at all in the absence of the Beis Hamikdash! However, if we look deeper, we will discover that these garments have much to teach us concerning fundamental aspects of Torah outlook and behavior.

COMPARING BIGDEI KEHUNAH WITH KORBANOS

We begin by referring to a most intriguing statement in the Gemara, which notes that the Torah's presentation of the *bigdei kehunah* is juxtaposed with that of *korbanos*. The reason, says the Gemara, is to equate the two. Just as the *korbanos* bring atonement for the sins of the Jewish People, so too do the *bigdei kehunah*.[1] For example:

---

1   *Zevachim* 88b.

- The *Ephod* atones for idol worship.
- The *Choshen Mishpat* atones for perversion of justice.
- The *Me'il* atones for *lashon hara*.

And so on.

Needless to say, this idea requires our reflection. Can it be that simple—the Kohanim wear their clothes and all is forgiven? That doesn't sound too hard at all. It sounds like, as long as the Kohen Gadol's wardrobe is in order, *everything* is in order; could that be?

What does all of this mean?

THE BEST KIND OF ATONEMENT

One of the classic commentators from among the late Rishonim, Rabbeinu Yitzchak Arama,[2] in his work *Akeidas Yitzchak*, explains as follows:[3] When the Gemara says that the priestly garments are capable of effecting atonement, it means that each of the garments contains a message regarding a particular sin. If heeded, this message can help us to avoid that sin in the future, and thus allow us to achieve atonement for past wrongdoings.

Let us consider some of these messages.

THE CHOSHEN MISHPAT: JUDGING IN TRUTH

The Gemara states that the *Choshen Mishpat* (the breastplate worn by the Kohen Gadol) atones, as its name suggests, for perversion of justice.

What lessons does the *Choshen* impart regarding fairness in justice?

The *Akeidas Yitzchak* explains that an incorrect ruling can come about for one of four reasons:

1. The judge favors one of the litigants.
2. The judge is afraid of one of the litigants.

---

2   Spain (c. 1420–1494).
3   *Shaar* 51. The *Akeidas Yitzchak* follows the weekly Torah portion, with the discussions divided between treatises on philosophical questions that relate to that parsha and a discussion of the contents of the parsha itself. This was one of the earliest works to adopt the format of opening with a list of questions and then answering them as the discussion unfolds.

3. The amount involved is not significant enough in the judge's eyes to warrant investigating the case thoroughly.

4. The judge is not sufficiently expert in the necessary area so as to be clear regarding what the ruling should be.

The *Choshen* contains messages cautioning against all the above shortcomings:

1. The *Choshen* contains twelve stones, each with the name of one of the tribes engraved on it.[4] The Torah states that these names are to appear in the order the tribes were born. Although some of the tribes enjoy positions of authority, such as kingship with Yehudah and priesthood with Levi, they are not favored or given precedence over the others. This is to teach us that when it comes to judgment, no one is to be favored over anyone else due to his position.

2. Inside the folds of the *Choshen* are the *Urim V'Tumim*,[5] which *Rashi* explains are Names of Hashem. This teaches that a judge should be mindful of the fact that he is representing Hashem in dispensing judgment and should fear no man in fulfilling this Godly endeavor truthfully.

3. Some of the stones on the *Choshen* are significantly more valuable than others, yet they all have an equal place. This teaches that one should judge all cases with equal care and thoroughness, regardless of the amount involved.

4. One of the functions of the stones was to have their letters illuminate when a question was asked of the *Urim V'Tumim* regarding something that affected the Jewish People. The judge, too, should see to it that his knowledge is sound to the degree that he can illuminate the case before him with authority and clarity.

If judges heed the messages of the *Choshen* to rid themselves of the above failings, then they will be deserving of atonement in the event

---

4   28:21.

5   Verse 30.

that a true error in judgment occurred. Moreover, as we know, even those among the Jewish People who are not in the judiciary often face situations where the above principles apply, even if not in a formal setting. In this broader sense, the *Choshen* addresses each individual, enjoining him to act forthrightly and fairly, having first pursued whatever means required to determine the correct course of action in that situation.

THE ME'IL: BELLS, POMEGRANATES, AND LASHON HARA

The Gemara states that the *Me'il*, the blue coat worn by the Kohen Gadol, atones for the sin of *lashon hara*. How are these two connected? The parsha describes how, at the hem of the *me'il*, is a row comprised alternately of gold bells and pomegranates spun from different materials.[6] Says the Gemara:

> Let an item which produces a sound [the me'il, whose bells chimed when the Kohen Gadol walked] come and atone for a matter involving a sound [lashon hara].

Once again, this is no magic cure, with every round of *lashon hara* ending by the gossiper being "saved by the bells." These bells contain a message aimed at helping us avoid *lashon hara* from the outset. What is that message?

As we mentioned, next to each bell is a pomegranate. The Gemara elsewhere tells us that the pomegranate is an expression of everything that is good about the Jewish People: "Even the empty ones among you are full of mitzvos, like a pomegranate is full of seeds."[7]

How can someone be both "empty" and "full of good deeds" at the same time? The answer is that there will always be redeeming features in any person. If you choose to ignore these positive points, you will see the person as empty. You may come to speak slander about your fellow because you feel there is nothing good to say about him. To this end, the Torah places a pomegranate next to each bell, as if to say, when you

---

6   Verse 33.
7   *Berachos* 57a.

"ring your bell" and make a sound about a fellow Jew, see to it that it is a "pomegranate sound." There is plenty of positive in others if you are prepared to see it. This is the antidote to *lashon hara*—and the pathway to its atonement.

Let us suggest an additional point to this idea. While there are bells and pomegranates at the hem of the *me'il*, the *me'il* itself is made entirely of *techeiles*—sky-blue thread. Let us ask, what role does this play in the message of positive speech?

The color *techeiles* is described by the Gemara as having a certain spiritually evocative quality. Commenting on the requirement to put a thread of *techeiles* in the *tzitzis*, the Gemara explains: "*Techeiles* resembles the sea, the sea resembles the sky, and the sky resembles the Throne of Glory."[8]

If people generally possess both positive and negative qualities, what would impel a person to ignore all the positives and focus solely on the negatives? Typically, one who denigrates and devalues others does so because he wishes to promote himself. To this end, the garment to whose hem the bells and pomegranates are attached is made entirely of *techeiles*. Acquiring and maintaining a vision which is focused on the Glory of Hashem will help release a person from the compulsion to denigrate others, and moreover, encourage him to see how that person, too, has qualities which can be used to further Hashem's glory.

How interesting to note that the paragraph which we recite after the *Megillah* reading describes the joy of the Jewish People, "*Bi'r'osam yachad techeiles Mordechai*—When they saw, all together, the *techeiles* of Mordechai." Absorbing the message of the *techeiles* allowed them to rise above the fault-finding which had kept them apart from each other, and to rejoice in the miracle of the eternity of the Jewish People—all together!

---

8   *Menachos* 43b.

FROM THE COMMENTATORS

MOSHE RABBEINU AND PARSHAS TETZAVEH

A distinctive feature of *Parshas Tetzaveh* is that it is the only parsha in the Torah after the birth of Moshe Rabbeinu which contains no mention of his name. Numerous commentators explain this anomaly by pointing out that the day of Moshe's passing, the seventh of Adar, generally falls in the week when this parsha is read; hence, his absence from the parsha represents his passing from the world which took place at that time.

The *Vilna Gaon* adds that although Moshe himself passed from the world during this time, nonetheless, he remains present in a hidden or inner way through the Torah that was his life-essence and which he transmitted from Hashem to the Jewish People.[1] This too, says the *Gaon*, is alluded to in our parsha, which contains one hundred and one verses. The letters of the name משה, when spelled out as words, are מם, שין, and הא, part of which are "revealed," i.e., written, and part of which remain concealed, as follows:

- מ"ם—the first *mem* is revealed, while the second letter *mem* is concealed.

---

1   Cited in *Kehillas Yitzchak, Parshas Tetzaveh*.

- שי"ן—the letter *shin* is revealed, while the letters *yud* and *nun* are concealed.
- ה"א—the *hei* is revealed, while the *aleph* is concealed.

If we take all the concealed letters—מ, י, נ, and א—their numerical value totals one hundred and one.[2] Thus, even while Moshe's name is absent from the parsha in an explicit sense—reflecting his physical passing from the world—his essence, the Torah that he taught, is alluded to by the number of verses in the parsha, which remain with the Jewish People.

There is an additional element here, for one hundred and one is also the numerical value of the word מיכאל. Indeed, the masoretic *"siman"* provided at the end of the parsha to represent the number of verses contained therein is מיכאל. How does this relate to Moshe?

After the Jewish People sinned with the Golden Calf, Hashem informed Moshe that He no longer wished to lead the people directly, but would rather do so through an angel.[3] Practically, this would mean that the miraculous means through which Hashem sustained the people through His direct involvement—manna from Heaven, Miriam's well, the Clouds of Glory—would be replaced by a more natural setup. Through his prayers at that time, Moshe was able to avert this decree and to have Hashem return and continue to guide the people directly.[4] However, the Midrash states that the decree was not entirely annulled; rather, it was postponed as long as Moshe was alive.[5] After he died, however, the angel appeared as Hashem's agent in guiding the people. This was the angel whom Yehoshua beheld in Yericho, who said, "אֲנִי שַׂר צְבָא ה' עַתָּה בָאתִי—I am the commander of Hashem's legion, now I have come,"[6] i.e., although originally my involvement was deferred by Moshe, the time has now arrived. The angel in question was Michael, who is

---

2 40 = 'מ, 10 = 'י, 50 = 'נ, and 1 = 'א.
3 *Shemos* 33:2–3.
4 See ibid., verses 15–17.
5 *Shemos Rabbah* 32:3; see also *Rabbeinu Bachya* to *Shemos* 23:20.
6 *Yehoshua* 5:14.

referred to elsewhere as "*sar Yisrael*—the spiritual minister of Israel,"[7] reflecting his role as the agency through which Hashem oversees and guides the Jewish People within the framework of nature.

Hence, at the same time as the number of verses in our parsha alludes to Moshe's physical absence, with only his inner essence remaining, it also alludes to the presence of the angel Michael, signifying the transition in the way Hashem oversees His people that occurred with Moshe's passing.[8]

A LIGHT INSIDE THE BUILDING

וְאַתָּה תְּצַוֶּה אֶת בְּנֵי יִשְׂרָאֵל וְיִקְחוּ אֵלֶיךָ שֶׁמֶן זַיִת זָךְ כָּתִית לַמָּאוֹר לְהַעֲלֹת נֵר תָּמִיד.

And you shall command the Children of Israel that they should take for you pure, pressed olive oil for the lighting, to kindle the continual lamp.[9]

The parshiyos of *Terumah* and *Tetzaveh* are dedicated to the building of the *Mishkan* and the making of the priestly garments. It seems strange, therefore, that the verse should interject at this juncture with the specifications of one of the mitzvos of the service in the *Mishkan*. Indeed, other mitzvos, such as the *Ketores* (incense) and the *Lechem Hapanim* (show-bread) are discussed later on. Moreover, the lighting of the *Menorah* itself is discussed in detail at the end of *Parshas Emor,*[10] seemingly rendering the entire mention of how to light the *Menorah* here redundant!

The *Kli Yakar* explains that these verses are indeed relevant to the parsha of building the *Mishkan*, for they are not discussing the mitzvah of lighting the *Menorah* per se, but rather its role in contributing to the basic definition of the *Mishkan* itself.

---

7   See, e.g., *Daniel* 10:21.
8   See *Chanukas HaTorah, Parshas Tetzaveh.*
9   *Shemos* 27:20.
10   See *Vayikra* 24:1–3.

The *Mishkan* is referred to as "*Mishkan HaEdus*—The *Mishkan* of Testimony,"[11] which the Sages explain to mean that the *Mishkan* constitutes testimony that the Divine Presence resides among Israel. The entity which embodies this testimony are the *Luchos* that reside in the *Aron* inside the Holy of Holies—which are referred to as such in the next verse: "בְּאֹהֶל מוֹעֵד מִחוּץ לַפָּרֹכֶת אֲשֶׁר עַל הָעֵדֻת—In the Tent of Meeting outside the Partition, which is over the Testimony." However, the very fact that the *Luchos* are blocked from view renders them unable to function visibly as testimony! That role is fulfilled, instead, through the *Menorah*—more specifically, through one of its lights. As we know, although the middle lamp received the same amount of oil as the other lamps, enough to burn through the night until morning, it miraculously continued to burn for the entire next day until the time for lighting the following evening. The Gemara explains that this miracle represented "testimony to the entire world that the Divine Presence resides among Israel."[12]

For this reason, in contrast to the section in *Parshas Emor* that states: "וְהֶעֱלָה אֶת נֵרֹתֶיהָ—And he shall kindle its **lamps**," our verse makes reference only to the "*neir tamid*—continual **lamp**." For while the *mitzvah* of lighting the *Menorah* involves all of its lamps, the *testimony* of the *Menorah* as is relevant to our parsha centers on one particular lamp which gives visible expression to the definition of the *Mishkan* as "the *Mishkan* of Testimony"!

A TERUMAH ITEM IN PARSHAS TETZAVEH

וְעָשִׂיתָ מִזְבֵּחַ מִקְטַר קְטֹרֶת.

You shall make an Altar on which to offer up incense.[13]

Already from the times of the Rishonim, the commentators discuss the question of the Torah's placement of the *Mizbeiach* for the *Ketores* in our parsha. Seeing as the *Mishkan* and its vessels have all been discussed in *Parshas Terumah*, while *Parshas Tetzaveh* is devoted to the

---

11   *Shemos* 38:21.
12   *Shabbos* 22b.
13   *Shemos* 30:1.

priestly garments, why was this one vessel of the *Mishkan* left until the end of *Tetzaveh*?[14]

A simple and elegant answer is provided by R' Leib Heyman.[15] *Parshas Tetzaveh* is about the selection of Aharon and his sons to be the Kohanim. The three vessels in the *Mishkan* that have crowns—the *Aron*, *Shulchan*, and *Mizbeiach* for *Ketores*—correspond to the three crowns mentioned in *Pirkei Avos*, namely, the crowns of Torah, *Malchus* (kingship), and Kehunah respectively. As such, since the *Mizbeiach* for *Ketores* is particularly associated with Kehunah, it is placed in the parsha which is devoted to the Kohanim.

A very different answer comes from one of the early Acharonim, R' Moshe Galanti.[16] The rule regarding the *avodah* in the *Mishkan* is that if the vessel for a particular *avodah* has for any reason been moved from its location, the *avodah* relating to that vessel cannot be performed in its location in its absence. Thus, for example, if the *Shulchan* has been moved elsewhere, there is no *avodah* of *Lechem Hapanim*, or if the outer *Mizbeiach* has been moved, no *korbanos* can be brought. However, the Gemara states that an exception to this rule relates to the *Mizbeiach HaKetores*, whereby even if the *Mizbeiach* is not there, the *Ketores* is nonetheless performed in the place where the *Mizbeiach* normally rests.[17]

Therefore, says Rav Galanti, in order to allude to this unique law that the *Ketores* is offered even if the golden *Mizbeiach* is not in its proper location, the Torah presented the *Mizbeiach* itself "off location" in *Parshas Tetzaveh*, and not with the other vessels in *Parshas Terumah*!

It is fascinating to consider how, in this instance, the Torah uses "parsha placement" of its discussions to parallel the physical placement of the objects it is discussing.

---

14   See, e.g., commentaries of the *Ibn Ezra* and *Ramban* to our verse.
15   *Chikrei Lev, Parshas Tetzaveh.*
16   Cited at the end of Responsa *Halachos Ketanos* of R' Yaakov Chagiz, Rav Galanti's son-in-law. See also *Meshech Chochmah* to our verse.
17   *Zevachim* 59a.

PARSHAS KI SISA

PSHAT, DRASH, AND THE MEANING OF THE WORD "ACH"

Dimensions in Rashi

BACKGROUND: RASHI'S COMMENT AND THE RAMBAN'S OBJECTION

Toward the beginning of our parsha, the Torah discusses the construction of the *Mishkan* and related matters. The parsha then moves to the topic of Shabbos, introducing it with the words:

אַךְ אֶת שַׁבְּתֹתַי תִּשְׁמֹרוּ.

However, you shall observe My Sabbaths.[1]

Commenting on the word "*ach*," *Rashi* writes:

אַף עַל פִּי שֶׁתִּהְיוּ רְדוּפִין וּזְרִיזִין בִּזְרִיזוּת הַמְּלָאכָה, שַׁבָּת אַל תִּדָּחֶה מִפָּנֶיהָ. כָּל אַכִין וְרַקִּין מִעוּטִין הֵן.

Even though you are driven and energetic regarding the work [of building the Mishkan], Shabbos shall not be pushed aside by it. All instances of the word "ach" and "rak" are exclusionary.

---

1   *Shemos* 31:13.

The source of *Rashi's* concept, that the words "*ach*" and "*rak*" in the Torah come to exclude or limit something, is the *Talmud Yerushalmi* in *Maseches Berachos*.[2] In this instance, *Rashi* informs us that the matter that is being excluded or limited is the building of the *Mishkan*, which we are being told may not take place on Shabbos.

The *Ramban* takes strong exception to this comment of *Rashi's*. The basis of his issue is the fact that when the Sages state that the words *ach* and *rak* are exclusionary in nature, it means that they come to exclude or limit the scope of *the matter that they introduce*, not the matter that has been previously discussed. Applying this idea to our verse, since the word *ach* introduces the mitzvah of Shabbos, then that is the area it is coming to limit—not the building of the *Mishkan* which was discussed in the previous section! And indeed, continues the *Ramban*, if we consult the relevant expositions of the Midrash on this verse, we will see that this is in fact the case. Thus, for example, in our case, the Gemara in *Maseches Yoma* cites our verse as a source for the idea that danger to life overrides the observance of Shabbos.[3] This is a limit on the scope of the mitzvah of Shabbos.[4]

How are we to understand *Rashi's* position?

DEEPENING THE QUESTION

To make matters worse for a moment, if we may, from elsewhere in his commentary it seems that *Rashi* actually agrees with the premise of the *Ramban*. For example, in *Parshas Emor*, the Torah introduces the festival of Yom Kippur with the words: "אַךְ בֶּעָשׂוֹר לַחֹדֶשׁ הַשְּׁבִיעִי הַזֶּה—However, on the tenth of this seventh month [of Tishrei]."[5] *Rashi* there writes:

---

2   9:7.

3   85b.

4   Interestingly, although *Rashi* and the *Ramban* do not appear to distinguish between the connotations of the two "limiting" terms *ach* and *rak*, the *Malbim* understands that they differ from each other in this very matter, whereby *rak* limits that which was mentioned previously, while *ach* limits that which is being discussed presently; see his Introduction "*Ayeles Hashachar*" to *Vayikra*, sec. 591.

5   *Vayikra* 23:27.

כל אכין ורקין שבתורה מיעוטים, מכפר הוא לשבים ואינו מכפר על
שאינם שבים.

*All instances of the words "ach" and "rak" are exclusionary.
[This means]: the day atones for those who repent and does not
atone for those who do not repent.*

We see that *Rashi* explains the limitation of the word *"ach"* as pertaining to *the matter it is introducing*—Yom Kippur! If so, then why
would *Rashi* depart from this idea in our verse, explaining rather that it
is the earlier matter (the *Mishkan*) that is being limited and excluded?

THE KEY: REMEMBERING RASHI'S GOAL

To understand *Rashi*'s position in all this, let us remind ourselves of
the goal he set for his commentary, as he expresses it in *Bereishis* 3:8,
namely, to explain the verse using the methodology of *pshat*, as well as
making use, where necessary, of *Aggadah* (*drash*) to resolve *pshat* issues
that arise.

It is quite clear, as the *Ramban* demonstrated, that Chazal use the
word *ach* to denote a limitation in that which is being presently discussed. However, that understanding exists in the realm of *drash*, which
allows for relating to the word beyond its simple linguistic meaning. By
contrast, there is no question that the *pshat* meaning of the word *ach*
is "however," which indicates a contrast to that which was mentioned
previously. Therefore, wherever it is possible to preserve the *pshat* understanding of this word, *Rashi* will do so, for in such a case, there is no
need to take recourse to a *drash* approach.

What determines whether the *pshat* meaning of this word can be
used? If there is something mentioned earlier to which the current matter can be meaningfully contrasted, then *Rashi* will be able to explain it
as "however." Such a case is in our parsha, where Shabbos follows the
Mishkan, so that we are able to say that indeed, we need to build the
Mishkan, *however*, not on Shabbos.

Moreover, this *pshat* understanding is so clear that in a situation
where the contrast between the current topic and the one that precedes
it is self-understood, *Rashi* will not comment at all! For example, in

Parshas Shemini, the Torah first discusses the animals which we may consume, namely, those that have both split hooves and chew their cud. The verse then says: "אַךְ אֶת זֶה לֹא תֹאכְלוּ—However, the following you may not eat,"[6] and proceeds to mention animals that have only one of those kosher signs. Here, the contrast between the permitted animals with both signs and the forbidden ones with less than that is abundantly clear; hence, *Rashi* makes no comment on the word "*ach*."

However, in a case where the Torah introduces a topic with the word *ach*, yet there is nothing mentioned beforehand for it to be contrasted with, that represents a situation where *Rashi* deems it necessary to take recourse to *drash* in order to explain the verse. In that setting, he will explain the limitation within the matter being discussed itself. Such is the case in the verse which introduces Yom Kippur with the word *ach*. With what is it being contrasted? The matter discussed immediately prior to this is Rosh Hashanah. There is no meaning in moving from there to discussing Yom Kippur with the word "however"! Therefore, in that case *Rashi* explains the limitation as existing within Yom Kippur itself, such that it only brings atonement for those who do *teshuvah*.

FINER POINTS: A MATTER OF ORDER

Indeed, there is a subtle but wonderful point here. In both of the cases we have discussed, *Rashi* cited the statement of the *Yerushalmi* that "the words *ach* and *rak* denote a limitation." However, it is interesting to note that in our parsha regarding Shabbos and the *Mishkan*, he first presents his explanation and then quotes the principle. By contrast, in the verse dealing with Yom Kippur, he first mentions the principle and only then presents the explanation. Why the shift in order?

It would appear that the answer lies in the above analysis:

- In the verse in our parsha dealing with the *Mishkan* and Shabbos, *Rashi* explains the limitation of the word *ach* on a *pshat* level (limiting the prior topic), and not on a *drash* level (limiting the present topic). Therefore, he first presents his explanation

---

6   Ibid., 11:4.

and only then cites the principle, indicating that his (*pshat*) interpretation is only *generally based* on that idea, but is not an application of the *Yerushalmi*'s actual (*drash*) methodology.

- In contrast, in the verse dealing with Yom Kippur, *Rashi* actually invokes the *drash* interpretation of the word *ach*. Therefore, he prefaces his comment by citing the *Yerushalmi*'s principle, indicating that what is about to follow is entirely faithful to that *drash* approach.

Very beautiful.

NOAH'S ARK: WHERE PSHAT AND DRASH MEET

Having established that *Rashi* will sometimes explain the word *ach* in a *pshat* sense, while other times he will employ a *drash* approach, let us conclude the present discussion by considering a case where *Rashi* brings both. In *Parshas Noach*, the Torah describes how everything outside the ark was wiped out in the flood. Verse 23 of chapter 7 reads:

וַיִּמַח אֶת כָּל הַיְקוּם אֲשֶׁר עַל פְּנֵי הָאֲדָמָה...וַיִּשָּׁאֶר אַךְ נֹחַ וַאֲשֶׁר אִתּוֹ בַּתֵּבָה.

He [Hashem] wiped out all existence that was on the face of the earth...only Noach and those who were with him in the ark remained.

Commenting on the words *"vayisha'er ach Noach,"* *Rashi* writes:

לְבַד נֹחַ. זֶהוּ פְשׁוּטוֹ. וּמִדְרַשׁ אַגָּדָה: גּוֹנֵחַ וְכוֹהֶה דָם מִטּוֹרַח הַבְּהֵמוֹת וְהַחַיּוֹת.

[The meaning is]: Only Noach. This is the simple [pshat] meaning. And in the Midrash [it explains]: he was groaning and coughing up blood from the effort of taking care of the animals and beasts.

We can see how these two interpretations reflect the *pshat* and *drash* respectively:

- The first explanation understands *ach* as distinguishing Noach, who survived, *from those mentioned prior* to him, namely, all those outside the ark, who did not survive.

- The second explanation explains the word *ach* as denoting a diminishing *within Noach himself*, in the form of the deterioration of his health due to his ongoing exertions in taking care of all the animals.

The question we need to ask, of course, is why did *Rashi* deem it necessary to include the *drash* approach, if he already explained the verse according to the *pshat*? Perhaps in this case, *Rashi* felt that in terms of *pshat*, the entire phrase could be seen as redundant, for obviously it was only those outside of the ark who were wiped out, not those inside.[7] Hence, *Rashi* invoked the *drash* approach. However, the potential redundancy notwithstanding, the basis for the *pshat* approach certainly exists, and therefore *Rashi* begins with that approach, only then moving on to the *drash*.[8]

It is truly inspiring to get a glimpse into the precision that *Rashi* brings to every word, evaluating each case as to which approach is best suited to reflect its primary meaning.

---

7   See *Gur Aryeh* to *Rashi* ibid.
8   See also *Rashi, Bereishis* 9:5, s.v. *v'ach; Bamidbar* 31:22, s.v. *ach;* and *Devarim* 16:15, s.v. *v'hayisa.*

MAKING SHABBOS

BACKGROUND: HOW MANY SHABBOSOS ARE THERE?

A number of verses in our parsha are devoted to the topic of Shabbos. The Torah introduces this section with the command:

אַךְ אֶת שַׁבְּתֹתַי תִּשְׁמֹרוּ כִּי אוֹת הִוא בֵּינִי וּבֵינֵיכֶם לְדֹרֹתֵיכֶם לָדַעַת כִּי אֲנִי ה׳
מְקַדִּשְׁכֶם.

However, you shall observe My Sabbaths, for it is a sign between Me and you for your generations, to know that I am Hashem Who makes you holy.[1]

The reference to Shabbos here in the plural form—"My Sabbaths"—is somewhat perplexing; after all, how many Shabbosos are there? Of course, it is possible to explain simply that the verse uses the plural form since there are numerous Shabbosos in a year. However, in every other verse the singular, Shabbos, is used, and we understand it to refer to the day of Shabbos on a weekly basis. What is behind the use of the plural form here?

A most beautiful explanation of this verse is found in the commentary *Hakesav V'hakabbalah* by R' Yaakov Tzvi Mecklenberg. He explains

---

1   *Shemos* 31:13.

PARSHAS KI SISA   **489**

that the verse uses the plural because there are *two aspects to every Shabbos*, derived from the two meanings of the word "Shabbos" itself.

- The first aspect is the prohibition against performing any of the thirty-nine types of productive labor (*melachah*). This is the basis of Shabbos observance, and as we know, the prohibition against performing *melachah* is among the most severe in the Torah. Regarding this aspect, the word "Shabbos" derives from the word *lishbos*—to rest.
- However, refraining from *melachah* does not constitute a full observance of Shabbos. Having cleared the day from prohibited labors, the question then becomes: what does one fill it with? This brings us to the second aspect of Shabbos, to actively use the day to restore a sense of vision and purpose in one's life that may have become blurred or faded in the day-to-day involvements of the week. This aspect of Shabbos is related to the word *la'sheves*—to settle, and refers to the consolidating of our spiritual values and perspective.

It is these two aspects which constitute a full observance of the Shabbos, and thus the verse states: "Keep my Shabbosos," meaning, keep both aspects of the Shabbos. In this vein, the verse proceeds to explain the full nature and goal of Shabbos: "For it is a sign between Me and you for your generations, to know that I am Hashem Who makes you holy." The ultimate goal of Shabbos is stated here as acting not only as a commemoration of Creation, but also as a sign of the bond between Hashem and us, and the sanctity that He bestows upon us. To achieve this goal, we need to keep "two Shabbosos"—every week!

With this in mind, Rav Mecklenberg explains the well-known statement in the Gemara:[2]

אלמלי משמרין ישראל שתי שבתות כהלכתן—מיד נגאלים.

If the Jewish People would only keep two Shabbosos properly, they would be immediately redeemed.

---

2   *Shabbos* 118b.

The classic question raised by the commentators is: Why two? What is it about the second Shabbos that does not exist in the first? Why is one Shabbos not good enough?

Based on the above idea, the *Hakesav V'hakabbalah* explains that "two Shabbosos" does not refer to two *consecutive* Shabbosos, but rather to the *dual aspects* of Shabbos as we have identified them. If the Jewish People would use Shabbos not only as a day of rest from physical labor, but also as a day of spiritual reinvigoration and restored perspective, they would indeed be well on the way to redemption.

WHEN WAS CREATION COMPLETED?

In fact, this fundamental idea that ceasing physical labor is in order to make room for a spiritual element may actually be observed within the original Shabbos itself. The verse states: "God completed His work on the seventh day, and He rested on the seventh day from the work that He created."[3] These two statements seemingly contradict each other. If Hashem rested on the seventh day from creating, then He must have finished creating on the sixth day! Why does the verse begin by saying that He completed Creation on the seventh day?

The *Alshich* explains that physical creation ceased on the sixth day.[4] However, the final element of Creation was the Shabbos itself, which is a day of spirituality. The introduction of this type of creation on the seventh day was made possible by ceasing all physical creation by the end of the sixth day. This then becomes the goal of every subsequent Shabbos: to use the space left by the cessation of physical labor to allow for the entry of spiritual pursuits.

This awareness of the ultimate goal of Shabbos will allow us to appreciate many of the enactments of the Rabbis regarding Shabbos. The Torah forbids engaging in *melachah*. The Rabbis further banned even handling objects which are normally used for *melachah*. Indeed, as early as the prophet Yeshayah, even talking about business pursuits

---

3   *Bereishis* 2:2.
4   Commentary to *Bereishis* ibid.

was banned on Shabbos.[5] The goal of these enactments is clear: don't just refrain from performing *melachah* on Shabbos—get it out of your system! Clear the day to make room for what Shabbos is meant to be used for.

In the same vein, the Rabbis instituted special Shabbos meals, lighting Shabbos candles, special prayers, and Torah reading, encouraging us to use the day for what it was meant to be used for—restoring perspective and consolidating our spiritual goals.

FOR WHOM THE SHABBOS?

Moreover, this second aspect of keeping Shabbos will explain why even though the Torah expects all the nations of the world to believe in Hashem as Creator, nevertheless, Shabbos was given only to the Jewish People. Why is this so?

Once we appreciate the full significance of keeping Shabbos, we understand that only the nation that Hashem chose to sanctify by giving them the Torah is entrusted with a day of bringing spirituality into the world.

In this regard, we say that Shabbos is not only a *zikaron l'maaseh Bereishis*—a commemoration of the Creation of the world, but also *zecher l'yetzias Mitzrayim*—a commemoration of leaving Egypt. Now, we can understand how the festivals commemorate the Exodus from Egypt, but how is this true concerning Shabbos?

The point in history when Hashem chose us to sanctify as His nation is when He took us out of Egypt. When we consider the fact that only the Jewish People were entrusted with the mitzvah of Shabbos, it will bring us back to the Exodus, when we were first elevated to the status which allows us to connect with the full observance of this day.

This is also the idea, mentioned in our parsha, of "*laasos es haShabbos*—to make the Shabbos."[6] Upon being presented with a physical vacuum on Shabbos, we then proceed to make it—by filling it with spiritual content.

---

5   See *Yeshayah* 58:13 and *Shabbos* 113b.
6   Verse 16.

As we will appreciate, this does not mean to negate or disregard the aspect of physical rest on Shabbos. The physical cessation of the labors and stresses of the week is an equal part of the mitzvah and is often a much-needed break. However, the call of the Torah to keep "My Shabbosos" is to see to it that the day also serves as one of spiritual re-alignment, reclaiming the perspective that we may have lost during the past week.

Restoring Vision

The Gemara states that taking oversized strides can diminish a person's eyesight by one five-hundredth.[7] However, it adds that this can restored by making *Kiddush* on Friday night. The *Maharal* explains that the number five hundred represents the world, as the Gemara elsewhere refers to the world as being "five hundred *parsangs* by five hundred *parsangs*."[8] Every person needs to "walk through the world" in the sense that he needs to be involved in the affairs of the world. It may happen, however, that over the course of the week, a person takes "oversized strides" through the world. This refers to over-investing in and ascribing outsized significance to matters of this world, seeing them as an end unto themselves, instead of a means toward the higher goal of successful Torah living. Such a person has lost "one out of five hundred" of his vision, i.e., he has lost a measure of clarity regarding his view of the world.

Can a person ever retrieve this vision? The answer, says the Gemara, is yes, at *Kiddush* on Friday night. By embracing the sanctity of the Shabbos, and by hearing its message reminding him of a higher destiny, a person can restore his perspective on the physical world.

THE END—AND BEGINNING—OF THE WEEK

Based on our discussion, we understand that the perspective and sense of purpose which one attains on Shabbos should make a difference

---

7   *Shabbos* 113b.
8   *Chiddushei Aggados, Shabbos* ibid.

to the days ahead. In this regard, we can say that Shabbos is not only the light at the end of the tunnel for the week that has just passed, but also a lighthouse to illuminate the week to come. The way we go about our weekly affairs should be guided by the restored consciousness of our values which took place over Shabbos. A successful Shabbos should lead to a Shabbos-impacted week.

The Gemara states:[9]

כל המענג את השבת נותנים לו משאלות לבו.

Anyone who delights in the Shabbos, they give him his heart's desires.

We may ask: Many people have kept Shabbos faithfully, yet we do not necessarily see that our hearts' desires came true!

The *Shem MiShmuel* explains that the Gemara does not say that one who keeps the Shabbos properly will have his heart's desires fulfilled. Rather, it says, "they give him his heart's desires." The things a person desires during the week may be very limited in scope, in keeping with the nature of weekday involvements—perhaps he wishes for a bonus, or a promotion, or a new car. One who succeeds in tapping into the essence of Shabbos and delights in it will leave behind the limited desires of having new physical things and pleasures to wish for. Now, instead, he may wish for greater insight in Torah, greater patience and understanding in dealing with people, greater connection to Hashem during prayer, and all the many other things which the Shabbos experience allowed him to remember. These are the wishes which are given to him when he delights in the Shabbos. This is the gift of Shabbos.

---

9   *Shabbos* 118b.

THE LETTERS THAT FLEW
UP FROM THE LUCHOS

BACKGROUND

One of the most traumatic moments in our formative history is described in our parsha, whereby, upon witnessing the people worshipping the *eigel* that they had made in his absence, Moshe smashes the *Luchos* that had been given to him by Hashem to deliver to them. Commenting on that moment, the Midrash says:[1]

ראה שפרח כתב מעליהן והשליכן מידו.

He [Moshe] saw that the script flew off them [the Luchos], and so he threw them down from his hands.

The Midrash clearly indicates that Moshe took the letters flying off the *Luchos* as a sign for him to break them—and indeed, what use would *Luchos* be with no writing on them? Let us ponder this idea a little further.

---

1 *Yalkut Shimoni, Ki Sisa*, sec. 391.

MANTZEPA"CH: FORGOTTEN LETTERS?

There is a most intriguing discussion in the Gemara regarding the five final letters: *mem, nun, tzaddi, peh* and *kaf*, known by their acronym as "*mantzepa"ch*" (מנצפ"ך).[2] The Gemara states that "*Mantzepa"ch tzofim amarum*—the letters of *mantzepa"ch* were said (i.e., instituted) by the prophets." The Gemara reacts to this statement by raising two objections:

The first question is one of principle: A prophet does not have the authority to add an institution to Torah law. Hence, if this form of writing these letters is acceptable regarding Torah mitzvos, such as a Torah scroll and tefillin, it must be part of the Torah from the time it was given. How then, can it be said to be an institution of the prophets?

The second question is one of history: We have a tradition that the letters *mem* and *samech* that were engraved in the *Luchos* were held in place by a miracle. The idea behind this is that the engraving on the *Luchos* went all the way through them. Almost all the letters of the Hebrew alphabet have some part which would remain attached to the body of the *Luchos* even after the letter had been engraved through the entire thickness of the *Luchos*. However, the engraved section of the letters *mem* and *samech* completely surrounds the middle of the letters, leaving that section of stone in the center unattached to anything! In this regard, we have a tradition that the middle sections of those letters stayed in the center of the letter, with nothing to hold them up, via a miracle. Now, we will appreciate that of the two letters mentioned, while the *samech* of course is a circle, the only type of *mem* which would require this miracle is the final *mem*, which is a square. Hence, asks the Gemara, if the final *mem* dates back to the *Luchos* given at Mount Sinai, why are the final letters of *mantzepa"ch* attributed to the prophets?

To answer these two questions, the Gemara explains its original statement: "*Shachechum v'chazru v'yesadum*—They were forgotten and then [the prophets] subsequently [re]instituted them." In other words, although these final forms were clearly known as far back as Sinai itself,

---

2   *Megillah* 2b.

they became forgotten, with the prophets not *introducing* them, but *re-instating* them.

Needless to say, this answer is enigmatic, to say the least. How is it possible for letters that are part of the alphabet to become forgotten? There are items that every Jewish household contains which include written sections that incorporate these letters, such as tefillin and mezuzos! As such, the notion that these letters were forgotten is very difficult, indeed.

On a separate note, the commentators point out that the way in which the prophets are referred to in this statement—"*tzofim*"—is very non-typical. The word "*tzofim*" comes from the word "*tzofeh*," which means to see. Now, while it is true that prophets experience visions, to which end they are in fact, "seers," nevertheless, they are usually referred to simply as "*neviim*—prophets." Why, in this particular context, are they called "*tzofim*"?

ELEMENTS OF CREATION: BEFORE AND AFTER SIN

One of the outstanding Torah personalities of the nineteenth century, R' Eliyahu Gutmacher, explains as follows.[3] We are aware of the concept that "Hashem looked into the Torah and created the world,"[4] which is then expressed in the well-known idea that the Torah is the "blueprint of Creation." On a more detailed level, this means that the letters of the *aleph-beis* represent the elements or basic spiritual building blocks of the universe, with each letter reflecting a particular force or concept. However, as we know, as a result of the sin of Adam HaRishon, the entire world, as well as man's relationship with it, underwent an enormous upheaval. Specifically, this impacted on five areas:

- Death, which was originally not meant to be experienced by man, now became part of the human experience.
- Life would now be marked by setbacks and difficulty.
- Earning a livelihood and obtaining sustenance from the world now became much more difficult.

---

3   Commentary to *Chagigah* 12a.
4   *Zohar, Parshas Terumah* 161a.

- Man became more animal-like in terms of his activities and interactions.
- Evil was more present in the world, making it harder to choose and maintain a course of righteousness.

These five areas are represented by the five letters of *mantzepa"ch*:

- *Mem* represents *misah*—death.
- *Nun* represents *nefilah*—a fall or setback.
- *Kaf* means hand, representing both Hashem's hand bestowing sustenance and man's hand in being able to receive it.
- *Peh* means mouth, representing eating, the most basic physical activity.
- *Tzaddi* is related to the term *tzaddik*, a righteous individual, representing a person's ability to attain righteousness.

In light of the above, we will appreciate that the letters that correspond to these five areas likewise underwent a change as a result of that sin. Initially, these letters were in the form as we have them at the end of a word:

- The *mem* was closed, representing death being closed away and sealed off from human experience.
- The *nun* was upright, representing man being vouchsafed from fall or setback.
- The *kaf* was open and upright, representing receiving Hashem's sustenance with ease.
- The *peh* was upright, representing the elevated level of man's physical activities.
- The *tzaddi* was upright, representing man's natural tendency toward righteousness.

However, in the wake of Adam's sin, the change in these five areas was likewise reflected in a change in these letters:

- The *mem* became open, allowing death to enter the world.
- The *nun* became stooped over, making man more prone to setback and mishap.

- The *kaf* became stooped over, representing the hardship that would be involved in making a living from the land.
- The *peh* became stooped over, representing the lowered nature of man's physical activities.
- The *tzaddi* became stooped over, representing the difficulty in attaining righteousness.

The crucial point emphasized by Rav Gutmacher is that there was never any difference regarding where in the word the letter appeared, whether in the beginning, the middle, or the end. When the letters were used in their "upright" form, this was so even in the middle of a word. Conversely, when they shifted to their "diminished" form, this was even at the end of a word.

HAR SINAI: RECLAIMING—AND RE-LOSING— THE ORIGINAL LETTERS

This diminished situation pertained from the time of Adam's sin onward. However, at a critical point in our history, the original letters finally had the opportunity to return to their original form, namely, when we stood at Har Sinai and received the Torah. The level achieved by B'nei Yisrael at that time was that of Adam before the sin, whereby they were to be free of death and hardship. Accordingly, the writing on the *Luchos* was able to re-introduce the letters of *mantzepa"ch* in their higher form, after having been in hiatus for two and a half millennia!

However, this elevated level was short-lived, for the making of the Golden Calf precipitated a fall once more back to the post-sin state. Hence, the writing on the *Luchos* that Moshe brought down on that occasion was again incompatible with the world in its diminished state. This, says Rav Gutmacher, is the meaning of the Midrash that says that Moshe saw script flying off the *Luchos* as he approached the camp. The script that flew off was specifically the letters of *mantzepa"ch*, which reflected a level that B'nei Yisrael were no longer on!

With this in mind, we return to the tradition cited by the Gemara that the letters *mem* and *samech* on the *Luchos* were suspended miraculously. We can now understand that this was true specifically regarding the first *Luchos*, where the letter *mem* was indeed sealed.

The second *Luchos*, which were given after the sin of the *eigel*, would already have those letters in their diminished form. Thus, Hashem said to Moshe that he should carve out two new tablets of stone: "וְכָתַבְתִּי עַל הַלֻּחֹת אֶת הַדְּבָרִים אֲשֶׁר הָיוּ עַל הַלֻּחֹת הָרִאשֹׁנִים—And I shall write on the Tablets the words that were on the first Tablets."[5] Hashem was emphasizing that the *words* on the second set of *Luchos* would be the same as on the first, but the *script* would be different, with the lower form of *mantzepa"ch* being used to reflect the fallen state of B'nei Yisrael.

It turns out that the only person who had seen the letters of *mantzepa"ch* in their higher form was Moshe, when he received the first *Luchos*. Beyond that point, only the diminished form of those letters was used. This is why the Gemara says that the higher form of those letters was forgotten at a certain point. Moshe may have told his disciples about them, who may have in turn passed this information on to their disciples; however, in the absence of actually being used, they faded from people's awareness.

TZOFIM: KEEPING THE END IN SIGHT

Once again, centuries went by with only the diminished letters of *mantzepa"ch* in use, while the higher letters were forgotten. This continued until the time of the Neviim, part of whose task it was to prophesy regarding the end of days and the future redemption of the Jewish People and the world. As part of this goal, they re-introduced the original form of the *mantzepa"ch* letters, which signify the rectification of the world that will take place at that time. That is the meaning of the Gemara that says the letters were "forgotten and then re-instituted." Moreover, it is for this reason that they instituted that these letters be used at the *end of the word* specifically, since they represent the situation that will exist in the end of days. This was, if we may say, the original postscript! Additionally, we can now understand why, within the context of this enactment, they are referred to as *tzofim* (seers), for the enactment itself is an expression of the vision that they had of the future and which they were seeking to instill within the Jewish People.

---

5   *Shemos* 34:1.

However, we recall that according to Rav Gutmacher, when the higher forms of the letters are truly relevant, they are used wherever the letter appears in the word—whether the beginning, middle, or end. And indeed, there is actually one place where this too, is expressed. In chapter 9 of *Yeshayahu*, the prophet foretells of the elevated states of the world in future times:[6]

לסרבה [לְמַרְבֵּה] הַמִּשְׂרָה וּלְשָׁלוֹם אֵין קֵץ עַל כִּסֵּא דָוִד וְעַל מַמְלַכְתּוֹ לְהָכִין אֹתָהּ וּלְסַעֲדָהּ בְּמִשְׁפָּט וּבִצְדָקָה מֵעַתָּה וְעַד עוֹלָם.

Toward abundant greatness and boundless peace [that will rest] on the throne of David and his kingdom, to establish and sustain it through justice and righteousness, from now to eternity.

There is a most unusual occurrence within this verse; unique, in fact, in the entire Tanach. The letter *mem* of the word *"l'marbeh"* is written as a final *mem*—"לסרבה," even though it is in the middle of a word! This, says Rav Gutmacher, is a "taste" and portent of the way these letters will be used when the time that they describe arrives—wherever in the word that they appear.

May we merit to see the return of these letters in full, and the elevated state that they signify, speedily in our days!

---

6   Verse 6.

FROM THE COMMENTATORS

THE DEATH OF CHUR

The Midrash, cited by *Rashi*,[1] informs us that alongside the sin of the Golden Calf, B'nei Yisrael committed another crime.[2] Chur, Miriam's son, attempted to stop the people from making the calf, and they killed him. This is alluded to in verse 7, which states regarding Aharon: "וַיַּרְא אַהֲרֹן וַיִּבֶן מִזְבֵּחַ לְפָנָיו." The simple meaning of these words is: "Aharon saw and built an altar before him." However, the Midrash explains that it also means: "Aharon saw and understood [*heivin*] from the one who was slaughtered [*zavuach*] in front of him [Chur]," that if he did not comply they would kill him too. At that point, their sin would be beyond any hope of forgiveness. Indeed, verse 1 states that the people "gathered toward Aharon." Before ascending the mountain, Moshe had told them that any issues they had should be presented to Aharon and Chur. Why then, was Aharon the only one addressed here? Where was Chur? The answer, as per the Midrash, is that they got rid of him.

We may ask: Why is this crime, which seems no less serious than the making of the Calf itself, not mentioned explicitly in the verse? The *Ohr Hachaim* explains that it is for this very reason it does not receive explicit mention. The sin of killing a fellow Jew for attempting to rebuke

---

1   32:5, s.v. *vayikra*.

2   *Vayikra Rabbah* 10:3; see also *Sanhedrin* 7a.

them is so horrific that to record it in the verses of the Torah for all time would be a condemnation too great for the people to bear.

This may explain to us something else. Chur is clearly a most significant personality, apparently Aharon's equal. When Moshe climbed the mountain to oversee the battle against Amalek, he was accompanied by Aharon and Chur.[3] Likewise, as we have stated, when he later ascended to receive the Torah, he instructed that all questions be directed toward Aharon and Chur.[4] How strange it is, therefore, that Chur receives no introduction whatsoever. With every other personality in the Torah of even relatively minor significance, we are told something about them—if only their basic lineage. Yet in this case, Chur seems to just appear in the Torah, with us only discovering from oral tradition that he was no less than Miriam's son! Perhaps the reason the verses do not draw much attention to his initial appearance, effectively "downplaying" his presence in the Written Torah, is likewise impacted by the way in which he would subsequently become absent. The more "there" he was in the Torah, the more "missing" he would then become, to the eternal and devastating shame of the Jewish People.

However, even though this sin was not explicitly mentioned in the Chumash, it nevertheless needed to be atoned for along with the sin of the *eigel* itself. This may explain to us the order of offerings on the inaugural day of the *Mishkan*, which came as an atonement for the *eigel*. The Torah relates that on that occasion, Moshe commanded the people to bring a calf and a goat.[5] The Midrash explains that the calf was to atone for the making of the Golden Calf, while the goat was to atone for an earlier sin—the dipping of Yosef's coat in the blood of a goat by the brothers.[6] The commentators wonder: Why is the sin of selling Yosef being brought up on this day, and why together with the sin of the *eigel*? In light of our discussion, perhaps it is because that sin was present at the *eigel*. The earliest incidence of people being prepared to take full

---

3 *Shemos* 17:10.
4 Ibid., 24:14.
5 *Vayikra* 9:3.
6 *Toras Kohanim* ibid.

and final measures against their brother is in the events surrounding and culminating with the sale of Yosef. That sin resurfaced in the killing of Chur, and hence, needed to be atoned for alongside the sin of the *eigel* itself.

DANCING AROUND THE GOLDEN CALF

The tragic episode of making and worshipping the Golden Calf came to a traumatic head with the breaking of the *Luchos* by Moshe Rabbeinu. Having received the *Luchos* from Hashem, Moshe descended the mountain in order to give them to the Jewish People. However, when he reached the camp, he saw that the Jews had made the Golden Calf and judged that they were not worthy to receive the *Luchos*, whereupon he threw them down and smashed them into fragments.

There is a very basic problem here. While he was still on the mountain, Moshe was told by *Hashem Himself* that the Jewish People had made the Calf, yet he nevertheless took the *Luchos* and began his descent. He was, apparently, of the opinion that the making of the Calf was not a critical impediment to the Jewish People receiving them. In that case, why, upon seeing the Golden Calf, did Moshe break the *Luchos*? If he felt that the people were not deserving of them, he should have left the *Luchos* on the mountain!

The *Seforno* explains that when Moshe was initially informed by Hashem that the people had made the Golden Calf, the verse reads:

סָרוּ מַהֵר מִן הַדֶּרֶךְ אֲשֶׁר צִוִּיתִם עָשׂוּ לָהֶם עֵגֶל מַסֵּכָה.

"They have strayed quickly from the path that I have commanded them; they have made for themselves a molten calf."[7]

Moshe was thus aware that the people had sinned. However, he reasoned that as grievous as their sin may be, they could recover from it by him bringing down the *Luchos*. Perhaps, their sin was born of a moment of confusion or lack of direction stemming from Moshe not being among them. As soon as they would see the *Luchos*, they would snap out

---

7   *Shemos* 32:8.

of it and be reminded of the correct path for them to be taking. This is why he took the *Luchos* with him.

However, when Moshe approached the camp, he saw the Calf—which he had been told about—but he also saw something else that he had not been aware of. The verse reads:

וַיְהִי כַּאֲשֶׁר קָרַב אֶל הַמַּחֲנֶה וַיַּרְא אֶת הָעֵגֶל וּמְחֹלֹת.

It happened as he drew near the camp, he saw the Calf and the dances.[8]

Moshe had been told that the people had made a Calf. He did not know, however, that having made the Calf, they then proceeded *to dance around it*.[9] This represented a completely different level of identification with their sin. They did not relate to it as a mistake at all. They were happy with it!

At this point, Moshe realized that merely seeing the *Luchos* would not have any effect on the people. They were too far invested in their path of sin, and with all the dancing, they may not even have noticed Moshe or the *Luchos*! The only course of action that could bring them back was to smash the *Luchos* in front of them. The people would then be confronted with a drastic expression of how far they had strayed and what they potentially stood to lose.

There is a profound message in these words for those people who make mistakes, otherwise known as human beings. Having committed those acts, a stubborn and egocentric part of us is reluctant to recognize them as wrong, choosing instead to justify them and even idealize and dance around them. The *Seforno* is teaching us that whatever mistakes we may have made, we should be sure to maintain a sense of honesty about them, so that the sight of the *Luchos* alone should be enough to bring us back, without anything having to be smashed in order to shake us out of our delusions.

---

8   Ibid., verse 19.

9   Rav Yehudah Copperman, in his commentary to the *Seforno*, points out that this contrast is reflected by the fact that the word "*ha'eigel*" is preceded with the letter *hei*, denoting a known entity, while the word "*mecholos*" has no *hei*, as that element was not known to Moshe.

THE THIRTEENTH ATTRIBUTE

וְנַקֵּה לֹא יְנַקֶּה.

And cleanses, though not completely.[10]

The Sages of the Talmud, cited by *Rashi*, expounded these words as reflecting two conflicting ideas: "*V'nakeh*—He will cleanse," and "*Lo yenakeh*—He will not cleanse."[11] The resolution of this conflict is that it depends on whether the person does *teshuvah*: "He cleanses those who do *teshuvah* and does not cleanse those who do not."[12] Indeed, this interpretation is reflected in our communal practice when reciting the Thirteen Attributes of Mercy out loud, where we conclude the recitation with the word "*v'nakeh*" and do not include the words that follow, as they reflect the negative outcome for one who does not do *teshuvah*.

Understandably, this matter requires some investigation: Since the simple meaning of the words sees them as one integral phrase—"*v'nakeh lo yenakeh*"—why does the Midrash state that they should be separated and treated as two opposing ideas?

In truth, however, the *pshat* approach which sees this as one phrase is quite difficult. Grammatically, as one phrase, this represents an absolute statement, which would mean, "He does not completely cleanse [the person]." How does this statement, which comes only to limit the extent of Hashem's mercy, reflect the concluding attribute of mercy? Moreover, is this even so? Can a person never be entirely cleansed of his sins, even if he does *teshuvah*?[13] For this reason, the Sages adopt the *drash* approach and explain that the cleansing is not limited, but it is conditional, for it depends on the person doing *teshuvah*. If he does,

---

10   *Shemos* 34:7.

11   See *Yoma* 86a.

12   This is also the approach of *Onkelos*, who translates: "סלח לדתבין לאורייתיה, ולדלא תיבין לא מזכי—He forgives those who return to His Torah, but does not cleanse those who do not return."

13   *Rashi* himself first offers a *pshat* approach, whereby Hashem does not entirely cleanse the person, but rather, exacts retribution from him little by little. However, even according to this explanation, Hashem *does ultimately* cleanse the person completely, He just does not do so *immediately*. This is already a departure from the absolute connotation of the negation contained within the *pshat*. For this reason, *Rashi* proceeds to cite the midrashic approach.

however, he can be entirely cleansed, and it is to this that we refer by mentioning only the word "*v'nakeh*" in our recitation of the Divine Attributes.

There is a fascinating idea related to this found in the early sources. There are two sets of "Thirteen Middos": The Thirteen Middos (Attributes) of Divine Mercy and R' Yishmael's Thirteen Middos (midrashic principles) through which the Torah is expounded.[14] These sources state that there exists a parallel between these two sets of thirteen, so that involving oneself in one of the principles of *drash* helps activate the corresponding attribute of mercy—a most unusual application of the idea of "*middah k'neged middah*"! The thirteenth and final exegetical principle states:

וכן שני כתובים המכחישים זה את זה עד שיבא הכתוב השלישי ויכריע ביניהם.

Similarly, two verses that contradict each other, until a third verse comes and reconciles them.

And indeed, this is the very situation described by the final Attribute of Mercy, which appears to contain "two conflicting verses"—the idea of Hashem cleansing and Him not cleansing—until the third "verse" comes to reconcile the contradiction, explaining that the matter is dependent on the person doing *teshuvah*![15]

---

14   These are enumerated in the morning prayers just before *Pesukei D'Zimrah*.

15   *B'nei Yissaschar*, Elul, *maamar* 2.

PARSHAS VAYAKHEL

ACTIVATING HOLINESS

Shabbos, the Mishkan, and the Cheit HaEigel

וַיַּקְהֵל מֹשֶׁה אֶת כָּל עֲדַת בְּנֵי יִשְׂרָאֵל וַיֹּאמֶר אֲלֵהֶם אֵלֶּה הַדְּבָרִים אֲשֶׁר צִוָּה
ה' לַעֲשֹׂת אֹתָם.

Moshe assembled the entire congregation of the Children of Israel and said to them, "These are the things that Hashem has commanded to perform them."[1]

INTRODUCTION: PRESENTING SHABBOS AND THE MISHKAN

This parsha is devoted to describing the construction of the *Mishkan* and its component parts. Before presenting this topic, however, Moshe first prefaces with two verses concerning observing Shabbos. The message of this juxtaposition is that although the people are about to embark on the lofty endeavor of constructing the *Mishkan*, Shabbos observance takes precedence over this; no work for the *Mishkan* can be done on Shabbos.[2]

---

1   *Shemos* 35:1.
2   *Rashi* to verse 2.

It is interesting to note a difference in the way the topics of Shabbos and the *Mishkan* are introduced:

- Although observing Shabbos is one idea, it is introduced with the plural "*Eileh hadevarim*—These are the things."
- By contrast, the building of the *Mishkan*, which comprises many details that take up the rest of the parsha, is introduced with the singular "*Zeh hadavar*—This is the matter."[3]

What is behind these differing and counterintuitive introductions?

Additionally, many commentators note that in the previous parsha, when the idea that building the *Mishkan* does not override the Shabbos is presented by Hashem to Moshe, the *Mishkan* is mentioned first and Shabbos second.[4] This is taken to mean that building the *Mishkan* must come to a halt on Shabbos. In our parsha, when communicating exactly the same idea, Moshe reverses the order, placing Shabbos first. What is behind this reversal?

KADOSH AND KODESH: TWO TYPES OF HOLINESS

In order to answer these questions, let us preface by referring to a comment of the *Meshech Chochmah*, who notes that we find two different ways in which the Torah refers to the holiness of the Jewish People:

- In *Parshas Mishpatim*, the verse states: "וְאַנְשֵׁי קֹדֶשׁ תִּהְיוּן לִי—You shall be people of holiness to Me."[5]
- In *Parshas Re'eh*, it states: "כִּי עַם קָדוֹשׁ אַתָּה—For you are a holy people."[6]

What is the difference in meaning between "*kodesh*" and "*kadosh*"?

The *Meshech Chochmah*, based on a comment of *Rashi* in *Maseches Kiddushin*,[7] explains the difference as follows:[8]

---

3   Verse 4.
4   *Shemos* 31:1–13.
5   Ibid., 22:30.
6   *Devarim* 14:21.
7   57b, s.v. *kadosh*.
8   *Devarim* ibid.

- "*Kadosh*" is an adjective and describes something that itself is inherently holy.
- "*Kodesh*" is a noun, referring to the concept of holiness. Something that is "of *kodesh*" is associated with that holiness, but not itself inherently holy.

To illustrate with examples of each of these two categories, let us consider two items that can be consecrated for the Beis Hamikdash:

- An animal can be consecrated to be brought as a *korban*. This animal attains inherent sanctity and is thus called "*kadosh*."
- An item can be consecrated for the funds of the Beis Hamikdash; it will be sold and its value used for the *avodah*. This item is not inherently holy, but rather holy by association, i.e., "of *kodesh*."

Is there any practical halachic difference between these two categories? Indeed there is, for an object that is holy by association can be replaced with something else—for example, if it is sold or redeemed. By contrast, an object that is intrinsically holy can never lose its status or be replaced.

How does all this relate to our discussion?

TRACKING THE HOLINESS OF THE JEWISH PEOPLE

The Gemara relates that after the *Cheit HaEigel* (Sin of the Golden Calf), when the Jewish People narrowly averted a Divine decree calling for their destruction, Moshe requested of Hashem that He pledge never to replace them with another people, and Hashem granted this request.[9] This teaches us that prior to this episode, the People of Israel could indeed have lost their unique sanctified status, whereas, after Moshe's request was granted, this sanctity could no longer be lost.

This historic development, says the *Meshech Chochmah*, is reflected in the two verses cited above referring to the Jewish People:

- The verse in *Parshas Mishpatim* refers to the period prior to the *Cheit HaEigel*. Therefore, the people are referred to there as

---

9   *Berachos* 7a.

"Anshei kodesh—People of holiness," reflecting the notion that their sanctity could be replaced.

- The verse in *Parshas Re'eh* describes the people well after the *Cheit HaEigel*; therefore, the terms used is "*Am kadosh*—a holy people," denoting the permanent and non-transferable nature of their inherent sanctified status!

EFFECTING THE CHANGE:
UNDERSTANDING THE SECOND LUCHOS

Let us proceed and ask: How was this change from associative holiness (*kodesh*) to intrinsic holiness (*kadosh*) brought about? To answer this question, my father, Rabbi Isaac Bernstein, *zt"l*,[10] referred to a most fascinating discussion of the *Beis Halevi* in his *drashos*.[11] Based on numerous sources in Chazal, the *Beis Halevi* develops the idea that there was a fundamental difference between the two sets of *Luchos* that were given to Moshe:

- The first set of *Luchos* contained, in some form, a representation of the entire Torah: not only what we know as *Torah She'bichsav* (the Written Torah) but also *Torah She'baal Peh* (the Oral Torah).
- The second set of *Luchos* contained only *Torah She'bichsav*. At that stage, *Torah She'baal Peh* became entirely oral in nature, with no written representation on the *Luchos* whatsoever.

The *Beis Halevi* asks: What are the implications of *Torah She'baal Peh* being present on the first *Luchos*, but absent from the second?

He answers that as long as both areas of Torah were written on the *Luchos*, the *Luchos* constituted the repository of Torah. Thus, even as the Jewish People learned Torah and were connecting with holiness, they were effectively an "accessory to holiness," equivalent to an ark that houses a Torah scroll. However, once the *Torah She'baal Peh* was no

---

10   *Shabbos Shuvah Drashah*, 5749/1988.
11   *Derush* 18.

longer written on the *Luchos*, the repository of that area of Torah became *the hearts and minds of the Jewish People themselves*. At this stage, they became like a Torah scroll itself and were no longer an accessory to holiness, but rather an inherently holy object!

Putting these two ideas together, my father suggested that the shifting of *Torah She'baal Peh* after the *Cheit HaEigel* from the *Luchos* to the people, as described by the *Beis Halevi*, was the means through which they graduated from associative holiness to intrinsic holiness, as discussed by the *Meshech Chochmah*, thereby assuring their immutable status as Hashem's people.

Perhaps this will give us a new insight into the famous statement of R' Yochanan in the Gemara:[12] "The holy One, blessed be He, only sealed a covenant with Israel over the Oral Torah, as it says,[13] 'For based [*al pi*] on these words, I have sealed a covenant with you.'" The verse cited by R' Yochanan is from the end of *Parshas Ki Sisa*, after the second *Luchos* had been written; for the eternal covenantal connection between Hashem and Israel is based on the shifting of the Oral Torah to the people themselves, thereby elevating them to a status of intrinsic holiness.

MOUNTAINS SUSPENDED BY THREADS

In light of the above, we can appreciate that an integral part of securing the lasting rehabilitation of the Jewish People came through connecting them to *Torah She'baal Peh*. With this in mind, perhaps we can now explain why, although Moshe was originally told by Hashem concerning the *Mishkan* and then Shabbos, at this stage he reversed the order and spoke about Shabbos first. The Mishnah characterizes Shabbos with the term "*Hararim hateluyim b'saarah*—Mountains that are suspended by threads," that is to say, a huge body of laws based on a very small amount of verses in the Torah.[14] In this regard, Shabbos represents a mitzvah whose details are predominantly known to us

---

12   *Gittin* 60b.

13   *Shemos* 34:27. The phrase "*al pi*" is explained as a reference to *Torah She'baal Peh*—the Oral Torah.

14   *Chagigah* 10a.

through *Torah She'baal Peh*. This is in marked contrast to the laws of the *Mishkan*, all of which are described extensively in the Written Torah in all their details. Hence, as Moshe addresses the people for the first time after they have attained forgiveness for the *eigel*, he immediately engages in the area of Torah that will "activate" their new status of intrinsic holiness, vouchsafing their enduring and immutable status as Hashem's people.

We can now return to the question with which we opened our discussion, regarding the contrasting introductions of Shabbos and the *Mishkan*. We noted that Shabbos, which is discussed in only two verses, is introduced with the plural—"These are the things," while the *Mishkan*, which is discussed at length over dozens of verses, is presented with the singular—"This is the matter"! R' Yehonasan Eibeschutz, in his commentary *Tiferes Yehonasan* to the Torah, explains that the use of the plural form for Shabbos reflects the fact that it is derived from both areas of Torah—*Torah She'bichsav* and *Torah She'baal Peh*. By contrast, the *Mishkan* is presented with the singular form, since it derives entirely from the one area of *Torah She'bichsav*. We can appreciate that the reason this distinction between the two is being highlighted here is because that is what lay behind Moshe's reversal of these topics, choosing to open with Shabbos so as to elevate the people to inherent *kedushah* via *Torah She'baal Peh*.

FROM INSTRUCTION TO CONSTRUCTION

Building Relationships

The parsha of *Vayakhel* is often characterized somewhat loosely as a repetition of *Parshas Terumah*, with the former parsha detailing the instructions for the *Mishkan* and the vessels and the latter describing their construction. However, a closer inspection of this parsha will reveal that it is not a simple repetition at all. There are numerous differences between the two parshiyos—both in terms of content as well as language—which indicate that these are in fact two significantly different accounts of the *Mishkan*. Let us consider some examples.

DIFFERENCES BETWEEN THE PARSHIYOS: FROM THE GENERAL...

The most obvious difference between the two parshiyos is the order of the *Mishkan* (i.e., the beams and the coverings which made up the body of the *Mishkan*) and the vessels contained therein:

- *Parshas Terumah*—first instructs to make the vessels and then discusses the *Mishkan*.
- *Parshas Vayakhel*—describes the actual construction in reverse—first the *Mishkan* and then the vessels.

Indeed, this very matter was the subject of an exchange between Moshe and Betzalel, as recorded in the Gemara:[1]

> When the Holy One, blessed be He, said to Moshe, "Go and tell Betzalel to make for Me the Mishkan and its vessels," Moshe went and reversed the order, saying, "Make the vessels and the Mishkan."
>
> Said [Betzalel], "Moshe our teacher, it is the way of the world that a person [first] builds a house and then brings its vessels inside, yet you are telling me to make [first] the vessels and [then] the Mishkan. The vessels that I am making, where will I put them? Perhaps the Holy One, blessed be He, [actually] said to you to make the Mishkan [first] and [then] the vessels? Said [Moshe] to him, "Perhaps you were in Hashem's shade[2] and [thus] heard what He said."[3]

This exchange is most intriguing. In fact, it is actually completely baffling.

- How can Betzalel question a direct command from Moshe based on the way he would expect a house to be built? Indeed, for that matter, what relevance could he possibly think the "way of the world" in building a house would have on this situation? The *Mishkan* is clearly not a normal house!
- If Betzalel's reasoning based on "the way of the world" was indeed sound, why did Moshe respond by saying that he must have overheard Hashem's instructions, thereby knowing the true order? His basis for questioning Moshe was based on reason!
- The most difficult question is, of course, *why* did Moshe reverse the order as given to him by Hashem? Having clearly been

---

1   *Berachos* 55a.

2   "בצל א-ל," an exposition on the name בצלאל.

3   I.e., that Hashem did, in fact, tell Moshe to instruct Betzalel to make the *Mishkan* first.

instructed that the *Mishkan* should come first, what could have prompted him to change the order?

Now, we have noted that the order of vessels followed by *Mishkan* does seem to have a precedent in *Parshas Terumah*. It would seem, therefore, that in reversing the order, Moshe was looking to give primacy to that parsha. The question remains as to why he would do so, what difference the order makes, and why the Torah itself reversed it between the two parshiyos of *Terumah* and *Vayakhel*.

...TO THE PARTICULAR

Aside from the general question regarding the order in which things were made, we note that the two parshiyos also differ in the way that they refer to various parts of the *Mishkan* and its vessels. For example:

Twenty Beams: The north and south side of the *Mishkan* comprised twenty beams of cedar wood standing side by side.

- *Parshas Terumah* refers to these beams as "*Esrim karesh*"[4]
- *Parshas Vayakhel* refers to them as "*Esrim kerashim*"[5]

Now, in principle, both forms are correct, for even the singular form can be used to denote the plural. However, the question remains, why change between the two?

The Two *Keruvim*: As the Torah describes, two *Keruvim* were to be formed on the cover of the *Aron*. How does the verse refer to them?

- *Parshas Terumah* refers to them as "*Sh'nayim Keruvim*."[6]
- *Parshas Vayakhel* refers to them as "*Sh'nei Keruvim*"[7]

In this instance, it would actually appear that the word "*sh'nei*" is the more appropriate, since it denotes two *of something*,[8] as opposed to "*sh'nayim*," which simply denotes the number two. Either way, here too,

---

4   *Shemos* 26:18.
5   Ibid., 36:23.
6   Ibid., 25:18.
7   Ibid., 37:7.
8   In this case, *Keruvim*.

we ask: Why did the Torah change its way of referring to these things between the two parshiyos?

ACTION AND MOTIVATION

One of the great Torah luminaries of the nineteenth century, R' Yehoshua Heller,[9] offers a fascinating approach which answers all the above questions. He prefaces by noting that every action consists of the action itself plus the motivation which leads to it. In pure terms of mitzvos, these two ideas will express themselves as the love for Hashem (motivation) and the performance of the mitzvah (action). If we should ask: Which of these two comes first? The answer would seem to be quite straightforward—the motivation begets the action! However, the matter is not quite so simple, for it depends on the level of the person.

- For someone on a higher level, love for Hashem does indeed lead to performance of His mitzvos.
- For a person on a lower level, there may not be a natural love for mitzvos that motivates their performance. For such a person, the flow will actually be reversed: It will be the performance of mitzvos which will then breed an appreciation for their worth.[10]

Interestingly, we find a "template" for both of these levels in the first two paragraphs of the *Shema*:

- The first paragraph mentions love for Hashem before the performance of mitzvos: "וְאָהַבְתָּ אֵת ה' אֱלֹקֶיךָ...וּקְשַׁרְתָּם לְאוֹת עַל יָדֶךָ...וּכְתַבְתָּם עַל מְזֻזֹת בֵּיתֶךָ—You shall love Hashem, your God…you shall bind [these words] on your arms [tefillin]…and write them on your doorposts [mezuzah]."[11]
- The second paragraph mentions performance of mitzvos before love of Hashem—"אִם שָׁמֹעַ תִּשְׁמְעוּ אֶל מִצְוֹתַי...לְאַהֲבָה אֶת ה' אֱלֹקֵיכֶם—If you will surely heed My mitzvos…to love Hashem."[12]

---

9   *Ohel Yehoshua, drush* 1.
10 See *Mesillas Yesharim*, chap. 7.
11 *Devarim* 6:5–9.
12 Ibid., 11:13.

It turns out that these two paragraphs, which we recite daily one after the other, actually reflect two different levels of relationship with Hashem and His mitzvos.

UNITY

Another concept that relates to the spiritual level of the Jewish People is that of unity versus plurality. This is true in two respects:

- Interpersonal Unity: The higher the level of the Jewish People, the more unified they will be among themselves, as their elevated goals will nullify any mundane or petty differences that might otherwise have separated them.
- Personal Unity: This will exist within the people themselves, since their inner motivation is in line with their performance of mitzvos. At a lower level, by contrast, the disparity between their inner inclinations and their outward positive deeds will lead to a plurality within themselves.

How interesting to note that this difference too, can be seen within the two paragraphs of the *Shema*: The first paragraph, which, as we have seen, reflects the higher spiritual level, is written in the *singular*, while the second paragraph, which reflects the lower level, is written in the *plural*!

THE MISHKAN, THE HUMAN BODY AND TARYAG MITZVOS

As we have noted, the *Mishkan* and its vessels are dealt with both in *Parshas Terumah* as well as in *Parshas Vayakhel*. However, these two depictions are not the same, for in between, in *Parshas Ki Sisa*, we have the episode with the *eigel* (Golden Calf). This sin was to have major repercussions for the Jewish People's relationship with Hashem—beginning with the construction of the *Mishkan* itself.

To understand how this is so, Rav Heller refers to the well-known idea that the six hundred and thirteen mitzvos parallel the six hundred and thirteen parts of the human body, with each mitzvah representing a certain limb. Even without knowing the relationship between each mitzvah and each body part, we can safely posit that the inner parts of the body correspond to the "inner" mitzvos, that is, the mitzvos which relate to feelings, such as love of Hashem.

To this equation, Rav Heller adds the component parts of the *Mishkan*, which he tallies in detail and shows how there too, there were six hundred and thirteen parts! Continuing the logic of relating inner components to inner mitzvos, we may conclude that the inner parts of the *Mishkan*, i.e., its vessels, correspond to the inner mitzvos of thought and feeling, while the outer parts—the beams and coverings of the *Mishkan*—correspond to more external and practical mitzvos.

THE MISHKAN AND THE JEWISH PEOPLE

Putting all of this together, we can now answer our opening question regarding the shift in order regarding the *Mishkan* and its vessels. The *Mishkan* is the center of *avodah* for the Jewish People. As such, it needs to reflect their level of *avodah*. Yet, this level itself underwent a fundamental change as a result of the *eigel*. Prior to the *eigel*, the people were on a higher level, naturally attuned to doing Hashem's will. Subsequent to the *eigel*, their natural inclination was no longer to perform Hashem's will, and thus needed to be elevated by their positive actions. Therefore:

- In *Parshas Terumah*, which preceded the *eigel*, the direction of *avodah* for the Jewish People was from the inside (motivation) to the outside (action), and hence the inner vessels were instructed to be made before the outer body of the *Mishkan*.
- In *Parshas Vayakhel*, which followed the sin of the *eigel* and its resultant fall, the direction of *avodah* was now *reversed*, with the outer action coming first and leading to the development of inner feeling and motivation. As such, in this parsha, the *Mishkan* was commanded to be constructed first, and only after that were the vessels to be made.

Additionally, we mentioned that the higher spiritual level is associated with the concept of unity, both personal and interpersonal. This is the theme that pervades the *Mishkan* as described in *Parshas Terumah*, hence, the generic singular "*karesh*" is used, even when describing a number of beams—"*Esrim karesh*." Likewise, the two *Keruvim* are referred to as "*sh'nayim Keruvim*," for the word "*sh'nayim*" indicates two things that work together as a pair. In contrast, the parsha of *Vayakhel* already sees the plurality of the post-*eigel* era, and hence, this becomes the mode with which to refer to those very same entities—"*Esrim kerashim*" and "*Sh'nei keruvim*."

MOSHE'S ATTEMPTED REVERSAL

We can now understand why, when Moshe was told by Hashem to instruct Betzalel to make the *Mishkan* and then its vessels, he reversed the order. The current order reflected the drop in the people's spiritual level due to the *eigel*. For his part, Moshe protested them being consigned to this post-*eigel* state, attempting to *keep them compatible with the higher state* that they had originally enjoyed. In this regard, Moshe's actions here were no different than when he protested against Hashem telling him that the people would be led via an angel and not directly by Hashem, as discussed in *Parshas Ki Sisa*.[13]

In this instance, however, the higher level of *avodah* was no longer meaningfully within reach of the people. This is what Betzalel communicated to Moshe by raising the question from "the way of the world" in building a house. Betzalel did not mean to question Moshe's order based on this logic-based idea alone—as that would clearly be insufficient grounds to do so. Rather, in this way, he was delicately indicating to Moshe that the people had fundamentally shifted toward an affinity with "the way of the world" as a result of having made the *eigel*. As such, the order of making the *Mishkan* first and then its vessels—which Betzalel grasped through *ruach hakodesh*—was sadly, but unavoidably, necessary.

Moreover, it is possible that had the *Mishkan* been built in accordance with the higher "inside-out" level, Betzalel would not have been involved at all! For us, it is a given that Betzalel was to oversee the construction of the *Mishkan*, but throughout the entire parsha of *Terumah*, there is no mention of this. Indeed, the simple meaning of Hashem's command to Moshe throughout that parsha, "*V'asisa*—You

---

13   *Shemos* 33:2–3 and 12–17.

shall make," indicates that Moshe himself was the one who was to make the *Mishkan*. Betzalel is first mentioned toward the end of Moshe's stay on Har Sinai,[14] at which point the people had already made the *eigel*, for this too was a response to the *eigel*. If the way in which the *Mishkan* is to be made is less than optimum, Moshe can no longer be the one who is making it.

A completely new perspective on the parshiyos of *Terumah* and *Vayakhel*—and on the *Mishkan* itself!

---

14   Ibid., 31:2.

FROM THE COMMENTATORS

CENTERED AROUND HOLINESS

וַיַּקְהֵל מֹשֶׁה אֶת כָּל עֲדַת בְּנֵי יִשְׂרָאֵל וַיֹּאמֶר אֲלֵהֶם וגו'

Moshe assembled the entire congregation of the Children of Israel and said to them etc.[1]

In all other occasion when Moshe speaks to the Jewish people, the verse just states that he spoke to them, even though he presumably assembled them first in order to do so. Why, on this occasion, is the assembling of the people mentioned explicitly in the verse?

When commanding the Jewish People regarding the construction of the Mishkan, Hashem says:

וְעָשׂוּ לִי מִקְדָּשׁ וְשָׁכַנְתִּי בְּתוֹכָם

They shall make for Me a Sanctuary, and I shall dwell in their midst.[2]

We note that Hashem does not say He will dwell בתוכו—in *it*, i.e., the Mishkan, but rather בתוכם—in *them*, i.e., the Jewish People. What is it

---

1   *Shemos* 35:1.
2   Ibid., 25:8.

exactly about the Mishkan that will cause the Divine Presence to dwell within the Jewish People?

The Vilna Gaon offers a fascinating explanation of this matter, saying that the very fact that the people are united around the holy endeavor of building the Mishkan is what will cause the Divine Presence to dwell among them.[3] In other words, it is not the existence of the Mishkan per se that brings Hashem close to His people, but the fact that it serves as a focal unifying point around which they encamp and live their lives! It is that unity that allows the entity known as the Assembly of Israel to become a dwelling for the Divine Presence.[4]

In light of this, we can understand why the verse emphasizes Moshe assembling the people on this occasion, for the topic he was presenting to them—the construction of the Mishkan—would only be capable of achieving its function of allowing the Divine Presence to reside among Israel if they were assembled and unified around it.

RAISED HEARTS AND GENEROUS SPIRITS

וַיָּבֹאוּ כָּל אִישׁ אֲשֶׁר נְשָׂאוֹ לִבּוֹ וְכֹל אֲשֶׁר נָדְבָה רוּחוֹ אֹתוֹ הֵבִיאוּ אֶת תְּרוּמַת ה' לִמְלֶאכֶת אֹהֶל מוֹעֵד.

Every man whose heart raised him up came, and everyone whose spirit motivated him brought the portion of Hashem for the labor of the Tent of Meeting.[5]

The verse appears to be describing the generosity of those who donated to the *Mishkan* in two different ways. And indeed, various commentators discuss how the two phrases in the verse reflect two

---

3   Commentary to *Shir HaShirim* 1:17.

4   Moreover, the Vilna Gaon writes that this unification continues to a certain degree even if the Mishkan or Beis Hamikdash is not there. As we know, the halachah stipulates that when we pray we face toward Israel, and if we are in Israel we face toward Jerusalem. On a simple level, this is due to the special sanctity of the land of Israel, making it the place through which we wish to direct our prayers to Hashem. However, the Vilna Gaon explains that here, too, the idea is that since everyone is facing toward the same place, Jews from all over the world are united in their prayer, which, as mentioned above, has the effect of bringing the Divine Presence close to us and helping to ensure that our prayers will be accepted.

5   *Shemos* 35:21.

different types of generosity. For example, the *Ohr Hachaim* explains that the two phrases reflect two different types of donation:

- Every man whose heart raised him up—refers to those who were inspired to donate beyond (higher) than their means
- Everyone whose spirit motivated him—refers to those who donated in keeping with their means.

In a somewhat different vein, the *Rama* explains that the two phrases refer, not to the donations themselves, but to the differing motivations behind the donation.[6] Some people are motivated to give due to natural generosity, while others may not be naturally generous, but will donate to a worthy cause based on higher spiritual faculties within them that motivate them to do what is right. Accordingly:

- Every man whose heart raised him up—refers to those who were motivated by their "heart," i.e., their natural generosity.
- Everyone whose spirit motivated him—refers to those who were moved to give on account of their "spirit," i.e., their higher faculties, even though they may not have been naturally generous.[7]

In contrast to the above, the *Ramban* explains that these two phrases are actually talking about two different aspects of the *Mishkan* for which people came forward.

- The second phrase, "whose spirit motivated [*nadvah*] him," indeed refers to the generosity of those who donated.
- The first phrase, "whose heart inspired [*nesa'o*] him," refers not to donations people made, but to their volunteering to become involved in the construction itself:

  For there were none among them who had learned these skills from a teacher, or had themselves trained in them. Rather,

---

6   *Toras Ha'olah*, cited in *Hakesav V'hakabbalah* to our verse.
7   See also commentaries of *Malbim* and *Haamek Davar* to our verse.

these people found within their nature that they could do these things and their hearts were elevated in the ways of Hashem, to come before Moshe and say to him, "I will do all that my master commands."

Beautiful words!

Indeed, in this idea, we can see a worthy conclusion of *Chumash Shemos*—the Chumash of Redemption. This concept embraces not only liberation from the temporal constraints of national slavery in Egypt (*Mitzrayim*), but also from the personal constraints (*meitzarim*) that people were able to throw off as they were inspired to access their talents and capabilities and step forward to make their contributions toward the most elevated of causes.

PARSHAS PEKUDEI

SYNONYMS IN
LASHON HAKODESH

אֵלֶּה פְקוּדֵי הַמִּשְׁכָּן...

These are the reckonings of the Mishkan...[1]

INTRODUCTION

Often in *lashon hakodesh*, we come across two or more words which appear to share the same meaning, superficially "two ways of saying the same thing." However, as numerous commentators demonstrate, there is no such thing as synonyms in *lashon hakodesh*. Rather, each word contains a particular nuance or variation within the general theme.[2] A number of examples of this idea can be found in our parsha. Let us consider some of them.

PEKIDAH AND SEFIRAH

The parsha begins with a tally of the materials used in the construction of the *Mishkan*. The opening verse reads: "אֵלֶּה פְקוּדֵי הַמִּשְׁכָּן—These are the reckonings of the *Mishkan*." We see that the word used for the

---

1   *Shemos* 38:21.
2   Classic exponents of this idea are the *Vilna Gaon*, *Afikei Yehudah*, *Hakesav V'hakabbalah*, the *Malbim*, and the *Netziv*.

count is "*pekudei*." We are also aware that is another word for counting: "*Sefirah*," used, for example, in the mitzvah of counting the *omer*: "וּסְפַרְתֶּם לָכֶם"—You shall count for yourselves."[3] What is the difference in connotation between these two terms?

The *Hakesav V'hakabbalah* explains that these two words reflect two different types of counting:

- One type of counting takes the form of simply adding units up until one knows how many there are; for example, the steady count of the days in the *omer*.
- Another type of counting involves first counting units within various groups and then adding it all together; for example, the census of the Jewish People, who were counted first as families and then as tribes, and then those amounts were added together to yield the national total.

The term *sefirah* denotes the first type of purely incremental counting.

The second type of counting is called *pekidah*. This is associated with the word *lifkod* (to remember), since after one has finished counting the first group, he needs to keep track of that amount as he starts from zero in counting the second group, and so on.

Since the tally of the materials used in the *Mishkan* involved calculating how much was used for the various parts and appurtenances, it partakes of the *pekidah*-remembering type of count and hence the term "*pekudei*" is used.

AVODAH AND MELACHAH

Having described the manufacture of the *Mishkan* and its vessels in the previous parsha, and the priestly garments in this parsha, chapter 39 concludes with a summation of the entire enterprise:

כְּכֹל אֲשֶׁר צִוָּה ה' אֶת מֹשֶׁה כֵּן עָשׂוּ בְּנֵי יִשְׂרָאֵל אֵת כָּל הָעֲבֹדָה. וַיַּרְא מֹשֶׁה אֶת כָּל הַמְּלָאכָה וְהִנֵּה עָשׂוּ אֹתָהּ כַּאֲשֶׁר צִוָּה ה'.

---

3   *Vayikra* 23:15.

In accordance with all that Hashem commanded Moshe, so did the Children of Israel perform all the work. Moshe saw all the work and behold, they had done it as Hashem commanded.

We see that the first verse refers to the work done with the word "*avodah*," while the second verse uses the term "*melachah*." What is the difference in connotation?

- *Avodah*—refers to the work that one puts *in* to a project.
- *Melachah*—refers to the product that comes *out*.

Helpfully, in this instance, the English term "work" itself shares these two connotations. On the one hand, one could say that something involved "thirty hours of work," referring to the work that went in to the enterprise. On the other hand, one could also refer to an important book as "a classic work," referring to that which was produced.

Similarly, in our situation, the first verse states that the Jewish People had finished investing the necessary work (*avodah*) into building the *Mishkan*, and the second verse says that Moshe surveyed what they had produced (*melachah*) and saw that it was in exact accordance with what Hashem had commanded.[4]

NESINAH AND SIMAH

This parsha concludes with a description of the setting up of the *Mishkan* on the first of Nisan. Verse 18 of chapter 40 reads:

וַיָּקֶם מֹשֶׁה אֶת הַמִּשְׁכָּן וַיִּתֵּן אֶת אֲדָנָיו וַיָּשֶׂם אֶת קְרָשָׁיו וַיִּתֵּן אֶת בְּרִיחָיו.

Moshe erected the Mishkan; he put down its sockets, he placed its beams, and put in its poles.

We note that the placement of the sockets and poles is described with the term "*vayiten*" while that of the beams uses the term "*vayasem*." What is behind this differentiation?

---

4   Based on the *Chasam Sofer* and *Malbim*.

The *Malbim* explains the connotations of these two terms as follows:

- *Nesinah*—as its name suggests, derives from the word *nosein* (giving). As such, it is used to describe not withholding something, but rather placing it before another, without any particular specification as to how this should be done.
- *Simah*—denotes a more precise or ordered way of placing something.

Thus, for example, when Hashem commands Moshe: "וְאֵלֶּה הַמִּשְׁפָּטִים אֲשֶׁר תָּשִׂים לִפְנֵיהֶם—And these are the laws that you shall place before them,"[5] the *Mechilta* explains this to mean: "Arrange [the laws] before them like a set table [*shulchan aruch*]." The use of the word "*tasim*" indicates Hashem's insistence that Moshe not only transmit the information, but that he do so in a way which is optimally ordered and organized.

How does all this relate to the items mentioned in our verse?

The halachah states that the beams of the *Mishkan* always needed to be arranged in the exact same order as they were originally placed.[6] Indeed, the *melachah* of writing on Shabbos is actually derived from the letters they would write on each of the beams in the *Mishkan* to identify where along the wall it was to be placed. However, this requirement applied only to the beams, not to the sockets or the poles, which could be placed or inserted in a different order each time the *Mishkan* was set up.

We can now understand why the Torah uses the term "*vayiten*" for the sockets and beams, which were placed in a non-specific way, while it uses the term "*vayasem*" for the beams, which carried the additional insistence of placing them in a specific order.[7]

---

5   *Shemos* 21:1.

6   This is the origin of the practice to make an *atarah* for a tallis, so that the same side always covers the head.

7   There is a well-known halachic principle that "*Maalin bakodesh v'ein moridin*—we ascend in matters of holiness and do not descend." The Gemara (*Menachos* 99a) cites our verse as a source for the second part of that principle—that we do not descend. However, the Gemara does not explicate how we derive this from the verse. Perhaps, it is as per the observation of the *Malbim*, namely, that the Torah is particular that the beams always retain their order, so

These examples should hopefully encourage us to give our full attention to the words the Torah uses and always ask why a particular word was chosen in each verse and what its unique connotation is.

---

as not to descend in holiness by being placed further away from the Ark than they originally were placed.

FROM THE COMMENTATORS

MOSHE'S BLESSING

וַיַּרְא מֹשֶׁה אֶת כָּל הַמְּלָאכָה וְהִנֵּה עָשׂוּ אֹתָהּ כַּאֲשֶׁר צִוָּה ה' כֵּן עָשׂוּ וַיְבָרֶךְ אֹתָם מֹשֶׁה.

Moshe saw the entire work and behold, they had done it as Hashem had commanded, so they had done, and Moshe blessed them.[1]

Rashi, citing the Midrash, informs us regarding the blessing that Moshe gave the people:

אמר להם יהי רצון שתשרה שכינה במעשה ידיכם. ויהי נועם ה' אלקינו עלינו ומעשה ידינו כוננה עלינו.

He said to them, "May the Divine Presence rest on the work of your hands. May the pleasantness of Hashem, our God, be upon us, and may He establish our handiwork for us."[2]

---

1   *Shemos* 39:43.

2   These words are to be found in *Tehillim* 90:17. The Gemara (*Bava Basra* 14b) informs us that a number of chapters in *Tehillim* were said by other prophets and then redacted and incorporated by David HaMelech into his *sefer*. Among these, eleven were composed by Moshe Rabbeinu. Indeed, chapter 90, the first of those eleven, opens with the words, "*Tefillah l'Moshe*—A prayer of Moshe."

Rav Chaim Friedlander explains that Moshe's blessing was not just about the *Mishkan*, that the Divine Presence should rest in this place which the people had constructed. Rather, the blessing was that with the *Mishkan* residing in the center of the camp, *everything* that the people did should be inspired and elevated accordingly, so that the Divine Presence would rest on the work of their hands in all that they would do.

The verse quoted by *Rashi*, "May the pleasantness of Hashem, our God, be upon us," which was originally said by Moshe, is the verse that we recite immediately after the *Amidah* prayer on Motzaei Shabbos. Our intent with this is similar to that of Moshe, for Shabbos is to the week what the *Mishkan* was to the camp. Therefore, as we take leave of Shabbos and prepare to embark on the week ahead, we voice our hope that like the *Mishkan*, the sanctity which we encountered and absorbed over Shabbos should spill out into the week and that the pleasantness of the Divine Presence should be upon us—in all that we do.

ABOUT THE AUTHOR

Born and raised in London, Rabbi Immanuel Bernstein learned in Yeshivas Ateres Yisrael, Jerusalem, and received his rabbinic ordination from Rabbi Chaim Walkin. Rabbi Bernstein currently teaches in Yeshivas Machon Yaakov, Jerusalem, as well as in various seminaries, and gives a popular weekly *shiur* on Chumash that is open to the public and available online. He is the author of six books, *Teshuvah: A Guide for the Heart and Mind during Elul, Rosh Hashanah, and Yom Kippur*; *Aggadah: Sages, Stories and Secrets*; *Darkness to Destiny: The Haggadah Experience*; *Purim: Removing the Mask*; *The Call of Sinai: A Deeper Look at Torah, the Omer, and the Festival of Shavuos*; and *Chanukah: Capturing the Light* (Mosaica Press). He lives in Jerusalem with his family. Visit him at www.journeysintorah.com.